The Complete Guide to Systems Thinking and Learning

"Following the natural order of the Universe in our work and in our lives"

The first practical book with The Systems Thinking Approach[SM] to guide transformation change in our personal lives and organizations. This book explains how to use four simple concepts and specific tools to move from theory to practice and from chaos and complexity to elegant simplicity.

The way you think . . . is the way you act . . . is the way you are.

—By—

Stephen G. Haines
President and Founder
Centre for Strategic Management®

HRD Press, Inc. • Amherst • Massachusetts

Published by:

HRD Press
22 Amherst Road
Amherst, MA 01002
1-800-822-2801 (U.S. and Canada)
1-413-253-3488
1-413-253-3490 (Fax)
Website: www.hrdpress.com

ISBN 0-87425-571-6

Production services by Anctil Virtual Office
Cover design by Eileen Klockars
Editorial services by Robie Grant

PREFACE

From Theory to Practice

System: A set of components that work together for the overall objective of the whole.

Systems Thinking:

- A new way to view, filter, and mentally frame what we see in the world.
- It is based on our world view whereby we see the entity or unit first as a whole, with its fit and relationships to its environment as primary concerns.
- In systems thinking, the whole is primary and the parts are secondary.
- It is finding patterns and relationships, and learning to reinforce or change these patterns to achieve your outcomes.
- This is a shift from seeing elements, structures, functions, and events to seeing the process and interrelationship of them and their outcomes.

"Systems Thinking" and "Systems Learning" have become popular terms partly because it is systems thinking that Peter Senge was referring to in his best-selling book, "The Fifth Discipline." Since the book was first published in 1990, systems thinking and systems learning have become buzzwords in the organizational change theory and practice field. People use (and misuse) them to refer to anything that links together and fits with something else, or even to mean a list of related topics that somehow are all important to training, educating, and achieving some change.

From Chaos and Complexity to Elegant Simplicity

The reality of true systems thinking is different. It is part of a disciplined science and way of thinking referred to as "General Systems Theory" which evolved out of the study of biology in the 1920s. (Refer to the bibliography and the conceptual companion book by this author, entitled *Destination Thinking,* for more on this.) General Systems Theory never really entered into mainstream business consciousness. Instead it virtually disappeared. Now these elegant secrets from our natural and living world and biological science have been rediscovered by the author and reframed and put into practical tools for success in today's chaotic and complex world. These natural laws have been organized into four elegantly simple concepts which constitute The Systems Thinking Approach^{SM} to life and business:

- Concept #1: There are Seven Levels of Living (Open) Systems
- Concept #2: There are Twelve Laws of Natural Systems
- Concept #3: The A-B-C-D Systems Model represents how Living Systems naturally operate
- Concept #4: There is a normal way all living systems undergo change (The Natural Cycles of Life and Change)

Living Systems Applied—the Basic Unit of Life

I have been fortunate to have experienced firsthand over the past 25 years just how useful and practical this simplified natural framework has been as my new "orientation to life." Since I was trained as an engineer at the U.S. Naval Academy in analytical and reductionist thinking, systems thinking and synthesis has been quite a revelation to me. **Living Systems are the natural order of life on earth**—and there are many natural and universal laws we take for granted. We've lost touch with them in our blacktop world. However, it has taken me a lifetime to discover those secrets. As I gradually did, however, it helped me be more successful in my career, first as a senior corporate executive, and then as a CEO, and now as a consultant to CEOs. Its frameworks have been an elegantly simple way to "clarify and simplify" the manner in which I see the world—and how the dynamics of its different levels of living systems, such as (1) individuals, (2) teams, and (3) organizations, work.

This book is an attempt to distill and share the techniques I have learned over the past 25 years. Systems thinking is a lost art with a very practical set of tools which our consultants and I use. It assists us and our clients' thinking, diagnoses, and actions in whatever we do ...and wherever we go in a much better, more holistic and practical way than traditional methods.

As an example, this book focuses on the #1 Systems Question: *What's Your Destination?* Ask this question over and over again wherever you are in your career and life. You'll be amazed at the focus and secrets it uncovers and the better actions and results that follow.

We use all these tools to focus on three lines of business, which are the major changes clients are undergoing in organizations of all types today. These changes include: (1) Strategic Planning and Change, (2) Strategic Leadership and Human Resource Management, and (3) Creating Customer Value to assist our clients in creating their competitive edge through a systems approach to transformational change. **We do this through the application of an "Organization as a System" model that ties these specific tools together into an integrated systems framework.**

This Destination Thinking Question and many other specific tools can help you see and use systems thinking and learning as your new orientation to life as well. Let it clarify and simplify how you see reality, the 1,000-foot view from a helicopter, so to speak . . . and how you can operate more successfully within today's complex and globally interconnected world. **Discover simplicity through this lost art of thinking and learning.**

Here's to elegant simplicity . . . and to systems solutions.

—Stephen G. Haines
September 1999

Centre for Strategic Management®
1420 Monitor Road, San Diego, CA 92110-1545
Phone: 619-275-6528; Fax: 619-275-0324
E-mail: csmintl@san.rr.com
Internet: www.csmintl.com

ACKNOWLEDGMENTS

"Systems Thinking" is a popular and often used, yet frequently misunderstood term. I first encountered an older, less well-known discipline called "General Systems Theory" while pursuing a master's degree at George Washington University in the 1970s. Professor R. F. Ericson taught Management 262: Contemporary Administrative Theory as a required course in the spring of 1975. It was all about an arcane science and framework for thinking called General Systems Theory. At that stage of my life, I looked at it as an esoteric course to be tolerated, successfully completed, and then promptly forgotten.

My Master's degree advisor at George Washington University was Professor Jerry Harvey, best known for his work and story about "The Abilene Paradox." However I best remember him for advocating that **"there is nothing so practical as a good theory"**—a position I totally disagreed with at the time.

As a result, my 1975 knowledge on General Systems Theory was quickly forgotten. Instead, I left the U.S. Navy for the private sector and began my career as an executive. It was not until 1979 that I heard Systems Theory discussed in a practical way by Professor Russell Ackoff, then at the University of Pennsylvania. As part of an executive seminar series at Sunoco (my employer), Russ Ackoff spoke for four hours without notes on General Systems Theory and its practical use in organizational change and as a way of thinking.

Viola! I finally "got" what Dr. Ericson and Dr. Harvey were trying to communicate. I rediscovered the concepts they advocated. Ever since, my partners and I at the Centre for Strategic Management have been using and learning more and more about the practical tools inherent in systems thinking and learning. I've refined these natural laws over time into *four elegantly simple Systems Concepts* of The Systems Thinking Approach™ to strategic management.

So, to my three professors and teachers/mentors, I dedicate *The Compete Guide to Systems Thinking and Learning* as I carry on the work and secrets you first discovered and shared with me.

Thank you Bob, Jerry, and Russ.

TABLE OF CONTENTS

"From Theory to Practice ... From Chaos and Complexity to Elegant Simplicity"

Comprehensive Outline of the Tools

Note: All tools fit and work together. They are organized here only for convenience. Use multiple tools in combination for maximum effect.

Chapter II: Standard Systems Dynamics

- Tool #1: Systems Preconditions
- Tool #2: Desired Outcomes
- Tool #3: The Need for Feedback
- Tool #4: Environmental Impact
- Tool #5: Looking at Relationships
- Tool #6: The What or the How
- Tool #7: The "Iceberg" Theory of Change
- Tool #8: Buy-In and Stay-in
- Tool #9: Centralized vs. Decentralized
- Tool #10: Multiple Causes, Root Causes
- Tool #11: KISS: From Complexity to Simplicity
- Tool #12: The Ultimate Question: Superordinate Goals
- Tool #13: System Dynamics Overall

Chapter III: The Outcome Thinking Tools

- Tool #14: Customer Wants and Needs
- Tool #15: Customer Focus
- Tool #16: Internal vs. External Customers
- Tool #17: Ideal Future Vision
- Tool #18: Whole Jobs

Chapter IV: Feedback and Learning Tools

- Tool #19: Feedback and Learning
- Tool #20: Reinforcement and The Learning Organization
- Tool #21: Environmental Scanning System
- Tool #22: Key Success Factor Measures
- Tool #23: People Support What They Help Create
- Tool #24: Look in the Mirror—Self-Feedback
- Tool #25: Assessment and Debriefing Frameworks

Chapter V: The A-B-C-D Systems Thinking Approach and Model

- Tool #26: "Organization as a System" Model
- Tool #27: Reinventing Strategic Management
- Tool #28: Strategic Life Planning
- Tool #29: HR Strategic Planning
- Tool #30: Hiring and Promotion as a System
- Tool #31: The Team as a System
- Tool #32: Systemic Team Building
- Tool #33: Cross Functional Teams

Chapter V: The A-B-C-D Systems Thinking Approach and Model (continued)

- Tool #34: Leadership Development as a System
- Tool #35: TQM as a System
- Tool #36: Systems Solution vs. Problem Solving
- Tool #37: Organization Design as a System
- Tool #38: Project Management—Simplicity

Chapter VI: Seven Levels of Living Systems

- Tool #39: "Glue" and the Cascade of Planning
- Tool #40: Six Leadership Competencies
- Tool #41: Total Rewards Systems—All Levels
- Tool #42: Methods of Communications
- Tool #43: HR and Training Roles—in Strategic Management

Chapter VII: The Rollercoaster of Change℠

- Tool #44: The Rollercoaster of Change℠
- Tool #45: The Rollercoaster of Self-Change
- Tool #46: The Rollercoaster of Interpersonal Change
- Tool #47: The Rollercoaster of Team Change
- Tool #48: The Rollercoaster of Organizational Change
- Tool #49: Cutting and Building Success Strategies
- Tool #50: Six Natural Phases of Change
- Tool #51: The Natural Life Cycle
- Tool #52: Performance Management System and Cycle
- Tool #53: People-Edge System and Cycle
- Tool #54: Annual Strategic Review Cycle

Chapter VIII: Summary Applications

- Tool #55: Organizational Culture Change
- Tool #56: Strategic Management System
- Tool #57: Tailor to Your Needs
- Tool #58: Wheel of Detail
- Tool #59: Change Management Organizational Structures
- Tool #60: Change Management Fail-Safe Mechanisms
- Tool #61: Open Systems Planning
- Tool #62 Socio-Technical Systems
- Tool #63: Versatile Assessment Tool
- Tool #64: Five Key People Management Subsystems

PROLOGUE

WELTANSCHAUUNG

(German for "Your View of the World")

First, I'd like you to look at the earth as the astronauts do . . . a 260 mile in space holistic view of earth as a living planet, floating out in space, with all its major natural characteristics visible. All of us can't be astronauts, but we don't need to be. Instead, we are all able to fly in a helicopter above the ground. So, I'd like you to visualize getting into a helicopter and climbing up to 2,000 feet. This will help you enormously in understanding systems thinking concepts and this book. It will give you a better and higher vantage point on life and work, virtually improving your practical IQ by over 50 points. I will use this helicopter **(H)** analogy throughout to remind you of how to read and understand systems thinking as *"a new orientation to life."*

Many attend but few understand.
—Martin Luther King

The term "systems thinking" is used a lot these days. It means many things to many people, often just meaning that there is a checklist of things that somehow relate to each other. And it is also a meaningless term to many of us as well. If you read this book from the **H** (helicopter) point of view, *you can be one of a growing number* who really understand systems thinking and all its elegant simplicity.

Complexity and Chaos

The world is complex today, and becoming more so with today's technological inventions and innovations. We have a complex, interconnected world economy and global Internet communications. Thus, it is seductive to think that the new sciences of complexity and chaos theory will finally help us understand the world. In fact, our complex world actually obscures the realities of how life functions naturally on earth (unless we are up where the astronauts view the earth).

Unfortunately, complexity is just one, albeit a very important one, of the twelve characteristics ("internal elaboration") of General Systems Theory regarding living systems on earth. Another key characteristic, for example, is "entropy," whereby all living things tend to run down over time, become inert, and eventually die. ("From the time we're born, we begin to die.") Scientists tell us that the individual cells in our bodies die and regenerate every seven years.

So, we can't ignore complexity, yet we have to deal with it. For example, no one today can fully understand the global economy or our brain's functioning. Our complex, yet simplistic minds can't understand either, yet they remain our reality.

Simplicity on the Far Side of Complexity

Simplicity and Complexity	**Simplicity and Genius**
I wouldn't give a fig for the simplicity this side of complexity, but I'd give my life for the simplicity on the far side of complexity. *—Justice Oliver Wendell Holmes*	Any idiot can simplify by ignoring the complications, but it takes real genius to simplify by including the complications. *—John E. Johnson, TEC Chairman (the Executive Committee)*

There is a huge difference between simplicity and being simplistic:

Simplistic thinking is done by someone who is naïve and simple in his or her thinking, ignoring the complexity involved, and often coming up with knee-jerk and poor, direct cause-effect solutions. These attempts usually create more problems than the ones the individual is attempting to solve.

Simplicity in thinking is different. It is actually accomplished by a person who is quite sophisticated, disciplined, and critical in his or her thinking. He or she looks for ways to include the complexity of the situation, but go beyond it to a higher **(H)** view to solve the problem or issue in a more effective way. We refer to this as *elegant simplicity* as it truly is an elegant way to a much better result.

1. This thinking works first from the *"outside—in"* by looking at *"the whole system"* and its purpose in its environment. This is the **H** view from 2,000 feet that allows you more simplicity in which to see the different and natural hierarchical levels of living systems below (individuals, teams, organizations, communities, societies, earth) and how they interact (and often collide) with each other.

2. Secondly, *"each whole system"* has a natural structure and six systems characteristics that define it as a system. It has inputs, throughputs (or processes), permeable boundaries, and multiple outputs into the environment. And, living systems have a feedback loop to correct, adapt, or modify their inputs to improve their outputs.

   Our A-B-C-D Systems Model, explained later in this book, represents this natural structure of living systems. It allows us to visually see, and elegantly clarify, the main parts of the whole living system interacting with its environment. Again, it is a simplicity that allows us to understand what we are seeing far better than the average person does.

3. Thirdly, now you can more effectively spend time, work, and deal *"inside—out"* with the *"inner workings"* (or throughputs or processes) of any living system. If you are trying to make it more effective (based on the outputs and feedback loop above), only now can you focus effectively on the activities of the inner workings of any living system. This is due to the fact that all the parts of a system are not separate, but are complex interrelated parts that ideally should work together to achieve the desired outputs.

The complexity and chaos problem now becomes quite clear and predictable as it follows the natural laws of how living systems operate. If it weren't for the pervasiveness of the six systems characteristics of the inner workings of all living systems explained in this book (including hierarchy, interrelatedness, internal elaboration, equifinality, entropy, and dynamic equilibrium), we would not be able to go from organization to organization as employees, vendors, customers, or consultants. Think about that! By seeing the similar patterns that lie behind different events in different firms, we actually simplify life beyond the complexities.

Summary

In summary, these natural laws of how living systems operate provide our templates to think and act, if only we could see them through the complexities and chaos of our daily lives. Our world is much more predictable than we think when viewed in systems thinking and natural terms and in the 1-2-3 sequence above. *That is our Systems Thinking Approach*^{SM} *in its essence.*

In Systems Thinking, the whole is primary and the parts are secondary

vs.

In Analytic Thinking, the parts are primary and the whole is secondary.

Read on for the details and story—and learn the tools.

CHAPTER I
INTRODUCTION TO SYSTEMS THINKING^{SM} AND LEARNING

- Overview
- Systems Concept #1: Seven Levels of Living (Open) Systems
- Systems Concept #2: Twelve Laws of Natural Systems (Standard Systems Dynamics)
- Systems Concept #3: A-B-C-D Systems Model
- Systems Concept #4: Changing Systems (The Natural Cycles of Life and Change)
- Some Guiding Principles of the Systems Age
- What Is Learning? *and* The Learning Organization

THINKING IS HARD WORK

All the problems of the world could be settled easily if people were only willing to think.

The trouble is that people often resort to all sorts of devices in order not to think, ***because thinking is such hard work.***

—Thomas J. Watson

Overview
Living Systems . . . the basic unit of life

System *n.,* A set of components that work together for the overall objective of the whole.

We at the Centre for Strategic Management believe we are already *in the Systems Age—people are just not aware of it yet. We have reached this destination already.*

Most of the technological changes and advances today involve the use of mechanical and electronic systems (particularly the latter), or are improvements to systems that link and work with other systems (NAFTA, Mercosur, GATT, telecommunications, satellites, Internet, etc.). The common thread, however, is that they all fit the above definition.

There are several different types of systems:

1. **Mechanical/electrical systems**—cars, clocks, assembly lines
2. **Human systems (including social and organizational)**—individuals, teams, families, organizations, communities, nations
3. **Electronic/telecommunications systems**—personal computers, local area networks (LANs), wide area networks (WANS), super computers, Internet
4. **Ecological systems**—the 21 eco-regions of North America, earth as a planet
5. **Biological systems**—birds, fish, animals, insects

These are basic, fundamental types of systems. There are many other kinds of manmade systems, as well as countless combinations of the five types described above.

There are also *open* and *closed* systems. A closed system is one that is closed and isolated from its environment. An experimental, sterile chemistry lab is an example of a closed system. An open system is one that accepts inputs from the environment around it, and acts on those various inputs to create new outputs into the environment. Every system in which humans operate is an open system—some are more open than others, and this is a key to their success, as we'll discover later. Closed systems are the exception.

Though it may at first seem trivial, we need to recognize the open systems around us that interact with our environment, because they are key to our basic understanding of how we live. They provide us with a framework for diagnosing, analyzing, problem solving, and decision making. ***Most importantly, this way of thinking gives us a way to manage the complex Systems Age—focusing on (1) the whole, within its environment, as well as (2) its components, and the interrelationships of the components that support the objective of the whole. To do this we need new and better/broader paradigms and mental models—hence Systems Thinking^{SM}!***

We believe that on a subconscious level, our mental models can either *hold us back* or *propel us forward.*

Mental models, frameworks, concepts—call them what you like—are our mind-set. They are our ways of understanding or *mis*understanding the world in which we live. Other words used to describe our mind-set are "world view" or "Weltanschauung" (German for "view of the world"). Paradigms, popularized by the futurist and author Joel Barker, do the same thing.

Whatever you call them, our mental models or ways of thinking are based on our prevailing beliefs and assumptions—generally unexamined and unvoiced. The challenge is to put ourselves in touch with these assumptions and hold them up to the light—this is crucial. Knowing the biases that make up our ways of thinking is key to our present and future success.

It is only by deliberately shaping our way of thinking in order to distinguish processes, patterns, and relationships *from* events that we will finally discover a *systems thinking* mind-set—and through the process of diagnosis and discovery, we will move in a more positive, productive direction.

When one life element changes, it simultaneously changes and affects many other elements. Why? Because life itself is made up of complex and interdependent systems. Just think of any ecosystem—such as a salt marsh—and the many types of biological and living systems dependent upon it.

Much as it is not possible to change one element of any biological system without having an effect on the entire system, it is equally impossible for one system to change without affecting other systems. We share a planet protected by a fragile layer of ozone preserving life as we know it; at this and every other level of life, we exist as part of many *inter*dependent systems.

Unfortunately, only with this understanding of interdependency can we appreciate and discover the complexity of life and all its systems.

It would be better for us if we looked at all societal and organizational problems as "systems problems," and sought answers that integrate within and between each interdependent system. Collaborative, team, and systems-oriented efforts are becoming more and more common in our organizations and communities for good reason, and not a moment too soon.

Many fields of thought deal with the interrelationship of processes and patterns—*the art of systems thinking in its broadest sense.* These include the fields of cybernetics, chaos theory, gestalt therapy, General Systems Theory, complexity theory, socio-technical systems theory, and systems change—as well as areas like project management, information systems, operations research, telecommunications, and more.

Those who spend much of their professional lives thinking about systems thinking include such diverse and well-known people as Fritjof Capra, Jay Forrester, Gregory Bateson, Peter Drucker, Peter Senge, Russ Ackoff, Ludwig Von Bertalanffy, Meg Wheatley, Mitchell Waldrop, Cliff McIntosh, Eric Trist, and others. What they have in common, despite their diversity, is that they recognize that the behavior of all systems follows certain common and "natural" principles of living systems and systems change.

We need to learn and follow these principles, even though the details and applications are still being discovered and articulated. These systems apply to every living system at every level—individual, couple, team, family, organization, community, and society. What we see changing on one system level will also affect another system level, which in turn affects yet another level, and so on.

Unfortunately, many of these attempts within our society today are "partial systems" solutions. While they do try to identify and solve *patterns of problems*—as opposed to simply identifying one isolated occurrence—there is as yet only one theory or body of thought that offers a fully integrated solution to our systems problems. This neglected theory which is not chaos theory or complexity theory, is *General Systems Theory,* an arcane theory and set of characteristics from the 1920s that has been lost. It was not very well known even then. But what these General Systems theorists knew, because they were initially biologists, is that living systems are the natural order of life on earth. Systems thinking helps you see patterns in the world and spot the leverage points that, when acted upon, lead to lasting beneficial changes.

This book's Systems Thinking Approach[SM] is the only heavily researched, valid, and holistic way to think. It is based on:

1. Biological research on living systems, begun in the 1920s.
2. The Society for General Systems Research, established in the fall of 1954 in Palo Alto, California, by four prestigious interdisciplinary thinkers:
   - Ludwig Von Bertalanffy—biologist, renaissance thinker, and the father of General Systems Theory
   - Anatol Rapoport—applied mathematician and philosopher
   - Ralph Gerard—physiologist
   - Kenneth Boulding—economist
3. Research as articulated in the annual yearbooks of this Society, as well as the teachings and writings of "renaissance" professors of management, such as:
   - Russ Ackoff, University of Pennsylvania
   - Jay Forrestor, Massachusetts Institute of Technology (MIT)
   - Gene Ericson, George Washington University
4. Systems Thinking as interpreted and translated for the first time into practical management tools by Steve Haines, founder and president of the Centre for Strategic Management in San Diego, California.

In order to survive, we human beings need physical, social, mental, and spiritual stimulation and nourishment. We also need the elements in our environment within which we exist, which has all of its own systems (land, water, air, wind, fire, sun, moon)—well, you get the picture.

> *We try hard to remove ourselves from all the dramas and sensational nature, and yet without them we feel lost and disconnected . . . subconsciously, we bring them right back indoors again . . . we obsessively visit nature . . . we go swimming, jogging or cross-country skiing, we take strolls in a park.*
>
> —*"The Best Reason of All to Care for the Earth,"*
> Diane Ackerman, *Parade*, April 23, 1995

Everywhere we look, we can see living, breathing examples of systems in our lives . . . and in our earth/world floating in the universe.

The astronauts view systems thinking as a new orientation to life
Creating a better future starts with the ability to envision it.

Ever since those early NASA pictures and astronauts seeing a far-away earth floating in space, we've known we are part of a vast, interdependent system called the Universe—a system in which we are but one small planet. Those pictures eloquently remind us that earth is a single organism.

As the many dramatic and revolutionary changes occurring in our interdependent, interrelated systems collide, our sense of chaos, confusion, and complexity will deepen. However, if we accept the reality of the living systems perspective as the ongoing, natural order of life on earth, we begin to recognize that this confusion is a normal part of the natural systems cycle.

To truly succeed in the 21st century, we will need to gain the same level of perspective that gave the early astronauts such a radically new perception of earth. Not only do we need to gain it, we need to make it a new way of life—and this is precisely where our new Systems Thinking Approach[SM] and mind-set will have its greatest value.

> *Thinking across boundaries, or integrative thinking, is the ultimate entrepreneurial act. Call it business creativity. Call it holistic thinking. To see problems and opportunities integratively is to see them as wholes related to larger wholes, rather than dividing information and experience into discrete bits assigned to distinct, separate categories that never touch one another.*
>
> —*Harvard Business Review,* November/December 1990

General Systems Theory

To better understand systems as the natural order of life on earth, we must look at the nature of the system itself. In the 1920s, biologist Ludwig Von Bertalanffy and others proposed the idea of a general theory of living systems that would embrace all levels of science, from the study of a single living cell to the study of society and the planet as a whole. They were seeking to reveal these secrets and generalizations in order to create a recognizable standard of scientific principles that could then be artfully applied to virtually any body of work. Out of this study came a scientific application called the General Systems Theory.

In 1972, Geoffrey Vickers, one of these theorists, put the theory in layman's terms:

> *The words "general systems theory" imply that some things can usefully be said about systems in general, despite the immense diversity of their specific forms. One of these things should be a scheme of classification.*
>
> *Every science begins by classifying its subject matter, if only descriptively, and learns a lot about it in the process . . . systems especially need this attention, because an adequate classification cuts across familiar boundaries and at the same time draws valid and important distinctions which have previously been sensed but not defined.*
>
> *In short, the task of General Systems Theory is to find the most general conceptual framework in which a scientific theory or a technological problem can be placed without losing the essential features of the theory or the problem.*[1]

As a systemic, theoretical framework for describing universal relationships, General Systems Theory is a marvelous vehicle. Its secret and basic principle states that in studying solutions to

---

[1] Vickers, Geoffrey, *General Systems Thinking,* 1972.

any problem, the whole is the primary consideration; its parts are only secondary. General Systems Theory argues that parts play roles in light of the purpose for which the whole exists—no part can be affected without affecting all other parts. In other words, when studying any system, be it organizational, organic, or scientific in nature:

The place to start is with the whole.
All parts of the whole—and their relationships to one another—evolve from this.

Systems Thinking℠ Contrasted with Analytic Thinking

> *From an early age, we're taught to break apart problems in order to make complex tasks and subjects easier to deal with.*
>
> *But this creates a bigger problem . . . we lose the ability to see the consequences of our actions, and we lose a sense of connection to a larger whole.* *Peter Senge*[2]

Make no mistake, breaking away from our outdated analytic and sequential thinking won't be easy; it's been an integral part of our modern society for a long time. In fact, we rarely differentiate analytic, linear thinking from *thinking*; we tend to see them as one and the same.

Many social theorists believe that our problems today stem from the Agricultural Age, when humans found ways to dominate nature and make it subservient to our immediate needs. The Industrial Revolution furthered that dominating mode because it was a "mechanistic revolution" fueled by the intent to take over and conquer Mother Nature. And it worked—or so we thought.

This mechanistic approach to creating change is no longer viable, if it ever was. As Russell Ackoff reminds us, *"We [have been] attempting to deal with problems generated by a new [systems] age with techniques and tools that we inherit from an old [mechanistic] one."*[3]

Ackoff believes that these old techniques and tools developed as the Agricultural Age closed and the Machine Age began. In his view, the latter spawned three fundamental concepts: reductionism, analysis, and mechanization. He believes these must now be changed if we want to be in step with the Systems Age. I agree!

The Fundamental Concepts of the Machine Age

1. **Reductionism**
   This concept's premise is that if you take anything and start to take it apart or reduce it to its lowest common denominator, you will ultimately reach indivisible elements. For instance, in reductionism, the cell would be the ultimate component of life.

2. **Analysis**
   A powerful mode of thinking, analysis takes the entity/issue/problem apart, breaking it up into its components. It is at this point in analysis that you solve the problem, then aggregate

---

[2] Senge, Peter, *The Fifth Discipline: The Art and Practice of the Learning Organization.* New York: Doubleday/Currency, 1990.

[3] Ackoff, Russell, *Ackoff's Fables: Irreverent Reflections on Business and Bureaucracy.* John Wiley & Sons, Inc., 1991.

the solutions into an explanation as a whole. Analysis tends to explain things by the *behavior* of their parts, rather than by the whole!

Even today, analysis is probably the most common technique used in corporations. Managers "cut their problems down to size," reducing them to a set of solvable components and then assembling them into one solution. It is still so much the norm that many managers continue to see *analyzing* as synonymous with *thinking*. But what *really* is needed is synthesis . . . holistic systems thinking.

3. **Mechanization**
This way of thinking seeks to explain virtually every phenomenon by distilling it down to a single relationship: cause and effect. However, mechanization has a key consequence: When we find the cause, we don't need anything else; thus, the environment becomes irrelevant. Indeed, the whole effort of scientific study is about relationships that can be studied in isolation and in laboratories—an artificially closed-systems view of the world.

Mechanization colored how we looked at the world as a whole. It brought us assembly lines, mass production, countless machines—and the idea that we live in a mechanistic rather than organic world. We have gone from thinking of machines as a means for mass production to thinking of the whole world as a machine, not as "Mother Nature" with a will and mind of her own.

Appearance and Reality

While the reductionist, analytic, and mechanistic approaches may appear to resolve ongoing problems, they actually fail to provide long-term, longer lasting solutions.

Analytic thinking is perhaps the biggest culprit among them, for it is such a common way of thinking that we're hardly aware of it. Because its central, linear approach is to problem-solve only one issue at a time, other issues must wait their turn, and this alone can cause further problems. It's an inherent deficiency of this thinking mode—and something important to remember and be alert for.

Simple analytic thinking focuses on cause-and-effect: one cause for every one effect. It asks the all too common "either-or" question. Its weakest link and the reason it's not working in today's world is that it doesn't take into consideration the environment, other systems, and the multiple and/or delayed causality that surrounds each cause and effect. Nor does it consider the consequences of its interrelationships and interdependencies with other parts.

Systems thinking—at first glance more complex and multi-level than analytic/linear or reductionist thinking—is actually more accommodating to a simpler understanding of reality, because systems themselves are circular entities. Always keep in mind this circular concept. It is integral to the input-transformation-output-feedback (in the environment) model that forms the framework for systems thinking and the natural order of life. Once you get used to viewing this simple model and framework as representing reality and some of the natural laws of this world, complexities fade away. Your perspective is like that of an astronaut . . . seeing the world as it really is, not as we want it to be. *Systems Thinking℠ moves us from chaos and complexity to elegant simplicity.*

Systems thinking is about thinking in a new way—thinking synergistically, wherein 1 + 1 = 3. The simple exercise of looking up the definitions of these words—as shown here—quickly illustrates the diametrically opposed concepts behind them.

Synthesis		vs.	Analysis
Synergism	Interaction of parts such that the total effect is greater than the sum of the individual parts (2 + 2 = 5).	**Reductionism**	To narrow down; the attempt to explain all biological processes by the same explanations that chemists and physicists use to interpret inanimate matter; it reduces complex data or phenomena to simple terms—i.e., over-simplification.
Synthesis	The combinations of parts or elements so as to make a whole.	**Analysis**	Separation of a whole into its component parts; an examination of a complex entity, its elements, and their relationships.
Synergetic	Working together, cooperating.	**Analytic**	Separating something into component parts; synonyms: analyze, dissect, break down.

Analytical thinking has run amuck!

Analytic thinking, when paired with reductionism, does make us "micro-smart"—good at thinking through individual issues and elements—but it also makes us "macro-dumb" at planning for the whole portfolio. Here are a few dramatic examples of how analytic thinking has run amuck and led to needless complexity.

1. **IRS** rules and regulations—over 4,000 pages of regulations that continue to cost American taxpayers over $400 billion each year in compliance activities.
2. **Educational code** in California—over 6,800 pages and 11 volumes that restrict school districts from any kind of innovative, creative, or holistic ideas for learning.
3. **The U.S. Naval Academy Regulations**—over 1,000 pages . . . as compared to 10 pages when it opened 150 years ago. Both versions cover the same topic areas, but the early versions assume that readers are mature with common sense; today's 1,000 pages spell out each and every probability.
4. **Health care**—thousands of small, specialized entities and programs, often based on categorical grants created for singular, simplistic problems and solutions.
5. **Social services**—similar to today's health care situation, the U.S. Department of Health and Human Services tends to deal with simplistic cause/effect symptoms, rather than the root causes.

6. **Specialized government districts**—Thousands of unaccountable districts: water districts, assessment districts, school districts, and so forth.
7. **Federal intelligence agencies**—we have 16 (yes, that is right) federal agencies concerned with intelligence. They sound like alphabet soup; CIA, NSA, DIA, NIS, NCS, etc.
8. **Congressional subcommittees**—Too many to enumerate. Every time a new issue comes along, Congress establishes a new subcommittee, to the detriment of good government.
9. **Duplication of services**—many not-for-profit and government organizations/agencies go after specific categorical missions that end up duplicating and overlapping with the missions of other agencies. The confusion and fragmentation is obvious and detrimental to their overall success, not to mention the extra cost.

When we engage in analytic or reductionist thinking, we resist considering more than one issue at a time, because when we do, we quickly see there are always multiple and delayed causes for every effect. Unfortunately, we have few resources within our archaic, linear thinking that prepare us to deal with more than two or three issues at a time. ***Is it any wonder we feel overwhelmed using this analytic approach to our systems problems?***

In sum, reality is made up of circles (and feedback loops) in which multiple causality is inherently and integrally tied to multiple effects in an open and free-flowing environment. It is this reality that we must pay attention to in the lost art of applying systems thinking.

Partial Systems Thinking . . . Some Progress

> *I am wary of the word "system" because . . . "system" is a highly cathected term, loaded with prestige; hence, we are all strongly tempted to employ it even when we have nothing definite in mind and its only service is to indicate that we subscribe to the general premise respecting the interdependence of things.*
>
> —Kast & Rosenzweig, quoting the psychologist, Murray, *Systems Thinking*

As we noted earlier, there have been an increasing number of business trends and concepts in the last couple of decades that approach problem solving from this "general premise of interdependence." Many of them—such as Total Quality Management, reengineering, process redesign, benchmarking, and work empowerment—are struggling in today's organizational environment, and perhaps even dying a slow death. In our view, this is because none of them look at their strategies and their problem solving from a fully integrated, holistic, or systems methodology that begins with a definition of their ideal future vision or ultimate purpose.

As you will see, none of these concepts meet the fundamental systems-thinking test. They are really partial systems views, checklists, and the like. *True systems thinking* includes:

1. Starting from the point of view of understanding what a complete, input-transformation-output system looks like within its environment.
2. Starting in the right place with your vision and desired outcomes (begin with the end in mind).
3. A feedback loop based on clarity of the desired outputs or goals.
4. A full understanding of the interrelationships of the parts to each other in support of the whole and its desired goals.

Partial systems rarely meet these tests—rather, they are usually checklists of integrated and related points important primarily to their authors. That's why these concepts miss the full systems focus. Ultimately, they become fads whose time has passed. Though we may benefit by their presence, they somehow are not enough. In the end, each concept fails to make the fundamental, full-system changes that are desired . . . and needed.

The weak link is that these short-lived ideas are attempts at *unconscious* systems applications—not yet systems applications at a conscious level, and partial at that. Because they are not clearly thought-out and related to the entire system, they leave too many unanswered questions and die an early death.

This paradigm shift to Systems Thinking℠ is a shift from seeing elements, structures, functions, and events to seeing processes and interrelationships. It is switching our perspective from (#1) events (pure analytical thinking) to (#2) patterns (some relational thinking), to (#3) mental models (partial systems thinking), and then breakthrough thinking from analytical to (#4) holistic systems thinking.

Mental Models
Worldview
Basic Assumptions
or
***Weltanschauung* (German)**

#1 Events	**#2 Patterns**	**#3 Mental Models**		**#4 Holistic**
Analytical Thinking	**Cause/ Effect**	**Partial Systems Thinking**	***Breakthrough Thinking***	**Systems Thinking**
or	*or*	*or*		*or*
reductionist thinking	smaller/ initial relationships	collaboration		organic
Machine Age	repeated events	cooperation		fit
mechanistic	relational thinking	integrated thinking		relationships of processes
simple cause/effect		etc.		

This chart illustrates the shift from thinking in terms of elements, structures, functions, and events **to *seeing*** the process and interrelationships and their outcomes.

Partial Systems Thinking Example #1

Total Quality Management (TQM) is an example of partial systems thinking. At its outset, it was an innovative concept built around the idea of delivering consistent and continuous quality to the customer. However, there was a tendency among practitioners to look only at the general process and overall end of improved quality, rather than focusing on the customer.

Even Dr. Deming, who created the 14 points of TQM, didn't mention the customer specifically. Also frequently neglected was the often unspoken expectation that there would be a bottom-line profit for shareholders—an outcome or dimension that was indirectly anticipated as a result of the process, but rarely achieved.

The greatest obstacle to achieving my goals is that I don't know what my goals are.

–Ashleigh Brilliant

Partial Systems Thinking Example #2

The Workbook for Implementing The Five Tracks, by Calvin Brown, presents a program for managing organization-wide improvement on a more holistic level. Described in Kilman's *Managing Beyond the Quick Fix,* Brown's program uses a five-track model that includes many of our organizational factors—culture, management skills, team-building, strategy-structure, and reward system—but still provides no systems framework of interdependencies, processes, outcomes, and feedback loop.

In the systems model, the input-output structure leads us to a complete understanding of the full breadth of systems. Every business trend or fad is initially intriguing in its own right because it identifies logical portions of the system or systems model, and reworks those portions for a better fit and integration.

Partial Systems Thinking Example #3

Studying and copying competitive organizations' best practices—or benchmarking—is another example of well-intentioned partial systems thinking. A November 1992 *Business Week* article, "Beg, Borrow, and Benchmark," says that even industrial giants can run aground with benchmarking. Quoting J. M. Juran, a consultant and quality pioneer, the author writes, "It's quite possible for one department to launch a benchmarking program that inadvertently undermines another. One example is when purchasing devises a better system of managing suppliers, but that leads to buying equipment or materials that hamper manufacturing efficiency."

The article also quotes Henry Johansson of Coopers & Lybrand, who advises that benchmarking needs to be done in conjunction with business reengineering—rethinking an organization's work flow as well as the procedures and systems used in various tasks. Once again, though this gets closer to true systems thinking, it falls short of the true systems framework.

Partial Systems Thinking Example #4

There are many, many partial systems thinking models out there today that produce what they think is a finite list, from which they shape an organizational approach for change. The cute McKinsey 7-S framework called the "Opportunity Model" is built around seven "S" concepts—Strategies, Structures, Staffing, Style, Skills, Shared Values, and Systems.

Other partial systems models include those of Professor Jay Galbraith (Star Model), University Associates founder John Jones (Organizational Universe), and Dr. Edward deBono (Six Thinking Hats). These partial systems programs offer lists of various thinking techniques designed to generate new and productive ideas.

Summary

Each of these widely varying concepts offers a partial systems approach by making a sincere effort to try to look at many issues at once and recognize that change needs to take place on more than one level. In reality, however, they are only partial systems approaches and thus are destined to make some progress and then falter.

Why do so many of these concepts die young? Primarily because while they insist they are a systems approach, in fact, they are nothing more than linear lists of four or six or ten or eighteen points presented in a visual or—as evidenced in the "Opportunity Model,"—a circular format on which the organization chooses to focus.

Don't get me wrong. The abundant partial systems thinking out there today *has* had a hand in moving us *toward* full systems thinking. However, it doesn't get us there all the way. The dilemma in partial systems thinking, on one hand, is that it provides us with better, clearer ways to focus on those things that trouble us today. On the other hand, it leaves us out in the cold on all other elements that haven't been incorporated or anticipated, therefore creating suboptimal results and new disturbances as actual byproducts.

A terrific support for this point came when we at the Centre for Strategic Management were developing our "Reinventing Strategic Planning for the 21st Century Model." In doing background research, we looked at 27 other strategic planning and strategic change-management models. Of the 27, none incorporated the input-output systems phases or took a system's environment and feedback loop into consideration. Only ours was developed based on the fundamental, full systems framework. It is described in more detail in the Tools section of this book.

When all is said and done, the real beauty of the full Systems Thinking Approach℠ is that by using our "elegantly simple" four basic concepts, anyone can consciously develop systems solutions for their systems problems. We'll look at these four basic concepts in the next four sections:

- Concept #1: Seven Levels of Living (Open) Systems
- Concept #2: Twelve Laws of Natural Systems (Standard Systems Dynamics)
- Concept #3: A-B-C-D Systems Model
- Concept #4: Changing Systems (The Natural Cycles of Life and Change)

Systems Concept #1:
Seven Levels of Living (Open) Systems

In addition to this systems model, we also need to be aware of the seven levels of living systems, outlined by Kenneth Boulding[4] in his 1964 book, *The Meaning of the 20th Century.* This key concept on systems' levels is being used more frequently in today's organizations. The seven different levels form a specific hierarchy of living systems:

1. **Cells**—the basic unit of life
2. **Organs**—the organic systems within our bodies
3. **Organism**—single organisms such as humans, animals, fish, birds
4. **Group**—teams, departments, families, etc.
5. **Organization**—firm, company, neighborhood, community, city, and private, public, and not-for-profit organizations
6. **Society**—states, provinces, countries, nations, regions within countries
7. **Supranational system**—continents, regions, earth

The Seven Levels of Living Systems, Expanded

1. The cells in our bodies and in primitive life forms in water, air, and land are the smallest units of independent life and living systems. In humans and other individual life forms, however, there are three smaller levels of reductionistic divisions that are the focus of much scientific investigation. However, these levels, listed below, are *not living systems*:
   - **Chromosomes**—present as strands in cells, humans have 23 pairs (one each from mother/father)
   - **DNA**—blueprint for producing the proteins and chemicals essential for life
   - **Gene**—a strand of DNA that contains the instructions for making proteins
2. The organs in our body are the subject of much medical inquiry. These living systems include:
   - **Nervous System**—brain, spinal cord
   - **Cardiorespiratory System**—heart, arteries, lungs, trachea
   - **Digestive System—**mouth, stomach, liver, gall bladder, pancreas, intestines
   - **Reproductive System**—genitals, pelvis, prostate, uterus, vagina, ovaries
   - **Muscular System**—head and neck, back, abdomen, limbs, gluteus maximus
   - **Skeletal System—**skull, ribs, vertebrae, pelvis, limbs

[4] Boulding, Kenneth, *The Meaning of the 20th Century.* New York: Prentice-Hall, 1964.

The Focus of This Book

The focus of this book is primarily on living systems at the following three hierarchical levels:

3. Organisms or individuals
4. Groups or teams and families
5. Organizations and communities

These levels of living systems form the foundation from which to expand our thinking of living systems ever further. Each systems level is in a hierarchy with all the others and interrelates and reacts to other living systems at their own level. Here we see the reality of our experiences—we "collide" or relate with individuals (one to one), teams/departments collide or relate; the organization interacts with its environment.

This expands our focus on change to each of these levels and their collisions of levels for a systematic large-scale change effort, i.e., the collision of levels 3, 4, and 5:

3A. one to one

4A. between departments

5A. between an organization and its environment

In addition, the further you go towards the higher level system levels (i.e., 4-5-6-7), the more complex the system is, the more of these "collisions" occur, and the greater must be the skills, the willingness, and the readiness to deal with this chaos and complexity.

These levels of living systems illustrate how every system is in hierarchy with every other system and thus impacts every other system. These levels validate the concept of "systems within systems"—another secret to applying the lost art of system thinking.

When we look at any of our human organizations as *levels* of systems within other systems that collide with other systems, we further cement the systems concept. We begin to look not only at isolated events, but also for patterns of behavior and events, how each pattern relates to the whole, and how each whole system relates or collides with other whole living systems.

If we want to find fully integrated solutions for today's systems problems, we need to understand on a fundamental level that the systems in which we exist are all interrelated. They cannot be treated separately; to do so is to court disaster. Once we begin thinking in terms of systems connected to systems in a hierarchy, it becomes easier to see how problems are connected to other problems—and it forces us to consider solutions to these problems in a new light. Usually, in fact, the solution to a systems problem is found at the next highest system—a concept Einstein understood when he used his famous quote about *problems not being solved at the same level (of systems) that created them.*

Systems Concept #2:
Twelve Laws of Natural Systems (Standard Systems Dynamics)
(as researched and established by the members of the General Systems Theory Society and adapted from *Academy of Management Journal*, December 1972)

The following twelve characteristics are the **"Standard Systems Dynamics"** always present in living systems. They have been adapted, with my own comments, from the *Academy of Management Journal.*[5] For ease of retention, I have characterized them in two conceptual groups: (1) the whole system and (2) the inner workings (of a living system). However, keep in mind that **it is the *relationship* and *fit* of all these parts and *characteristics* into one *whole system* that is key**—not just each characteristics alone. **Systems Dynamics are all about relationships.**

1. The Whole System

CHARACTERISTIC #1: Holism (Synergism, Organism, and Gestalt)

The whole is not just the sum of the parts; the system itself can be explained only as a totality. Holism is the opposite of elementarism, which views the total as the sum of its individual parts. For instance, we write letters, but our hands cannot write alone as separate parts; they can only do so as part of our overall human system.

This is the basic definition of a system: a holistic unit that is the natural way of life. It has overall purposes and a transformational synergy when it is optimally effective.

➥ **For example:** Many managers believe that a corporate strategic plan is just a "roll-up" of lower level plans. This is an excellent example of elementarism, one that usually results in poor implementation and the perpetuation of many turf battles and "silos." People lack holistic vision and a strategic plan that would serve as an overall framework for efficiency and cooperation.

Experienced Dynamics

Instead of holism, we usually see ineffective change that is parts—or activity—focused; this can only lead to suboptimal results.

CHARACTERISTIC #2: Open Systems

Living systems can be considered in two ways: (1) relatively closed or (2) relatively open to their environment. Open systems exchange information, energy, or material with their environment. Biological and social systems are inherently open systems; mechanical systems may be open or closed. We prefer to think of open-closed as a dimension; that is, systems are relatively open or relatively closed.

---

[5] Vickers, Geoffrey, *Academy of Management Journal*, December 1972.

For example, as human beings we survive by adapting to our physical environment with such necessary input as food, clothing, and shelter. This is a basic, unalterable fact of life, and Maslow's first level in his hierarchy of needs.

Thus, the three keys to success for any living system are its ability (1) to be interactive with its environment; (2) to fit into that environment; and (3) to be connected with that environment. A crucial task of any system is to scan its environment and then adapt to it.

➥ **For example:** Excellent organizations are marked by their intense desire to be open to feedback and by their constant search for information from their environments that will help them thrive and lead.

Experienced Dynamics

Many organizations and their cultures are relatively closed systems with a low environmental scan—a myopic view in today's rapidly changing environment.

CHARACTERISTIC #3: System Boundaries

When we consider the above, it naturally follows that all systems have boundaries that separate them from their environments. The concept of boundaries furthers our understanding of the distinction between open and closed systems. The relatively closed system has rigid, impenetrable boundaries, whereas the open system has permeable boundaries between itself and a broader suprasystem. Thus an open system can more easily integrate and collaborate with its environment.

Boundaries are easily defined in physical and biological systems, but are very difficult to delineate in social systems like communities and organizations. This may be partly why U.S. society provides so much protection to the individual and less so to "the common good" of a community.

In organizations, the boundaries are relatively open, making it somewhat vague in terms of knowing and fully understanding its limits. In society today, with world-wide, instantaneous communications, our boundaries have become more and more open.

➥ **For example:** A key to shifting from analytic to systems thinking is to be able to mentally recognize the system and its boundaries. Only then can you work with and hope to change the system.

Many governmental organizations are very unclear where their boundaries end, and where the boundaries of the individual citizen begin. This is pretty much how our current "big government" got started, ultimately making us more and more dependent on it, while simultaneously robbing us of the vitality, spirit, and self-initiative that created the United States.

Experienced Dynamics

We often see closed boundaries leading to fragmentation, battles over turf, and separation and parochialism. The ideal is integration, collaboration, and harmony with the environment.

CHARACTERISTIC #4: Input-Transformation-Output Model

The open system can be viewed as a transformation model. In a dynamic relationship with its environment, it receives various inputs, transforms these inputs in some way, and exports outputs. This is the way that natural and living systems operate.

*This is **the** core systems thinking model, framework, and structure for you to internalize* if you want to use systems thinking in a practical way. This model creates a flow chart explaining how systems change and transform over time when combined with Characteristic #5; Feedback.

➥ **For example:** On the most basic level, we must take inputs (e.g., food and water) and transform them into the vital nutrients if we are to survive.

Experienced Dynamics

Because our piecemeal, linear, analytic, reductionist, and sequential view of the world is so narrow, we often miss the outcomes (feedback) and environmental factors.

CHARACTERISTIC #5: Feedback

The concept of feedback on effectiveness is important in understanding how a system maintains a steady state or improves. Information concerning the outputs of the system is fed back as an input into the system, perhaps leading to changes in the transformation process to achieve more effective future outputs. Often this information helps to get to the root of problems.

Feedback can be both positive and negative, although the related field of cybernetics is based on negative feedback. *Negative feedback* is informational input that indicates that the system is deviating from a prescribed course and should readjust to a new steady state.

Feedback is a key to stimulating learning and change, and it is essential to hear and understand even the bad news and root/underlying causes we don't like to hear.

➥ **For example:** When you get rid of all the rhetoric about learning organizations you see that what's needed is to gather as much positive and negative feedback as possible, then act on it to create new learning. Only through feedback can organizations hope to learn and grow at all systems levels—individual, team, and organization.

Experienced Dynamics

We often get very little feedback on our performance or the performance of the organization vs. its customers. We do get good financial feedback, accounting for part of its primacy in most organizations.

CHARACTERISTIC #6: Multiple Outcomes/Goal-Seeking

Biological and social systems appear to have multiple goals or purposes. Social organizations seek multiple goals, if for no other reason than that they are composed of individuals and subunits with different values and objectives. Today's multicultural and diverse society is making it more and more difficult for us to resolve the differing goals we carry with us.

Since this is a characteristic of all systems, it follows that a detailed and common vision for any organization or society is crucial if its members are to focus and coordinate their actions.

➥ **For example:** The clash of individual and organizational goals causes conflict and lost productivity for all concerned—a lose-lose situation. Add this to the dehumanization, delayering, and mechanization of work and you have a very alienated workforce.

Experienced Dynamics

We often engage in *artificial either/or thinking* instead of embracing multiple outcomes, which leads to conflict rather than cooperation.

2. The Inner Workings (of a Living System)

CHARACTERISTIC #7: Equifinality of Open Systems

In mechanistic systems we see a direct cause and effect relationship between the initial conditions and the final state. Biological and social systems operate differently. *Equifinality* suggests that certain results can be achieved with different initial conditions and in different ways. It offers us the basis for the flexibility, agility, and choice needed in today's dynamic world.

This view suggests that social organizations can accomplish their objectives with diverse inputs and with varying internal activities (processes). For this reason, there is usually not one "best" way to solve most problems; in other words, as the saying goes, there's more than one way to skin a cat!

➥ **For example:** The lack of one best way to solve today's problems in organizations and in society in general is why strategic consistency as well as "operational flexibility"—or empowerment—is crucial to achieving commonly agreed upon, multiple goals (see #6). We need to challenge our minds and use our mental skills to determine how to achieve goals, as long as those goals are clear and agreed upon—in other words, we need to operate with a shared vision and a shared set of strategies to guide operational levels.

Experienced Dynamics

Instead, we often fight and insist on the *one and only best way*. We tend to simplify complex issues into a direct one-to-one, cause-effect relationship. That's unfortunate. Things are much more complex; single or simple solutions just don't work in a systems world.

CHARACTERISTIC #8: Entropy

Entropy refers to the natural characteristic of all living systems to eventually slow down and die. Physical systems are subject to entropy, which increases until the entire system fails. The tendency to move toward maximum entropy brings disorder, complete lack of resource transformation, and death.

In a closed system, the change in entropy must always be positive, toward death. However, in open biological or social systems, entropy can be arrested and may even be transformed into "negative" entropy—a process of more complete organization and enhanced ability to transform resources—because the system imports energy and resources from its environment, leading to its renewal. This is why education and learning are so important; they provide new and stimulating input (termed "neg-entropy") to transform each of us.

The old cliché "from the time we're born, we begin to die," is an apt one and applies here. Our cells completely regenerate every seven years through neg-entropy, and, in a sense, we become a completely new person. Regular follow-up and constant feedback is key to this needed renewal.

➥ **For example:** Most change efforts fail because they aren't given enough follow-up, reinforcement, and new energy. Though many managers want to get everything up and running on autopilot, this is the antithesis of what actually makes change happen. In systems terms, it takes negative entropy—what we call "new energy" in normal terms—to make change occur. Case in point: most executives are concerned about employee "buy-in," but "stay-in" is even more difficult. (For more on this topic, see *Sustaining High Performance,* by Stephen Haines.[6])

Experienced Dynamic

The absence of negative entropy is what leads to a system's obsolescence, rigidity, decline, and (ultimately) death.

CHARACTERISTIC #9: Hierarchy

A basic concept in systems thinking in nature is hierarchical relationships between systems. A system is composed both of subsystems (lower order systems) and is itself part of a suprasystem (higher order system). Thus, there is a hierarchy of the components of any living system in our world. In today's politically correct environment, the concept of hierarchy is quite unpopular, but it is a permanent fact of life in any living system. The secret is to flatten the hierarchy as much as possible and to go with the *flow of life* and what makes sense—i.e., almost "self-organizing" in a natural way—not the imposition of rigid, bureaucratic, and artificial structures.

➥ **For example:** Look at the concept of nature's food chain—it is an inescapable hierarchy, found on land, in water, and in between.

---

[6] Haines, Stephen G., with McCoy, Katie, *Sustaining High Performance.* St. Lucie Press, 1995.

➥ **For example:** Since systems are hierarchical, the organizational system is higher than the department/unit/team as a system, which is higher than an individual employee as a system (whether we like it or not). If we don't like the hierarchy or fit, we need to either work to change how the hierarchy works or lessen it, but it can't be eliminated—as some would naively propose—it's simply a fact of life within systems.

Experienced Dynamics

We often experience rigid hierarchies and bloated bureaucracies based on the old "command and control" attitude as if we really can fully control others.

CHARACTERISTIC #10: Interrelated Parts (Subsystems or Components)

By definition, a system is composed of interrelated parts or elements in some relationship with each other. This is true for all systems—mechanical, biological, and social. Every system has at least two elements, and these elements are interconnected.

The whole idea of a system is to optimize—*not* maximize—the fit of its elements in order to maximize the whole. If we merely maximize the elements of systems, we suboptimize the whole (i.e., 2 + 2 = 3—less than it should be, and less than we want it to be). Consider the practice of young college football players, who try to artificially maximize their muscles and weight with steroids and end up doing serious long-term harm to their bodies with the risk of premature death.

➥ **For example:** Organizations must involve all of their related parts to achieve their business goals. However, individual departments tend to attempt to maximize their influence in the organization individually and separately. This is detrimental to other departments and, ultimately, to the organization as a whole.

Balancing the demands of each department is difficult, but it should be a key role of senior organizational leaders. Unfortunately, this can lead to conflict issues; leaders in both private and public institutions know they often do not have conflict-resolution skills, so conflicts often get ignored or pushed aside.

Experienced Dynamics

We often experience these artificial and separate parts and components that managers try mightily to maintain—but it's impossible to do so in a system with natural and related parts.

CHARACTERISTIC #11: Dynamic Equilibrium (Steady State)

The concept of a dynamic equilibrium in "steady state" is closely related to that of negative entropy. A closed system eventually must attain an equilibrium state with maximum entropy—death or disorganization. However, an open system may attain a state where the system remains in dynamic equilibrium through the continuous inflow of materials, energy, information, and feedback. This leads to balance, stability, and resistance to change.

We tend to resist change in our lives and in our organizations and go back into balance in this dynamic equilibrium. This is normal and natural. However, we must be flexible and adaptable if we are to keep up with today's rapidly changing environment. Overcoming the desire for the rut of habit—accompanied by the desire for stability—can only come to us through becoming adaptable and flexible to change in a very personal way.

- **For example:** Dynamic equilibrium is why culture change in organizations is far more difficult to achieve than isolated change. Culture change requires modifying *all* aspects and parts of the organization's internal workings so the whole will enter a new steady state.

- **For example:** When trying to change the culture of an organization, providing everyone with training on "empowerment" is good. But the culture around the training usually defeats the intent of the training and it fails to change the culture. There is a dynamic tension present but eventually the old habits, ruts, policies, and procedures defeat the training's good intentions.

Experienced Dynamics

Resistance to change often leads to short-term myopic views and actions that lead only to stagnation.

CHARACTERISTIC #12: Internal Elaboration

Closed systems move toward entropy and disorganization. In contrast, open systems appear to move in the direction of greater differentiation, elaboration, details, and a higher level of organization sophistication. As humans, we grow and develop physically, emotionally, and intellectually.

This can also lead to organizational complexity and bureaucracy in its worst form. Complexity must be continuously resisted as it occurs naturally—it is a part of the natural process of ossification, rigidity, and death.

- **For example:** This is why the KISS method and guidance to clarify and simplify are so crucial to success in our lives and organizations. Also, the elimination of waste, in total quality management and reengineering terms, is a positive trend toward reversing this ossification.

Experienced Dynamics

Often, the growth of the organization leads to chaos, complexity, and confusion and we have no concepts of how to deal with them. That is what systems thinking can address.

In summary, **Standard Systems Dynamics** can be viewed as follows:

Natural Laws/Desired State vs.	Experienced Dynamics
1. **Holism**—Overall Purpose Focused Synergy/Transformational	1. Parts/Activity Focused/Suboptimal Results
2. **Open Systems**–Open to Environment	2. Closed Systems/Low Environmental Scan
3. **Boundaries**—Integrated/Collaborative	3. Fragmented/Turf Battles/Separate/ Parochial
4. **Input/Output**—How Natural Systems Operate	4. Piecemeal/Analytic/Sequential and Narrow View
5. **Feedback**—on Effectiveness/Root Causes	5. Low Feedback/Financial Only
6. **Multiple Outcomes**—Goals	6. Artificial Either/Or Thinking
7. **Equifinality**—Flexibility and Agility	7. Direct Cause-Effect/One Best Way
8. **Entropy**—Follow-up/Inputs of Energy/Renewal	8. Decline/Rigidity/Obsolescence/Death
9. **Hierarchy**—Flatter Organization/Self-Organizing	9. Hierarchy/Bureaucracy/Command and Control
10. **Interrelated Parts**—Relationships/ Involvement and Participation	10. Separate Parts/Components/Entities/ Silos
11. **Dynamic Equilibrium**—Stability and Balance/Culture	11. Short-Term Myopic View/Ruts/Resistance to Change
12. **Internal Elaboration**—Details and Sophistication	12. Complexity and Confusion

Once you have grasped these Standard Systems Dynamics, you need to know how they play out in change so the desired dynamics occur.

Systems Concept #3:
A-B-C-D Systems Model

Is your personal mental mind-set and model the four-phased systems model? Is it your orientation to life?

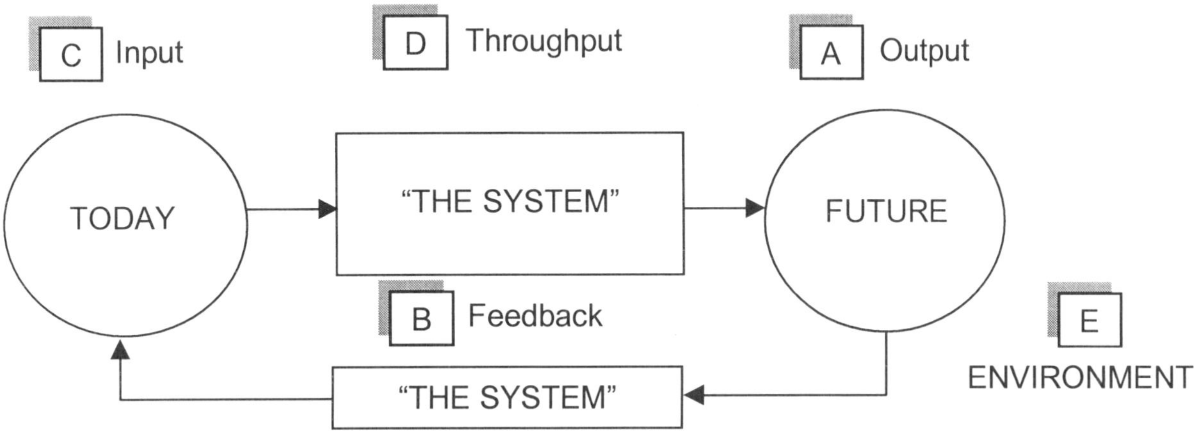

➥ **For Example:** Is this A-B-C-D model how you think and act in every aspect of your life . . . both at work and at home? If it is, then you will have a clear set of outputs or life goals (Phase A) for yourself.

Systems, as we have said, are made up of a set of components that work together for the overall objective of the whole (output). Thus, this framework, dubbed the A-B-C-D Systems Model, is a reflection of that definition.

This model asks us to ask five questions:

A Where do we want to be? (i.e., our ends, outcomes, purposes, goals, holistic vision)

B How will we know when we get there? (i.e., the customers' needs and wants connected into a quantifiable feedback system)

C Where are we now? (i.e., today's issues and problems)

D How do we get there? (i.e., close the gap from C ➔ A in a complete and holistic way)

E And an ongoing question: What is changing in the environment that we need to consider?

Analytic/Linear/Sequential Thinking Is Different from Systems Thinking.

Analytic/linear/sequential thinking:

- starts with today and today's current state, issues, and problems
- breaks the issues and/or problems down into their smallest components
- solves each component separately (i.e., maximizes the solution)
- has no far reaching vision or goal (just the absence of the problem)

  Note: In systems thinking, the whole is primary and the parts are secondary (not vice versa).

"If you don't know where you're going, any road will get you there."

For you, systems thinking will probably be a new way of thinking and looking at every issue or problem you have all day long. Start with the outcomes, Phase A, and work/think backwards to create the future you want.

Indepth Understanding

The General Systems Theory Model (input, throughput, output, and feedback with the environment) provides elegant simplicity to reduce the chaos and complexity we experience when we use analytic/piecemeal thinking.

Teach everyone in your organization to frame all issues into an A–B–C–D systems context that can be understood by all. It will help you focus on the result/output—not just a knee-jerk solution—and it will result in better, longer-term answers/solutions.

To truly comprehend the systems concept, it is critical to understand that a system goes beyond simply being an entity as a whole—it is also a living, breathing, ongoing process, requiring inputs, outputs, and feedback (phases A through D).

Phase A

The defining phase in a systems model is Phase A, the output that results from that system's activity. This phase asks the question: "Where do we want to be?" This, in part, is why some refer to systems thinking as "backwards thinking"—we begin with the desired outcome and work backward to achieve that result. This is the # 1 systems question always asked in any situation—and it must be asked in the context of its environment and the other levels of systems around it.

***Phase* B**

The next part of the systems model is Phase B, the feedback loop. It is at this step in systems thinking that we start thinking *backward* to determine what must take place in order for our desired outcome to occur. This phase asks the # 2 systems question: "How will we know when we achieve our desired outcome?" This is the time to decide how we will measure our achievement. We then feed that decision back into the system. This phase also operates as a way to see if the first phase needs more work; for example, we may find the goal has been too broadly defined and needs redefinition. Be sure to keep asking the question, *What is changing in the environment that we need to consider?*

***Phase* C**

This phase, with its question, "Where are we right now?" is the input phase—the phase in which the system begins to create strategies and specific actions for closing the gap between what's happening right now versus what should ultimately happens. This is where linear thinking begins and where we see what differentiates linear and reductionist thinking from systems thinking. Linear thinking starts with the present, problem solving isolated events, whereas systems thinking sees inputs and the present in light of outcomes (Phase A).

***Phase* D**

This phase—the "throughput phase"—asks "How do we get there from here?" It's all about the #1 system itself: interdependently implementing the necessary, ongoing processes, activities, relationships, and changes to create the required outcome. Another criteria of this phase of the systems model is to plan on what processes must be developed and put into motion to reach the desired future state.

Suggestions for Use

General Systems Theory provides a generic, universal framework to which literally any set of requirements can be adapted, as long as the A–B–C–D locator phases are used (in the environment).

The systems framework also simplifies *how* we approach and evaluate all of our problems and issues because it is *an orientation to life*. Use it in all you think about, do, and evaluate.

Some of its many uses are shown in the rest of these tools. **However, its use is virtually unlimited as a framework and orientation to life.**

Note: See all the tools based on the application of the input-output model. Each of them is a specific example/tool to begin to apply this fundamental *master tool*.

Systems Concept #4:
Changing Systems (The Natural Cycles of Life and Change)

Our natural world does not operate in a linear, sequential fashion, despite all our training and all the traditional engineering models available to us which assume that it does. The natural way of life is that there are cycles of change—day and night, up and down, awake and asleep. Even the Bull and Bear markets on Wall Street aren't immune to this. We call this natural rhythm of life (birth, growth, maturity, decline, death) **The Rollercoaster of Change**℠ in order to acknowledge the complexities of change in our dynamic world.

Some of these historical and natural cycles of change and learning include:

The Environment	Civilizations	Historical Ages
• Ocean tides • Volcanoes • Whale and bird migration • Lunar cycle • Day and night	• Inca, Aztec, Mayan empires • Chinese dynasties • Roman empire • British empire	• Hunting and gathering • Dark Ages • Agriculture Age • Industrial Age • Information Age
Industries	**Travel**	**Life**
• Start-up • High growth • Maturity • Decline • Renewal	• Automobile • Ocean liner • Mass transit • Airplanes • Space shuttle	• Birth, death, new generation • food chain • food cycle • growth/decline

Economics	Flight
• Bull/Bear markets • K-wave (long wave—Nikolai Kondratieff, 1926) • Recessions, depressions • Profit-taking • Inflation	• Balloon • Wright Brothers—biplanes • Single-wing propeller • Jet planes • Concorde • Satellites, rockets • Space shuttles

Human, living systems keep on changing. It is a natural part of life (and death). Change is constant. The key is to *find simplicity on the far side of complexity*. That's what Systems Theory is all about.

There are many, many uses of this Rollercoaster concept during changes of all types, as we shall see in the tools. However, the basic Rollercoaster of Change[SM] looks like this:

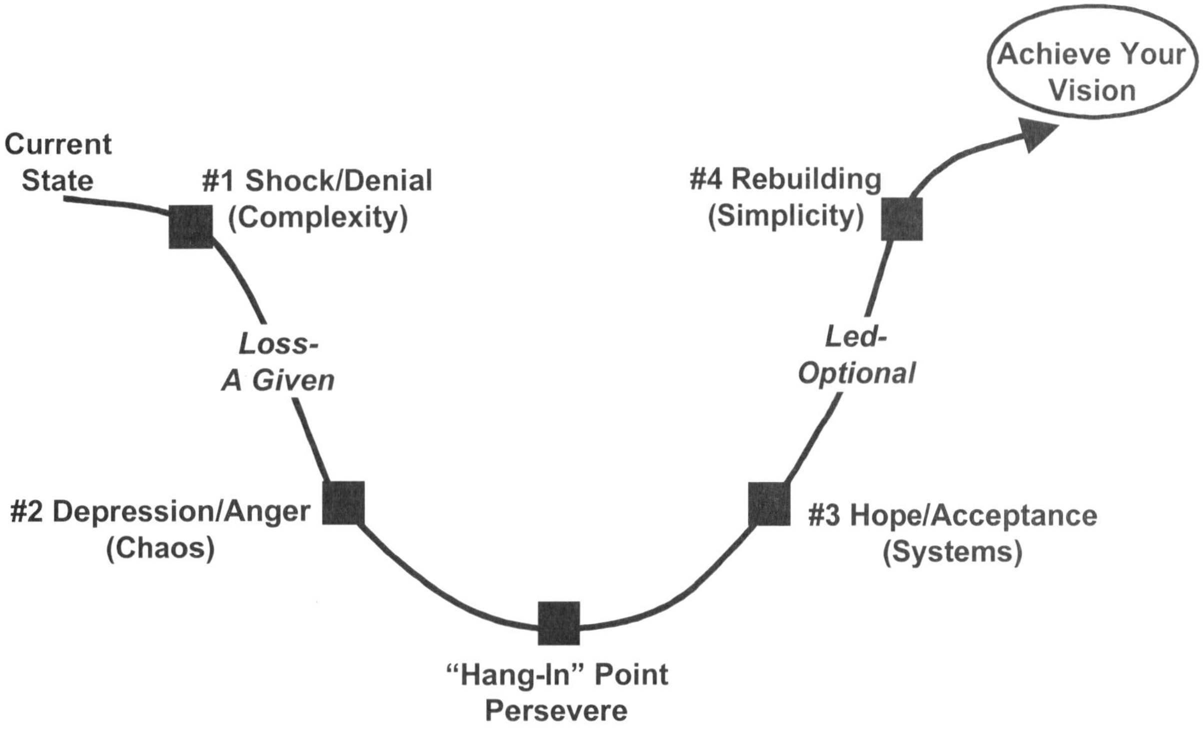

To summarize all of these elegantly simple four systems concepts, see the following aid.

The Systems Thinking Approach℠

Systems: Systems are made up of a set of components that work together for the overall objective of the whole (output).

CONCEPT #1: Seven Levels of Living (Open) Systems

Hierarchy

1. Cell
2. Organ
3. Organism/Individual
4. Group/Team
5. Organization
6. Society/Community
7. Supranational System/Earth

(3–6: Organizational Focus)

Levels of Thinking

Problems that are created by our current level of thinking can't be solved by that same level of thinking.

—*Albert Einstein*

So . . . if we generally use analytical thinking, we now need real "Systems Thinking" to resolve our issues.

—*Stephen G. Haines*

Six Rings of Focus and Readiness

Increased:

- Complexity/chaos
- Readiness/willingness
- Skills growth

Note: Rings 3-4-5 are 3 of the "Seven Levels of Living Systems"

Rings 3A-4A-5A are "Collisions of Systems" with other systems

Adapted from General Systems Theory and Haines Associates, 1978.
Based on 1984 and 1995 literature searches and subsequent client feedback ever since.
CSM has offices in the USA • Canada • Australia • Korea

CONCEPT #2: Laws of Natural Systems
(Standard Systems Dynamics)

Natural Laws/Desired State vs.	Experienced Dynamics
1. Holism—Overall Purpose Focused Synergy/Transformational	1. Parts/Activity Focused/ Suboptimal Results
2. Open Systems—Open to Environment	2. Closed Systems/Low Environmental Scan
3. Boundaries—Integrated/ Collaborative	3. Fragmented/Turf Battles/ Separate/Parochial
4. Input/Output—How Natural Systems Operate	4. Piecemeal/Analytic/ Sequential and Narrow View
5. Feedback—on Effectiveness/Root Causes	5. Low Feedback/Financial Only
6. Multiple Outcomes—Goals	6. Artificial Either/Or Thinking
7. Equifinality—Flexibility and Agility	7. Direct Cause-Effect/ One Best Way
8. Entropy—Follow-up/Inputs of Energy/Renewal	8. Decline/Rigidity/ Obsolescence/Death
9. Hierarchy—Flatter Organization/Self-Organizing	9. Hierarchy/Bureaucracy/ Command and Control
10. Interrelated Parts—Relationships/Involvement and Participation	10. Separate Parts/Com-ponents/Entities/Solos
11. Dynamic Equilibrium—Stability and Balance/ Culture	11. Short-Term Myopic View/Ruts/ Resistance to Change
12. Internal Elaboration—Details and Sophistication	12. Complexity and Confusion
12. A. Cycles of Change—Chaos and then Elegant Simplicity	12. A. Individual/Sequential Change/New Problems Created

1420 Monitor Road, San Diego, CA 92110
(619) 275-6528 • FAX (619) 275-0324

The Systems Thinking Approach℠

Systems Thinking℠ . . . is finding patterns and relationships, and learning to reinforce or change these patterns to fulfill your vision and mission.

CONCEPT #3: A-B-C-D Systems Model

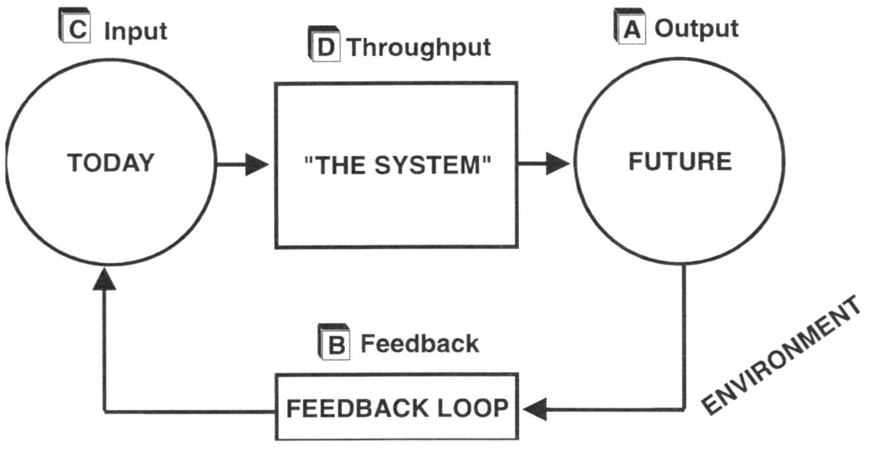

Four Questions in Sequence

A. Where do we want to be? (i.e., our ends, outcomes, purposes, goals, holistic vision)

B. How will we know when we get there? (i.e., the customer's needs connected into a quantifiable feedback system)

C. Where are we now? (i.e., today's issues and problems)

D. How do we get there? (i.e., close the gap from C ➔ A in a complete and holistic way)

Why Thinking Matters

The way you think creates the results you get.

The most powerful way to impact the quality of your results

is to improve the ways you think.

"How you think … is how you act … is how you are."

Adapted from General Systems Theory and Haines Associates, 1978.
Based on 1984 and 1995 literature searches and client feedback ever since.
CSM has offices in the USA • Canada • Australia • Korea

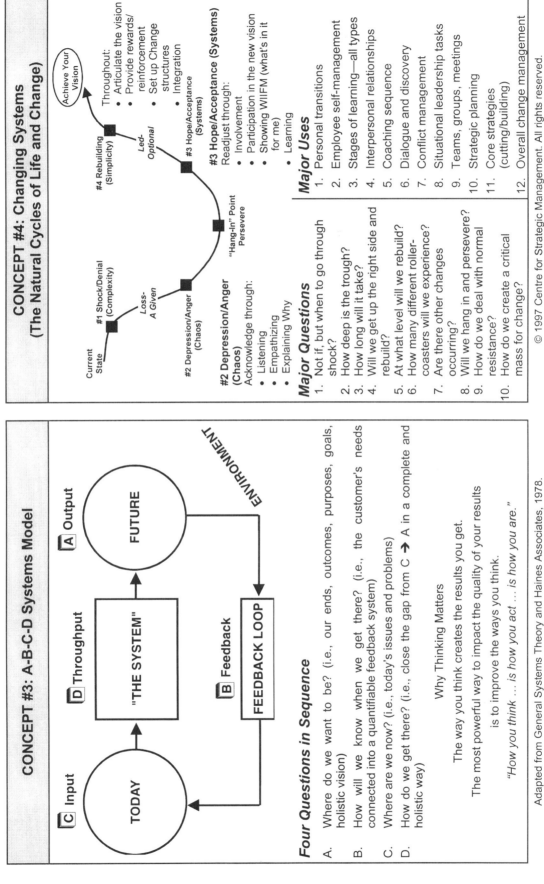

CONCEPT #4: Changing Systems (The Natural Cycles of Life and Change)

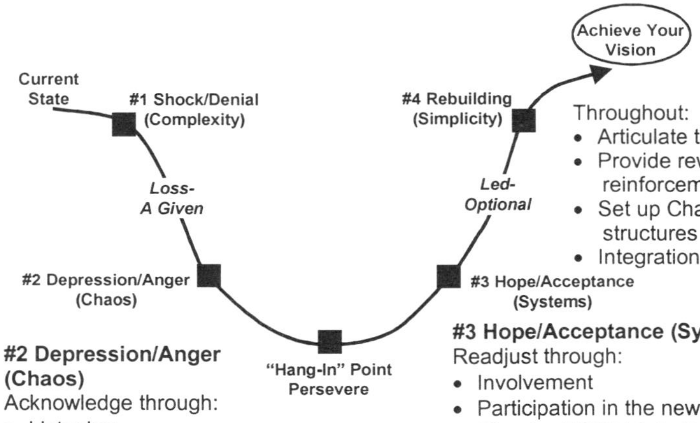

Throughout:
- Articulate the vision
- Provide rewards/ reinforcement
- Set up Change structures
- Integration

#2 Depression/Anger (Chaos)
Acknowledge through:
- Listening
- Empathizing
- Explaining Why

#3 Hope/Acceptance (Systems)
Readjust through:
- Involvement
- Participation in the new vision
- Showing WIIFM (what's in it for me)
- Learning

Major Questions

1. Not if, but when to go through shock?
2. How deep is the trough?
3. How long will it take?
4. Will we get up the right side and rebuild?
5. At what level will we rebuild?
6. How many different roller-coasters will we experience?
7. Are there other changes occurring?
8. Will we hang in and persevere?
9. How do we deal with normal resistance?
10. How do we create a critical mass for change?

Major Uses

1. Personal transitions
2. Employee self-management
3. Stages of learning—all types
4. Interpersonal relationships
5. Coaching sequence
6. Dialogue and discovery
7. Conflict management
8. Situational leadership tasks
9. Teams, groups, meetings
10. Strategic planning
11. Core strategies (cutting/building)
12. Overall change management

1420 Monitor Road, San Diego, CA 92110
(619) 275-6528 • FAX (619) 275-0324

Some Guiding Principles of the Systems Age

Now that we have looked at the four basic concepts of the Systems Thinking Approach℠, let's break them down to some useful and basic principles.

Success or failure in this coming Systems Age will depend, ultimately, on what we adopt as our primary guiding principles. As Von Bertalanffy said, *"In one way or another, we are forced to deal with complexities, with 'wholes' or 'systems' in all fields of knowledge."* [7]

We must recognize and understand the twelve interrelated general systems characteristics and the seven levels of living systems. Only then can we understand the guiding principles of the Systems Age. They will aid us immeasurably in our effort to work with systems that require change in order to achieve our desired outcomes.

What follows are principles derived from these twelve interrelated characteristics which I developed at the Centre for Strategic Management. These guiding principles for the Systems Age will help us identify what *needs* to be changed, and clarify *how* it can be changed. However, it is important to remember that these principles are growing and changing; thus the title word, "Some."

PRINCIPLE #1: The entity to be changed must be clear. (Remember "holism.")

Challenge the obvious. Always look for and identify which of the Seven Levels of Living Systems you're dealing with. Be clear on the entity you are working to change. Is it an individual, team, family, business unit, community, company, state, nation, or international? What are its boundaries? Is it relatively open, or is it closed in its environmental interactions?

PRINCIPLE #2: Ask the first systems question: "What are the desired outcomes?" (Remember . . . systems are multiple-goal seeking.)

Develop clarity/agreement to this before beginning any actions. Keep in mind that there are usually multiple outcomes; not either/or questions from reductionistic thinking. Other words for outcomes include *vision, ends, goals, objectives, mission, purpose,* (the "what"), etc.

Without agreement on ends, our actions will never have a chance of succeeding. Once the "what" is clear, you will have many options regarding "how."

PRINCIPLE #3: There are many different ways to achieve the same desired outcomes; involvement of the right people involved in planning and implementing the solutions/actions is key. (Remember . . . equifinality.)

People support what they help create. It follows that decision making should be as close to the needed actions as possible, and to the entity we desire to change in #1. People have a natural

[7] Von Bertalanffy, L., *General Systems Theory.* New York: Braziller, 1968.

desire to be involved and provide input into decisions that affect them *before* the decision is made. For leaders, this is called "participatory management."

PRINCIPLE #4: *Feedback is the breakfast of champions—be flexible and adaptive. (Remember the feedback loop.)*

In today's complex and continually changing world, initial solutions are not even as important as the ability to gain constant feedback and adapt in order to achieve your desired outcomes. The ability to be flexible and adaptive (i.e., to learn, grow, change, and adapt to changes in the environment) is crucial. Economies of speed are replacing economies of scale as a key competitive edge. Feedback is the key input into today's need for learning organizations. It will help them learn, grow, and adapt at all levels of the organizational system (individuals, teams, and the organization as a whole).

PRINCIPLE #5: *The whole is more important than the parts—and the relationships and processes are key. (Remember holism and subsystems.)*

Synthesis, how the parts fit/link together in an integrated process, in support of the whole outcome, is the most important process in any system.

Analysis of each part's effectiveness cannot be analyzed in a void, but only in relationship to the other parts and the processes that lead to the whole. *Always remember that a system cannot be subdivided into independent parts.* Change in one part affects the whole and the other interdependent parts or processes. This is true whether talking about families, teams, departments, neighborhoods, organizations, or society; something we all need to learn and understand.

PRINCIPLE #6: *Work and align the entity to be changed from the outside-in—not inside-out. (Remember . . . open systems view.)*

Remember to employ "backwards thinking." Start with the wants and needs of the customer and desired outcomes to gain clarity. Then work backward into the organization to determine how to meet those current and future needs, while still meeting the multiple outcomes of other key stakeholders.

Align all employees, suppliers, the entire organization, and business processes across departments to meet these outcomes. This is the conceptual basis for business process reengineering in today's organizations. However, it is often fragmented into departmental elements or internal cost-cutting activities only; customer impact is too often ignored.

PRINCIPLE #7: *All systems are linked to other systems—some larger, some smaller—in a hierarchy.*

No system is independent of any other. We are all, as human beings, linked in a hierarchy of systems to all others on this planet, to a greater or lesser extent, *whether we like it or not*. Pay close attention to both the system and system-system linkages as well. (Supplier, organization, customer is one set of linkages; individual, family, and community would be another example of system-system linkages).

PRINCIPLE #8: Root causes and effects are usually not linked closely in time and space. (Remember open systems and systems boundaries.)

Our simplistic cause-effect analyses and desire for quick fixes often create more problems than we solve. Because our world is composed of seven levels of complex and interdependent systems, multiple causes with multiple effects are the true reality, as are circles of causality-effects. See, for example, how the ocean/clouds/rain/wind, etc., affect our local weather and crops.

Delay time—the time between causes and their impacts—can have enormous influences on a system. The concept of "delayed effect" is often missed in our impatient society. It is often too subtle, ignored, and almost always underestimated. When we feel that results aren't happening quickly enough, it shakes our confidence, causing unnecessarily violent "knee-jerk" reactions.

Decisions often have long-term consequences years later. Mind mapping, fishbone diagrams, and all sorts of creativity and brainstorming tools are quite useful here.

However, *keep in mind that the complexity we encounter is often far beyond our ability to fully assess and comprehend intuitively*. For this reason, it is crucial to flag or anticipate delays, understand and appreciate them, and learn to work with them rather than against them.

PRINCIPLE #9: The KISS method really is best—reverse the entropy! (Remember entropy and neg-entropy.)

Systems can continuously increase in complexity until they become bureaucratic and ossified, ultimately resulting in the death of the system. All living systems require constant energy and inputs (i.e., feedback) into them if they are to reverse this entropy. Otherwise, all living systems eventually run down and die.

For example, while human beings and families obviously have a finite life cycle, it doesn't have to be this way for neighborhoods, communities, and organizations. For them, the renewal process that reverses the entropy is key to long-term success. As Meg Wheatley discusses in her recent book, *The Simpler Way*, chaos and disorder are often a precursor to renewal and growth at a higher level.

This is the good news. We now have a virtually limitless supply of constant feedback, which provides us with new input toward change. On the reverse side, however, we get information overload and feel that life is getting too complicated.

We need to eliminate the waste that complexity brings. Remember that the KISS method is more powerful than many economies of scale. Focus on the fundamentals, not the fads. In the future, the virtual corporation may very well be more effective than the more traditional, vertically integrated complex organizations.

A corollary to KISS (keep it simple, stupid!) is the "*Rule of 3*." List topics, issues, or anything else for that matter, in groups of three. It is much easier for people to remember this way (hence three Systems Concepts and a fourth on "Changing Systems") and Mother Nature, herself, prefers it!

PRINCIPLE #10: The steady state equilibrium we all want can kill us. In a rapidly changing society, the biggest risk is to stay the same.

Change keeps us creative, but it is awkward, uncertain, ambiguous, and even painful. Thus, our normal and natural inclination is to maintain the status quo and its comfortableness. Change requires us to (1) admit we need to change and *will* it, and then (2) acquire the new skills and abilities to function more effectively.

Knowledge and information are just inputs, and not enough to be effective by themselves. New skills need to be developed if we want to learn, grow, and change. Short-term creative destruction can sometimes be key to long-term advances that are made; today's "steady state" is one of constant change.

PRINCIPLE #11: Focus and strengthen the basic units/systems of organizations. (Remember holism.) The basic unit of organizations is not just the individual alone. It is also the relationships of individuals to one another. Thus, we believe the basic units to be: (1) individuals, (2) individual–individual relationships, (3) teams, (4) cross-functional teams, (5) the organization.

We need to balance our strong Western tendency to glorify the individual at the expense of team and organization (Asian societies often do the opposite).

PRINCIPLE #12: Change is an individual act. (According to the Seven Levels of Living Systems, the individual is the smallest conscious system.)

Organizational change is a myth. Organizations and institutions change when people change. Processes and procedures change when people change their behaviors. Accepting responsibility for yourself and your actions and being accountable for them is key. Each of us needs to understand how we *link to* and *fit in* with the rest of society.

Unfortunately, in terms of wisdom and maturity, *interdependence* is the highest order, coming after dependent and independent stages. The truth is, independence is really a myth! Thus, focusing on assisting individual change within the family/team/unit-as-a-system and context is the way to assist individual change.

PRINCIPLE #13: Systems upon systems upon systems are too complex to fully understand and manage centrally.

Liberation from regulation, shaping corporate bureaucracies into smaller units, privatization and free market economies are generally more efficient and effective than government or big business can ever be in understanding the complexities of systems. It is the thousands and thousands of little decisions we all make each day in our businesses that shape and meet these market needs, not central government regulations. Clearly, government has a role to play in today's society, just not an all-encompassing one! The same is true for big corporations.

PRINCIPLE #14: We are holistic human beings in search of meaning. (Remember multiple-goal seeking.)

Our search for meaning in our lives is crucial to our own success and failure. This meaning only comes from the "ends" and "whats" of serving others outside of ourselves. Again, however, this requires that we understand our own interdependence with others in our world.

The more we can balance ourselves in body, mind, and spirit, the better we can serve others. Starve any of our three essential elements and we starve as human beings. Dehumanize us in our work settings and we don't perform anywhere near our true potential.

PRINCIPLE #15: The ultimate systems principle: "Problems can't be solved at the level they were created." (Albert Einstein)

. . . so go to the next higher system's level and its desired outcome in order to succeed (superordinate goals).

PRINCIPLE #16–18: "You tell me . . ."

Above all in systems thinking is the understanding that we learn about our systems and ourselves as we evolve and grow and change. The learning never stops, nor should it. So you tell me what other General Systems principles there are in *your* line of vision!

Summary

Now that we have explained these beginning principles of Systems Thinking℠, we need to relate them to one additional application of the change concept: Learning and The Learning Organization, because organizations are where most change and learning is taking place.

Change = Learning
Learning = Change

What Is Learning? *and* The Learning Organization

"If you think education is expensive, consider the price of ignorance!" [8]

The idealized concept of **The Learning Organization** is an important application of **Systems Thinking**℠. These two concepts—**systems thinking and systems learning**—are the foundation of the Centre's work. We have clarified and simplified these complex concepts into three frameworks from Systems Thinking to guide people in their quest for these elusive "holy grails" of learning and The Learning Organization.

Let's examine these three systems frameworks in more detail.

Framework #1:	**Multiple Outcomes**—There are multiple learning outcomes (the *whats*) for individuals, teams, organizations, and systems of all types.
Framework #2:	**Environmental Scanning and Feedback/Reinforcement**—These are key to "how" people, teams, and organizations learn.
Framework #3:	**The "Seven Levels of Living Systems**"—These are guidelines for "where" learning occurs within complex systems such as organizations.

Framework #1: Multiple Outcomes
("What" people learn)

Learning is the term we use for different kinds of new outcomes, facts, or understanding and the demonstrated mastery we acquire as a result of both formal study and life experiences. However, there are three kinds of learning (i.e., multiple outcomes) in this world. Another example of our Rule of Three is *what* three things we learn:

- Knowledge—first comes awareness, and then the acquisition of knowledge, new concepts, facts, and opinions. This is where schools and organizations usually focus (erroneously, as we shall see), giving rise to the term "knowledgeable idiot."

- Attitude—the willingness and motivation to act or not to act. Note: Attitude is often the key to a successful life—positive attitudes of resilience, determination, optimism, and self-initiative, which are sometimes thought of as values and character, are other ways of looking for attitude.

- Skills—the use, demonstration, or performance of an action. We use our skills to apply some new knowledge to one of life's tasks.

---

[8] Bumper sticker.

Competencies vs. Knowledge

In today's information society, new knowledge is the valued commodity. However, as Peter Drucker puts it:

"The essence of management is to make knowledge productive." [9]

The application of this knowledge is your ability (or lack of ability) to put the learning into skilled practice in a more and more competent way over time. Eventually your ability to use all this learning effectively will increase your level of "competency."

This new focus on people's "competencies" as part of The Learning Organization needs to focus on related groups of skills and abilities, not just knowledge alone. Those who focus solely on this (and many do) are narrow in their views of learning and do us all a disservice.

There is a very old management matrix that outlines "what" knowledge, skills, and attitudes management and professionals in organizations should learn. The matrix is just as applicable today as it was years ago.

Three Levels of Leadership and Management Development

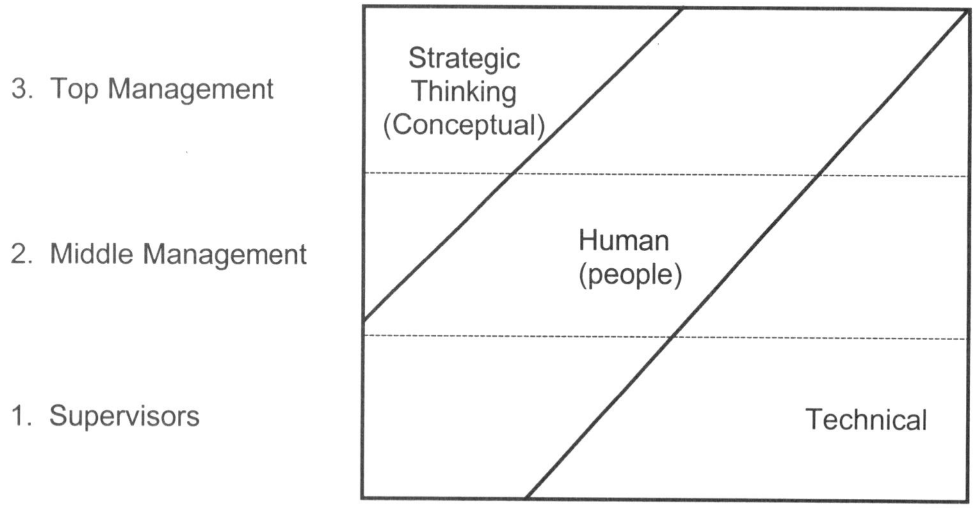

As we move up the management ladder, we find that different learning is required. One of the reasons why bright individuals and good organizations fail is because they don't learn, practice, and apply all the competencies their level of responsibility calls for. The need to acquire additional (and new) people skills and competencies is one constant growth for which managers must plan. This is why my partner, Dennis Rowley, calls leadership "a contemplative and life-long art."

Those management members who are involved in creating a Learning Organization need to understand that their learning will continue throughout their careers, at every level (first line, middle, and senior management). Additional breadth and depth of all three types of learning (knowledge, skills, and attitudes) and different categories of learning (technical, people, conceptual/strategic) will be needed.

[9] Drucker, Peter, *Managing in a Time of Great Change.* New York: Dutton, 1995.

Learning vs. Teaching

Learning is not the same as teaching. Teaching is the work or process of instructing, presenting, or imparting knowledge or skills, or causing someone to learn by memorization, example, or experience. In general, the best learning often occurs when the teacher lets go of being "The Sage on the Stage" and becomes "The Guide on the Side."

The teacher may teach, but did the learner learn? And what did he or she really learn? There are always multiple outcomes and unintended or wrong byproducts.

Whatever you do, don't confuse learning and teaching. They are not the same. **Teaching is the activity; learning is the outcome.** Teaching solely by presentation and lecture rarely imparts all the information we want people to learn, and never the skills, attitudes, and actions need to be successful. **So, don't forget:**

Become The Guide on the Side—not The Sage on the Stage.

Now, let's move on to how people learn, through feedback and environmental scanning.

Framework #2: Environmental Scanning and Feedback
("How" people learn)

Everyone seems to agree that adults learn best by doing. Now there is growing agreement that everyone (not just adults) learns by *doing*. Educational professionals use terms like *cooperative learning, outcome-based education,* and *authentic learning.*

Some ways for learning specialists to assist, guide, or facilitate learning include:

Types of Learning	Methods
Knowledge	Read/Lecture/Video
Skills	Demonstration/Practice
Attitudes	Group Discussion/Peer Pressure

Obviously, interactive learning requires that we maintain constant awareness of the environment we are in and how it is changing. Different situations and environments require different strategies to achieve the same end. Thus, scanning the environment and providing feedback (a key Systems Thinking^{SM} concept) always comes into play. Many "learnings" and applications as to what is correct are situational or make sense only within a certain context. For instance, centralized and vertically integrated organizations of the '60s and '70s worked well, but the need for speed in the '90s has made flattened, decentralized organizations with partnerships and alliance the key to success.

This "environmental feedback" is best conceptualized by **The Learning Organization** cycle.

Learning is comprised of (1) awareness, knowledge, and thoughts; (2) skills; and (3) attitude, motivation, and feelings.

The application of this learning is your ability (or lack of ability) to put the learning into practice consistently.

Eventually your abilities to use this learning effectively will become your competencies.

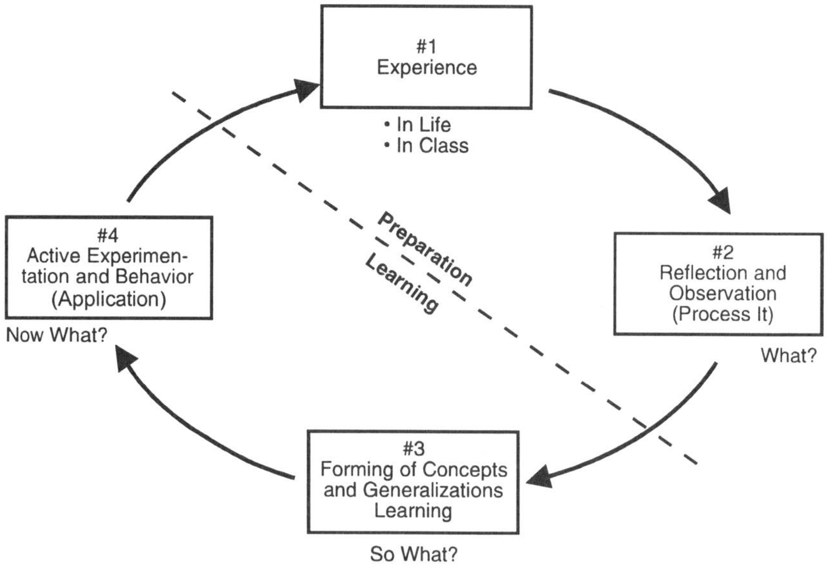

Adapted from the Kolb, Rubin, McIntyre Model of Learning[10]

What this circular model shows (using involvement and feedback as the keys) is that training activities are not enough to create learning. Processing them (feedback), making broader generalizations, and applying them are necessary. Thus after an activity/action occurs—whether in a meeting, in training, or on the job—there are three simple questions to ask **in sequence**. These three questions create the learning and improvement for next time. After all, the heart of **The Learning Organization** is continuous improvement. The three questions are:

1. **What** happened (What did we see and feel? What were the trends?)

2. **So what** can we learn, generalize, or figure out?

3. **Now what** are we going to do/apply differently (as a result of this)?

This cycle never stops—all our lives, we learn. It is just a question of conscious vs. random or passive learning (at the TV set, etc.).

Note: For those of you already familiar with The Rollercoaster of Change[SM], these four steps on the sequence of learning are the same four phases of the **Rollercoaster**. Why? Because learning is about change. Learning *is* change. They are one and the same. There is even a *Stairway of Learning* we predictably climb again and again, topic after topic.

Stairway of Learning

Organizations begin to change only when individuals begin to change and grow. Without individual learning, there can be no organizational learning. And, the learner is responsible for the change; the voyage of learning, to be successful, is a personal one.

---

[10] Kolb, David A., *Experiential Learning: Experience as the Source of Learning and Development.* New York: Prentice Hall, 1983.

The Stairway of Learning, developed by my partner, Jim McKinlay, leads to a doorway of vast possibilities. It includes four steps and four risers that serve as the transition stages between steps. It's helpful to reflect on a specific new skill you've developed, such as learning how to drive a car, or learning how to use a computer, as we explore the following stages (with an illustration provided at the end of the exploration).

Step #1: Unconscious Incompetence

At this stage, "You don't know what you don't know," a very dangerous place to be. You are not conscious of things you cannot do and you probably are not even concerned about this lack of competence.

> ***Riser #1: Awareness.*** Here you become aware that there is something you *don't* know. This is the beginning of awareness of yourself and of feedback from others.

Step #2: Conscious Incompetence

You are now conscious of your own limitations in certain areas. It's up to you to decide whether or not you want to become competent. If so, then seek support and assistance to become more knowledgeable and skillful. If not, your incompetence will continue. **It's a personal choice!**

> ***Riser #2: Attitude and Knowledge***. This is a deliberate and conscious shift. You must have the right attitude and be ready to learn. What's your best approach to developing competence? Is it through a course, private coaching, or through on-the-job assignments?

Step #3: Conscious Competence

After developing the basic skills, you now have some competence, but your movements are still methodical and mechanical. You lack the fluid rhythm of one who is truly competent, but you *are* moving in the right direction!

> ***Riser #3: Skills Acquisition***. "Practice makes perfect." Through dedication and perseverance, you begin to transfer the skill from your mind into your body. Your motions become more fluid. Candid feedback is critical here so that you don't develop bad habits. You must also reinforce the proper skills.

Step # 4: Unconscious Competence

At this stage, you are capable of performing the function in an automatic or natural way without having to think much about it. It has become second nature to you.

> ***Riser #4: Mastery.*** Now you're on the way to achieving a superior level or mastery of the task. This is high-level performance. A whole new level of learning opens up. In the martial arts, after progressing through the various levels of colored belts to achieve your black belt, you find out there are multiple levels of black belts.

People with a high level of personal mastery live in a continual learning mode. They never "arrive." But personal mastery is not something you possess. It is a process. It is a lifelong discipline. People with a high level of personal mastery are acutely aware of their ignorance, incompetence, and growth needs.

The learning cycle begins again—only this time the stairway is at a higher plane of knowledge and skills. The learning process continues and continues, as does the Stairway of Learning.

Stairway of Learning

"Organizations and teams learn . . . when individuals learn."

—Jim McKinlay

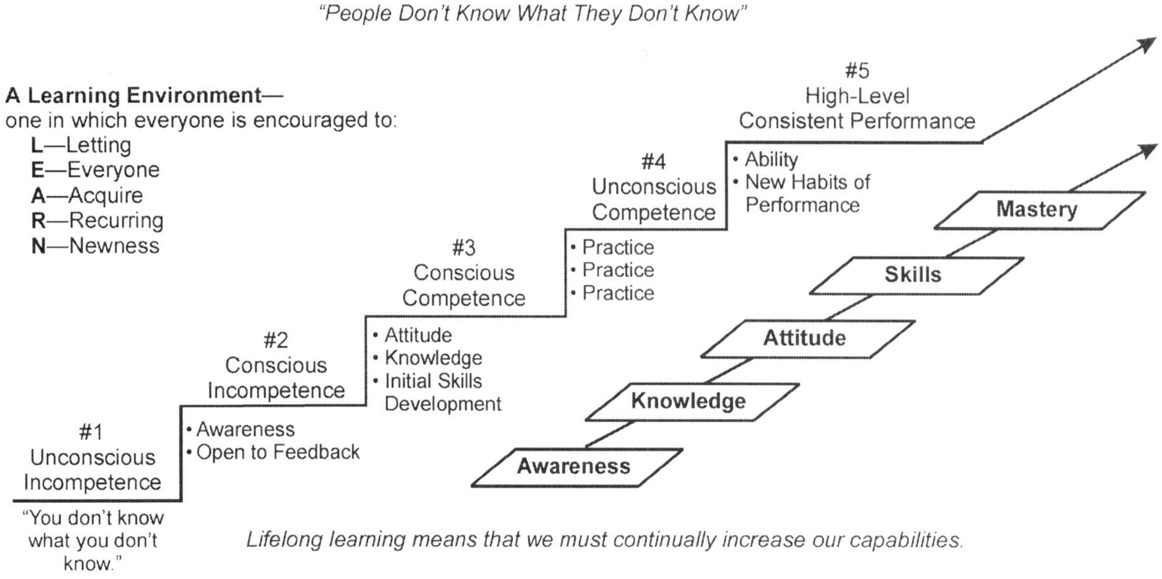

Reinforcement of Learning

Traditional training is a one-time event or a topic-by-topic school course. Both of these methods frequently neglect to focus on the environment and root causes within which the desired learning is occurring:

- A child who is hungry won't be ready to learn.
- The employee who has a supervisor who doesn't believe in or know what the training is will be prevented from learning more.

Once the course/event is over, it's over—despite the fact we know people generally need to see/hear something **four times** before they fully learn it. We also learn better when more senses are involved (not just passive listening). Over 60% of us are visual learners. The need for reinforcement is crucial.

Reinforcement Pyramid
(To Sustain New Behaviors)

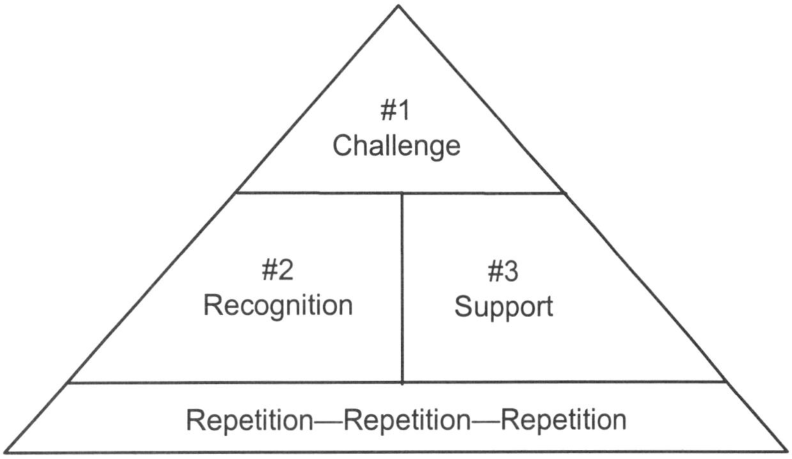

This list could be the topic of a complete article or book. However, a few types of reinforcement ideas are in order to develop the concept further:

1. Resource library for books/periodicals
2. Subscriptions to newsletters, book summaries
3. Visual reinforcement symbols (walls/ plastic cards)
4. Management networks and buddy systems
5. Celebrations of successes, events
6. Skills assessment, development planning
7. Weekly, monthly, quarterly review meetings

What else can you think of? My favorite ways to reinforce learning are to ask learners three questions and have them answered within the last 3 to 5 minutes at the end of a meeting, a seminar, or a workshop:

How did today/the meeting/the training go?

#1 What to continue?
#2 What to do more of?
#3 What to do less of?

Framework #3: Seven Levels of Living Systems
("Where" learning occurs)

Now, let's put all these ideas together and look deeper at The Learning Organization. First, ***where*** does learning need to occur? The answer is everywhere! So, how many levels and kinds of interactions does any organizational system have?

The answer starts with General Systems Theory: Again, what are the Seven Levels of Living Systems?

Level #1 Cells
Level #2 Organs
Level #3 Individuals
Level #4 Teams
Level #5 Organization
Level #6 Society
Level #7 Earth

Our focus in this book is on levels #3, 4, and 5: Individuals, Teams, and Organizations as well as the collisions of the levels of systems at the one-to-one level, cross-functional team level, and the level of your organization—environmental interfaces. To create a learning organization, we must see all three types of learning (knowledge, skills, and attitude) at these six levels of organizational functioning. Thus the following matrix is where learning needs to occur:

The Complexity of the Learning Organization

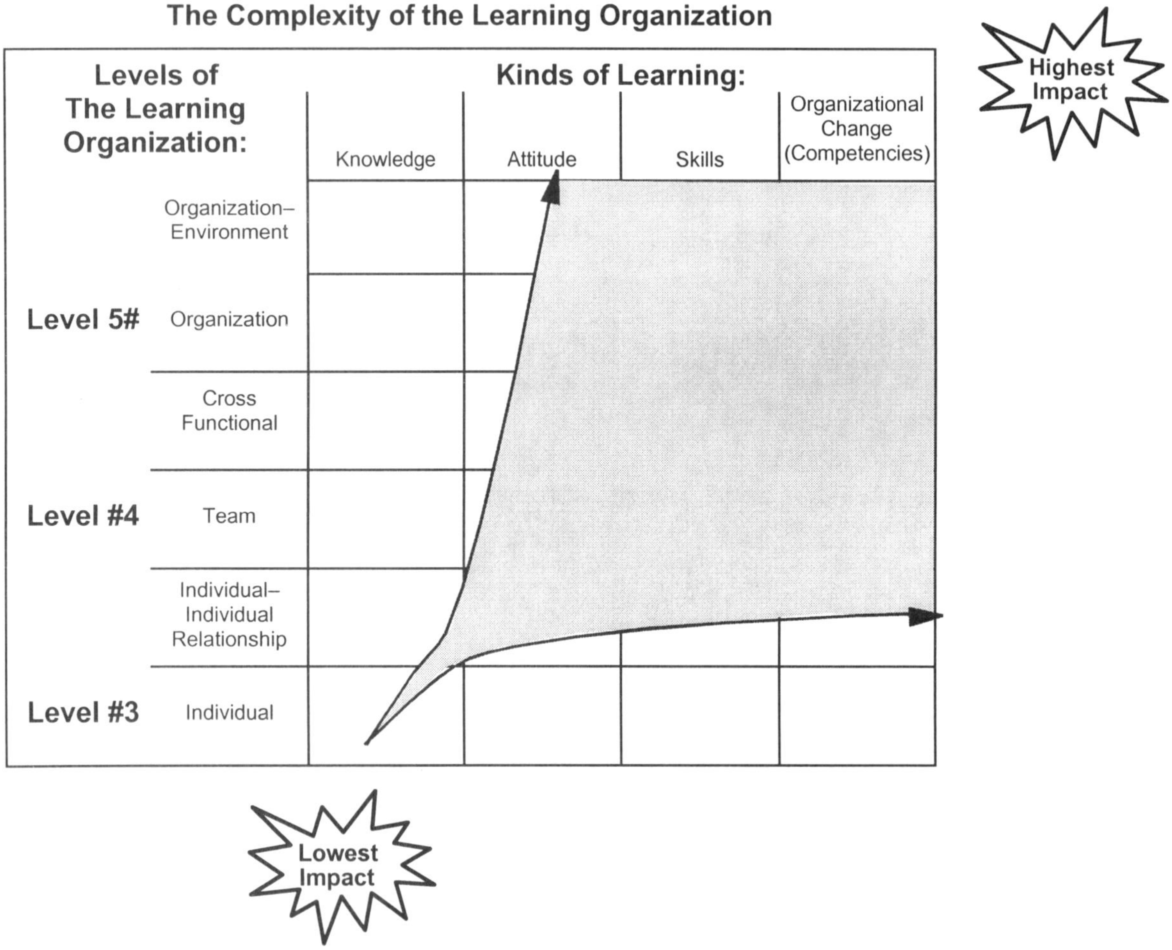

This helps to explain why **The Learning Organization** is so complex a concept to achieve in reality. Learning first occurs in an individual, but it must then spread up the levels to all parts of the organization needing the learning and then the learning itself must move from mere knowledge, to positive attitudes, to skills that are mastered as competencies for changing the organization. Only then is a "Learning" organization starting to become a reality, as the matrix shows. Peter Senge's book, *The Fifth Discipline*, focuses on only Level Three–Individuals and Level Four–Teams, but the reality is that we also have an infinite number of **"collisions" of these systems**, including:

- All the one-on-one relationships in organizations
- All the team-to-team relationships (i.e., the horizontal organization)
- All the organization-environmental relationships with societal forces, stakeholders, suppliers, customers, etc.
- All the vertical "collisions" of systems within systems have learning possibilities as well (i.e., individuals within teams, teams within total organizations, etc.)

So focus your learning to leverage for the desired organizational change.

Finally: Learning—Your Competitive Edge

Why is The Learning Organization important to organizations? Econometricians consistently report that only 40% of competitive improvements derive from direct investments; the other 60% comes from "advances in knowledge" or "innovation."[11]

In other words, 40% of a competitive edge can be bought, but 60% has to be learned through knowledge and science, invention, skills and innovation, commerce, and the experience of others (i.e., best practices).

A substantial share of competitiveness does, indeed, derive from the ability to buy equipment, capital, technology, and expensive resources, but the lion's share of economic success comes from the effective deployment and utilization (attitude, motivation, and competencies) of resources, especially people-resources and what they learn.[12]

What, then, defines a true Learning Organization? The July/August 1993 issue of the *Harvard Business Review* put it in these terms:

> *A learning organization is an organization skilled at creating, acquiring, and transferring knowledge,* ***and*** *at modifying its behavior (i.e., skills, attitudes, and competencies) to reflect new knowledge and insights.*[13]

[11] Denison, 1974; Baumol et al., 1989.

[12] Patrick, Anthony, *America and the Economy*. San Francisco: Jossey-Bass Publishers.

[13] *Harvard Business Review,* July/August 1993.

Summary

Now it's time to look at the specific tools. We at the Centre have developed and used them extensively. They have proven to be effective in solving our clients' systems issues and in successfully helping them achieve their visions and competitive edge. We hope they also do this for you. But remember, they are tools and techniques to be used within the learning context of feedback from the environment based on your desired outcomes.

CHAPTER II
APPLICATION: STANDARD SYSTEMS DYNAMICS

This chapter presents the 12 key questions and tools good Systems Thinkers know and use, as well as the principles they are based on.

Tool No.	The Applications
1	Systems Preconditions: Question—Which Entity? — *What entity (system or "collision" of systems) are we dealing with, and what are its boundaries?*
2	#1 Systems Question—Desired Outcomes — *What are the desired outcomes?*
3	#2 Systems Question—The Need for Feedback — *How will we know we have achieved the desired outcomes?*
4	#3 Systems Question—Environmental Impact — *What is changing in the environment that we need to consider?*
5	#4 Systems Question—Looking at Relationships — *What is the relationship of x to y and z?*
6	#5 Systems Question—The What or the How — *Are we dealing with ends (the what) or with means (the how)?*
7	The "Iceberg" Theory of Change — *What new process and structures are we using to ensure successful change?*
8	Buy-In and Stay-in — *What must we do to ensure buy-in and stay-in (perseverance) over time, and thus avoid the problem of entropy?*
9	Centralized vs. Decentralized — *What should we centralize and what should we decentralize?*
10	Multiple Causes, Root Causes — *What multiple causes lie at the root of our problem or concern? (That is, what are the root causes of our problem or concern?)*
11	KISS: From Complexity to Simplicity — *How can we move from complexity to simplicity, and to a new strategic consistency and operational flexibility, in the solutions we devise?*
12	The Ultimate Question: Superordinate Goals — *What is our common higher-level (subordinate) goal?*
13	System Dynamics Overall — *What are the typical (and predictable) dysfunctional patterns of human behavior in any organization?*

REALITY

Remember: Things are the way they are because someone wants them that way.

Tool #1 Systems Preconditions: Question—Which Entity?

Application of Seven Levels of Living Systems and Systems Dynamics #3: System Boundaries

Identify which overall system or systems are trying to change (which organization, alliance, partnership, business process, etc.). Also be clear on its boundaries and limitations physically and mentally. Where does it begin and end?

While this question may seem so obvious that it doesn't even need to be asked, we have seen over and over again that people's thought processes are so unclear as to make this a **precondition** to any intelligent and effective action and change.

This leads to the first Precondition Question: ***What entity, system, or "collision" of systems are we dealing with?***

PRINCIPLE: The entity to be changed must be clear.

Challenge the obvious—always look for and identify which of the Seven Levels of Living Systems you're dealing with. Be clear on the entity you are working to change—is it an individual, team, family, business unit, community, company, state, nation, or international entity? What are its boundaries? Is it relatively open or closed in its environmental interactions?

➥ **For example:** Are you trying to change yourself, your family, your department, or the entire organization? Are you trying to change your neighborhood, your community, or an entire city? Set your goals realistically on what is *really* achievable… even with stretch.

"Think globally, act locally" is an apt phrase here.

Suggestions for Use:

1. Be clear on the entity you are discussing, especially its boundaries with its environment.
2. Solutions to issues of change and issues of leadership will be very different for each system level you are dealing with. Personal change/learning solutions are different from team/family change or organizational change solutions.
3. Troubleshoot all solutions to see what change you predict they will bring—in your personal or your organizational life. Can you predict that the answers you have chosen will achieve the desired changes in your entity of choice?

Second Question—*Which Levels of Change?*

Organizational change to create high performance organizations requires paying attention to all levels/rings of systems within the organization and all the interactions of systems colliding with other systems. There are different purposes and solutions at each of these levels/rings, and each is important to success.

➥ **For example:**
The biggest failure is often in the "team to team" ring—horizontally across departments.

This leads to the second Precondition Question: Within our identified overall system, what levels/rings of the system are we trying to change and what is our desired outcomes?

High Rings

- Increased complexity
- Readiness/willingness
- Skills growth

Suggestions for Use:

1. Engineer success up front by clarifying which levels and purposes you are trying to change, as well as those other "rings" you will need to change first to achieve your desired outcomes.

2. **General Purposes of Each Ring**

   Ring #3: Individuals ("Self-Mastery")
   - Improve personal competency and effectiveness.
   - Trustworthiness issues within us

   Ring #3A: One-to-One Relationships (Interpersonal Skills/Effectiveness)
   - Improve the interpersonal and working relationships and effectiveness of each individual.
   - Address trust issues between us

(continued)

Suggestions for Use: *(concluded)*

Ring #4: Work teams/Groups (Team Effectiveness)

- Improve the effectiveness of the work team as well as its members.
- Empowerment and interpersonal roles/issues

Ring #4A: Intergroups (Conflict/Horizontal Cooperation)

- Improve the working relationships and business processes across teams/departments horizontally to serve the customer better.
- Address horizontal collaboration/integration issues

Ring #5: Total Organization (Fit)

- Improve the organization's systems, structures, and processes to better achieve its business results and potential; develop its capacity to provide an adaptive system of change and response to a changing environment while pursuing your vision and strategic plan.
- Address issues of alignment

Ring 5A: Organization-Environment (Strategic Plans)

- Improve the organization's sense of direction, response to its customers, and proactive management of environment/stakeholders by reinventing strategic planning for the 21st century.

- Adapt to environmental issues

3. **Organization Change by Levels/Rings**

   The manager of each level/ring of the organization engaged in the change must understand, accept, integrate, and subsequently "own" and direct the vision and changes at their level. Each of the following individuals or groups will manage the changes differently:

   Board
   CEO
   Senior Management (interpersonal relationships)
   Middle Management (department by department)
   Crossfunctional Department (conflict resolution and cooperation)
   Workers across the entire organization

4. The changes will have to be sold and re-sold throughout many levels of the organization. Coming to terms with the change involves a set of themes from the Rollercoaster of Change, shown in more detail in later tools.

   1. Awareness, shock, depression
   2. Education, skills
   3. Experimentation
   4. Understanding, hope
   5. Commitment to building the new vision
   6. Fuller appreciation
   7. Integration into ongoing behaviors

Tool #2 #1 Systems Question—Desired Outcomes

Application of Systems Dynamics #6: Multiple-Goal Seeking

Always ask **The #1 Question first—*"What are the desired outcomes?"*** Since systems usually have multiple outcomes, this is a more complex question than it looks at first glance.

PRINCIPLE: Systems are multiple-goal seeking.

Develop clarity/agreement to this question before beginning any actions. Keep in mind that there are usually multiple outcomes; not either/or questions from reductionistic thinking. Other words for outcomes include *vision, ends, goals, objectives, mission, purpose* (the "what"), etc.

Without agreement on ends, our actions will never have a chance of succeeding. Once the "what" is clear, there are many ways to skin a cat (the "how") through empowerment, etc.

➥ **For example:** Organizational outcomes often include the needs of customers, employees, and stockholders, as well as the community, the suppliers, etc. Asking this question is the beginning of "Backward Thinking."

Success

The great successful men [and women] of the world have used their imagination. . . . They think ahead and create their mental picture, and then go to work materializing that picture in all its details, filling in here, adding a little there, altering this a bit and that a bit, but steadily building—steadily building.

—Robert Collier

Further, these desired outcomes are all about setting goals. Goal-setting and careful goal selection (i.e., establishing a vision or purpose and meaning) appears over and over again in the literature as the #1 criteria for success.

➥ **For example:** In simplistic, personal, and meeting management terms, it means making daily "To Do" lists so you focus on actions/results, not just talk and good ideas or minutes.

Meeting "To Do" List

What to Do/Achieve	By Whom	By When

Suggestions for Use:

Always ask the #1 Question: "What are the desired outcomes?" before beginning anything you do in life, job, family, etc. It's the #1 Question, and it is the #1 way to succeed!

Tool #3 — #2 Systems Question—The Need for Feedback

Application of Systems Dynamics #5: Feedback

After answering The #1 Question, ask **The #2 Question—*"And how will I know I've achieved it?"*** (i.e., feedback loop of outcome measures).

The concept of feedback is important in understanding how a system maintains a steady state or how it changes successfully. Information concerning the outputs of the system is fed back as an input to the system.

This crucial concept, which is taken from the control theory of the engineer, consists of modifying the behavior of a system by reinserting the results of actual past performance.

Feedback can be negative or positive. Negative feedback is informational input, which indicates that the system is deviating from a prescribed course and must change and adjust, or the desired new state/future vision will not be achieved. Thus, negative feedback is good! In fact, it is a personal and business "survival skill" in today's rapidly changing environment.

PRINCIPLE: Feedback is the breakfast of champions—be flexible and adaptive.

In today's complex and continually changing world, initial solutions are not even as important as the ability to gain constant feedback and adapt in order to achieve your desired outcomes. The ability to be flexible and adaptive (i.e., to learn, grow, change, and adapt to changes in the environment) are crucial. Economies of speed are replacing economies of scale as a key competitive edge. Feedback is the key input into today's need for learning organizations that can learn, grow, and adapt at all levels of the organizational system (individuals, teams, and the organization as a whole).

➥ **For example:** Feedback is a gift; allow others to give it to you! It is the skill of being open and receptive to (and even encouraging) feedback from all your customers, all your employees, all your direct reports and peers, and anyone who can help you to learn and grow as a person, as a professional, and as a leader of your organization.

The Corollary Question is—***How do you develop self-mastery?***
(i.e., the external *style,* and *inner psyche* to genuinely encourage others to help you with this *gift* of feedback, even when it *hurts*).

Suggestions for Use:

1. Welcome feedback in all aspects of your life—it is a gift. Don't be defensive.
2. Thank the person for giving it to you.
3. Decide later, after reflecting on the feedback, what to do (if anything) with it.

Tool #4 — #3 Systems Question—Environmental Impact

Application of Systems Dynamics #2: Open-System View; and #3: System Boundaries

Keep asking **The #3 Question: *"What will be changing in the environment in the future that will impact us?"***

In today's rapidly changing environment, people and organizations who fail to constantly scan their environment to see what is changing are unlikely to be successful.

➥ **For example:** In *organizational* terms, the acronym "SKEPTIC" is one framework. It includes scanning for changes in:

S Socio-Demographics
K "K"ompetition
E Economics
P Politics
T Technology
I Industry
C Customers

➥ **For example:** In *individual* terms, it means paying attention to changes in the environment that may impact all the roles one plays in life, such at "PITO."

P Personally—body, mind, spirit
I Interpersonally—family, friends, colleagues
T Team—associations, community, department
O Organization—job, career, wealth

PRINCIPLE: Work and align the entity to be changed from the outside in—not the inside out.

Remember to employ "backwards thinking." Start with the environment and the wants and needs of the customer and desired outcomes to gain clarity. Then work backwards into the organization to determine how to meet those current and future needs while still meeting the multiple needs of other key stakeholders in the environment.

Align all employees, suppliers, and business processes across departments to meet these outcomes in the environment. This is the conceptual basis for business process reengineering in today's organizations. However, it is often fragmented into departmental elements or internal cost-cutting activities only, without regard to customer impact.

Suggestions for Use:

1. **For organizations:** Set up a full environmental scanning system and assign responsibility for the collection of environmental changes/data on each aspect of SKEPTIC to a senior person or team.
2. Conduct quarterly environmental scan sessions where everyone shares their information; identify trends/impacts on your organization as a result.
3. Revise your strategic plan yearly with this as key input.
4. **Personally:** Keep yourself open to what is changing in the environment—not just through the typical media, but through other means as well (i.e., magazines and newsletters).

Tool #5 — #4 Systems Question—Looking at Relationships

Application of Systems Dynamics #9: Hierarchy; #10: Subsystems; as well as the Seven Levels

A. "What Is the Relationship of X to Y?"

In overview terms, you are always looking at the relationship of the part/event to both (1) the overall system outcomes, and (2) all other parts and events within the system.

- In systems, the whole is primary and the parts/events are secondary. And the parts are only important within their relationship to other parts/events.
- Balance and optimization is the key—not dominance and maximization of a single part.
- In systems, relationships and processes are what are important—not departments/units and events.
- **Change your thinking from events and parts to *relationships* and *processes*.**

PRINCIPLE: The whole is more important than the parts—and the relationships and processes are key.

The most important assessment to be continually made by any system is the synthesis of how the parts fit/link together in an integrated process in support of the whole outcomes.

You cannot analyze each part's effectiveness in a void, but only in relationship to the other parts and the processes that lead to achieving the whole. *Always remember that a system cannot be subdivided into independent parts.* Change in one part affects the whole, as well as all the other interdependent parts or processes. This is true for families, teams, departments, neighborhoods, organizations, or society as a whole; it is something we all still need to recognize, learn, and understand.

➥ **For example:** In organizations, it's not how I can maximize my job or our department impact. *It's how we can all work and fit together in support of the overall objectives of the organization.* To that end, each year all major departments should share (and have critiqued) their annual plans with a critical mass of senior executives and middle managers/professionals to ensure everyone knows what everyone else is doing. This is actually a large group team-building process.

➥ **For example:** On the personal level, systems thinking is finding patterns and relationships in your work and your life—and learning to reinforce or change these patterns to achieve personal fulfillment. This can actually help to simplify life, because you will see its interconnections. For example, what is the relationship between your lack of fitness and your energy level, and between your overall feelings of health and your ability to have the stamina needed to do your job and run your life each day?

Create "synergy" in your life. Synergy is the working together of two or more parts of any system to produce an effect greater than the sum of the individual effects. It is increasing your own outcomes by working together with others in a particularly effective way.

Suggestions for Use:

1. **The Interdependence Paradigm:** We are all **interdependent** with each other. We all know that we are a part of a vast interrelated whole earth/universe—NASA's pictures of earth from space proved that!
2. So why don't we focus on the interrelatedness of key people in our lives? Our relationships with them, desired outcomes, visions, purposes we have that affect them? Why don't we focus on sharing/agreeing on these visions together, gaining feedback on this vision, and our personal part in it on a continuing and regular basis?
3. Pay close attention to the impact you have on others and they on you. Rarely do we really know the full impact of our actions on others.
4. Keep asking the #4 Systems Question: *What is the relationship of X to Y in all aspects of life?*

B. The Either/Or Corollary

Either/or questions (X vs. Y) usually should be answered by "yes, both" since there are usually multiple causes and multiple effects/outcomes to most issues.

- Forget the analytic tyranny of the either/or and adopt the systems thinking genius of the "and"—the ability to embrace two or more different opinions, extremes, or seemingly contradictory statements at any one time.

Social Problems as a Puzzle

> *A puzzle is a problem that we usually cannot solve because we make an incorrect assumption or self-imposed constraint that precludes solution.*
>
> —Russ Ackoff

➥ **For example:** When someone asks, "Is it **X** or **Y**?" they are making an assumption that there is only one answer. This happens in organizations, in families, and in all interpersonal relationships and it often results in needless conflict, differences of opinions, and hard feelings.

Suggestions for Use:

1. Don't get caught up in either/or debates.
2. State areas of agreement first, rather than debating.
3. Then state your area of disagreement *if* there is one.
4. When someone asks you an either/or question, answer with "yes, both" to surface this artificial disagreement.

C. Instead, Find the Third and Fourth Alternatives

There's always a third alternative. Find it. Use higher level goals and/or brainstorming to raise the level of discovery to a higher-order system. Focus on finalizing an outcome you both can agree to, rather than trying to impose your answer on the other person.

➥ **For example:** Picture the decision process involved when a couple selects the color for a new house:

The man wants to paint it green, because of the earthiness of the color. The woman wants to paint it yellow, so it will be more cheerful. If they compromise by mixing the colors, the house will be painted chartreuse. Most people would never accept that solution. But in our personal and business lives, we often produce solutions that are the equivalent of "painting things chartreuse."

***A real solution**—a common denominator—for the couple might be a shade of peach, which is both cheerful and earthy. This would satisfy the needs of each. In the end, it's a better choice than creating a chartreuse eyesore.*

—Edith Weiner

Suggestions for Use:

1. Always first ask: "What's the higher level goal we can both agree on?"
2. Ask Stephen Covey's question: "What's the third alternative?" whenever you are stuck.
3. Brainstorm a variety of solutions if you are stuck. Ask: "What else, what else?" to keep brainstorming going.
4. Ask for the "nuggets" of the brainstorming session that you like or that have further merit. Ignore the *"too crazy"* ideas.

D. The Dominant Coalition—Unbalanced Relationships

Focus on the "whole vs. the parts" and the polarity/extreme swings of the pendulum to correct imbalanced parts and relationships (i.e., parts trying to maximize their whole; not the system's whole).

➥ **For example:** Guard against one skill or function dominating all relationships in an organization. The classic cases we run into are organizations dominated by engineering or finance while the organization tries to become "market/customer-oriented." If no one in senior management has background/skills in these areas (they rarely do), guess what doesn't happen?

➥ **For example: Which is the dominant coalition among all the relationships?** (i.e., Who gets promoted to senior management? What are the backgrounds of senior management? How is the organization driven (finance, products, customers, engineering)?)

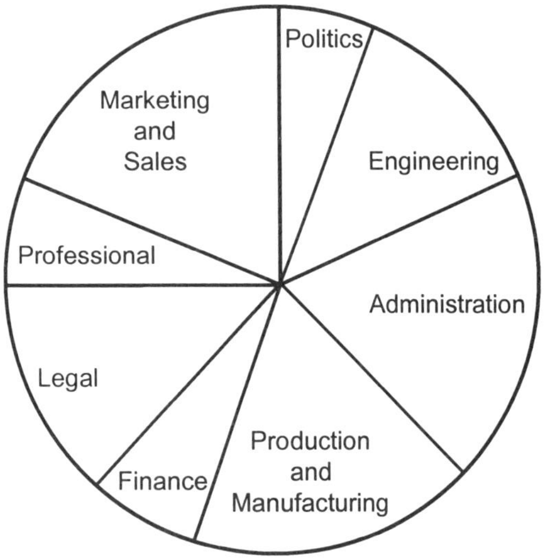

➥ **For example:** Many organizations start out with strength in products and engineering or manufacturing. In today's world, adding competencies in sales, marketing, and service is often crucial if they wish to build a competitive edge for the future.

Defenders of Decline

As the dominant coalition:
Are you a defender of decline or *an architect of the future?*
How do you know?

➥ **For example:** In the same way, we as individuals need a balance of skills and knowledge to get ahead in our career. We have often observed that the most innovative people in organizations did not take a narrow, "stovepipe" approach to their career. They had jobs in more than one function, and were able to learn and relate better to all parts of the organization.

Suggestions for Use:

1. Assess yourself: What different functions have you had a job in? Are you narrowly skilled or broadly skilled?
2. Organizations today need "systems interpreters." How well do you know all the organization's departments?
3. Analyze the organization's strengths in the different disciplines. Which are strong? Which are weak?
4. Balance the strengths/core competencies and relationships in the organization by strengthening weak areas.

E. Relationship of System Levels: A Matrix

To understand and better problem-solve relationships within different levels of living systems, set up a systems matrix.

➥ **For example**: Vertically down the left side of the matrix is the "Organization as a System" model. Across the top of the matrix you can include either:

a. this Systems Model again (see Matrix #1)
b. the "tree-ring" six levels of systems/interaction of systems (see Matrix #2)
c. the organization's business processes
d. each department/function of the organization
e. levels of the organizational hierarchy
f. educational outcomes (knowledge-skills-attitude-competencies) or levels of impact (individual, team, organization)

Market segmentation is another way to use this matrix concept (see below).

Suggestions for Use:

1. Market Segmentation
   a. Fill out Columns 1, 2, 3, and 4 individually, and then build consensus as a team.
   b. Next, decide from this analysis the relative ratings in Column 5.

The Cost/Value of Customers

#1 Customer Segments/ Account Names	#2 Relative Cost to Service This Segment (High-Med.-Low)	#3 Current Relative Value (High-Med.-Low)	#4 Future Potential (High-Med.-Low)	#5 Final Priority (Force Rank All Segments)

Suggestions for Use:

2. Applied Systems Thinking (Matrix #1)
(and the Relationships of the Parts to the Whole)
Decide from this analysis the relative ratings in Column 5.

Matrix #1

Instructions: Use either (1) the horizontal or (2) the vertical blocks to compare the fit/integration of the parts to the whole.

Level of System / Orgn/ Systems Elements	1. Strategic Planning	2. Operational Tasks	3. Leadership & Management	4. Resources & Technology	5. Organization Design	6. HR/Admin. Systems	7. Team Development	8. Strategic Change Management	9. Feedback Loop	10. Achievement of Results	Added Comments
1. Strategic Planning											
2. Operational Tasks											
3. Leadership & Management											
4. Resources & Technology											
5. Organization Design											
6. HR/Admin. Systems											
7. Team Development											
8. Strategic Change Management											
9. Feedback Loop											
10. Achievement of Results											
Added Comments											*Systems Definition:* A system is a set of interrelated elements that work together for the overall good of the whole system's outcomes.

Suggestions for Use:

3. Applied Systems Thinking (Matrix #2)
(and the Relationships of the Parts to the Seven Levels of Living Systems)
Decide from this analysis the relative ratings in Column 5.

Matrix #2

Instructions: Use either the horizontal or the vertical blocks to compare the fit/integration of the parts to the different levels of systems.

Level of System / Orgn/ Systems Elements	Self	1-to-1	Teams	Team-to-Team	Organization	Environment	Customers	Suppliers	Added Comments
1. Strategic Planning									
2. Operational Tasks									
3. Leadership & Management									
4. Resources & Technology									
5. Organization Design									
6. HR/Admin. Systems									
7. Team Development									
8. Strategic Change Management									
9. Feedback Loop									
10. Achievement of Results									
Added Comments									*Systems Definition*: A system is a set of interrelated elements that work together for the overall good of the whole system's outcomes.

F. Decision Matrix Criteria

All analyses and assessments must have as their criteria for success the goals/vision of the whole entity first. The parts/elements, linkages, and how they will fit and integrate with each other only come after the overall vision.

- ➥ **For example:** Use a "decision matrix" as a systems tool when trying to resolve desired multiple outcomes vs. the root causes that are blocking them. (See the sample matrix that follows.)

- ➥ **For example:** Your strategic plan should be the criteria upon which all your organizational decisions are made. It is crucial to do a full analysis to discover all the root causes. Remember, root causes are often delayed in time and space from the issue itself.

Suggestions for Use:

1. In any decision you make, first ask and agree upon the criteria or outcomes upon which to make the decisions. Then, and only then, should you look at the decision options you have.
2. What is your criteria for a decision regarding: ______________________________

   a.

   b.

   c.

   d.

   e.

   f.

   g.

   h.

The Decision Matrix

Instructions: Use the horizontal and the vertical blocks to compare the fit/integration of the parts to the whole. Use H-M-L to evaluate the blocking of root causes.

Multiple Desired Outcomes / Root Causes									Needed Actions? (H-M-L)
1.									
2.									
3.									
4.									
5.									
6.									
7.									
8.									
9.									
10.									
Added Comments									*Systems Definition*: A system is a set of interrelated elements that work together for the overall good of the whole system's outcomes.

Tool #6 — #5 Systems Question— The *What* (Ends) or the *How* (Means)

Application of Systems Dynamics #4: Input—Transformation—Output Model

Are we dealing with means ***or*** ends***?*** (the *What* or the *How*?)

#1 The *What* (the ends)—multiple outcomes

#2 The *How* (the means)—many different ways to achieve the same end/outcome; key is the process, the fit, and the relationship between the parts

➥ **For example:** In organizational and in personal terms, systems thinking is about focusing on outcomes, by whatever definitions you want to use. In "A–B–C–D" terms, the following clear terminology will help you understand how to communicate with others.

Phase C = Inputs ⇨	Phase D = Means/How ⇨	Phase A = Ends/What
(Input Phase)	**(Throughput Phase)**	**(Output Phase)**
• Strategies • Resources • People–Money–Facilities	• Tasks–Activities–Actions • Processes—Operations—Departments • Elements—Parts—Components	• Goals–Results–Objectives • Vision–Mission–Values • Outcomes–Purposes

➥ **For example:** The means or how to is a hierarchy of systems operating within larger systems. An outcome to you is a means to an end for the larger system. This is why divisions of a larger company are perplexed with higher-up decisions that can be only understood by knowing the multiple outcomes (*the what*) of the overall corporation.

***PRINCIPLE: All systems are linked to other systems—some larger, some smaller—in a hierarchy.* The What of one person/department/team is actually the How To of the larger organization.**

No system is independent of any other. We are human beings linked in a hierarchy of systems to all others on this planet, to a greater or lesser extent, *whether we like it or not*. Pay close attention to both the system and system-system hierarchies as well. (Supplier-organization-customer is one set of linkages—individual-family-community is another example of hierarchic linkages.)

Suggestions for Use:

1. In difficult meetings, ask whether we are dealing with means or ends. With *the how*-to or *the what*?
2. Be careful when giving or getting project assignments to separate the *what* from the *how*.
3. If you are looking at measuring success, then measure outcomes, rather than the how-to's.
4. When it comes to your personal life and normal family–children–spouse conflicts, stop them when they are spiraling downward and check if the argument is over *means* or *ends*. Then get agreement on the end goal first. Agreement there often mitigates fights over the how-to.
5. If you aren't clear, ask why you are doing the task. It will move you toward the ends. Ask two to three "why's" in sequence to get to the real ends.

Means and Ends: Teaching and Learning

What is the difference between teaching and learning? What skills are needed to do each?

Learning is the outcome. Teaching is the way to accomplish learning. It is the means to the end only.

➡ **For example:** Schools focus on teachers and teaching. The real outcome or goal is the student's actual learning. Teachers and trainers of all types should ask themselves:

Are you:
The Guide on the Side
—or—
The Sage on the Stage?

"Facilitators" and "Platform Presenters" are different!

There are added key differences between these as well.

Teaching and Learning: Distinctions

Teaching/(Means?)		**Learning (Outcomes)**
Pedagogy Leader of Child	← Means — Ends →	**Andragogy** Leader of Man (Adult)
Dependent	Self Concept	Self-Directed
Little	Past Experiences	Rich
Biological Development	Readiness	Social Roles
Postponed Application	Time Perspective	Immediate Application
Subject-Centered	Learning Orientation	Problem-Centered
Trainer	Locus of Control	Learner

Suggestions for Use:

1. Recognize the crucial distinction between means and ends.
2. Focus on ends—the learnings.
3. Revise your strategic plan yearly and use this key input.
4. Be careful of content experts who don't have learning skills beyond platform presentations. People rarely learn this way.

Tool #7 The "Iceberg" Theory of Change

Application of Changing Systems Dynamics:
The Natural Cycles of Life and Change

A. CONTENT—PROCESS—STRUCTURE

When any system changes, three elements are a reality of life and are present at all times and in all interpersonal and system interactions.

- Element #1 is the **"content"** of the change—it is obvious and is the one most focused upon.

However, change is like an iceberg, where 87% of the issues and solutions are below the surface of the water. They are in elements #2 and #3.

- Element #2 is just below the surface and is the "process" of change.
- Element #3 is deep below the surface—the "structures" or arrangement/context needed to set up to manage change before change manages us. See the list of key change structures that follow to focus on this. They are an often overlooked, yet vital context for systems change.

This gives rise to Systems Question #6—*What are the new structures and processes we are using to ensure successful change?*

PRINCIPLE: The steady state equilibrium we all want can kill us.
In a rapidly changing society, the biggest risk is to stay the same.

Our natural inclination is to maintain the status quo and its comfortableness vs. the pain, awkwardness, uncertainty, and ambiguity of change. And change requires the difficult issues of (1) admitting and becoming willing to change, along with (2) acquiring the new skills and abilities to function more effectively.

Knowledge and information is just an input, and not enough of an input to be effective by itself. More skills in how to work with systems need to be developed if we want to learn, grow, and change effectively. Short-term creative destruction can sometimes be key to long-term advances; today's "steady state" is one of constant change.

➥ **For example:** Designing, building, and sustaining a customer-focused, high performance learning organization for the 21st century requires a balance in how organizations spend their time and energy. You must balance between the:

1. Content/**tasks/goals and focus of the business**
2. Processes **and the way we go about our behaviors while working on the tasks**
3. Structure **(or context/arrangements) within which the content and process operate**

The "Iceberg" Theory of Change
(To Achieve Your Competitive Business Edge)

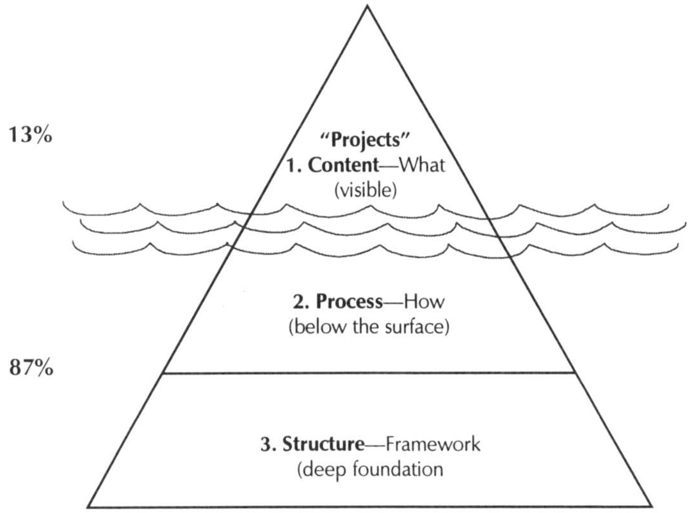

Systemic change requires a major focus on structure and process in order to achieve the content/results.

Suggestions for Use:

1. If you desire effective and successful change, then you must build a change management game plan and a yearly map/project plan of the implementation.
2. This is especially important if you want to effectively implement a strategic plan. The game plan needs to be the very last page of the strategic plan so that it gets implemented.
3. Included in this game plan are both key processes and structures.
4. See the *Rollercoaster of Change* section for a description of the processes of change.
5. The structures of change are described below. Follow them.
6. On a personal level, you need to set up a simpler, yet similar set of follow-up meetings/structures on a regular basis with yourself and/or your family regarding the changes in your lives as each of you progress through your life cycles. These are often called *family summits* and they're very helpful.

   How often do you have a family meeting in today's rapid-paced, changing world?

Here's a **"menu"** of typical change structures we believe you will need to choose from for successful strategic change. They include:

Primary Strategic Change Management (Structures and Roles)

A Menu

1. **Visionary Leadership**—CEO/Senior Executives with Personal Leadership Plans (PLPs)
   - For repetitive stump speeches and reinforcement
   - To ensure fit/integration of all parts and people toward the same vision/values
2. **Internal Support Cadre** (informal/"kitchen cabinet")
   - For day-to-day coordination of implementation process
   - To ensure the change structures and processes don't lose out to day-to-day tasks
3. **Executive Committee**
   - For weekly meetings and attention
   - To ensure follow-up on the top 15 to 25 yearly priority actions from the strategic plan
4. **Strategic Change Leadership Steering Committee** (formal)
   - For bimonthly/quarterly follow-up meetings to track, adjust, and refine everything (including the vision)
   - To ensure follow-through via a yearly comprehensive map of implementation

*5. **Strategy Sponsorship Teams**
   - For each core strategy and/or major change effort
   - To ensure achievement of each one; including leadership of what needs to change

*6. **Employee Development Board** (Attunement of People's Hearts)
   - For succession—careers—development—core competencies (all levels)—performance management/appraisals
   - To ensure fit with our desired values/culture—and employees as a competitive edge

*7. **Technology Steering Committee**
   - For computer—telecommunications—software fit and integration
   - To ensure "system-wide" fit/coordination around information management

*8. **Strategic Communications System (and Structure)**
   - For clear two-way dialogue and understanding of the plan/implementation
   - To ensure everyone is heading in the same direction with the same strategies/values

*9. **Measurement and Benchmarking Team**
   - For collecting and reporting of key success factors, especially customers, employees, competitors
   - To make sure the focus is on the outcome/customer at all times

10. **Annual Department Plans**
    - For clear and focused department plans that are critiqued, shared, and reviewed
    - To make sure they fit and coordinate with the core strategies and annual top priorities and that everyone is committed to them
11. **Whole System Participation**
    - For input and involvement of all key stakeholders before a decision affecting them is made; includes parallel processes, search conferences, management conferences, etc.
    - To make sure a critical mass supports the vision and desired changes

*Subcommittees of #4: the Leadership Steering Committee

Suggestions for Use:

1. Make sure you fully understand this menu of 11 possible change management structures.
2. Select those you need for your change management process.
3. Set up and be very clear on each one's purpose.

B. The #1 Absolute—Have a Strategic Change Leadership Steering Committee (SCLSC)

A Strategic Change Leadership Steering Committee (SCLSC) run by the top executive is our #1 absolute requirement. It will help prevent change from losing out to day-to-day tasks, stress, pressure, and crisis. We have yet to see an effective change management process that was made without this committee. It is essential to reversing the entropy and providing the feedback to keep a change process on track.

It's a new way to run your business: to give equal weight to managing desired changes and managing the organization's ongoing daily operations.

Ineffectiveness of Hierarchical "Cascade" Implementation Strategy Alone

The normal "cascade" strategy for implementing change is usually ineffective, because memories remain embedded in the way the organization works after the change. This applies particularly if the change relates to the culture rather than to work practices or systems.

—Dick Beckhard
"Changing the Essence"

Suggestions for Use:

1. **Purposes of the Steering Committee**
   a. To guide and control the implementation of any large-scale, organization-wide strategic planning/change efforts undertaken through the "Strategic Planning Model for the 1990s" or "Seven Tracks to Creating a High-Performance Organization."
   b. To coordinate any other major performance improvement projects going on in the organization at the same time; to ensure fit with the time and energy demands of ongoing daily business activities (i.e., systems fit, alignment, and integrity).
2. **Criteria for SCLSC Membership**
   a. Senior management leadership teams for today *and* the future.
   b. Informal or formal leaders from all parts of the organization that are key to implementation.
   c. A Core Steering Group Implementation Staff Support Team, including overall change management coordinator, KSF/ESS coordinators, and internal facilitators.
   d. Credible staff who are well-versed in the actual strategic plan that was developed.
   e. Key stakeholders who share your ideal vision of the future and who are willing to actively support it.
3. **Committee Meeting Frequency**
   a. Phase I: Monthly or bimonthly as the process begins
   b. Phase II: Quarterly once the process is functioning smoothly
4. **Core Steering Group Roles (in-between SCLSC meetings)**
   a. Led by the top leader of the organization (i.e., CEO, Superintendent, Executive Director) who coordinates regular weekly/monthly meetings of all the other members.
   b. Internal Staff Overall Change Management Coordinator/Manager responsibility by a competent and credible senior-level executive with the time/energy to coordinate the activities, supported by a competent assistant/secretary support person.
   c. An Internal Communications Coordinator for ongoing communications to all key stakeholders.
   d. A Key Success Factor Coordinator to make certain that KSFs are tracked/reported regularly.
   e. An Internal Staff Facilitator involved and trained to take over from the external consultant.
   f. "Strategy Sponsorship Team Leaders" who are leaders of the cross-functional teams set up previously for each core strategy. If not set up, do so at this time.
   g. Facilitation by an external master consultant who is skilled in both this process and your content areas of change.
5. **Involvement of Key Stakeholders**

Who	How
1. Board of Directors	
2. Middle Managers	
3. All Employees	
4. External Stakeholders	

C. Another Key Structure: Employee Development Board

The people-management practices of any organization should be viewed as a system of people-flow from initial hire, through career progression and retirement and/or termination. Making this all happen is the responsibility of senior management; it is usually best done through an Executive/Employee Development Board (EDB) focused solely on this framework and developing people as a competitive business advantage (the "people" edge).

➥ **For example:** Having such a board reinforces senior management's responsibility to carry out their "stewardship" responsibilities. The best way to explain this fully is through the example at the end of this tool, from the author's days as an Executive Vice President of Imperial Corporation of America (ICA), a $14 billion financial services company formerly in San Diego, California.

In essence, this Executive Development (Stewardship) Board is responsible for the flow and continuity of human resources. It's responsibility is to link staffing to business strategy via:

• hiring	• training: classroom (internal, external)
• selection (up/lateral)	• organization design/structure
• succession planning	• socio-demographic trends
• developmental jobs/experiences	• employee surveys of satisfaction
• development: on-the-job	• rewards/performance system

Here is an example of a mechanism/structure of how to achieve management continuity throughout the organization:

1. Executive Development Board (EDB)—executive team
2. Management Development Board (MDB)—all department heads/teams
3. Employee Development Committees (EEDC)—all supervisors/section head areas

The desired outcomes for the entire organization include:

Finding the Right person—in the Right job—at the Right time

➥ **For example:** The author was at MCI in its heyday of growth, and during the break up of Ma Bell (AT&T), coordinating its Executive Development Board. It had as its key the linking of organizational needs for succession planning and the individual needs of managers to grow and develop.

Suggestions for Use:

1. Study the next page for details on Executive/Employee Development Boards.
2. Set up an Executive Development Board for the organization or even for one department/division or function.

Sample structure of an Executive Development Board

Imperial Corporation of America (ICA)

What's the purpose of the Employee Development Board (EDB)?

It serves as a forum to carry out our employee stewardship responsibilities. We realize that our success and profitability come from the strength and capabilities of all of our employees.

This Board's only purpose is to discuss and decide on human resources issues, policies, and programs so that we can continue to "grow" the talent we have in the organization and make ICA a great company in which to work, learn, and develop.

The EDB provides a direct link to the Personnel Committee of the Board of Directors, ensuring that sound investment in our human resources remains a corporate priority.

What are the goals of the EDB?

Simply stated, the goals of the EDB are to effectively carry out the following ICA Management Principles.

3. Achieve and reward outstanding performance. Also confront and correct poor performance.
5. Use human and financial resources wisely in support of the corporate direction.
9. Involve our employees by providing opportunities to contribute.
10. Develop productive employees. Delegate, train, and motivate employees to their maximum potential.

The EDB philosophy sounds good. But how will this translate into action?

Some of the employee benefit programs and development concepts that have come out of EDB meetings include:

- Shared Savings Plan—401(k)
- Employee banking program enhancements
- Employee pension and benefits program changes/enhancements
- Performance management system and the rewards-for-performance concept
- Team and individual non-financial rewards, recognition, and incentives
- Merit increase programs and plans
- Career development and succession planning commencing with executive level assessment and slated to progress through the entire organization in later years
- Training and development program for managers/supervisors in:
  - — Performance Planning and Review
  - — Goal Setting
  - — Coaching and Counseling

  . . . to name a few

Who is a member of the Employee Development Committee?

- **Chairman:**

  President and CEO
- **Members:**

  Exec. VP, Retailing Banking

  Senior VP, Legal

  Exec. VP, Administration

  Exec. VP, Mortgage Banking

  Exec. VP, Mortgage Banking

  Exec. VP, Finance

  Exec. VP, Corporate I. S.
- **Secretary:**

  Sr. VP, Human Resources

  This committee is supported by an implementation team from the following departments:

  Benefits

  Communications

  Compensation

  Employee Relations

  Employment

  Training and Development
- **When does the EDB meet?**

  Quarterly, or more often, if necessary.
- **How do I find out what the Board is doing for us?**

  Primarily through articles in "Inside ICA" and other employee publications. We want to inform you on an ongoing basis that much time, effort, and attention is being spent on you—to help you develop and grow as you contribute to the success of the ICA team.

Tool #8 Buy-In and Stay-In

Application of Systems Dynamics #8: Entropy

Focus continually/regularly on reversing entropy—the normal tendency of a system to run down and deteriorate over time—with feedback. "Buy-in" isn't the killer of change—it's the lack of "stay-in" over time that kills change.

- **This gives rise to Systems Question #7—*What do we need to do to ensure buy-in/stay-in and perseverance over time (to reverse entropy)?***

All business problems conform to the laws of inertia—the longer you wait, the harder the problem is to correct. Incremental degradation is the main barrier to achieving the "fit" of all organization processes and actions with espoused organizational values/vision. Every system requires attention, booster shots, stop checks, etc., on a regular basis in order to be effective and to have stay-in over time.

PRINCIPLE: Reverse the entropy!

Systems tend to increase in complexity until they become very bureaucratic and ossified, ultimately resulting in the death of the system. All living systems require constant energy and inputs (i.e., feedback) if they are to reverse this entropy. Otherwise, all living systems eventually run down and die.

For example, while human beings and families obviously have a finite life cycle, it doesn't have to be this way for neighborhoods, communities, and organizations. For them, the renewal process that reverses the entropy is key to long-term success. As Meg Wheatley says, chaos and disorder are often a precursor to renewal and growth at a higher level.

However, there is more good news in our worldwide instantaneous information transmissions—we now have a virtually limitless supply of constant feedback, which can provide us with new inputs toward effective change. The downside is that we have to deal with information overload, leading to more and more complexity in our lives.

The worlds of engineering, math, economics, and science in general often look at the future as mainly extrapolations of the present in a linear or straight line from the past and present. Often financial and other projections, as well as budgets/sales/growth projections, assume a straight-line growth of "X"% per year.

The reality of life is more like a sine curve/wave with constant ups and downs.

➥ **For example:** The rhythm of our heartbeat, the waves on the beach, daily temperature fluctuations, and the changes of the seasons are nature's natural curves.

➥ **For example:** Normal System Atrophy

Entropy

A tendency for any system to run down and eventually become INERT

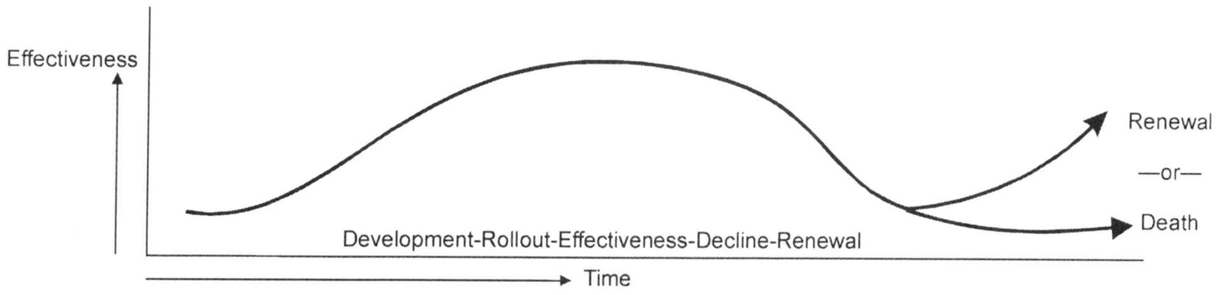

Suggestions for Use:

1. Recognize change as the reality of life and stop doing linear projections on any project you are doing.
2. If you must project this way, be sure everyone recognizes its artificiality.
3. Plan for the ups and downs in your life on the job—as well as in your organizations. Don't be too upset when they take place (or get too high or low). Persevere . . . persevere. Woody Allen once said, "Ninety percent of life's success is just showing up!"
4. Stop believing that *when things are bad they'll always be bad*, or the converse, *when things are good, they'll always be good.*

The Telltale Signs of Organizational Entropy

How do you know if your organization is experiencing entropy? The following list, adapted from Max DePree, CEO of Herman Miller, in his 1987 book *New Management,* presents the telltale signs.

- A tendency toward superficiality.
- A dark tension among key people.
- No time for celebration and ritual.
- A growing feeling that rewards and goals are the same.
- People no longer telling or understanding tribal stories.
- A recurring effort by some to convince others that business is, after all, quite simple. (The acceptance of complexity and ambiguity and the ability to deal with them constructively is essential.)
- People having different understanding of words like *responsibility* or *service* or *trust.*
- Problem-makers outnumbering problem-solvers.
- Folks confusing heroes with celebrities.

- Leaders who seek to control rather than liberate.
- The pressure of day-to-day operations pushing aside concern for vision and risk. (Vision and risk can never be separated.)
- An orientation toward the dry rules of business school rather than a value orientation, which takes into account such things as contribution, spirit, excellence, beauty, and joy.
- People speaking of customers as impositions on their time rather than as opportunities to serve.
- Manuals.
- A growing urge to quantify both history and thoughts about the future. (You may be familiar with people who take a look at a prototype and say, "In 1990 we'll sell $6,493 worth"—nothing is more devastating, because then you plan either to make that happen or to avoid it.)
- The urge to establish ratios.
- Leaders who rely on structures instead of people.
- A loss of confidence in judgment, experience, and wisdom.
- A loss of grace, style, and civility.
- A loss of respect for the English language.

Building a Critical Mass for Change

Change leaders must focus on buy-in to create widespread support (i.e., a critical mass) for change. It can take up to two years to fully build support for large-scale strategic change. Here are some ways to do it:

1. Modify strategic plan drafts—listen, review (share, gain feedback from those affected).
2. Continue to hold parallel process meetings with key stakeholders throughout implementation.
3. Develop trust in your leadership by being open via a Strategic Change Leadership Steering Committee and every day involve skeptics and listen to them.
4. Develop three-year business plans for all business units/major support departments by involving key stakeholders/staff.
5. Develop annual plans for all departments/divisions/sections under the strategic plan/core strategy umbrella.
6. Put out "updates" after each Strategic Change Steering Committee meeting and ask for feedback.
7. Use Strategic Sponsorship Teams as "change agents" for each core strategy/major change.
8. Implement quick changes/actions so people know you are serious (silent majority).
9. Review reward systems and the performance appraisal form to reinforce core values and core strategies.
10. Help each person answer the "What's In It For Me?" (WIIFM) question.

Remember that skeptics are our best friends. If you encounter skeptics, be sure to ask them why they are skeptical. Get them to identify the roadblocks; don't try to force them to agree with you.

Roadblocks are key items you must overcome to ensure successful achievement of your vision.

Critical Mass Building—It takes almost one to two years to build enough support in an organization to create the critical mass for change.

Year #1

- Core Strategic Planning/Major Change Team
- plus 20–40 key "others"

Year #2

- the rest of the organization
- other key external stakeholders

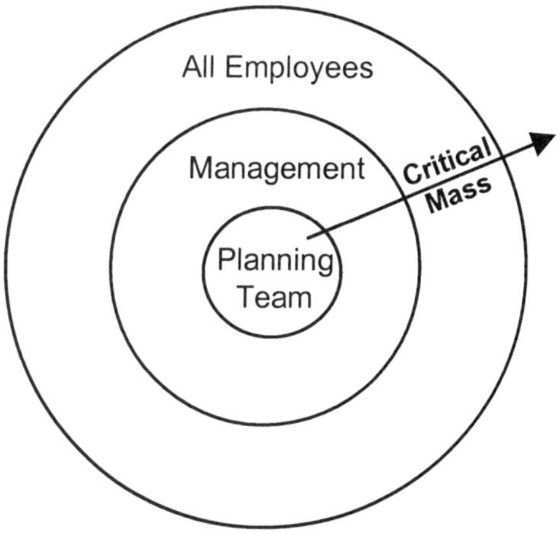

Institutionalizing the Desired Changes

Getting long-term stay-in on change projects requires that you institutionalize the desired changes. Ways to do this include the following:

1. Conduct an organizational assessment to determine the status of the change and problems that need resolving in order for the change to reach its full effectiveness.

2. Conduct refresher-training courses on the change topic.

3. Hold yearly conferences on the subject (renewal).

4. Have the basic change and the improvements noted in #1 above as part of senior management's goals and performance appraisal.

5. Conduct a reward system's diagnosis and make appropriate changes so that the rewards (both financial and nonfinancial) are congruent and consistent with the changes.

6. Set up an ongoing audit system. Also find ways to statistically measure the change effectiveness. Line managers are used to statistics and generally like them.

7. Have ways to discuss and reinforce the change at periodic staff meetings of top management and department heads.

8. Set the changes into policies and procedures for the ongoing organization; then have someone accountable for them. Set up permanent jobs to maintain the changes or put the accountability into existing job descriptions.
9. Use a variety of communication avenues and processes for one-way and two-way feedback on the change.
10. Hold periodic team meetings on the subject across the organization.
11. Have top managers conduct "deep sensing" meetings on the subject down through the organization on a regular basis.
12. Have periodic intergroup or interdepartment meetings on the subject and its status.
13. Set up a process of yearly renewing and reexamining the change in order to continually improve it.
14. Have outside consultants conduct periodic visits on the subject and assess the status of the change.
15. Be very sure that the top team continues to model the changes.
16. Set priorities and deadlines for short-term improvements to the change.
17. Look closely at the key environmental sectors to be sure they are reinforcing the changes (particularly any parent companies or division heads).
18. Create physical indications of the permanency of the change (offices, jobs, brochures, etc.).
19. Develop "stay agents" or multiple persons who have a strong interest in maintaining the change (particularly among line managers and informal leaders).
20. Refine change procedures to make them routine and normal.
21. Link other organizational systems to the change. Encourage specific and formal communications, coordination, and processes between them.
22. Keep the goals and benefits of the change clear and well known.
23. Assess the potential dangers and pitfalls of the change and develop specific approaches and plans to minimize these dangers.
24. Be alert to other changes that can negatively affect this change. (Unintended negative side effects and consequences.)
25. Have a different person manage the stability than the one who managed the change. They are different tasks involving people with different personalities. Change agents are poor stay agents!

Tool #9 Centralized vs. Decentralized

Application of Systems Dynamics #10: Relationships

Build strategic consistency (the what) and operational flexibility (the how) into your organization. Focus on what is strategic and what is operational ("either/or" questions such as centralize vs. decentralize are too simplistic). One size no longer fits all; consistency isn't always key, especially in the "how-to."

Strategic consistency (the "what") to your vision/mission and operational flexibility (the "how") replace the either/or centralized vs. decentralized dilemma of the past.

- **This gives rise to Systems Question #8—*What do we centralize (mostly whats) and what should we decentralize (hows)?***

➥ **For example:** Organizations need both better strategic consistency and more operational flexibility in today's fast-paced world.

> ***PRINCIPLE: There are many different ways to achieve the same desired outcomes; thus, involving the right people in planning and implementing solutions/actions is key.* People support what they help create.**

It follows that decision making should be as close to the actions (and the entity we desire to change) as possible. People have a natural desire to be involved and provide input into decisions that affect them *before* the decision is made. For leaders, this is called participatory management.

➥ **For example:** Today's leadership paradigm requires a different way of looking at organizations. It requires a much higher level of wisdom and maturity not to abdicate or to overcontrol—to find the higher ground of interdependence.

The Third Level of Maturity/Wisdom
(is required for this to work best):

#3 Interdependent (Systems/Teamwork)

#2 Independent (Individual/Separate)

#1 Dependent (Child-like)

Suggestions for Use:

1. **In their personal or professional lives**, leaders need to identify the few things they need to ensure consistency in their organization or their lives—i.e., personal/organizational values and beliefs, shared vision and/or mission, as well as key strategies everyone should help carry out.
2. In addition, most organizations need consistency in the following areas:
   - financial arrangements
   - senior executives/succession planning
   - organization identity and visibility
3. Beyond these few strategic consistencies, operational flexibility and empowerment should reign.
4. **In our personal lives**, we need to allow other family members to live their lives as they want, as long as they stay true to the family's agreed-upon values.
5. **For children**, specify as few rules as possible but adhere to them with integrity.

Tool #10 Multiple Causes, Root Causes

Application of Systems Dynamics #2: Open System View; #11: Steady State, Dynamic Equilibrium; and #12: Internal Elaboration

Use free-flowing and participative management and active-learning techniques to find linkages and the multiple causality factors that are really the root causes.

- **This gives rise to Systems Question #9—*What are the root causes?***

Managerial leverage and the long-term impacts of what you do each day look like this:

Long-Term Impact on What You Do Each Day

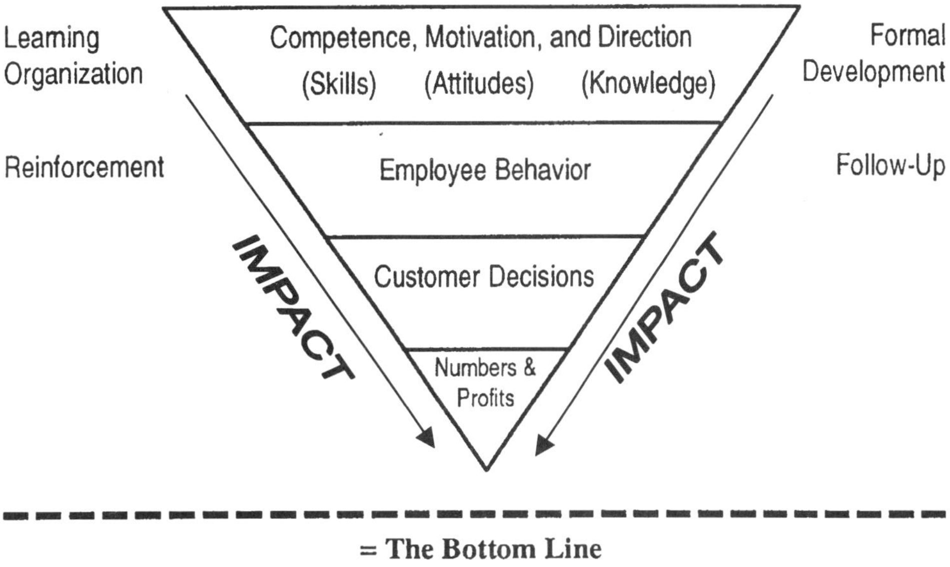

PRINCIPLE: *Root causes and effects are usually not linked closely in time and space.*

Our simplistic cause–effect analyses and desire for quick fixes often *cause* more problems than they solve. Because our earth is composed of seven levels of complex and interdependent systems, multiple causes with multiple effects are the true reality, as are circles of causality-effects. See, for example, how our local weather and crops are affected by the ocean/clouds/rain/wind (i.e., El Nino).

Delay time—the time that elapses between causes and their impacts—can have enormous influences on a system. The concept of "delayed effect" is often missed in our impatient society. It is often subtle, ignored, and almost always underestimated. When we feel that results aren't happening quickly enough, it shakes our confidence, causing unnecessarily violent knee-jerk reactions.

Decisions often have long-term consequences. Mind-mapping, fishbone diagrams, and all sorts of creativity/brainstorming tools are useful in anticipating these results.

However, *keep in mind that things are often far too complicated for us to fully assess and comprehend intuitively.* For this reason, it is crucial to flag or anticipate delays; understand and appreciate them, and learn to work *with* them rather than against them.

➥ **For example:** If you want to retire at age 55 with enough money to do what you want the rest of your life, don't go after this goal at age 54. Start at age 21 and work toward it in numerous ways—pension, savings, investments, home ownership, material possessions, etc.

Suggestions for Use:

1. To find root causes, try active learning techniques suggested by your training and development function. The key is to involve people affected by a change in the search for solutions.
2. Use these techniques to search for root causes vs. "surface symptoms." Some root causes are very hard to find.
3. Continually ask, *"What else might be the root cause?"* or *why-why-why?*
4. Keep an open-systems view of the environment, as it often contributes to overall root causes as well.

Simple and direct "cause and effect" is a myth—a linear/analytical myth. There are multiple causes to achieve almost any effect; not all of them are closely related in time and space to the result. It is often a ripple effect of multiple environmental and internal factors.

➥ **For example:** The cheapest/quickest solutions often turn out to be the most expensive. There is no free lunch; obvious solutions are often the worst because their implications are not considered beforehand, buy-in is bypassed, and negative by-products of the decision are ignored. There are no simplistic, single answers.

The Failure of the Quick Fix
Doing the most obvious quick fix
usually
does not produce the most obvious desired outcome.

Machine-Mechanistic View of the World (is Obsolete)

Direct Cause and Effect

i.e., Acorn ➔ Oak Tree
Cause must be necessary
must be sufficient

- Acorn is necessary but not sufficient.
- What's missing is the environment.

"Direct cause and effect" is an environment-free concept!

➥ **For example:** In organizations, the simplistic view of training of frontline employees to improve the way they serve the customer is obviously more involved than it looks. Often overlooked are these factors: the processes, the product quality, the rest of the organization, the leadership, the rewards system, etc. Training is usually just an initiator of changes, not the full solution.

➥ **For example:** In our personal lives, dieting alone doesn't lead to even short-term weight loss, as your body slows down due to its reaction to the "starvation." Being fit is different from being overweight: It requires regular exercise and a totally different life-style. But—it sounds good on the surface, doesn't it?

Suggestions for Use:

1. Expand your horizon to a total systems view.
2. Gain agreement not to use simple quick-fix gut reactions.
3. Use third-alternative thinking.
4. Stay away from "either/or" thinking.
5. Be careful when budgeting to deal with and fund solutions to the *underlying* issues—not just the "quick-fix" ones.

Tool #11 KISS: From Complexity to Simplicity

Application of Systems Dynamics #7: Equifinality; #9: Hierarchy; and #12: Internal Elaboration

Flexibility, looseness, adaptability, speed, and KISS (simplicity) are more important than rigid plans, tight controls, one-size-fits-all consistency, and economies of scale. Eliminate the waste of complexity, bureaucracy, hierarchy, and levels in every system.

- **This gives rise to Systems Question #10—How can we go from complexity to simplicity and from consistency to flexibility in the solutions we devise?**

The Goal (in whatever we do)

Clarify and Simplify—Clarify and Simplify—Clarify and Simplify

PRINCIPLE: Systems upon systems upon systems are too complex to fully understand and manage centrally.

Liberation from regulation, shaping corporate bureaucracies into smaller units, privatization, and free-market economies are generally more efficient and effective than government or big business can ever be in understanding the complexities of systems. It is the thousands and thousands of little decisions we all make daily in our businesses that shape and meet these market needs—not central government regulations. Clearly, government *has* a role to play in today's society—just not an all-encompassing one! The same is true for big corporations.

We need to eliminate the waste that complexity brings. Remember, the KISS method is more powerful than many economies of scale. Focus on the fundamentals, *not* the fads. In the future, the virtual corporation may very well be more effective than the more traditional, vertically integrated complex organization.

Suggestions for Use:

1. **Ten Ways to Reduce Bureaucracy** (and create Simplicity and Flexibility)

   The **KISS** mindset

   Answer these questions in terms of your own job/your own life:

   1. What made me mad today?
   2. What took too long?
   3. What was the cause of any complaints?
   4. What was misunderstood?
   5. What cost too much?
   6. What was wanted?
   7. What was too complicated?
   8. What is just plain silly?
   9. What job took too many people?
   10. What job involved too many actions?

2. **Three Magic Questions to Build in Simplicity**

   1. What is going well in the organization or my personal life that should not be changed?
   2. What are the abrasive or problem areas that should be examined?
   3. If you could change your organization or your life with a stroke of the pen, what would you do?

3. **Ask the #1 Systems Question over and over: "What's our purpose/goal here?"**

4. **Reduce all key documents/action plans to one page** (2-sided max)

5. **Use the 80/20 Rule: Focus on the top 20% of life that will give you 80% of the benefits.**

6. **Keep in mind "Strategic Consistency yet Allow Operationally Flexibility."**

7. **Focus on the fundamentals.**

The Rule of Threes

Four-leaf clovers are a rarity and, many believe, good luck. The world mostly operates from the "Rule of Three"—beginning, middle, end; sun, moon, stars; body, mind, spirit; air, land, water. In fact, this method of reducing and seeing the world in threes is the key to the KISS Method.

Management's Ultimate Challenge:

Search for the simplicity on the far side of complexity.

LEADERS ARE SIMPLE

Most great leaders I've met are simple men. People like Sam Walton and General Schwarzkopf—they're far from stupid, but they are basically very simple. I include myself in that category. I hate complexity. I think the world is already complex enough as it is, without me making it more so. The principles of management and leadership are simple. The hard part is doing them, living up to them day after day, not making lots of excuses for ourselves. You know all those complex management theories? They're just an excuse for not facing up to how hard it is to live by some very basic principles.

From a conversation with H. Ross Perot, founder of Electronic Data Systems, Inc., and Perot Data Systems, during a recent Inc. conference
Source: INC, January 1992

SIMPLICITY RULE

Let's make a rule that we can't use anything I can't explain in three minutes—Phil Crosby

"Life's Rules of Three"

Application	**(1)**		**(2)**		**(3)**
Individuals:	Body	—	Mind	—	Spirit
Learning:	Skills	—	Knowledge	—	Feelings/Attitude
Human Interactions:	Structure	—	Content	—	Process
Levels:	Individuals	—	Teams	—	Organization

Suggestions for Use:

1. When giving a talk or a presentation—in fact, whenever you are trying to influence someone—*reduce your views to three main points.* Everyone will remember it.
2. Always ask yourself, "What are my three main points?" in everything you are doing. Build frameworks people can remember.
3. When someone else is being complex, or rambling on, ask him or her for the three main points, or the three *pro* points and three *con* points on an issue

Suggestions for Use: **Simple Yet Powerful Rewards**

Managers and leaders (and even parents) should follow these three simple, yet powerful rewards:

1. Celebrate the moment.
2. Recognize the effort.
3. Have time with the boss.

—Alan Landers

Tool #12 The Ultimate Question: Superordinate Goals

Application of Systems Dynamics #9: Hierarchy; and #6: Multiple-Goal Seeking

Problems can't be solved at the level they were created, said Albert Einstein. So, we need to go to the next higher systems level and its desired outcome in order to succeed. Focus on abundance (win-win) vs. scarcity (win-lose) activities through the use of higher systems-order outcomes.

- **The Ultimate Systems Question: What is our common superordinate goal here?**

Paradigm Shifts–Real Advances

> *To raise new questions, new possibilities, to regard old problems from a new angle, requires creative imagination and marks real advance in science.*
>
> —Albert Einstein
>
> *No problem can be solved from the same consciousness that created it. We must learn to see the world anew.*

PRINCIPLE: (The ultimate systems principle): Problems can't be solved at the level they were created. (Albert Einstein).

> *. . . so go to the next higher system's level and its desired outcome in order to succeed (superordinate goals).*
>
> —Albert Einstein
>
> *So . . . if we generally use analytical thinking, we now need real Systems Thinking^{SM} to resolve our issues.*

- **Creating Systems Thinking^{SM} (and Strategists)**

Do you have disciplined systems thinking in your organization, or just empty rhetoric?

➥ **For example:** In union–management fights and strikes over pay, it is a win-lose game. By moving to the higher level goal of competing and selling more products profitably, then both sides can gain more money (increase the size of the pie).

➥ **For example:** In your day-to-day life, do you think about your future vision and your highest-level goals?

> *If you do not think about the future, you cannot have one.*
>
> —John Galsworthy

Suggestions for Use:

1. If it feels like any discussion you are a part of is going nowhere, ask what the common superordinate goal is all can support.
2. In planning your day, week, month, or year, ask this question of all involved at the beginning. Sometimes this is seen as a shared vision.
3. You may also want to ask sides involved in a conflict, "Is there a third alternative we all can live with?" as a way to a higher goal.

Tool #13 System Dynamics Overall

Application of Systems Dynamics #4: Input-Output Model; and #5: Feedback

Standard "systems dynamics" are the basis of Concept #1 of our Systems Thinking[SM] framework.

- The dysfunctional patterns of behaviors show up time and time again in organizations and systems. Recognizing these trends, patterns, and loops, first defined by Peter Senge of MIT, is crucial to changing and modifying them.
- Changing them is a process of diagnosis and discovery.

A. Typical Dysfunctional Patterns of Behavior—Part of Your Diagnostic Repertoire

1. **The Quick Fix That Backfires**
    - only short-term improvement; need to address root problem
    - the squeaky wheel gets the grease
    - downsizing to improve profits
    - always has unintended consequences
2. **Limits to Everything**
    - the harder you push, the harder the system pushes back
    - plateaus occur naturally
    - if you zoom past your natural constraints, you'll eventually collapse ("overshoot and collapse")
    - easy improvements first, then they get harder
    - fight harder and harder for less and less
    - understand the balancing process
    - constraints get tougher
    - mental models; limit the change culture
3. **Dependency**
    - addition/denials
    - key unintended consequences compound the problems
    - system's capacity to fix goes down over time
    - causes "crisis heroism" vs. long-term cures
    - requires practice/self-initiative to break
4. **Maximizing Elements**
    - ruins the whole/the public good—common resource
    - too much of a good thing
    - requires cooperation of parts to solve it
    - individual needs vs. optimization of the whole
    - need overriding legislation for the common good

5. **Turf Battles**
   - vs. collaboration, mutual support
   - unintended obstruction, undermining of others' tasks
   - focus on self only and sometimes end up shooting the other person/group in the foot
   - well intended, righteous indignation
   - need to understand others' needs

—adapted from *The 5th Discipline Fieldbook*

Suggestions for Use:

1. Recognize and stop these vicious cycles and circles. Instead, find other solutions that combat these loops.

B. More Standard System Dynamics

Suggestions for Use:

1. Using the twelve characteristics of General Systems Theory, answer the following questions:
   - **Predicting Outcomes:** Since multiple outcomes occur in almost everything you do, can you predict not only your desired outcomes, but also the negatives or by-products as well? What are they?
   - **Run-Down Entropic Effect**: Since everything runs down and dies over time when left to its own devices, how do we continually add power, energy, and follow-up into any system, project, or change process?
   - **Elaboration and Rigidity**: Since most things acquire more complexity, elaboration, and bureaucracy/rigidity over time, how do we keep things useful and simple with the KISS method (Keep It Simple, Sweetheart)?
   - **Dynamic Resistance:** Since most organizations (and especially organizational structures) exist in a steady-state or dynamic equilibrium, how can you use it positively to bring about change? (The answer is that it is very difficult. The steady-state structure naturally resists change because it is often not in its own best interests. Who is resisting? Why?)
   - **The Gift of Feedback**: "Feedback Is the Breakfast of Champions." The organizations with the most open boundaries seek good and bad feedback from their environments. They see feedback as not good or bad, but just feedback, make their needed corrections, and adapt better to our dynamic changing environment. What feedback do *you* get?
   - **Equifinality and Empowerment**: There are many ways to achieve a desired future vision (the "what"), that is why empowerment (the "how") is so important. The person closest to the issue usually has the best view and is the most committed to solving the issue (not higher up in the hierarchy). Who is closest to the issue?

C. System Dynamics: Cooperation and Competition

Cooperate within your system; compete between systems (at times), and know which is appropriate/when. Be conscious of this. It is possible to compete and cooperate at the same time.

➥ **For example:** Professional sports leagues can be used as examples. Owners own their teams and they compete—yet the league's reputation rises/falls collectively, based on their cooperation (or lack thereof). See baseball's 1994–1995 season "failure" as an excellent example.

➥ **For example:** The turf battles and politics between departments/individuals in an organization reflect the absence of a broader corporate view. If your organization has this and I compete with you, I'm very happy to see these struggles. While I'm competing with you, you've taken your "eye off the ball" and marketplace. Thanks!

Adversarial cultures include:

1. Managers vs. those whom they are managing
2. Line departments vs. staff departments
3. Manufacturing vs. marketing
4. Headquarters vs. field employees
5. Division vs. division

➥ **For example:** While we want cooperation and teamwork in organizations, what do we reward? We reward individuals (rarely teams); our merit budget percentage limit means that for every person above the percentage, one person must be below it—in effect, competing for limited money.

Systems—The Natural Order of the Universe and Life

We need to learn:

The Synergy of Systems Solutions
vs.
The Failure of Fragmented Functions

The dominant paradigm in our lives is "Analytic Thinking."
However,
The Natural Order of Life in the World is a *Systems* one.

Thus, analytic approaches (and analytic thinking) to systems problems in everyday life and organizations are now bankrupt!

The good news is that this new "Systems Thinking Paradigm" is beginning to emerge; witness the use of new systems-oriented words, such as:

united, fit, integration, collaboration, cooperation, teamwork, partnerships, alliances, linkages, stakeholders, holistic, seamless, boundary-less, system, etc.

Our Systems Model bridges this gap, opening up whole new vistas and THE newly emerging paradigm that more properly fits with reality . . . and the ***Natural Order of the Universe and Life.***

Suggestions for Use:

1. Make everyone aware (in your family, team, department, organization) of this western proclivity toward competition in all we do.
2. Define where cooperation and collaboration might work better.
3. Be sure your pay and recognition systems reward what you desire (**experts agree, most do not!!**).
4. Ask yourself: Do you see the world in a win-lose (i.e., scarcity) view or in a win-win (i.e., abundance) one? And can you tell when the situation is one or the other? Often your win and lose posture causes the same reaction in others. The resulting struggle is actually a lose-lose result.

   Think about this next time you have a conflict with others.

D. Hierarchy

There is a natural hierarchy in the world. The food chains (both in the water and on land) are examples of this as are the families of man and animals. **It is a natural law and fact of life.**

So the real question is, *How do we make it work effectively?"* After all, we can't escape it.

➥ **For example:** The old "command and control" (C&C) hierarchy is no longer appropriate today. What should take its place?

➥ **For example:** We've seen too many executives and managers fail because the only alternative they knew to C&C was to be "The nice guy." Yet there is a big range between these two extremes. The middle is participative management.

Suggestions for Use:

The question is not, *How do we get rid of the hierarchy in an either/or mentality. It's:*

1. How best to use the appropriate/least hierarchy in pursuit of our goals/outcomes?
2. What kind of a participative management hierarchy are we ready for?

   (i.e., self-directed teams ← → input only); there is a very broad range even here.
3. **What people want most of all is quite simple:** Most of us want input into decisions that affect us before the decision is made. People want to be recognized, respected, and asked their opinion ("People support what they help create!").
4. Consensus decision making
   - is a dynamic and evolving process
   - means that although it may not be the decision you would make, you are willing to live with it and actively support it
   - includes an agreement on the decision by the manager/leader who will lead implementation of the decision

   So it follows—Involve people in decisions that affect them prior to making the decision.
5. On a personal basis, this participative/consensus style also applies at home, especially with teenagers who are trying to grow and experience independence.

CHAPTER III

APPLICATION: PHASE A — THE OUTCOME THINKING TOOLS

This chapter identifies the most important practical tools for becoming customer-focused and results-oriented.

Tool No.	The Applications
14	Customer Wants and Needs — *What is the range of choices a customer may want or need from any business?*
15	Customer Focus — *What are the best practices of a customer-focused organization?*
16	Internal vs. External Customers — *Who is your customer?*
17	Ideal Future Vision — *What is your shared vision, or mission, and what are your core values?*
18	Whole Jobs — *What is needed to make everyone's job fulfilling?*

INCREMENTAL THINKING VS. THE FUTURE

Incremental thinking *is when you design a company to be run tomorrow based on what you have today.*

Strategic thinking *is when you look into the future and design your company based on what you want to become.*

—Linda Honold

Tool #14 Customer Wants and Needs

Application of Systems Dynamics #4: Input/Output Model; and #6: Multiple-Goal Seeking

Focus on outcomes—defining and meeting customer wants/needs. The value to the customer is always some mix of five "STAR" outcome points:

- choice and customization
- service excellence, ease of doing business
- high quality goods and services
- speed, timeliness, responsiveness
- total cost (in all ways)

➡ **For example:** When you start thinking about how to create customer value, consider all the outcomes customers are likely to desire. Though customer needs are rarely looked at in their entirety, the Centre for Strategic Management has copyrighted the following "Star Model" to help organizations aim for *full* customer satisfaction and position themselves vs. others in the marketplace.

Star ★ Results Model

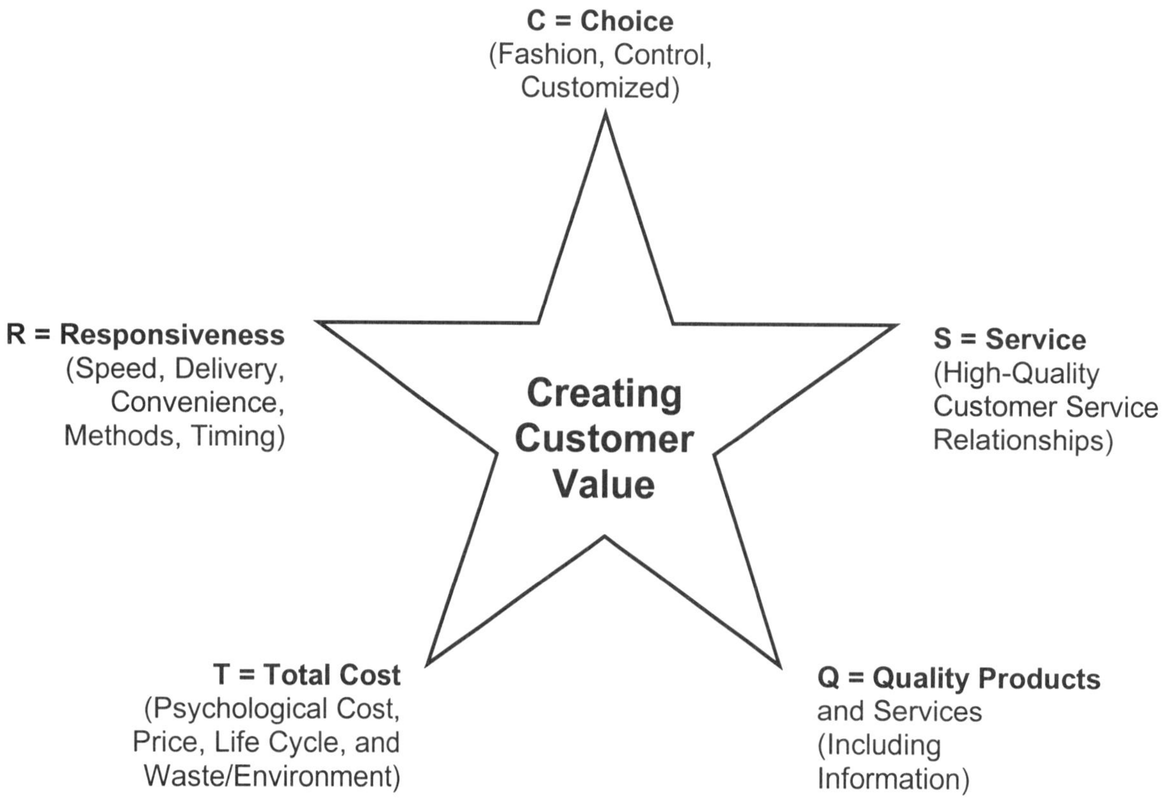

A. Choice

It has been common knowledge for years that in dealing with senior executives, the best method is to give them options and choices rather than tell them what to do. This is now true for the "me generation" consumer who considers himself or herself a "unit of one" to be marketed to in an individual way.

➥ **For example:** Nordstrom decided in 1996 to set up new departments within each store called "The Individualist."

➥ **For example:** Japanese car manufacturers can get you the exact car of your choice (customized) within two weeks of your decision in a showroom. Once you decide, a message is transmitted to the factory and the next car in final assembly is marked as yours, customized to your every desire as it comes down the line.

Suggestions for Use:

1. **With anyone you can serve or deal** with (supervisors and staff alike), give options and choices, if at all possible, in order to gain their agreement. This is especially true where empowerment is important, or in using our "People support what they help create" credo.
2. **At home**, give your children more options vs. always telling them what to do, especially if they are teenagers.
3. **With customers**, it is critical to offer them choices, not just one color, one delivery system, etc. "Either/or" choices are wrong . . . multiple choices are right!
4. **Organizationally**, "strategic consistency and operational flexibility" are in—the old centralize vs. decentralize is out!

B. Speed/Responsiveness

Do you want it:

- Good
- Fast
- Cheap

Pick two of the three; you can't have all three.

In today's world we almost always choose "speed" as one of the two; often paying more in the process. Speed is of the essence in today's world. And time is usually the most scarce/precious of all resources.

➥ **For example:** Faxes, fast food, home delivery, ATMs, fast check-ins, etc. It's all around us; finding ways to "save" time however we can.

➥ **For example:**

> **Time Management and Organization Effectiveness**
> A systems approach to Strategic Planning is the ultimate
> Time Management (i.e., speed/responsiveness) tool for an entire organization.

Levels of Time Management Professionalism

Four Levels of Strategic Planning, Mastery, and Effectiveness to deal with the #1 issue in every organization, in every person today: Lack of time. Anything we can do to increase speed/responsiveness and focus employees translates to the customer.

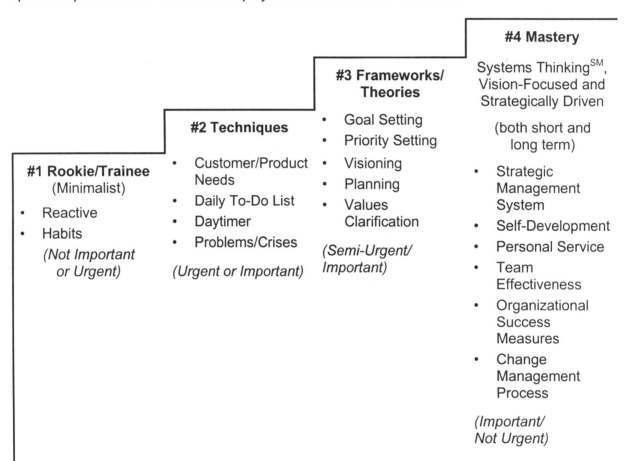

#1 Rookie/Trainee (Minimalist)	**#2 Techniques**	**#3 Frameworks/ Theories**	**#4 Mastery**
• Reactive • Habits *(Not Important or Urgent)*	• Customer/Product Needs • Daily To-Do List • Daytimer • Problems/Crises *(Urgent or Important)*	• Goal Setting • Priority Setting • Visioning • Planning • Values Clarification *(Semi-Urgent/ Important)*	Systems Thinking^{SM}, Vision-Focused and Strategically Driven (both short and long term) • Strategic Management System • Self-Development • Personal Service • Team Effectiveness • Organizational Success Measures • Change Management Process *(Important/ Not Urgent)*

➥ **For example:** We must have a clear set of priorities for our personal lives so that we can focus our time properly. It's not just speed that is key; it's focusing on *what's important to us*.

➥ **For example:**

Do We Focus on the Compass, or the Clock?
—adapted from Steven Covey

Is the Focus Our Compass or Our Clock?
(Important Direction or Urgent Activity?)

- Lead your life—don't just manage your time.
- Our struggle to *put first things first* can be characterized by the contrast between two powerful tools that direct us: the clock and the compass.
- The clock represents efficiency, our appointments, and schedules, things, tasks—what we do with our time, and how we manage our time.
- The compass represents effectiveness, our vision and our principles, people, mission, conscience, and direction—what we feel is important and how we lead our lives.
- People who are effective do different things—they subordinate the clock to the compass and *lead* their lives, not just manage their time.

Suggestions for Use:

1. Where are you? What do you need to do differently?
2. How do you and your team go about "speeding up" organizational effectiveness?

Use of Managerial Time (Especially in Meetings)

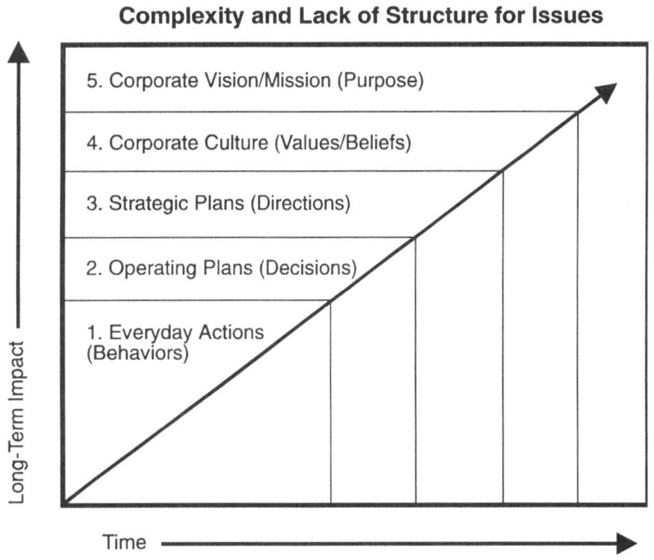

C. Total Cost Alone

Holding down costs and lowering prices are not enough to achieve success and realize your vision. Keeping costs low is definitely necessary, but success requires that you do more.

➥ **For example:** Businesses, governments, and not-for-profit organizations can and do fail despite successful efforts to control costs.

➥ **For example:** Competitors are often willing to engage in a price war to take away your business. Auto rebates and airfare wars are proof that lowering your price won't pay off in the long run. You have to do something else.

Suggestions for Use:

1. When you develop your change strategy, remember to focus on cost containment.
2. Some strategies in this area include:
   - Cut costs across the board.
   - Do some selective cost-cutting based on yearly action priorities.
   - Reorganize and flatten your hierarchy and expand others more.
   - Eliminate waste and bureaucracy.
   - Improve your business processes.

How to Reduce Costs and Complexity

1. Begin Business Process Improvement through process mapping/cross-functional teams.
2. Arrange for "Blow Out Bureaucracy" Workshop presented by the Centre for Strategic Management.
3. Eliminate "waste" of all types (outside waste assessment)
   - all non-value-added activities
   - wasted movement
   - corrections
   - overproduction
   - waiting
   - excess inventory
   - transporting parts and materials
   - processing parts
4. Examine/delete layers of management.
5. Examine materials and equipment costs.
6. Reduce usage—telephone, copier, etc.
7. Increase productivity and efficiency everywhere.
8. Benchmark best practices vs. your costs.
9. Adopt Quality Improvement in Your Daily Work (QIDW)/continuous improvement (individual/teams).
10. Solicit cost-savings ideas and solutions.
11. Examine all overhead costs.
12. Examine all administrative costs.
13. Focus training dollars on your strategic plan.
14. Increase response, speed, KISS.

15. Promote innovation, creativity.
16. Promote automation, robotics.
17. Deal with poor performers (up or out).
18. Reduce supplier costs.
19. Reduce inventory (just in time).
20. Invest in people and technology.

Suggestions for Use:

Option #1: **Current Assessment of Customer Value**

You can use the format below to assess:

- What your customers currently value
- Anticipated customer value
- How you are currently meeting this customer desire
- Where you desire your competitive positioning to be on this matrix

Option #2: **Current Assessment of Your Own Career**—Who do you serve, and how well do you provide these outcomes to your organization?

Assessment of What the Customer Values / Customer Segments	Score 1 (Low) to 10 (High)					Overall Comments
	#1 Choice/ Control	#2 Service/ Relationships	#3 Quality Products/ Services	#4 Delivery/ Speed/ Convenience	#5 Total Cost	
1.						
2.						
3.						
4.						
5.						
6.						
7.						
8.						

Once you've identified your desired customer value, are you able to write a position statement about yourself vs. your competition in either (1) your career or (2) your organization? This position should state what differentiates you from your competition.

It is also called (at times) your *driving force*, *strategic intent*, or *grand strategy*.

D. Competitive Positioning Statement Defined

- Our driving force(s) is the way we differentiate ourselves vs. the competition. It is sometimes called "the Mother of all Core Strategies."
- It is the main way we achieve a sustained competitive advantage/edge vs. the competition over time.
- It can't be more than one to two thrusts in number (any more and you're attempting to be all things to all people). The other elements of the Customer Value Star Model need to be accomplished at a competitive level if they are also desired by your customers. Otherwise, you're at a competitive disadvantage.
- This positioning should be the key single strategic thrust your organization uses to achieve its vision/mission/values . . .
  - ❑ to which all other functions, directions, decisions, and criteria are subordinated and focused upon
  - ❑ usually only either a *who, what,* or *how* from your mission/values (*why* is a given)
  - ❑ that is or can be the organization's core or distinctive competency which makes it unique from the competition
  - ❑ is sustainable as an edge over a period of years that cannot be readily duplicated
  - ❑ and that you are known for—your reputation—your distinctiveness

Competitive business advantages are difficult to achieve. A sustainable advantage requires the organization to build and deliver something that others cannot duplicate easily or quickly. You can gain a competitive business advantage only by doing something difficult; if it's easy, too many other people can and will do it.

E. How Are You Driven? Competitive Positioning

How are you driven?—Are you outcome-oriented to the customer and markets, or to the products, employees, order-taking, processes, or regulations? If you are trying to design, build, and sustain a customer-focused, high-performance organization for the 21st century, then you had better be at the high end of this evolutionary scale!

➥ **For example: How Are *You* Driven?**

Where Are You on the "Evolutionary Scale"?

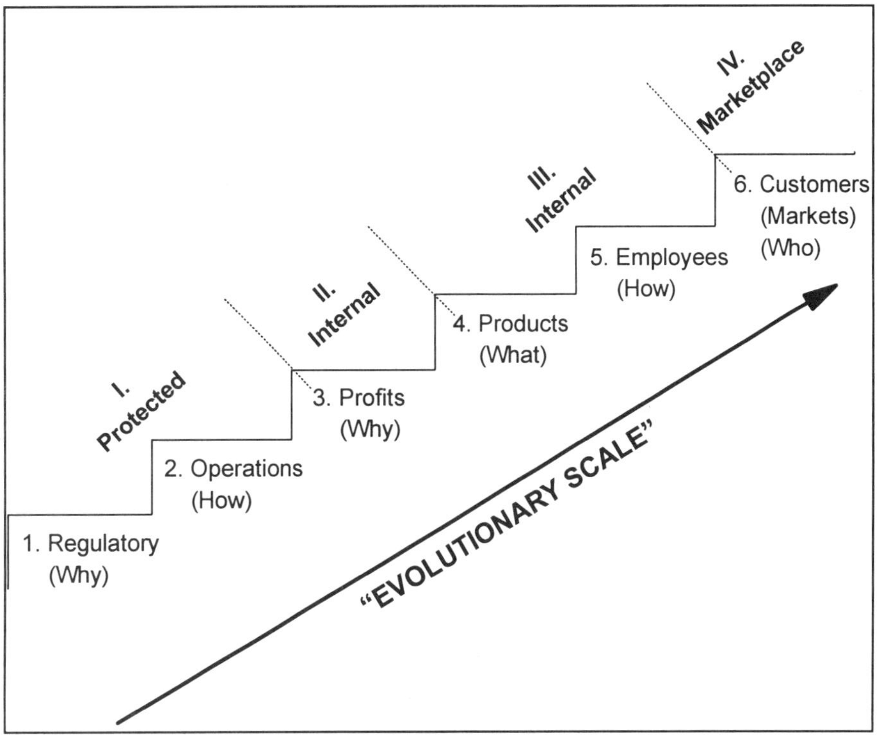

➥ **For example:** In personal terms, are you driven to serve and help others (customers) using products, your own gifts/skills? Or are you driven by the prospect of making money/health? Even worse, do you live your life day-to-day, or spend it following the rules (and regulations) of others, accepting your life as your fate?

How We Are Driven (Questionnaire)

Instructions: Answer the questions *How am I driven now? How would I like to be driven?* Distribute 10 points.

Driven By:	How Am I Driven Now?			How Would I Like To Be Driven?		
	Distribute 10 Points	**Priority #**	**Evidence/ Examples Today**	**Distribute 10 Points**	**Priority #**	**Why?**
❑ Regulations/ Rules/ Government (The Why/)						
❑ Our Operations/ Administration (The How)						
❑ Our Profits/ Budgets (The Why/Owners)						
❑ Our Products and Services (The What)						
❑ Employee Needs (The How)						
❑ Our Customers (The Who)						
	Total 10 Points			Total 10 points		

1. Are you happy with your answers? Why or why not?
2. If you are not happy, then try to find out what to do about this.

When you change your organization's marketing strategies to better serve your customers, competitors don't just stand by and watch you. Competitive analysis is key to success, both organizationally and individually.

➥ **For example:** Try to write a position statement about your career and your organization. It should spell out what differentiates you from your competition.

F. The Art of Trade-Offs

There is an art to living simply in this imperfect, interrelated world. Systems Thinking^{SM} helps you practice the "art of trade-offs." We need to make intentional, conscious choices in terms of solutions and direction—deciding which problems we want to live with and which to try and solve. But these choices must be based on our desired outcomes.

Some Strategic Answers and Trade-offs vs. One Right Answer

➥ **For example:** System relationships are often complicated and unpredictable.

- There's rarely any single right answer to a question.
- There is almost always some unintended consequence within and outside the system.
- Some multiple processes and answers result in more long-term and strategic (i.e., successful) solutions.

The secret of systems thinking is to learn to recognize the trade-offs of every action and, in effect, to make wise choices concerning our next problems.

➥ **For example:** You can't be all things to all people. Choose your niche. Will it be as a low-cost producer, providing unsurpassed customer service, or creating innovative new products? Focus—focus—focus!

➥ **For example:** What are your product pricing objectives: maximum profits today, or market share tomorrow?

➥ **For example:** In your personal life, you are always trading off your priorities. Do you want to get ahead in your career by earning an MBA in night school? It will mean spending less time with family/friends. Do you want to spend or save your disposable income? What's your desired outcome?

➥ **For example:** All situations have three fundamental elements: content, process, structure. Keep in mind that balance and trade-offs are usually needed on these three elements in all situations.

Suggestions for Use:

1. Recognize that trying to be all things to all people is a sure-fire way to fail and this applies to all areas (i.e., Seven Levels) of life.
2. Focus your direction, vision, goals, purpose. Then budget to support your future, not the past.
3. Once you've focused your direction, set priority actions and a budget, and focus on first things first.

G. Whole Package

Examine in detail your entire "package" the way customers see and experience it. You'll be amazed at how different things look from their perspective.

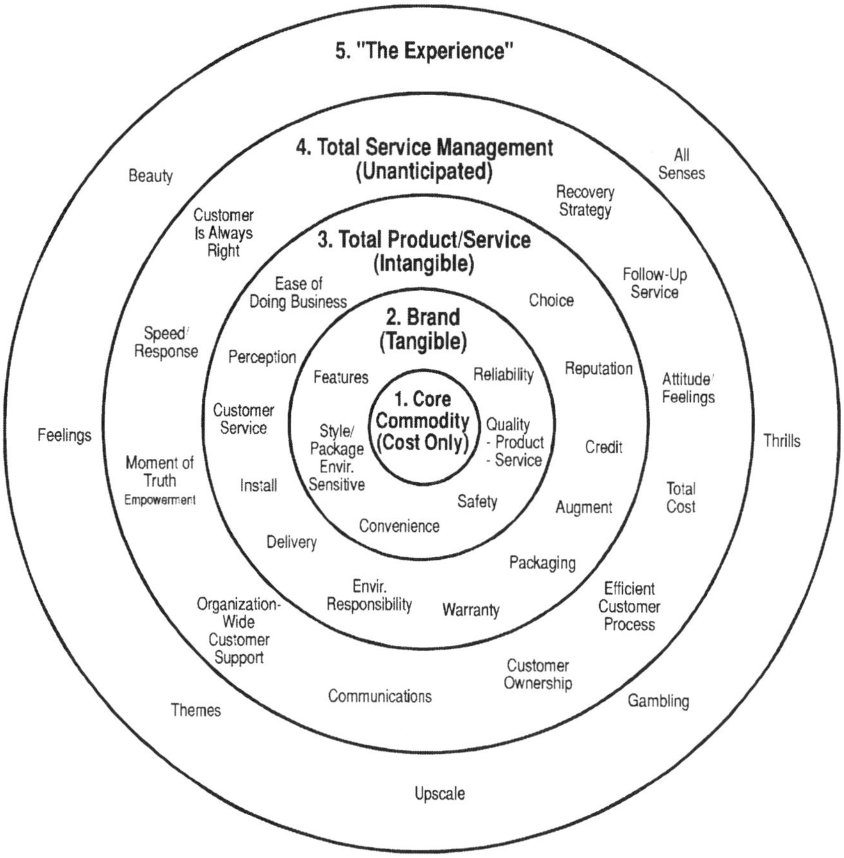

➥ **For example:** The big question is, "Where do you compete (core product or outer features)?

1. Commodity
2. Brand
3. Total product/intangibles
4. Total product and services package/unanticipated

Core commodity is not the best place to compete.

Suggestions for Use:

1. Complete the Values Map Assessment on the next two pages.

Value Map Assessment

Instructions: On a scale of 1 (low) to 10 (high), answer the following two questions:

Value	***How is it today for our customers?***			***How do we want it to be, ideally, in the future?*** (i.e., Where's your competitive edge?)		
	Low	***Avg.***	***High***	***Low***	***Avg.***	***High***
1. **Core commodity** • Cost only	1 2 3 4	5	6 7 8 9 10	1 2 3 4	5	6 7 8 9 10
2. **Brand (Tangible)**	1 2 3 4	5	6 7 8 9 10	1 2 3 4	5	6 7 8 9 10
• Reliability	1 2 3 4	5	6 7 8 9 10	1 2 3 4	5	6 7 8 9 10
• Safety	1 2 3 4	5	6 7 8 9 10	1 2 3 4	5	6 7 8 9 10
• Quality (Product/Service)	1 2 3 4	5	6 7 8 9 10	1 2 3 4	5	6 7 8 9 10
• Style/Package Environmentally-Sensitive	1 2 3 4	5	6 7 8 9 10	1 2 3 4	5	6 7 8 9 10
• Features	1 2 3 4	5	6 7 8 9 10	1 2 3 4	5	6 7 8 9 10
• Convenience	1 2 3 4	5	6 7 8 9 10	1 2 3 4	5	6 7 8 9 10
3. **Total Product/Service (Intangible)**	1 2 3 4	5	6 7 8 9 10	1 2 3 4	5	6 7 8 9 10
• Choice	1 2 3 4	5	6 7 8 9 10	1 2 3 4	5	6 7 8 9 10
• Reputation	1 2 3 4	5	6 7 8 9 10	1 2 3 4	5	6 7 8 9 10
• Credit	1 2 3 4	5	6 7 8 9 10	1 2 3 4	5	6 7 8 9 10
• Augmentation	1 2 3 4	5	6 7 8 9 10	1 2 3 4	5	6 7 8 9 10
• Packaging	1 2 3 4	5	6 7 8 9 10	1 2 3 4	5	6 7 8 9 10
• Warranty	1 2 3 4	5	6 7 8 9 10	1 2 3 4	5	6 7 8 9 10
• Environmental Responsibility	1 2 3 4	5	6 7 8 9 10	1 2 3 4	5	6 7 8 9 10
• Delivery	1 2 3 4	5	6 7 8 9 10	1 2 3 4	5	6 7 8 9 10
• Installation	1 2 3 4	5	6 7 8 9 10	1 2 3 4	5	6 7 8 9 10
• Customer Service	1 2 3 4	5	6 7 8 9 10	1 2 3 4	5	6 7 8 9 10
• Perception	1 2 3 4	5	6 7 8 9 10	1 2 3 4	5	6 7 8 9 10
• Ease of Doing Business	1 2 3 4	5	6 7 8 9 10	1 2 3 4	5	6 7 8 9 10

(continued)

Value Map Assessment (concluded)

Value	*How is it today for our customers?*			*How do we want it to be, ideally, in the future?* (i.e., Where's your competitive edge?)		
	Low	*Avg.*	*High*	*Low*	*Avg.*	*High*
4. **Total Service Management (Unanticipated)**	1 2 3 4	5	6 7 8 9 10	1 2 3 4	5	6 7 8 9 10
• Recovery/Strategy	1 2 3 4	5	6 7 8 9 10	1 2 3 4	5	6 7 8 9 10
• Follow-Up Service	1 2 3 4	5	6 7 8 9 10	1 2 3 4	5	6 7 8 9 10
• Attitude/Feelings	1 2 3 4	5	6 7 8 9 10	1 2 3 4	5	6 7 8 9 10
• Total Cost	1 2 3 4	5	6 7 8 9 10	1 2 3 4	5	6 7 8 9 10
• Efficient Customer Process	1 2 3 4	5	6 7 8 9 10	1 2 3 4	5	6 7 8 9 10
• Customer-Ownership	1 2 3 4	5	6 7 8 9 10	1 2 3 4	5	6 7 8 9 10
• Communications	1 2 3 4	5	6 7 8 9 10	1 2 3 4	5	6 7 8 9 10
• Organization-Wide Customer Support	1 2 3 4	5	6 7 8 9 10	1 2 3 4	5	6 7 8 9 10
• Moment of Truth Empowerment	1 2 3 4	5	6 7 8 9 10	1 2 3 4	5	6 7 8 9 10
• Speed/Response	1 2 3 4	5	6 7 8 9 10	1 2 3 4	5	6 7 8 9 10
• Customer Is Always Right	1 2 3 4	5	6 7 8 9 10	1 2 3 4	5	6 7 8 9 10
5. **The Experience**	1 2 3 4	5	6 7 8 9 10	1 2 3 4	5	6 7 8 9 10
• All Senses	1 2 3 4	5	6 7 8 9 10	1 2 3 4	5	6 7 8 9 10
• Thrills	1 2 3 4	5	6 7 8 9 10	1 2 3 4	5	6 7 8 9 10
• Gambling	1 2 3 4	5	6 7 8 9 10	1 2 3 4	5	6 7 8 9 10
• Upscale	1 2 3 4	5	6 7 8 9 10	1 2 3 4	5	6 7 8 9 10
• Themes	1 2 3 4	5	6 7 8 9 10	1 2 3 4	5	6 7 8 9 10
• Feelings	1 2 3 4	5	6 7 8 9 10	1 2 3 4	5	6 7 8 9 10
• Beauty	1 2 3 4	5	6 7 8 9 10	1 2 3 4	5	6 7 8 9 10

Total Points Today:_______________ Ideal:_______________

Difference = GAP: _______________

Actions needed as a result of this gap include:

Tool #15 Customer Focus

Application of Systems Dynamics #4: Input/Output Model; and #6: Goal Seeking

The only reason for the existence of any organization is to serve someone else. This is your primary outcome. Thus, once you've defined who your customer is, the entire focus of the organization should be on serving that customer.

➡ **For example:** If Cadillac's customers are upscale older folks, is the total organization—people, physical plant, cars, etc.—focused on these customers?

➡ **For example:** If part of your purpose in life is to raise your children effectively, have you focused on them properly (i.e., amount/quality of time, character/values, education, skills and fitness, work ethic, etc.)?

A. Customer Focused

Suggestions for Use:

1. Another way to focus on outcomes is to see if your organization is a customer-focused one. Most people talk about it; few actually do it. Test yourself by responding to the following **Ten Commandments of a Customer-Focused Organization**.

1	5	10
Low	Avg.	High

The Ten Commandments of Customer-Focused Organization

Question: Which do you do well? Score each one.

______ 1. **Closeness to the customer**—What is the senior executive's customer involvement?

______ 2. **Know customer's needs**—Is surpassing them a driving force?

______ 3. **Survey customer's satisfaction**—Done regularly on products and services?

______ 4. **Focus on "value-added"**—Star ★ Results Model?

______ 5. **Measurable service standards/expectations set**—All units?

______ 6. **"Moments of Truth"**—All staff/1 day/year + ?

______ 7. **Cross-functional business processes reengineered**—Customer-focused?

______ 8. **Structure based on marketplace?**

______ 9. **"Recovery" strategies**—Clear/rewarded to surpass customer expectations?

______ 10. **Customer-friendly people**—Hired and promoted?

Total Score = ______ (out of 100 points)

Suggestions for Use:

2. Do your children have goals, visions, and ideas of their desired future? If not, talk to them and expose them to different careers and who they would serve. They often can visualize themselves doing these careers—good or bad. This will heighten motivation and the desire to succeed.

B. Customer-Recovery Strategy in More Detail *(Best Practice #9)*

A Customer Recovery Strategy (or CRS) is the secret of unsurpassed customer service. If people are happy with you, they will tell three to four people; if they are unhappy, they will tell eleven or more. Thus, the key issue for every organization is how it handles customer problems and complaints.

➥ **For example:** How do you handle "Moment of Truth" encounters? Each problem or complaint will have a customer's story attached to it when described to friends. The only question is whether the punch line has a good or bad ending.

Suggestions for Use:

1. The following is a checklist about unsurpassed customer service. Which of these do you do at the "Moment of Truth" when there is a problem?

    _____ 1. Focus on the 5–10 year ROI of the customer.

    _____ 2. Focus on your long-term image and reputation. (Remember, unhappy people tell 11 others; happy customers tell 4 others.)

    _____ 3. Empower the person at the moment of truth to be creative and innovative to surpass the customer's expectations as to solving the *problem.*

    _____ 4. Provide expenditure authority to do the above.

    _____ 5. Ensure accountability = responsibility—at the moment of truth.

    _______ 6. Focus recovery on future business (i.e., 50% next time; free next time, etc.).

    _____ 7. Speed up the recovery during the moment of truth.

    _____ 8. Develop a "Customer Guarantee" and live up to it/surpass it.

    _____ 9. Ensure your CRS deals with fast responsiveness, being knowledgeable, having empathy and sensitivity, as well as both the tangibles and intangibles.

    _____ 10. What else?

2. There are four levels of Customer Recovery Strategy Mastery: Which do we do now? What do we want it to be?

Now	**Wants**	
_____	_____	1. Deny it's our problem. (I just work here.)
_____	_____	2. Fight their concern but eventually give in to them. (They won.)
_____	_____	3. Meet their expectations. (Customer is always right.)
_____	_____	4. Meet their expectations and then do something else beyond it that they don't expect (including an apology).

3. Given your answers to #2 above, what are some next steps you need to do to improve your CRS?

C. Customer Service Standards

Customer service is like motherhood and apple pie. Everyone is for it, but often, no one really coordinates it organization-wide. While organizations often set up customer service goals and targets with their external customers, each department in an organization needs its own standards.

➥ **For example:** Customer service standards will vary by departments. HR, Finance, Manufacturing, Engineering, Sales, and Customer Service will probably have different standards.

Suggestions for Use:

1. Have each department in an organization develop and commit to its own unique set of customer service standards; include measures of success.
2. In order to do this properly, solid customer services training is usually needed.
3. The Ten Commandments of Customer Services are listed below. Have each department assess themselves and use it as a "starter" to develop their own standards

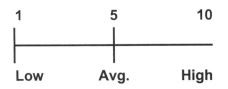

1 — 5 — 10
Low — Avg. — High

The Ten Commandments of Customer Service Survey

Question: Which do we do well? Score each one.

	1. **Bring 'em back alive.** Ask customers what they want and give it to them again and again.
	2. **Systems, not smiles.** Saying *please* and *thank you* doesn't guarantee that you'll do the job right the first time, every time. Only systems guarantee you that.
	3. **Underpromise, overdeliver.** Customers expect you to keep your word. Exceed it.
	4. **When the customer asks, the answer is always yes.** Period.
	5. **Fire your inspectors and consumer relations department.** Every employee who deals with clients must have the authority to handle complaints.
	6. **No complaints? Something's wrong.** Encourage your customers to tell you what you're doing wrong.
	7. **Measure everything.** Baseball teams do it, football teams do it, basketball teams do it. You should too.
	8. **Salaries are unfair.** Reward people for good service.
	9. **Your mother was right.** Show people respect. Be polite. It works.
	10. **Japanese them.** Learn how the best really do it; make their systems your own; then improve them.
	Total Score = ____________ (out of 100 points)

Tool #16 Internal vs. External Customers

Application of Systems Dynamics #3: System Boundaries

Be clear on who your "real" customer is; your supervisor, your immediate staff/department, others externally, or the external customer who buys your products and services. You may have more than one primary set of customers.

Who is the Real Customer?
Internal or External?

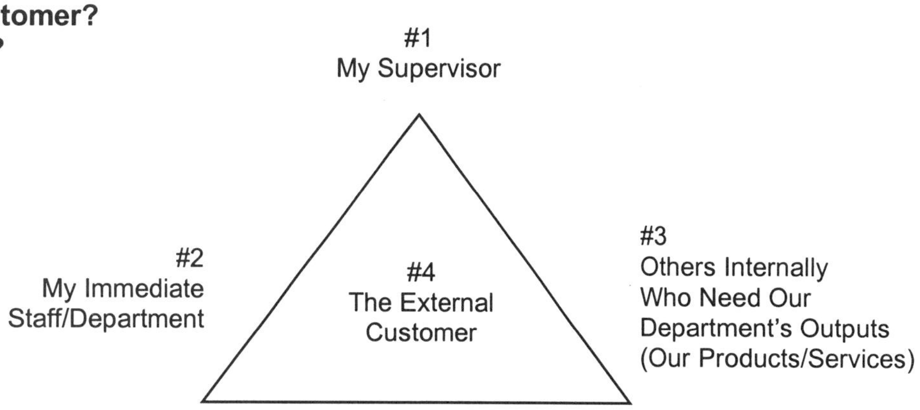

➥ **For example: The external customer is the *only real customer*.** Number 1, 2, and 3 exist to serve the real customer of the organization. However, you may exist to serve someone else "internally" in the organization but "externally" to your department, (such as #3 and #1 above).

"My job is to serve the customer or to serve someone who does."
(Everybody is a customer to somebody for something.)

➥ **For example:**

Question: Do you know your customer's customer? Once you've defined your customers, you must proceed to define their needs by asking them.

Question: Personally, who do you serve with your life—is it just yourself and your own selfish self-aggrandizement, or do you serve others? (Who specifically?)

Suggestions for Use:

1. **Organizationally**, define clearly who your real customers are outside of your department/organization. Establish clear words as to who they are.
2. List them in priority order—or primary, secondary.
3. Share this with all your staff, over and over again.
4. **Personally,** answer the question above. Who do you serve in your life, outside of yourself (servant-leader concept)?

Customer Clarity

Can you differentiate your customers from other key stakeholders (owners, beneficiaries, employees, suppliers, or competitors)? You must clearly identify your true customers, especially in the public sector where senior government officials are seen as your customers. The citizens are your owners and they elect the government officials as your supervisors and "bosses" to set up government departments/agencies for the real purpose of serving true customers/clients/citizens. Owners and customers and beneficiaries are all stakeholders, but with different roles.

➥ **For example:**

What are the differences among . . .

1. Owners (the stockholders)
2. Customers (the who)
3. Beneficiaries (the why)

Other key stakeholders include:

4. Employees (the means)
5. Suppliers (the support means)
6. Competitors (the alternative choices)

Be clear on the differences in terminology and in strategy. Focus on all the multiple outcomes so that you understand the desired (and conflicting) outcomes of different stakeholders:

- customers—they want better "value"
- employees—they want more pay, recognition, learning, growth, freedom, and benefits
- stockholders—they want a return on their investments
- stakeholders—they all have their own unique needs and wants
- suppliers—they have to earn their own respectable living
- community—they have their own broader/narrower societal and environmental wants

Even for customers alone, the "total package" of products and services they want might include everything, but organizations can't afford it.

Suggestions for Use:

1. While defining who your customer is, also identify all other stakeholders—those who have a stake in your success and failure—both internally and externally.
2. **Personally**, ask yourself if you know all those around you who are stakeholders in your life. How do you deal with each?

Tool #17 Ideal Future Vision (Shared Vision, Mission, and Core Values)

Application of Systems Dynamics #6: Multiple-Goal Setting

Without clarity and agreement about the ends, the means will be full of conflict. "Begin with the end in mind," as Steven Covey states, and develop an Ideal Future Vision you really desire. It begins with a shared vision and a specific pragmatic mission statement for your future, as well as a set of core values.

A. Shared Vision and Visioning

Visioning is a process that enables us to put aside reason temporarily and look beyond the present to the future, as we would like it to be.

"It can't be done" is irrelevant. How to turn a vision into a reality is something that happens after the vision is created.

➥ **For example:** A Vision Must Be

1. Leader-initiated
2. Shared and supported
3. Comprehensive and detailed
4. Positive and inspiring—a reach, a challenge

The future belongs to those who believe in their dreams.
—Eleanor Roosevelt

The only limits, as always, are those of vision.
—James Broughton

You can and should shape your own future; because,
if you don't, somebody else surely will!
—J. Barker

➥ **For example:** Most everyone knows today that organizations need a vision. What is not as well known is the following:

- The "shared vision" requires supporting details so that it isn't just "fluff" but is clear and understandable to others.
- Also, if it is to be shared, then a parallel process involving all key stakeholders is crucial to its development and ownership.
- Lastly, it needs to have a set of outcome measures developed so that it is clear and concrete.

Thus:

"Is your visioning the result of disciplined, focused thinking . . . or empty rhetoric?"

Suggestions for Use:

The Future Visioning Process Steps

A. Opening the Group's Perspective

1. Define what a vision is.
2. Conduct the "9 Dots Exercise" (focus on boundaries).
3. Show Joel Barker's film "Creating Your Future: The Business of Paradigms."
4. Debrief key points of the film.
5. List changes in paradigms over the past 20 years (next 10 = last 20 years in amount of change).
6. List all the boundaries of today's paradigm of how you operate—individually, then collectively.

B. Individual Vision Work

1. Create a quiet place/inviting music and relaxing posture for mental clarity, freedom, and acceptance.
2. Use guided imagery to mentally create the vision at year ________, free from current boundaries.
3. Write down the images.
4. Create a symbol/picture for the old and new vision.
5. Return to #3 and add to the images list from the picture/symbol of the new vision.

C. As a Team, Create a Shared Vision

1. Form subgroups.
2. Share your individual visions lists and pictures/symbols.
3. Combine your visions into one vision; develop consensus . . .
   a. First write it on a flip chart.
   b. Then create a symbol/picture of it.
   c. List the three to six key elements of the vision picture.
   d. Report out your vision to the total group.

(continued)

Suggestions for Use: *(concluded)*

The Future Visioning Process Steps (concluded)

D. Synthesize Lists Over a Break

1. Select one person per subgroup to join the facilitator. Send everyone else on a 15-minute break.
2. Have the subgroup representative and the facilitator synthesize the various visions into one list of areas that can be used with the total group. Be sure to include all the words/concepts of the subgroups.

   NOTE: At this point the areas of the vision will probably be composed of

   a. "Outcomes"/why we exist/future vision, and . . .

   b. "Means," or How-To's.

   You can choose to shorten the list once you are back with the total group, or let it ride for awhile, as this will help surface (and possibly resolve) key organizational issues.

E. Total Group—Volunteer Subgroups

1. Based on the areas above, allow participants to volunteer for a subgroup to focus on one aspect of the vision. For that area or aspect, have them:

   a. Write a complete vision statement.

   b. Report out to the total group.
2. In the total group, go over each vision area and work on it until a final consensus is reached. (This product is actually a back-up page to the final vision statement [outcomes] developed below.)

F. Final Vision Statement Developed

1. Over a break, form a subgroup of two to four people (maximum) to write a draft final vision statement based on the consensus of the vision areas above.
2. Have this draft reported out to the total group.
3. Finalize the draft vision statement.
4. Use the parallel process to check the draft; then redo it one last time.

In Summary

1. **Vision is Aspirational—Idealistic—*"Our Guiding Star"***
   - Our view/image of what the ideal future looks like at time "X"
   - It has dreamlike qualities, future hopes, and *aspirations,* even if they are never fully attainable.
   - An energizing, positive, and inspiring statement of *where and what we want to be* in the future

2. **Mission is Pragmatic—Realistic—*"Our Unique Purpose"***
   - What business are we in? (not the activities we do)
   - Why we exist—our reason for being (raison d' être)
   - The purpose toward which we commit our work life
   - What we produce; its benefits/outcomes
   - Who we serve—our customers/clients

3. **Rallying Cry is Our Essence—Motivational Force—*"Our Memorizable Essence"***
   - The crisp slogan (8 words or less) that is remembered by the employees and is *the essence* of the vision, mission, and core values.
   - It is our driving force upon which all else revolves.
   - It should be a powerful motivational force for our staff.
   - It is memorable, memorized, believable, and repeatable on a daily basis across the organization, everywhere and in every way.

B. Mission

1. The mission statements need to be clear as to:
   - **who**—the customers really are
   - **what**—the benefits of their products and services are, and
   - **why**—they should exist (stockholder and societal reasons)

2. Mission statements in and of themselves are *not* important. What is crucial is creating a management team and an organization with a sense of mission (or purpose).

   ➥ **For example**: In mission-focused organizations, there is:
   - an extra level of motivation, commitment, action, and enthusiasm
   - a moral reason, not just a commercial one
   - a more inspirational purpose than just meeting the selfish needs of a shareholder, stakeholder, unit, or department
   - core values that instill pride and commitment

3. In mission-focused organizations, managers move from maintenance activities to:
   - change management
   - visionary leadership
   - cross-functional teamwork

4. If the above is true, then mission statements actually make "cents." According to a study by Charles Rarick and John Vitton in the *Journal of Business Strategy* (January 1995):
   - It appears that firms engaged in the type of formal strategic planning process that produces a mission statement are more likely to achieve good financial and bottom-line performance.
   - The average return on stockholder equity for firms with mission statements was 16.1%.
   - The average return for firms without mission statements was 9.7%.
5. While simply having a mission statement is good, having one with content is even better, i.e., depending on the following content, with average return on stockholder equity (ROE) listed
   - concern for public image = 73% ROE
   - concern for quality = 73% ROE
   - commitment for survival, growth, profitability = 70% ROE
   - identity of customers and markets = 60% ROE
   - identity of products/services = 60% ROE
   - statement of company philosophy/values = 43% ROE
   - differentiation from competition = 33% ROE
6. When high content mission statements are compared with low content mission statements, the average return for firms with high content statements is 26.3%. The average return for firms with low content statements is 13.7%.

Mission Development Steps

Steps

#1 If you already have a mission statement, set it aside and use it at the end of the steps as a check on the work completed.

#2 Provide a lecturette on mission statements

- what their criteria is
- what they are and *why they are important*
- in what ways they are different from vision, values, and your rallying cry

#3 Have each person individually conduct the mission development activity.

#4 Form the participants into three subgroups and have each subgroup develop visual answers on a flipchart to questions #1, 2, and 3 above (i.e., why, who, what on points of triangles); report out your answers to the total group.

Mission Development Steps

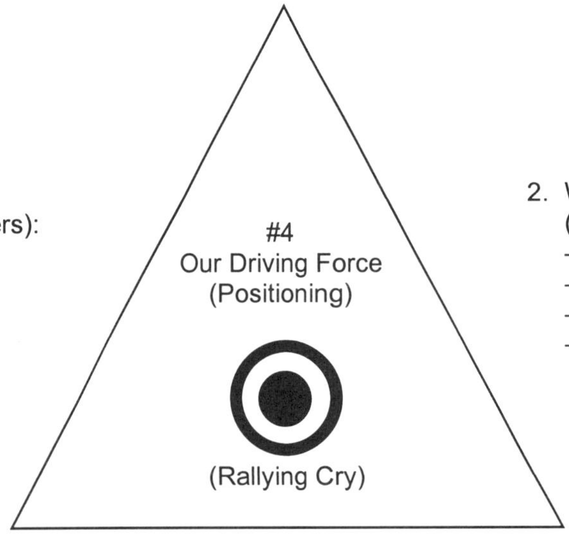

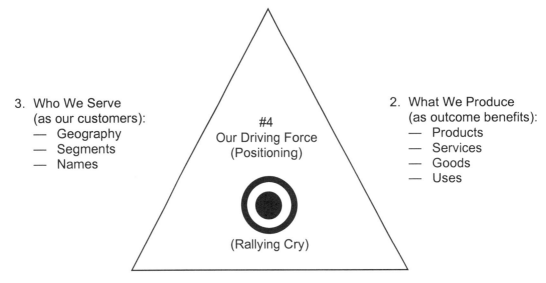

#5 Have the participants take a 15-minute break. One person from each subgroup will join the facilitator in synthesizing the three flipcharts into one master chart, taking care not to eliminate any answer. Filtering and closure comes later.

#6 After the break, have the total group go through each of the three questions, one by one from the synthesized listing. Some tests to ensure clarity and closure include:

a. Does each *who* relate to a *what* and vice versa?
(i.e., multiple *who's* need multiple *what's*)

b. Is the *why* a higher order societal good? What will be better as a result of your existence as an organization? Does it tie to the vision statement?

c. Are the *what's* the "outputs" from your activities (i.e., your goods, services, benefits) and **not** the activities themselves that you do daily to get the outputs? (i.e., systems thinking—ends, not means)

d. What risk is being taken by this future mission? Is anything changing? Use the "X" test to look at the risk factor.

#7 Now, gain agreement on the exact words for each who, what, why (or if you are following a parallel process, just get *general* agreement on the wording).

#8 Create a subgroup of three people to write a first draft "mission statement" document and bring it back to the group for final review, discussion, agreement, and closure.

Tests include:

a. Did we mix *how's* into it? Is it legitimate to do so? (It may be!)

b. How does it fit with our old mission document?

c. Is it future-oriented?

d. Will it clearly drive behavior in the organization?

e. What will be different in the future as a result of this mission?

#9 Conduct a parallel process with key stakeholders to get their feedback. Bring it to the next strategic planning meeting in an organized fashion for review by all members.

#10 Revise and finalize the mission statement based on the feedback from the parallel process/key stakeholders.

Alternative Application: Staff Mission Confusion

Staff departments have a difficult time understanding their mission and outcomes vs. others' responsibilities/self-initiative. **It is the "control vs. service" dilemma.** Thus, each staff department needs to understand this dilemma and take steps to clarify and resolve it satisfactorily.

➥ **For example:** Often staff departments try to be both:

a. the **control agent** for the CEO, and
b. a **service provider** to the same line management departments.

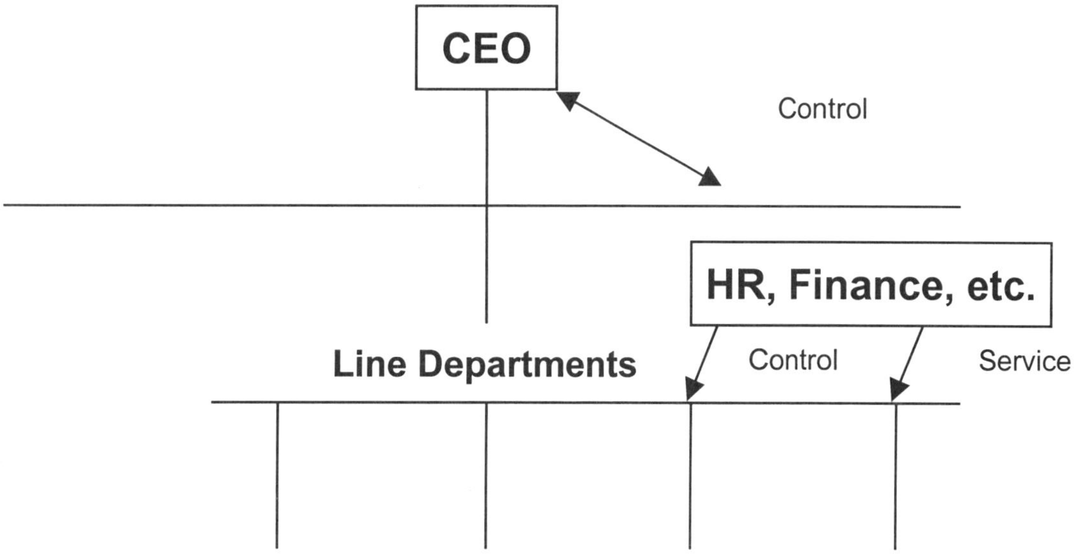

Suggestions for Use:

1. Recognize that this is a dilemma for almost all support staffs.
2. Separate these two functions if at all possible, to remove the conflicts.
3. If not able to do #2, then put the control in the line departments and have the staff department monitor and track—and report only (vs. control).
4. The last solution is to legitimize this dilemma so everyone understands and accepts it. While this isn't the best solution, often it's the only solution.

Alternative Application (#2): Public Sector Confusion

Public sector organizations also have difficulty understanding their distinct mission and outcomes/roles vs. the private sector and citizen initiatives.

➥ **For example:** Often "big government" results from government doing what the private sector and/or individuals should be doing. Either the government extends its mission too far into individual responsibility, or the converse, it focuses narrowly on activities as the end rather than just the means.

➥ **For example:** In today's world of limited budgets, government missions often need to do unique things that the private sector can't (or won't) do.

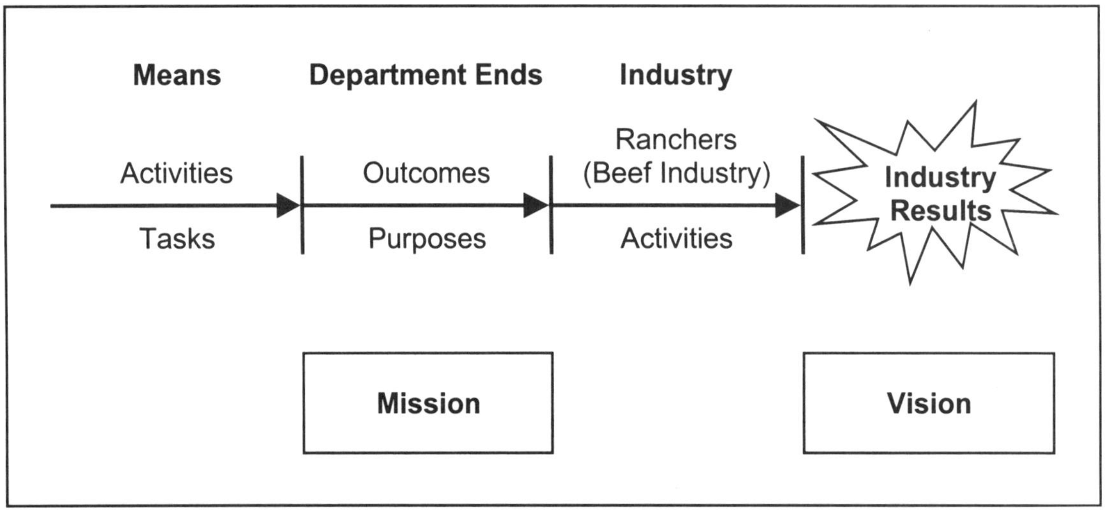

Suggestions for Use:

1. All public sector organizations need to *carefully* define the outcomes that they are willing to be *accountable* for.
2. Refine your mission and outcomes to fit your proper role and budgetary constraints.
3. Use the "Five Why's" to determine where your government department ends its responsibilities.
4. Don't confuse this with a shared vision for an entire industry which will require a combined synergistic and cooperative effort to achieve.

C. Core Values[1]

Core values are what really drive our behaviors. In fact, in organizations we often call them "Guiding Principles."

[1] Adapted from: S. Haines, "Internal Sun Co., Inc. Working Paper," 1979; J. W. Pfeiffer, L. D. Goodstein, and T. M. Nolan, *Applied Strategic Planning: A How To Do It Guide.* San Diego, CA, Pfeiffer & Co., 1986.

Conflicts in values often are the conflict between (1) short-term profits/results, and (2) the maintenance of a value system (i.e., the climate and culture that motivates employees to do their best).

➥ **For example:** If you want a core value in your organization, then it must meet the following five criteria:

1. It is a collective belief organization-wide—simple, clear, and understandable.
2. It determines the norms or standards of acceptable behavior.
3. People know and care when the value isn't being followed.
4. It is an enduring value and is consistent over time. It is one of the last things you want to give up.
5. There are myths, rituals, and other stories to support its existence. It is driven and crystallized from the top.

There can't be very many values like this. Core values are few in number.

Suggestions for Use:

1. Core Values Clarification Process

If you need to develop or clarify your values, the following eight steps are recommended **(personal or organizational)**:

Step #1

a. Identify core leadership team that will develop/agree on these values (correct decision).
b. Identify "key environmental stakeholders" who will be involved in this process in order to have buy-in for implementation (acceptance/ownership).

Step #2

Develop a "game plan" to involve people in 1a and 1b.

Step #3

- Send core team/family off-site 1 to 1½ days.
- Their task is to define the ideal future in year "X" prior to doing values (i.e., vision and mission).

Step #4

Core Values Development for Year "X":

1. Go through a personal values exercise (understanding each other).
2. Go through an organizational values exercise (individually, subgroup, total group).
3. Develop a draft core values statement to use below (it doesn't need to be perfect yet).
4. Troubleshoot (ideal vs. reality); Are you serious?

Note: However, if you really believe in your values, build in a feedback/reinforcement process for them (i.e., put them on your performance appraisal form for everyone—janitor to CEO).

(continued)

Suggestions for Use: *(continued)*

Step #5

Share draft with key environmental stakeholders in controlled situations (input only):

- Understand it first.
- Anything fundamentally wrong?
- What would you change (add/delete)?
- Where are the gaps today between our ideal and reality?

Step #6

Core team—off-site 1 day:

- Hear feedback from stakeholders.
- Revise values draft.
- Gap analysis reviewed/determined.
- Develop action plans to close the gaps during Year #1 of implementation.

Step #7

Rollout values (despite draft status):

- With personal actions from senior management clear

To key environmental stakeholders:

- Ensure understand/identify gaps
- Explain the decision
- Thank for their input
- Specify their required actions

To rest of organization:

- With clear action plan from above

Wait One Year

Step #8

Go through a shortened version of steps #4, 5, 6, and 7 above.

Goal: A values statement that is fixed and implemented into the new way we do business.

(continued)

Suggestions for Use: *(continued)*

2. Personal Values Exercise[2]

Please rank-order these items from 1 to 15 with 1 being the most important to you personally and 15 being the least important to you personally.

	Actual	Desired
1. Having good relationships with colleagues	________	________
2. Professional reputation/respect	________	________
3. Achievement of organization/unit goals	________	________
4. Teamwork and collaboration	________	________
5. Leisure time for enjoyment/fun	________	________
6. Wealth and prosperity	________	________
7. Fitness and health	________	________
8. Contribution/service to society/community	________	________
9. Acknowledging/recognizing other's achievements	________	________
10. Autonomy/freedom to act	________	________
11. Personal growth	________	________
12. Time with family/close friends	________	________
13. Ethical behaviors	________	________
14. Excitement and challenge	________	________
15. Spiritual/religious time	________	________

(continued)

[2] Adapted from: S. Haines, "Internal Sun Co., Inc. Working Paper," 1979; J. W. Pfeiffer, L. D. Goodstein, T. M. Nolan, *Applied Strategic Planning: A How to Do It Guide.* San Diego, CA: Pfeiffer & Co., 1986; T. Rusk, "Ethical Persuasion Working Paper," 1989; subsequent client feedback.

Suggestions for Use: *(continued)*

3. Organizational Values Exercise ("Guides to Behavior")[3]

Complete Column #1 (The Way It Should Be): Select 10 of the following values that have the most importance to your organization's future success.

Complete Column #2 (The Way It Is Now) at a later time (or as directed).

Column #1 *The Way You Think It Should Be Ideally*	**Column #2** *The Way It Is Now (Can Also Be Ideal)*	
______	______	1. Adaptation to Change
______	______	2. Long-Term Strategic Perspective/Direction
______	______	3. Energizing/Visionary Leadership
______	______	4. Risk-Taking
______	______	5. Innovation/Creativity
______	______	6. Marketplace Aggressiveness/Competitiveness
______	______	7. Teamwork/Collaboration
______	______	8. Individual/Team/Organization Learning
______	______	9. Recognition of Achievements
______	______	10. Waste Elimination/Wise Use of Resources
______	______	11. Profitability/Cost Consciousness
______	______	12. Quality Products/Services
______	______	13. Customer-Service Excellence/Focus
______	______	14. Speed/Responsiveness
______	______	15. Continuous/Process Improvement
______	______	16. Growth/Size of Organization/Revenue

(continued)

[3] Adapted from: S. Haines, "Internal Sun Co., Inc. Working Paper," 1979; J. W. Pfeiffer, L. D. Goodstein, T. M. Nolan, *Applied Strategic Planning: A How to Do It Guide*. San Diego, CA: Pfeiffer & Co., 1986; T. Rusk, "Ethical Persuasion Working Paper," 1989; subsequent client feedback.

Suggestions for Use: *(continued)*

3. Organizational Values Exercise ("Guides to Behavior") *(concluded)*

Column #1 *The Way You Think It Should Be Ideally*	**Column #2** *The Way It Is Now (Can Also Be Ideal)*	
________	________	17. Contribution to Society/Community
________	________	18. Safety
________	________	19. Stability/Security
________	________	20. Ethical and Legal Behavior
________	________	21. High Staff Productivity/Performance
________	________	22. Employee Development/Growth/Self-Mastery
________	________	23. Dialogue/Openness and Trust
________	________	24. Constructive Confrontation/Problem Solving
________	________	25. Respect/Caring for Individuals/Relationships
________	________	26. Quality of Work Life/Morale
________	________	27. High Staff Satisfaction
________	________	28. Employee Self-Initiative/Empowerment
________	________	29. Participative Management/Decision Making
________	________	30. Data-Based Decisions
________	________	31. Diversity and Equality of Opportunity
________	________	32. Partnerships/Alliances
________	________	33. Excellence in All We Do

D. Values Audit

A key part of creating your people-edge is adhering to your core values. Regular audits of these values (at least yearly) are crucial.

➥ **For example:** It is now relatively easy to develop and administer surveys of your employees. The main concern is to ensure confidentiality.

Suggestions for Use:

1. **Auditing Your Core Values**

   a. In looking at your core values, discuss which ones you are following:

—the most closely	—the least closely
(1)	(1)
(2)	(2)
(3)	(3)

   b. Based on this analysis, develop an action plan to improve your "least followed" core values immediately.

Least followed value	Where to use it more?	How to influence it?	Type training needed	What policies/ processes changed?	Action Plan Leader	Comments
1.						
2.						
3.						

2. **Values Assessment Survey**

   Aspirational vs. Current

   Step #1:

   Develop draft of aspirational values and list them on appropriate lines under Step #2

   Step #2:

   Conduct assessment of current status of each value and assess the energy/passion you have to make it one of your core values.

Value #1: (List) ____________________

Personal Energy I Have			Current Status of Success		
1	5	10	1	5	10
Low	Avg.	High	Low	Avg.	High

Why?

Value #2: (List) ____________________

Personal Energy I Have			Current Status of Success		
1	5	10	1	5	10
Low	Avg.	High	Low	Avg.	High

Why?

Value #3: (List) ____________________

Personal Energy I Have			Current Status of Success		
1	5	10	1	5	10
Low	Avg.	High	Low	Avg.	High

Why?

3. Values/Cultural Risk Matrix

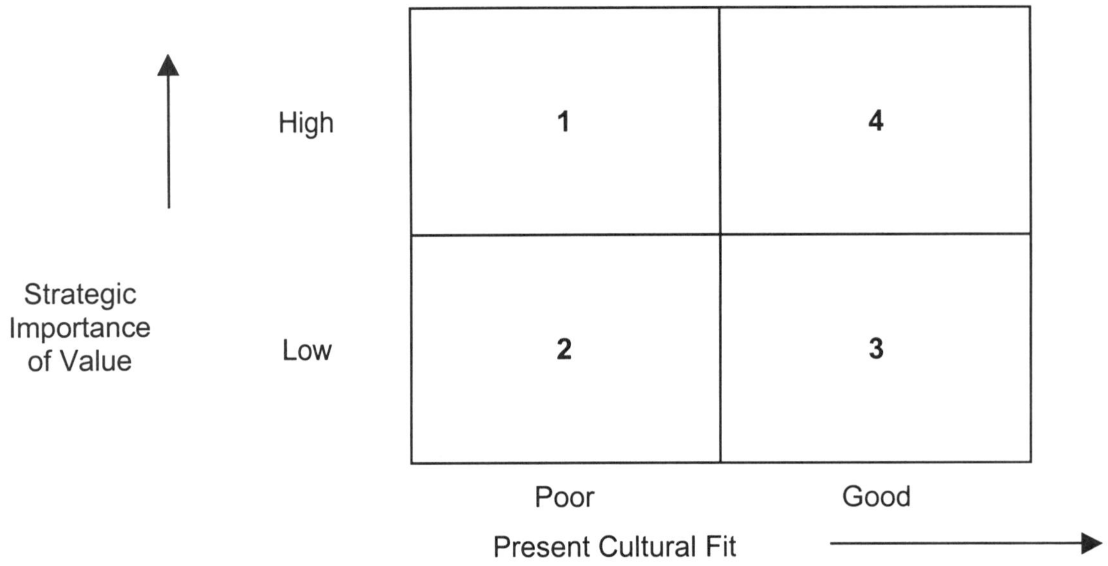

Evaluate each aspirational core value you have decided upon vs. this risk matrix.

Core Value	Risk Matrix #	Implications/Needed Actions
1.		
2.		
3.		

4. Core Values Assessment and Uses

Throughout All Areas of a High Performing Organization

Your organization should apply its guiding principles or core values everywhere. Here are some examples:

1. **Strategy**
   - Explicit corporate philosophy/ values statement—visuals on walls; in rooms
2. **Operational Tasks**
   - Corporate and product advertising
   - New customers and suppliers vs. current customer and supplier treatment and focus (vs. values)
   - Operational tasks of quality and service
3. **Leadership**
   - Flow of orientation and assimilation versus sign-up
   - Job aids, descriptions
   - New-executive orientation
   - To whom and how promotions occur (values consequence assessed); criteria
   - Executive leadership ("walk the talk"); ethical decisions; how we manage
4. **Resources/Technology**
   - Press releases, external publications/brochures
   - Image nationwide (as seen by others)
   - Resource allocation
5. **Structure**
   - Dealing with difficult times/ issues (i.e., layoffs, reorganizations)
   - Organization and job design
6. **Processes**
   - Recruiting handbook; selection criteria
   - How applicants are treated (vs. values)
   - How "rewards for performance" operates (vs. values), especially nonfinancial rewards
   - Role of training; training programs (vs. values)
   - Performance evaluation; appraisal forms (assess values adherence); team rewards
   - Policies and procedures (HR, finance, administrative, etc.); day-to-day decisions
7. **Teams**
   - Cross-departmental events, flows, tasks forces/teams
8. **Macro**
   - Managing change
   - Stakeholder relationships
9. **Feedback**
   - This analysis
   - Employee survey

Where else should core values appear and be reinforced in your organization?

Tool #18 Whole Jobs

Application of Systems Dynamics #1: Holism—Level 3

Workers who feel fulfilled in their jobs have usually been given a distinct set of responsibilities designed to fully empower them. However, in today's complex working environment, this old "whole job" or "job enrichment" concept has been lost.

➥ **For example:** Are all jobs in the organization "whole jobs" in Frederick Herzberg's terms?[4]

A. Empowerment—Enrichment—Self-Initiative

Suggestions for Use:

1. Fill out this questionnaire to see if your job contains the elements to qualify as "whole."

Yes	No	Elements
______	______	1. Direct Customer Feedback
______	______	2. Customer Client Relationship
______	______	3. New Learning
______	______	4. Scheduling Responsibility
______	______	5. Unique Expertise
______	______	6. Control over Resources
______	______	7. Direct Communications Authority
______	______	8. Personal Accountability

NOTE: You can also use this to analyze all jobs in a business process that is being improved.

"Every employee is a manager (of themselves)."

Suggestions for Use: *(continued)*

2. Check your job against the following list as well. There are eleven clues to a partial or unenriched job.

[4] Source: Frederick Herzberg, *Harvard Business Review,* September/October 1974.

B. Where Are Your Unenriched Jobs?[5]

Yes	No	Structural Clues
________	________	1. Communication Units or Jobs (cross department, unit, customer communication)
________	________	2. Checking Functions or Jobs (reviewers, inspectors)
________	________	3. Troubleshooting Jobs (expediters, coordinators)
________	________	4. Super Gurus (consultants, analysts)
________	________	5. Job Title Elephantiasis (overspecialization, excessive titles)
________	________	6. One-on-One Reporting Relationships (both jobs may suffer)
________	________	7. Dual Reporting Relationship (clarity of the matrix elements is crucial)
________	________	8. Unclear Division of Responsibility (Whose job was it? lots of meetings)
________	________	9. Overcomplicated Workflow (flow is hard to explain, paper handled/approved by many)
________	________	10. Duplication of Functions (work done twice, departments compete for work)
________	________	11. Labor Pools (programmers, accountants, word processors, etc.)

NOTE: You can also use this to analyze all jobs in the business process being reviewed.

C. Empowerment—Rights and Responsibilities

Make decisions as close to the action as possible. The people there have the data and can be more responsive to the customer (system) you are all serving. However, empowerment is not just about rights but also about responsibilities. If you do not know what the ends/objectives are—as well as the commitment you have to them and what skills you will need achieve them—simple empowerment will lead to chaos.

EMPOWERMENT DEFINED

Empowerment is *responsible* freedom: a balance of rights and responsibilities.

---

[5] Source: David A. Whitsett, *Harvard Business Review,* September/October 1974.

- If you empower your people, make sure you follow these guidelines:

Criteria for a Successful Empowerment Process

1. Everyone must understand/agree with the organization's vision, mission, values, and strategies.
2. You need to be proactive within set guidelines; use them to grant decision-making power.
3. The individual should continue to be a team player.
4. The individual must be willing to be held accountable for his or her actions/self-initiative.
5. The individual must be provided with the training and tools to be successful.
6. He or she needs management's willingness to:
   - give up some decision-making power/vetoes
   - allow some mistakes without punishment
   - provide positive reinforcement/recognition for good empowerment initiatives
   - allow others to come up with "how to" solutions that are different from the ones you would make (as long as the goal is the same)

The Conclusion

Empower individuals (not groups of individuals) only when:

- they are personally ready and committed (both person and supervisor)
- you are confident that empowerment will work

Suggestions for Use:

1. If you are already empowering your employees, analyze their status:
   - Are you empowering whole teams at once? or individuals one at a time?
   - Are all the criteria met? Which are not? Why not?
2. If you are planning to increase employee empowerment, use this criteria to decide when/how to implement it.
3. Remember: People often want empowerment, but are they willing to be held accountable? Do they know the positive and negative consequences?

D. Empowerment: Accountability = Responsibility

Empowering people is giving them responsibility for decision making. However, it should always come with accountability.

Flaws in Accountability

The fundamental flaw in the way many organizations try to approach the question of teamwork is that they ignore or try to fudge the issue of accountability. Everybody has to be accountable to someone for the quality of his or her work, and this accountability must be clear. But when people believe that teamwork and hierarchy are incompatible, they make the further mistake of holding accountability suspect.

Granted, a lot of organizations are poorly structured, their processes are obscure, and their management practices are poor. But it is a great mistake to conclude that these are inevitable flaws of all hierarchical organizations.

An inescapable characteristic of all employment systems is that they are also accountability systems. Accountability begins between the shareholders and the executives, and it has to form an unbroken chain down to the shop floor.

> *The myth is that accountability is bad. The reality is that it's inescapable.*
>
> —*Training,* August 1994

- **For example:** Don't hold me accountable for overhead costs if I'm not responsible for those areas.
- **For example:** Children should be brought up to understand the concept of accountability. They are responsible for doing the best they can in school, and parents and teachers need to hold them accountable for that. And give them responsibilities around the home. They will one day grow up and enter the work force. Love them unconditionally and teach them the work ethic. It will help them become productive and responsible adults.

Suggestions for Use:

1. The psychologist B.F. Skinner was right. We try to modify behavior all the time. But consider whether we do it intentionally and effectively.
2. Adults in some organizations, like some children, know they won't be held accountable for their actions; there will be no consequences. This permissiveness is like a spreading cancer. The wrong message is given, and in the end, there surely are negative consequences. Is this true in your organization?
3. There's a crisis of accountability in society today. Ask whether you are part of the problem or part of the solution.

E. Empowerment = Not One Best Way

There are often many ways to achieve the goal or end you have in mind. Always insisting on *your* one best way is a sure path to conflict and control (with its accompanying resistance).

➥ **For example:** The entire empowerment concept is about:

1. Involving people in the purpose/goal or "what" we want to achieve, and
2. Allowing them to determine the how to go about achieving it.

➥ **For example:** This issue is a big one, not only in organizations, but in child rearing and other areas of life. Once the "what" is agreed upon, the "how" can be more flexibly determined by the person closest to the issue or the one who has to carry it out.

Suggestions for Use:

1. First, always determine your goal (the "what") in any situation. Getting agreement/consensus on your purpose before continuing with the "how to" is an absolute of good Systems Thinking℠.
2. Brainstorm various "how to's" or allow the doers to come up with them. Again, be sure there is total commitment to the goal.
3. Don't insist on *your* one best way. This is micromanaging at its worst.
4. However, have a clear set of values as guides to behavior to keep the "how to" within the proper boundaries of behaviors.

F. Individual Commitment

Each of us is unique, with different backgrounds, experiences, and personalities. We do not change or make changes in our lives the same way in the same length of time. We also adjust to change differently.

As human systems, we control the degree of commitment we put into our work and our personal lives. We can choose to make the least amount of effort, or we can pull out all the stops. The results will reflect that degree of commitment.

➥ **For example:** There is a motivational gap between our minimum level of effort to stay alive at home and at work. This gap is the available "discretionary effort" and results achieved between committed and uncommitted people. The question of change has to do with when (or if) we are committed to something or we are just a "couch potato" at home and/or at work.

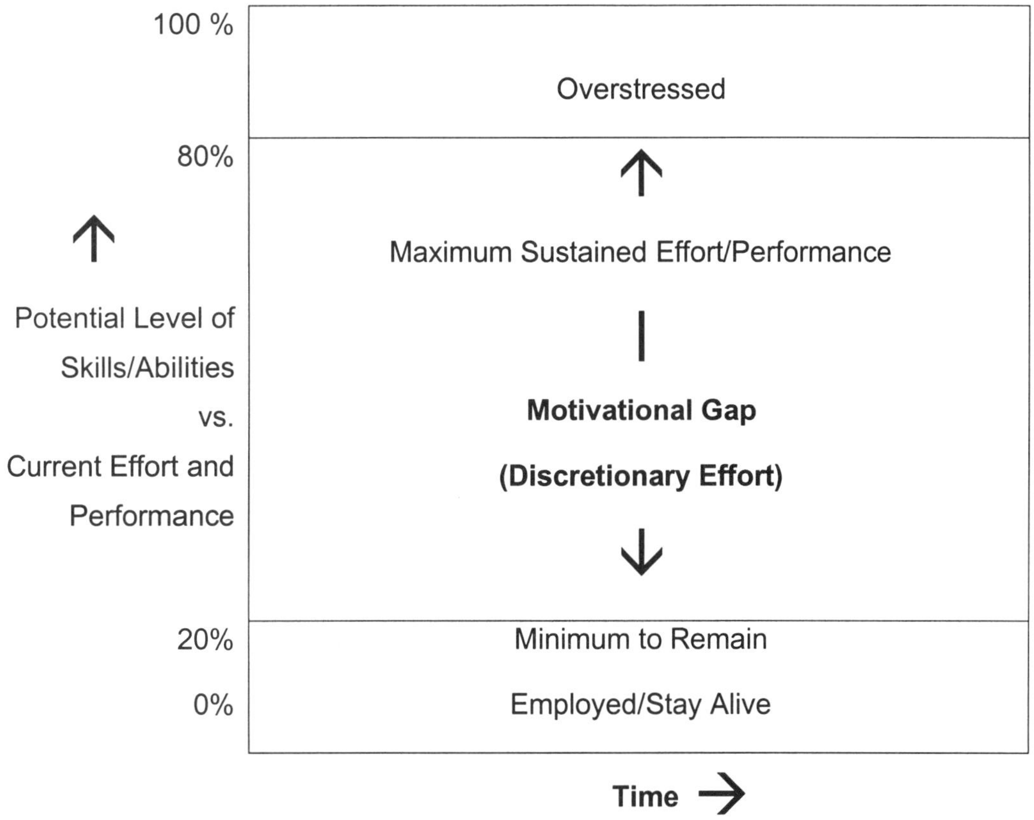

Suggestions for Use:

1. Recognize the reality of the situation and your goals. What commitment is needed by each person to achieve them?
2. Don't overstress or understress yourself and others (stay within 20–80%).
3. Work with others and involve and empower them toward maximum productivity and sustained effort and performance.

➥ **For example:** Much of the precepts behind Total Quality Management involve teams and processes. However, each person, from the CEO on down, should be committed to QIDW: Quality Improvement is My Daily Work.

➥ **For example:** Most TQM efforts that fail have not had the complete involvement of CEOs and senior management. The efforts fall to middle and first-line management who don't have the cross-functional power, skills, or influence to make change happen.

➥ **For example:** Doing the very best that we can do in our jobs and lives, and constantly striving for improvement is key to a successful life of service. We all have talents of one sort or another. The greatest waste of all is to waste them!

Suggestions for Use:

1. Have everyone understand the QIDW precept of TQM.
2. Have each person working in the organization put in writing the three specific things they will do to ensure QIDW.
3. Make this part of your performance appraisal.
4. Personally:
   - Get clear on your own gifts and talents.
   - Look yourself in the mirror and ask,

     Am I really doing the best I can?

     What's keeping me from this?

     What can I do differently?

     How can I get regular feedback on my use of these talents?

Chapter IV

Application: Phase B — Feedback and Learning Tools

This chapter stresses the tools needed to create a Learning Organization.

Tool No.	The Applications
19	Feedback and Learning — *Why is feedback the "Breakfast of Champions"?*
20	Reinforcement *and* The Learning Organization — *What kinds of training reinforcement are usually done?*
21	Environmental Scanning System — *How much of an environmental scanning "system" do you have?*
22	Key Success Factor Measures — *Do you have a "Continuous Improvement Matrix" of annual outcome measures?*
23	"People Support What They Help Create" — *How many ways can you use this basic truism?*
24	Look in the Mirror—Self-Feedback — *Do you look in the mirror first to see how you personally contribute to problems within your organization?*
25	Assessment and Debriefing Frameworks — *How can you learn from every project, issue, change, or solution?*

THE LEARNING ORGANIZATION

The illiterate of the 21st century will not be the individual who cannot read and write,
but
the one who cannot learn, unlearn, and relearn.

—Alvin Toffler
Future Shock

Tool #19 Feedback and Learning

Application of Systems Dynamics #5: Feedback

Feedback = Learning = Learning at all levels = The Learning Organization

Feedback is the breakfast of champions.

➥ **For example:** Knowledge alone is an input.

- There are many "knowledgeable idiots" in this world.
- Learning is composed of three types (and all are needed): knowledge, skills, and attitude.
- The other two real issues are:
  1. The attitude or willingness to put the knowledge to its appropriate use in order to achieve some objective.
  2. The abilities (or skills/readiness) to use the knowledge effectively to achieve some objective.

NOTE: Your outcomes (or objectives) must be clear and agreed upon before actions are taken.

In Systems Terms

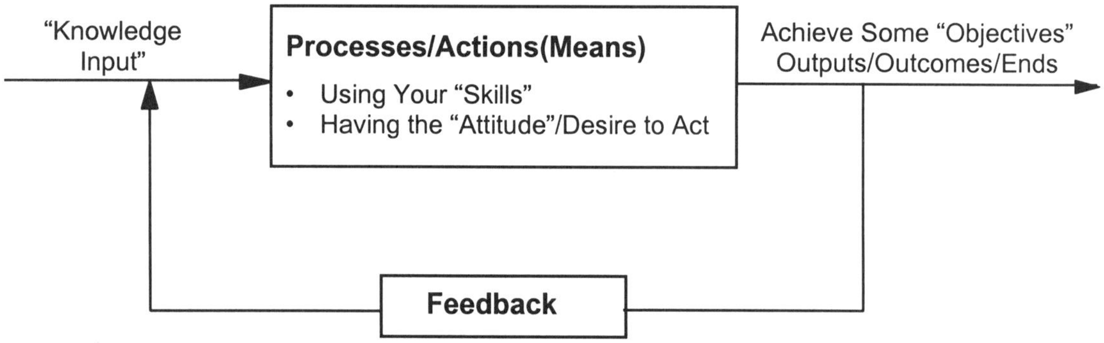

Suggestions for Use:

1. Ask yourself and your team whether or not everything you do has a feedback mechanism.
2. Ask yourself and your team whether each feedback mechanism has a way to turn the information obtained into (a) new learnings and (b) new applications.
3. Is learning knowledge enough, or do you want or need to improve your skills and attitudes? This requires practice—practice—practice; not just briefings.

NOTE: The "Stairway of Learning" that follows can serve as a framework for how learning occurs and feels.

Stairway of Learning

Learning goes well **beyond knowledge; it includes the skills and abilities** illustrated on this "Stairway of Learning."

➡ **For example:** Use this illustration to examine your own growth and development as a lifelong learner.

"People Don't Know What They Don't Know"

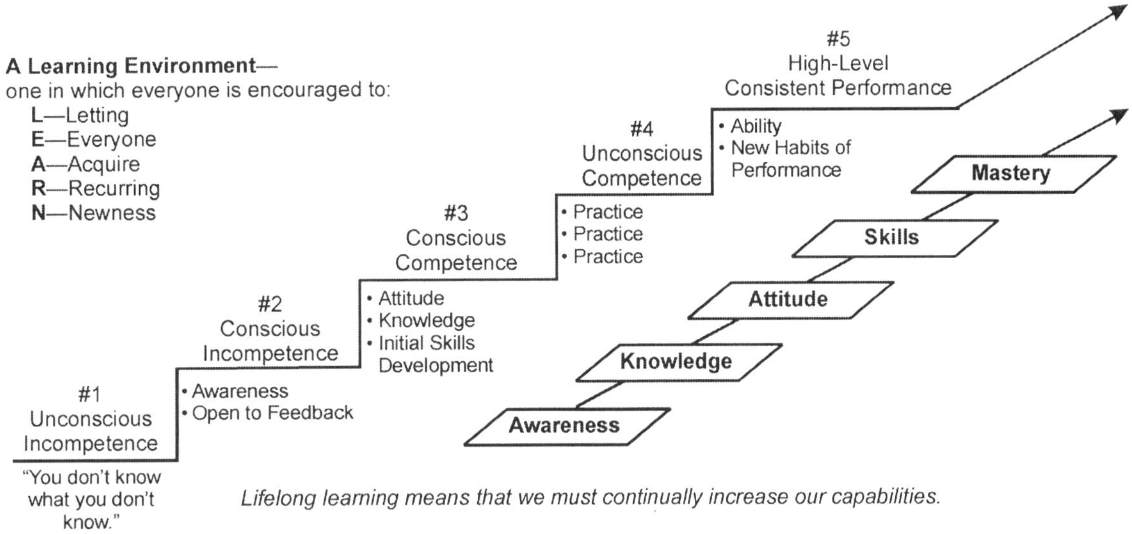

Lifelong learning means that we must continually increase our capabilities.

Suggestions for Use:

1. Recognize the different kinds of learnings and the steps involved in learning and applying new knowledge and skills. (Call the Centre for a four-page article on this subject, (619) 275-6528.)
2. This Stairway is the key to lifelong learning. Use it yourself.
3. Teach this Stairway to your family, team, and organization. Be especially aware of Step #1—"*You don't know what you don't know.*"
4. Finding organizational "best practices" are the best ways to get beyond Step #1.

Indepth Understanding: Three Kinds of Learning

Most of us don't really understand learning. We know much more about the activity of teaching (only one of the ways we learn). A primer on the basics:

"Adults Learn Best by Doing" But to really learn from experience, you must process the experience. Otherwise you may "learn" the wrong thing.

➥ **For example:** The Montessori Method of Management

One of the major departures in education this century was a shift of focus from teaching to learning. Maria Montessori, an Italian educator working in Holland, was the first to advocate this point of view. She demonstrated that schools were designed to ease the burden of teaching at the expense of learning. She embarked on an inquiry that led to a number of discoveries about how people learn.

- First, images are better than words. If a learner can see, feel, touch—in short, bring all five senses to bear on the acquisition of knowledge—learning will increase.
- Second, *showing* is better than telling.
- Third, too much guidance is worse than too little.
- Fourth, when the stakes get too great and anxiety is high, learners tend to avoid experimentation and openness to new experiences and revert to previously successful behavior.
- Finally, positive reinforcement of what is done right is far more effective than sanctions when things are done wrong.

Montessori's insights apply to management as well. Thus, learning theory has been clear since the 1970s, although probably not well known.

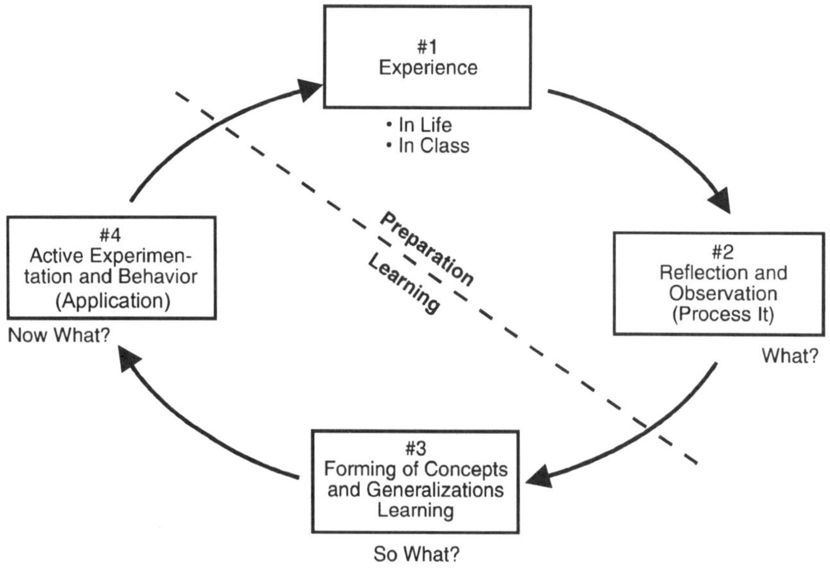

Learning is comprised of three elements: (1) Awareness, knowledge, and thoughts
(2) Skills
(3) Attitude, motivation, and feelings

To apply this learning, you have to continually put the learning into practice and build your competency.

Eventually your abilities to use this learning effectively will become your competencies.

Adapted from D. Kolb, "On Management and the Learning Process," in David Kolb, Irwin Rubin, and James McIntyre, *Organizational Psychology: A Book of Readings*, 2nd Edition. Englewood Cliffs, NJ: Prentice-Hall, 1974.

Suggestions for Use:

1. Ask yourself what you or your organization does well regarding learning.

   Instructions: Distribute 10 points across these three types of learning.

	How it is today	How you want it to be ideally
1. Knowledge	______	______
2. Skills	______	______
3. Attitudes	______	______
Total Points	10	10

2. What Are We Teaching or Changing?

   What? .... **Sample Hows**
   Information/Knowledge .... Lecture/Video
   Skills .... Demonstration/Practice
   Attitude .... Group Discussion/Peer Pressure
   Behavior .... Dilemma/Feedback Experience

3. Experiential Lectures and Participative Training Techniques

   With a little imagination, the facilitator can make almost any conceptual input experiential.

- Lecturettes, theories, and models with ice-breaker questions
- Group/subgroup discussions
- Pairs/triads
- Individual private work
- Buzz groups
- Films/AV with follow-up discussion
- Demonstration
- Role playing
- Skits
- Simulations
- Structured experiences
- Questionnaires/surveys
- Brainstorming
- Action planning
- Fish bowl
- Instruments
- Case studies
- Games
- In-baskets
- Sensitivity training
- Task forces
- Listening
- Problem analysis

Tool #20 Reinforcement and The Learning Organization

Application of Systems Dynamics #5: Feedback

Are you trying to create a learning organization? Or are you just trying to maximize your retention of each learning experience you have? **In either case, pay particular attention to the need for *continuous feedback* and *reinforcement* of all learnings.**

- **For example:** In order to sustain new behaviors, one needs (1) challenge, (2) recognition, and (3) support.

Build this into all of your own personal learning events.

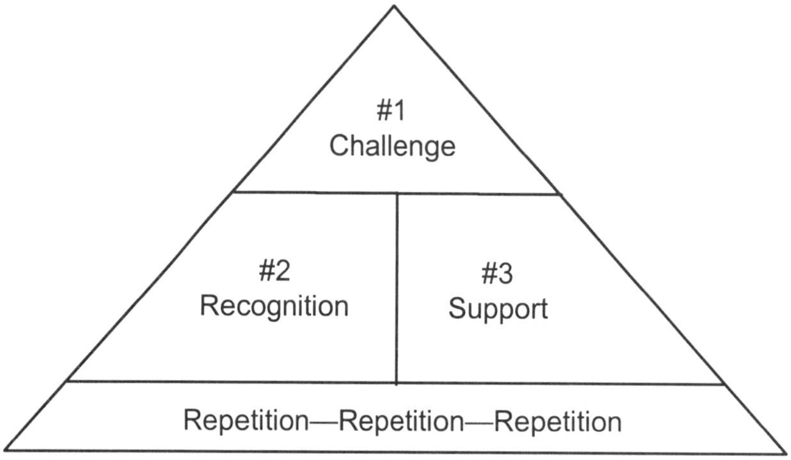

Suggestions for Use:

A. Yearly Reinforcement in Bite-Sized Chunks

1. A 52-week training and reinforcement program (an example follows) is an excellent way to handle reinforcement.
2. Other possible follow-up ideas for learning reinforcement include:
   - Setting up a buddy system, lunches, etc. Free floating agenda, set up at each meeting.
   - Creating small group/teams to teach and review each learning, i.e., what's working, what's not working.
   - Taking another course in the interim.
   - Following up every few months (alumni sessions).

52-Week Training Reinforcement Program

	Topic	Week	Trainer	Time
1.				
2.				
3.				
4.				
5.				
	etc.			

B. Mini-Team Feedback—Rule of Three

At the end of every meeting, training, or group session held in an organization, there should be a two to three minute mini-feedback session on how the meeting went and how to improve it (i.e., how to learn from it).

➥ **For example:**

Meeting "Processing" Guide

(To be used at the end of this part of the meeting or at the very end.)

Considering the past ___________ minutes of this meeting, let's make the next meeting's *process* (not content) work even better. I recommend we:

#1 Continue to do (the following):

#2 Do more of (or begin doing):

#3 Do less of (or stop doing):

Suggestions for Use:

1. At the end of every meeting, conference, or team/project effort, ask the group the three questions above (in this 1–3 order).
2. It only takes a few minutes to do this, and it gets you useful feedback to improve whatever you are doing.
3. The final question to ask afterwards is, "If you were talking to a good friend after the meeting, what would you tell them about the meeting?"

C. The Learning Organization

Organize and create The Learning Organization. Learning, feedback, and organizational renewal create the internal capacity for responding to and initiating change. *Is the glass half full or half empty?*

➥ **For example: Renewal: Systems Design and Redesign**

As soon as a design is *implemented,* its *consequences* (entropy) indicate a need for redesign.

1. Build in a *learning* system.
2. An *adapting* process is needed (i.e., debriefings/ongoing feedback).

Thus: The ideal system is an *inexact* adaptive-learning, ideal-seeking system.

Suggestions for Use:

1. How do you create The Learning Organization? Learning speed may be your competitive edge.

   Question: What are our needed actions to create a learning organization? (H–M–L).

________ 1. Reward managers who try to create it.

________ 2. Process meetings at the end to improve them.

________ 3. Conduct training and learning experiences at each staff meeting.

________ 4. Create whole jobs with direct customer contact. Give people the autonomy and freedom to act/control their own jobs. (Every employee a manager)

________ 5. Provide jobs/tasks to everyone that include on-the-job training and new learning experiences.

________ 6. Conduct training, training, and more training, always with follow-up and applications review so it is meaningful and useful to people's jobs.

________ 7. Understand and use adult learning theory as a way to present any and all new situations. Supply people with questions, not solutions.

________ 8. Set up a 52-week training program (bite-sized learning).

________ 9. Set up periodic and regular personal feedback to employees on how they come across to others and on their job performance vs. objectives.

________ 10. Set up a complete, strategic, and all-management-levels Management Development System. Use managers and executives as the trainers to help them learn better.

(continued)

Suggestions for Use: *(concluded)*

________ 11. Train and evaluate managers and executives in their new 21st century roles (i.e., TLC—trainer, leader, and coach).

________ 12. Work on *continuous performance improvement* and *delegation* daily. Track it.

________ 13. Set up debriefings and post mortems to ensure that everyone learns from mistakes and experiences.

________ 14. Help the organization and culture develop a forgiveness and problem-solving culture instead of a blaming culture. Promote experimentation, discovery, and mistake-making as a way to learn.

________ 15. Inspire a shared vision/common purpose that people can relate to and enthusiastically embrace.

________ 16. What else?

D. Feedback and Renewal Systems

Organizations have life cycles just as humans do. One of the big differences, however, is that organizations can renew and rebuild themselves into completely different organizations, starting all over again. Phase B, the Feedback Loop (from the environment), is a crucial variable in beginning this process. So is having a new vision (Phase A) of the future to act as a magnet, putting everyone forward to the "renewed" organization.

➥ **For example:**

The best example of this for a large corporation is what Jack Welch has done at General Electric. Another example is IBM. IBM, historically a mainframe provider, is well on its way to adding a brand-new company—a systems service provider. Large cities like Baltimore, Maryland, have also renewed themselves. It takes a learning organization using environmental scanning and feedback to achieve this kind of transformation.

Learning organizations must cultivate the art of open, attentive listening. Managers must be open to criticism.

E. Renewal Practices Questionnaire

Guidelines: Do I do or make use of any of these things?

Yes/No

________ 1. Issues management process (government, community, stockholders, stakeholders)

________ 2. Environmental scanning system

________ 3. Competitor analysis

________ 4. Financial reports (short-term, long-term)

________ 5. Industry financial comparisons

________ 6. Customer data, surveys, perceptions, feedback, focus groups

________ 7. Non-customer data, surveys, perceptions, focus groups

________ 8. Technology trends

________ 9. Sociodemographic trends

________ 10. Employee opinion surveys (morale, motivation, communications), yearly by unit

________ 11. Rewards—matching surveys, programs, diagnosis

________ 12. Culture surveys, focus groups

________ 13. Administrative MIS reports

________ 14. Deep-sensing of employee perceptions

________ 15. Advertising, marketing ROI and research

________ 16. Management data, opinions

________ 17. Task forces, think tanks, discussion groups

________ 18. Strategic planning processes

(continued)

E. Renewal Practices Questionnaire (concluded)

Guidelines: Do I do or make use of any of these things?

Yes/No

________ 19. Unfiltered upward-feedback meetings

________ 20. Team building, diagnosis, executive retreats

________ 21. Action, research

________ 22. Structured experiences, feedback, and learning

________ 23. Job design, work simplifications

________ 24. Organization effectiveness suggestion programs (not just productivity)

________ 25. Employee involvement programs

________ 26. Peer evaluations

________ 27. Meeting evaluations

________ 28. Employee, management meetings

________ 29. Offsite meetings, overnights, outward bound team experience

________ 30. Performance evaluation, including commitment to company values

________ 31. MBWA—Manage by Wandering Around

________ 32. Feedback—feedback—feedback

________ 33. Best practices research

________ 34. Benchmarking

________ 35. Work flow mapping

Now go back and circle those renewal practices you think you need to initiate.

F. Strategic Education Model

Real learning in an organization requires knowledge and skills, as well as the right attitude. And it needs to move up from the individual, to teams, to the organization as a whole in order to affect organizational change. These levels are also key to creating a learning organization.

Suggestions for Use:

Place high, medium, or low in each box to show the levels of learning going on for either (1) yourself, (2) your department, or (3) your organization as a whole.

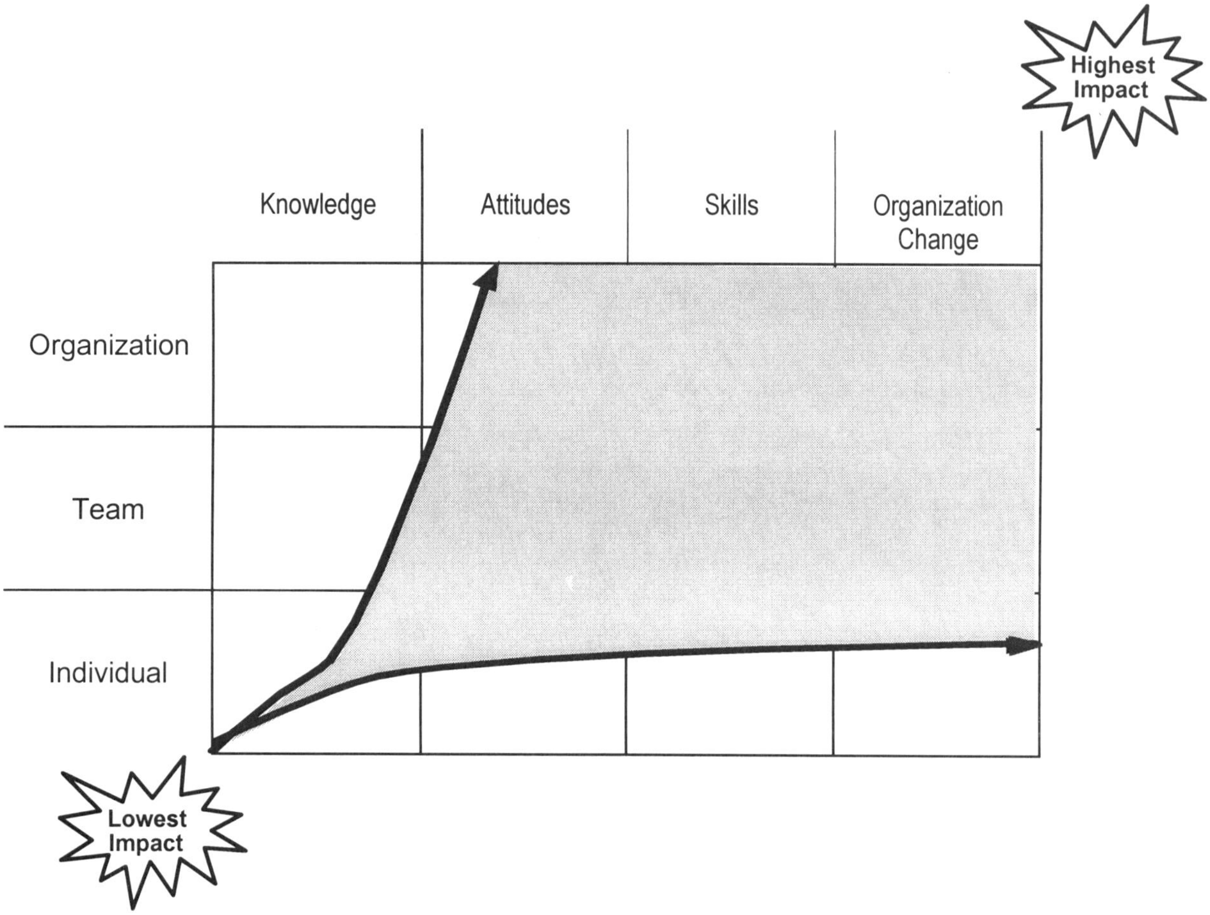

Tool #21 Environmental Scanning System

Application of Systems Dynamics #2: Open System View

A. Environmental Scanning System

Do you have a formal Environmental Scanning System to continually scan the environment on a regular basis—and do you do it in the context of your future vision and not just today?

- ➥ **For example:** All organizations today critically need this.
- ➥ **For example:** Each of us as individuals does as well.

The next six ideas are ways to accomplish this, personally and professionally.

Suggestions for Use:

1. Develop this way of scanning your organizational operations and report on it quarterly at your regular Change Management Leadership Steering Committee meetings. Change is happening so fast in today's world, and a yearly scan is really too infrequent. The steps to develop this scanning system include:

   a. Identify your organization's Environmental Scan needs.

   b. Generate a list of information sources that provide core inputs (i.e., trade shows, publications, technical meetings, and customers).

   c. Identify those who will participate in the Environmental Scanning process. It is often necessary to involve all senior managers. If so, assign each one of the seven SKEPTIC areas to a different executive.

   d. Collect data on a regular basis.

   e. Disseminate the information all at once (like a "data dump") in a large group meeting, such as quarterly at the Strategic Change Leadership Steering Committee meeting.

   f. Determine the major patterns or trends that could affect you and problem-solve/develop action plans accordingly.

2. Some specific ways to scan and get this feedback include:

Environmental Domains

I. Customers

- customer data, surveys, perceptions, feedback, focus group
- noncustomer data, surveys, perceptions, focus groups
- advertising, marketing ROI
- customer profitability
- accounts receivable
- product quality
- segmentation data
- complaint handling, trends
- visits, meetings
- customer comment cards

II. Suppliers/Vendors

- visits, meetings
- sales potential
- annual reports
- accounts payable

III. Unions (Employee Involvement Programs)

- joint union–management committees
- safety, security data
- meetings with union leadership

IV. Employees

- employee opinion surveys—morale, motivation, communications—yearly, by units
- rewards—matching surveys, programs, diagnosis
- culture surveys, focus groups, action research
- deep-sensing employee perceptions
- task forces, think tanks, discussion groups
- unfiltered upward-feedback meetings—employee/management meetings
- Manage by Wandering Around
- job design, work simplifications
- organization effectiveness suggestion programs—not just productivity

V. Public Community/Society

- technology trends
- sociodemographic trends
- issues-management process
- environmental impact
- social responsibility program
- advisory boards
- community involvement

VI. Government (Issues Management Process)

- lobbyist data
- legislative visits, reports (state/federal)
- legal reviews, compliance

VII. Owners/Stockholders

- investor relations surveys
- annual meetings
- phone calls, trends

VIII. Competition

- competitor analysis
- industry financial comparisons
- niches
- trade shows
- strategic alliances
- MBWA
- price analysis
- association meetings, seminars
- annual reports

IX. Wall Street Financiers/Creditors

- visits, meetings
- analyst briefings
- annual reports
- diversify
- advisory board

X. Management

- administrative MIS reports
- financial reports (short-term/ long-term)
- management data, opinions
- strategic planning process
- team building, diagnosis, executive retreats
- off-site meetings, overnights
- outward bound team experience
- peer evaluations
- meeting evaluations
- performance evaluation, assess commitment to company values

XI. International

- productivity, growth, and development
- economics, forecasts
- societal, cultural, country trends
- international financial exchanges
- Internet

3. Initial Environmental Scanning Required

   List the initial environmental scanning that needs to be conducted at the beginning of any strategic planning/strategic change process.

What areas should be scanned? What data collected?	Who will be responsible?	When will it be reviewed?

4. **Personally**: Here are some things to do when conducting such a scan in your career and personal life.

   1. Check out the resources in area libraries.
   2. Get subscriptions to:
      - newsletters
      - magazines
      - executive book summaries
   3. Join professional associations.
   4. Build networks, such as:
      - buddy systems
      - bag-lunch groups, film groups
      - breakfast meetings
   5. Conduct skills self-assessment and do development planning (use assessment tools, surveys).
   6. Conduct weekly-monthly-quarterly review meetings, mini-meetings, etc.

B. Alternative Application: Environmental Domains and Stakeholders

Focus on changes in the environment that have a major impact on your organization as a system—especially over time—as well as those that will be affected by any desired changes.

- Are you clear on all your stakeholders, and the ones that will best help you through this problem-solving and change process.

➥ **For example:**

Stakeholder Analysis: The World as a Complex System

Stakeholder = any group or individual who can affect or is affected by the achievement of the organization's objectives. The groups listed here are examples of categories of stakeholders.

Suggestions for Use:

1. Identification of Key Stakeholders

   a. Who are all our stakeholders?

   b. Identify the top five to seven stakeholders in terms of importance to the success or failure of our strategic planning/strategic change process and its implementation.

We often use the acronym "SKEPTIC" as a way to remember the key stakeholders.

S Socio-Demographics
K "K"ompetition
E Economics/Environment
P Politics
T Technology
I Industry, and, of course, your
C Customers

See Tool #4 for further details on SKEPTIC.

C. Specific Environmental Scanning: Market Research

Each customer or market segment has specific and different wants and needs. Have you done sufficient market research in the environment to know what those needs are and even anticipate them?

➥ **For example:** Many, many organizations we work with have no regular and ongoing customer data-collection efforts.

➥ **For example:** Are you honoring your children's goals? Do they even have any? Or are you pushing your goals on them as some parents do? As children, are they allowed to change?

Suggestions for Use:

1. As an organization, decide how you're going to collect market research
   - By surveys, mystery shoppers, warranties?
   - How often? by whom? How will they be used?
2. Use our copyrighted "Star" Model below to identify what they want.

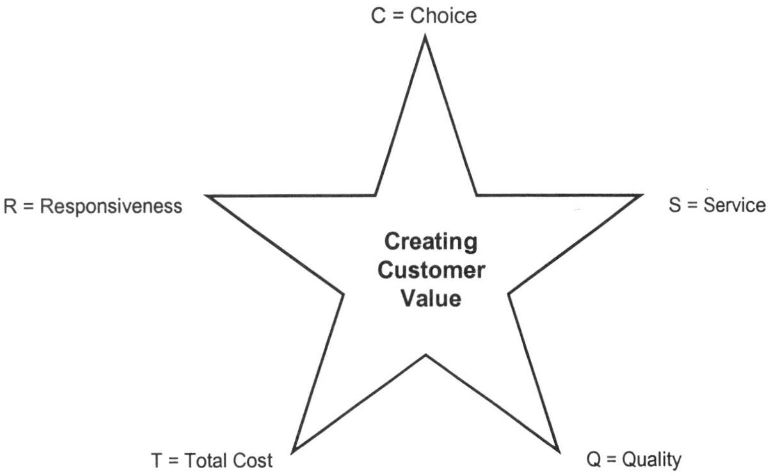

3. Once you have collected the data, how will you use it? Market research is the leverage between your customers and the rest of your organization. Use the questions below as a survey to see how well you use market research.

Environmental Scanning System

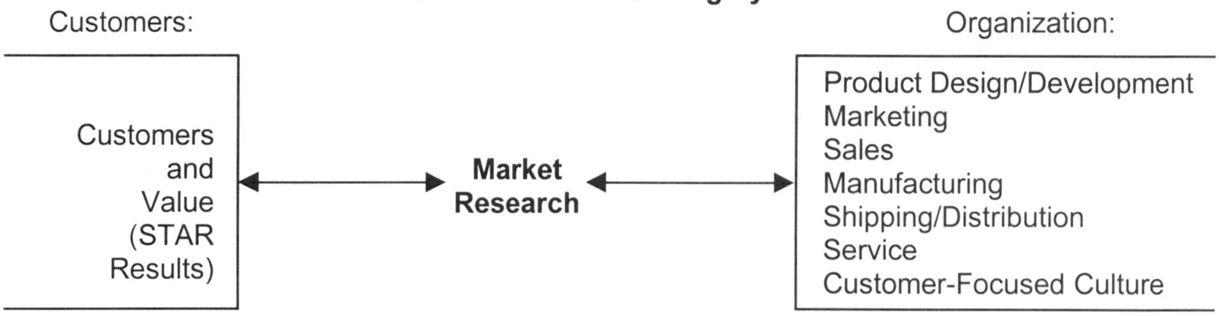

4. How does market research link to:
   a. product development
   b. the rest of marketing
   c. sales
   d. manufacturing
   e. shopping/distribution
   f. services
   g. senior management
   h. desired culture
   i. what else?

5. Personally, if you want to advance in your career, make ongoing market research and networking a part of your life. Don't start it when you need a job. It's too late then. It is not likely that you will be with one company your entire career. Therefore, keep up-to-date with the changes in your industry and improve your skills so you will be ready for your *next* job.

Tool #22 Key Success Factor Measures—Continuous Improvement Matrix

Application of Systems Dynamics #1: Holism

Key Success Factors (KSFs) measure key, multiple organizational outcomes holistically. Measure no more than ten outcomes and include customer, employee, and competitive measures, not just financials. Use these measures as a scoreboard, a more detailed version of corporate goal setting, which everyone takes responsibility to achieve.

Then, review your goals on a regular basis and assess how well you are progressing. But look at all your goals and your life holistically. Keep track!

Key Success Factors Defined

Key Success Factors are the **quantifiable outcome measurements of success** in achieving an organization's vision, mission, and values on a year-by-year basis to ensure continual improvement toward achieving the ideal future vision.

➥ **For example:**

1. How do you know if you're being successful?
2. How do you know if you're going to get into trouble?
3. Now, if you are off course (in trouble), what corrective actions do you need to take to get the organization back on track to achieve your ideal future vision?

➥ **For example:** What Do We Measure?

	Not These	*but*	*These*
1.	What's easy	or	what's important?
2.	Lots of activities	or	a few focused outcomes?
3.	80% activities	or	key 20% results?

Key Success Factor Measurement Screening Criteria

To be considered a Key Success Factor, an outcome must meet the following criteria:

1. It is a "key one" organization-wide (10 or less).
2. It is preferably an output (vs. a means to an end).
3. It has three parts:
   a. area
   b. indicator
   c. measurable targets (baseline, intermediate, and target goal for end of the planning horizon)

4. It has no overlapping or duplicate KSFs.

5. It is specific and measurable/quantifiable.

6. It is a key indicator of organization success; it is not a comprehensive list. The "comprehensive list" is more appropriate at the department or division level (and is even questionable there).

7. It is one whose status you can physically see, so you know factually whether or not it has been achieved.

8. It is a report card (not activities/work plan).

Key Success Factors Are Specific and Quantifiable

Key Success Factors can be measured in the following ways:

1. Quality —as perceived by customer (surveys?)
   —internal (zero defects)

2. Quantity —numbers (#)
   —ratios
   —specific existence/nonexistence of "x"

3. Time —1995-year/Jan-month
   —3 times a year

4. Cost —dollars ($)
   —percents (%)
   —ratios

Key Success Factors and Feedback Systems

➥ **For example:** To sustain a competitive business advantage, measure and track all four of these Key Success Factor areas:

1. Customer Satisfaction/Feedback
2. Employee Satisfaction/Feedback
3. Competitor Analysis/Comparison (Benchmarks vs. Best Practices)
4. Financial Viability Indicators (necessary but not sufficient)

Suggestions for Use:

Key Success Factor Areas: The following questions and instructions will help you determine how to use these measurement areas.

1. What are the key words and phrases from our statements on vision, mission, core values, and driving force that define "success"? List them.

2. What are other key important financial/operational success areas? List them.

3. Combine your answers and those of the rest of the senior management into a consolidated list. List those collective answers.

4. Prune the list to 10 or less Key Success Factor areas for the entire organization.

5. Once the areas are set, decide how to measure each one and assign responsibility and accountability for the development and reporting of each measure.

6. Collect baseline data for the current year (if available).

7. Next, set goals for your future target year as well as the intermediate years.

Note: You can use this for a total organization, a business unit, a department, or even a team.

Key Success Factor Continuous Improvement Matrix (Backwards Thinking)

KSF Overall Coordinator for Accountability is ______________________ (Name/Title)

KSF areas (headers) with specific factors for each	Baseline Target	Intermediate Targets				Target	Ultimate Target	Competitive Benchmark	Key Success Factors Accountability
	2000	2001	2002	2003	2004	2005			
1. Header: Factors:									1.
2.									2.
3.									3.
4.									4.
5.									5.

Tool #23 "People Support What They Help Create"

Application of Systems Dynamics #6: Multiple-Goal Seeking; and #7: Equifinality

Plans are nothing, planning is everything.

—Dwight D. Eisenhower

A. Participative Leaders

"People support what they help create" is an extremely important statement. People want to be involved and give input into decisions that affect them, before the decision is made.

Involve all key stakeholders on a regular basis through the use of a parallel process.

Decision-making goals should always be to arrive at the best possible decision, and to gain 100% support for the decision from all those involved.

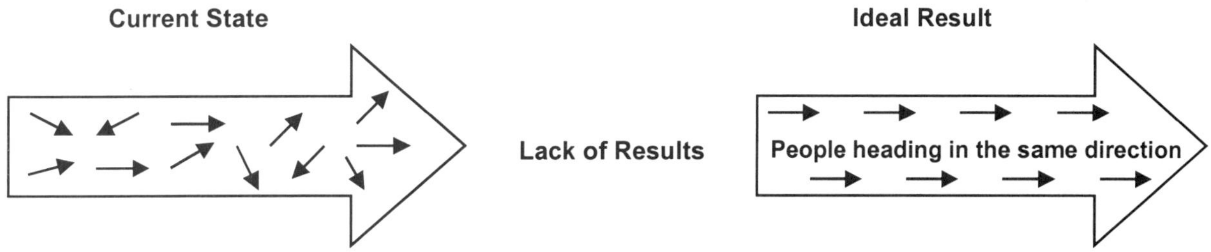

Unacceptable Alternatives (vs. Participative Leaders)

> *We seem stuck . . . between two unacceptable alternatives—the leader who dictates to others, and the one who truckles to them.*
>
> *If leaders dictate, by what authority do they take away people's right to direct their own lives? If leaders truckle, who needs or respects such weathervanes?*
>
> —*"What Makes a Good Leader?"* by Gary Wills
> *The Atlantic Monthly,* April 1994

What we need are participative leaders. Participative leaders are those who gather input on issues from the people who will be affected—before the decisions are made. This requires asking questions and listening openly to the answers, whether you like them or not.

Management Ideology Abandoned

> *What must be abandoned by management is a whole ideology, a whole way of thinking about power. Power no longer belongs in boxes, in titles, in ranks. What counts for power is what you do yourself with your own skills.*
>
> —Jim Champy
> author of *Reengineering Management*

➥ **For example:** The Parallel Process Concept

"People Support What They Help Create"

SET UP THE PLANNING COMMUNITY

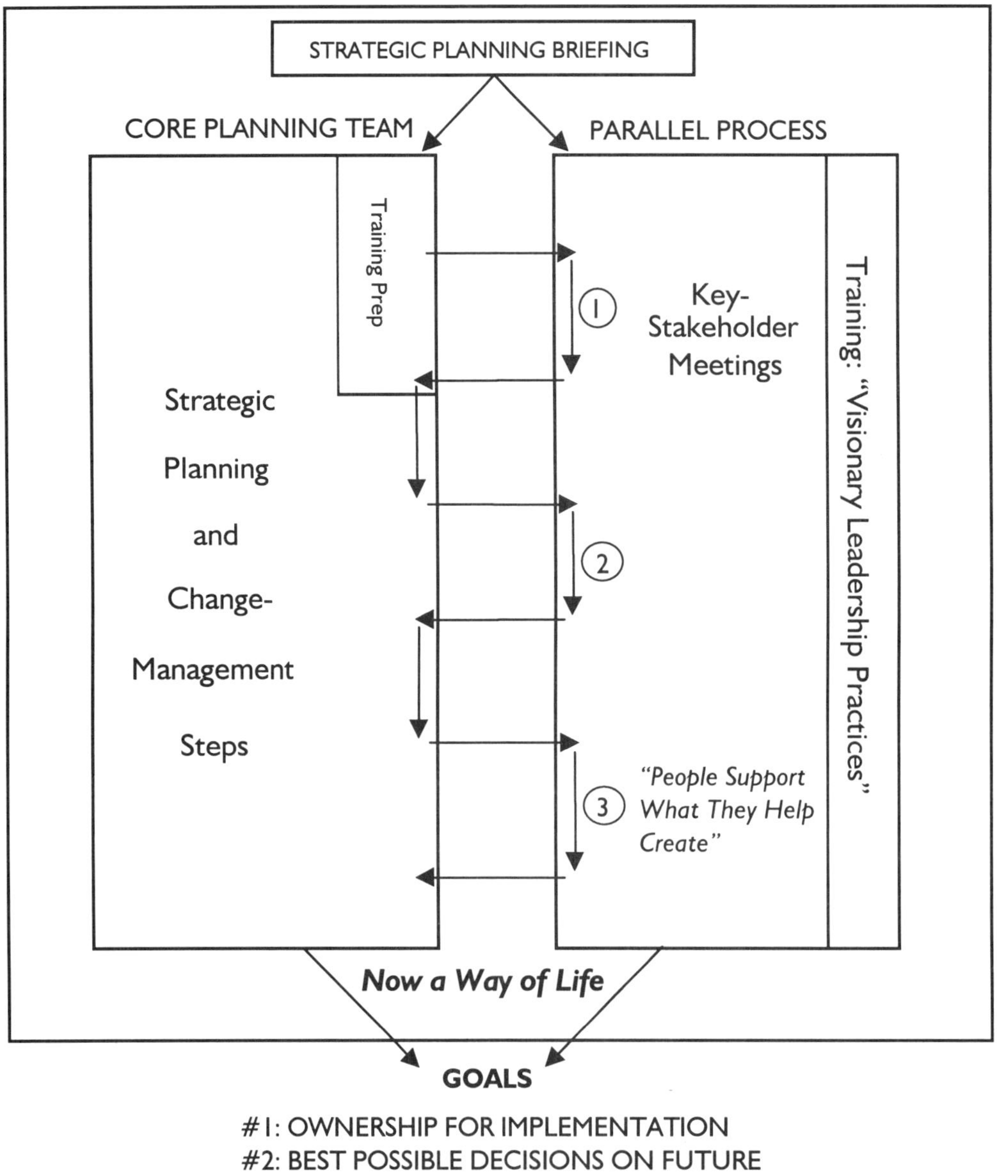

Suggestions for Use:

Key Stakeholders

1. **Overall Parallel Process Meeting Purposes**
   a. This is an information-sharing and input/feedback meeting.
   b. It is not a decision-making meeting. This will be done by the Core Planning/Change Team at its next meeting, based on your feedback.

2. **Who are our stakeholders?**

3. **Identify the top five to seven stakeholders in terms of importance to the success (positive and negative influences) of the strategic planning/process and its implementation/change.**

4. **How do we use parallel process meetings to involve our key stakeholders?**
   a. To explain the strategic planning/change effort and your role/involvement in it
   b. To understand the draft documents/change clearly
   c. To give us input and feedback to take back to the full core planning/change team
      - Guarantee: Your feedback will be seriously considered.
      - Limitation: Input is being gathered from many different people. Therefore, it is impossible for each person's input to be automatically placed in the final documents/action plan exactly as desired.

B. Open Book Management—More Involvement AND Support

Do you practice "**open book management**" where all employees are treated and trained as owners, and fully understand the business and its economics/outcomes (as well as all your products and services)?

Remember, an organization is a system. People function more effectively when they **fully understand the system.**

A quality process alone is no guarantee of sustained organizational prosperity. We'd like to cite the conclusions of **Jack Stack**, CEO of Springfield Remanufacturing and one of America's most innovative young leaders.

In his new book *The Great Game of Business,* Stack takes issue with the assumption that you get quality by making your people pay attention to details, rather than by telling them how the company works (opening your books and financials and your strategic plan).

He argues that employees first must understand how the organization works and how it makes its money. Only then are they able to see the big picture and put the parts into a balanced context.

Lacking the big picture and the business economics, an organizational focus on the parts can easily degenerate into departmental turfism—a reality that virtually ensures gridlock in major process quality improvements.

To stop or prevent this gridlock requires an **entire work force that is energized, knowledgeable, and engaged** from the neck up. We believe that this higher level of employee involvement **requires organizations to thoroughly communicate the business economics and the critical issues that constitute the whole of the organization's strategy before fully engaging their people in improving its parts.**

This is true for employees *and* their families, who also don't know your economic realities.

—Adapted from *The ForeSight Intrapreneur*
Winter 1992

Suggestions for Use:

1. Assess your level of openness; how much do you tell your family, your department, your organization about economics?
2. Build on what you're already doing; improve their understanding of your economic system.
3. When it comes to confidentiality, ask yourself, "What's the worst thing that can happen if you share your economic information?" Usually, not much.

Tool #24 Look in the Mirror—Self-Feedback

Systems Dynamics #5: Feedback; and
Application of Seven Levels of Living Systems

A. Self-Feedback

Focus on your own personal role in any problem (we are all interconnected and inter-dependent). Look inward first for the problem and some solutions.

➡ **For example:** Use the technique of seeing yourself as the object that is the problem and "problem-solve" yourself.

The world would be a far better place if each of us could only change one individual—ourselves!

➡ **For example:** The individual must change in order for the organization to change and the first individuals to change must be senior management! (They are at the center of the organization as a system.) Leaders must "walk the talk"—*be* the right role model.

Organizations Change When People Change

Who goes first?

➡ **For example:** The Wise Person and the Fool

Question: What's the difference between the wise person and the fool?

Answer: They both make mistakes, *but* the wise person continuously learns from his or her own mistakes and experiences, as well as those of others.

Suggestions for Use:

1. Review this individual self-change process:

PROGRESS

I. Awareness (unfreezing)

1. Awareness of Need/Desire to Change
2. Understanding and Education—knowledge—self-disclosure—and feedback on what to change

II. Choice (decision)

3. Attitude and Skills

—Willingness/discipline/conviction to change

—Willingness to acquire new skills/be naive

4. Organize a Program

—Organize a change effort

—Incentives to change

III. Change (action)

5. Self-Change

—Take action

—Get feedback on how you're doing

6. Build Habits—through maintenance/feedback and follow-up/reinforcement

2. *Question*: Where are you in this self-change process?
3. *Question*: What are your weaknesses regarding Steps #1–6 above?
4. What next steps do you need to take?
5. How does an individual really change?

B. Self-Management

Let him who would move the world first move himself.

—Socrates

You have to be able to manage yourself to succeed, and to set a good example for those who work for you. Intelligence, education, and drive are prime requisites for achievement. But they're worthless without the discipline that enables you to transport your abilities to the marketplace. A true achiever is an individual who has reached his or her full potential as a human being.

—Raymond C. Johnson, *The Achievers*

What I Can Do	How Others Can Help (Feedback)
1. Recognize my mind trap. 2. Visualize the new identity I'd like to have. 3. Have strong feelings and passion for the new identity. 4. Develop self-awareness of the change/ time to reflect on it. 5. Decide to change the self-doubting identity. 6. Have faith that I can make the change. 7. Be willing to feel anxious and out-of-control. 8. Practice and practice with the new attitudes and behaviors. 9. Become a compassionate self-observer (supportive and enthusiastic about one-self) in: • suspending my disbelief on the new identity • being less self-conscious with the new behaviors 10. Have a sense of humor about the change. 11. Reward myself for my new identity. 12. Persistence—persistence—persistence.	1. Peer pressure to change. 2. Critical mass; informal leaders. 3. Valid feedback (+/–) from others. 4. "Why" explained: questions, rationale; Hear them—don't discount them; Allow them to talk out issues and feelings. 5. Involve them in some aspect of the change, give them choices. 6. Continued positive reinforcement. 7. Support and reassurance. 8. Guidance, mentoring. 9. Respect for one's values and dignity. 10. Change the rewards system. 11. Accept the person "as is." 12. Provide continuity of certain support. 13. Provide education and awareness training.

Adapted by Stephen G. Haines from Tom Rusk, *1990 Annual*, University Associates.

C. Seeking Feedback

Feedback is so important. Do you seek it individually and collectively to make sure you are focusing on the right outcomes, even when the feedback might be painful? Constant feedback is what creates the competitive advantage of The Learning Organization . . . and The Learning Individual.

He who knows others is learned; he who knows himself is wise.

—Lao-Tsze

➥ **For example:** The key is encouraging and promoting feedback about your performance from others as well as from yourself. Rate yourself on the following feedback suggestions:

Scale: 1–6 (low to high)

____ 1. Tolerate pain

____ 2. Search for the truth

____ 3. Have humility; be naive

____ 4. Let go of your defenses

____ 5. Be open and courageous

____ 6. Have faith in your learning and growth

Suggestions for Use:

1. After rating yourself in the criteria above, score yourself on the 30 skills listed in our Leadership Development Competencies, found in Chapter 6. Then give the same blank questionnaire out to five people who know you in order to get feedback on yourself.
2. Have them fill it out and turn it in to a confidential source who can score it for you.
3. Compare their scores to yours.
4. Then create an action plan.

D. Intellectual Honesty

Balancing advocacy and inquiry is crucial to individual learning and personal/self-mastery. Inquiry is the spirit of nonjudgmental feedback, curiosity, and new learning. Dialogue, discovery, and the search for truth are the outcomes.

Intellectual honesty is the key!

Advocacy, instead, is trying to influence others toward your point of view and judgment.

➥ **For example:** Many people spend much of their time defending their point of view—looking to blame others and not listening or caring about the views of family members, friends, or work colleagues.

On the other hand, if you are intellectually honest with yourself and you focus on your vision/desired outcomes (which usually include growth, learning, getting better at something, etc.), you will find that inquiry and curiosity is a better way to live your life. It will help you discover so much more learning and growth—especially the natural and normal world of systems and systems dynamics.

To be the best, you have to be totally honest with yourself . . . and others.

—Thurman Thomas, *Sports Illustrated,* February 1993

➥ **For example:**

The Six Disciplines of Credibility—Where am I on these?

They say credible leaders:

1. Explore their inner selves continuously.
2. Learn to listen well to their constituents.
3. Share values that resolve conflict and build unity.
4. Develop lifelong learning habits.
5. Commit to shared values by accepting responsibility and accountability for the promises they make.
6. Sustain hope for the future by demonstrating their convictions.

Source: James M. Kouzes and Barry Z. Posner, *Training & Development*, January 1994.

Suggestions for Use:

1. Commit yourself to "intellectual honesty," even if you can't always reveal this to others. Be honest in your own mind with yourself.
2. Ask yourself where you are on the six disciplines of leader credibility. Which do you need to improve upon?
3. Learn how to use the process of inquiry to search for better ideas and reality (instead of your own perception).
4. The key is to suspend judgment at first in any operation for inquiry and learning. Advocate only after you've learned all you can.

E. Four Levels of Self-Feedback and Evaluation

Most training programs have little feedback as to their effectiveness after the course. There are actually four levels of feedback, at further and further ends/outcomes.

➥ **For example:**

Level #1. Did you like the course?

Level #2. Did you learn anything?

Level #3. Did you change your behavior for the better?

Level #4. Has the organization or your life improved as a result?

Each is a further and further outcome until the ultimate purpose (organizational improvement) is obtained.

Specifically:

Level #1 **Reaction Evaluation or "Happiness Scale" (informal conversation/observation)**

- perceptions indicated on evaluation form
- unsolicited participant feedback
- stop-action evaluation
- instructor reactions
- information and observations from participants during scheduled breaks
- seminar audit by staff or consultant
- telephone interview with a random selection of course participants

Level #2 **Learning Evaluation (interviews, formal discussion)**

- pre-tests by evaluator/instructor
- post-tests by evaluator/instructor
- performance test can be multiple-choice, true-false, matching, objective, subjective

Level #3 **Practical Application (behavior on the job)**

- use information/skills on the job
- change in learner's behavior
- questionnaire to participant two to six months afterwards
- informal feedback, post workshop
- questionnaire/telephone interview with approving manager
- observation in work setting

Level #4 **Bottom-Line Improvements (performance indicators)**

- Was training/course information productive/cost effective?
- Have bottom-line results improved?

Suggestions for Use:

1. Assess the current state of all training programs you attend personally, or have in your department/organization, regarding their level of evaluation.
2. Insist that all future courses have the appropriate level of evaluation.
3. What other events/actions (beyond training) are needed to make Level 4 happen?

*Adapted from Donald L. Kilpatrick's famous four-level evaluation model © 1959.

Tool #25 Assessment and Debriefing Frameworks

Application of Systems Dynamics #5: Feedback

A. Debriefing

Feedback vs. Desired Outcomes—In most organizations, the press of time gets in the way of learning from our experiences. We finish the task at hand and rush on to the next task, oblivious to true, indepth learnings by all participants in the task. In its place, each person takes their own perceptions with them to the next task, without checking their perceptions for accuracy.

➥ **Examples:** Good opportunities to use debriefing include:

1. Project Completion
2. Incidents/Failures
3. Workshops
4. Post Mortems of Issues/Problems Everywhere

The solution is to hold a "Debriefing" meeting with all key participants involved in the project or issue. Even if you have just one hour, use the standard agenda below to maximize the correct learnings for the future.

Suggestions for Use: **Debriefing Agenda**

Five Steps From the Incident/Project	**To the Goal of** Improvement for the Future*
1. Goal	clarity of project objectives
2. What	happened in the incident?
3. So What	did we learn (brainstorm * lots of them)?
4. Now What	do we do differently? *a. to correct the incident/problem if we need to (recovery strategy) *b. to prevent it in the future (new systems/ processes)
5. Celebrate	Meeting success

* = meeting success

B. Systems Thinking[SM] Assessment Questionnaire

Suggestions for Use:

1. Six questions to debrief/revisit our project plan content in retrospect after completion.
2. A way to properly plan and test for completeness, with feedback on an entire change project from the very beginning.

1. **Where do we (did we) want to be in our ideal future?** (i.e., our goals, purpose, mission, ends, outcomes, destination, etc.)

2. **How will we know when we get there?** (How do we know we are there now? i.e., a quantifiable and measurable feedback system)

3. **Where are we now?** (Where were we when we started? i.e., today's assessment of status, SWOT, strategic issues or problems)

4. **How do (did) we get there?** (i.e., what actions to take to close the gap from today to our ideal future in a holistic and strategic way)

5. **What are (were) the change management structures and processes needed** to ensure the actions and results above are achieved?

6. **Ongoing**: What is/will/may/did change in our environment that can affect this process/ project?

Chapter V
Application: The A-B-C-D Systems Thinking Approach℠ and Model

Provides tools for a number of key management processes and activities so you can become much more successful.

Tool No.	The Applications
26	"Organization as a System" Model* — *How do I visualize my organization as a system with all its elements if I'm going to change it?*
27	Reinventing Strategic Management — *How do I conduct strategic planning and then ensure accountability for implementation throughout the organization?*
28	Strategic Life Planning — *Where do I want to be in the future in my life—and how will I get there?*
29	HR Strategic Planning — *How do I plan to create the "people edge" for my organization?*
30	Hiring and Promotions as a System — *How do I maximize my chances of successfully hiring or promoting the right person who will be successful?*
31	The Team as a System — *How do I think of, assess, and plan my team's success as an interdependent team?*
32	Systemic Team Building — *How do I systematically build my team into a high performance one?*
33	Cross-Functional Teams — *What is an effective cross-functional team? And why is it important?*
34	Leadership Development as a System — *If leaders can be developed, how can an organization do it systematically?*
35	TQM as a System — *Is TQM a fad, a technique, or a system of management?*
36	Systems Solution vs. Problem Solving — *How can you rethink the old problem-solving model to be more effective?*
37	Organization Design as a System — *Can you design your organization to better fit its goals and vision?*
38	Project Management—Simplicity — *How can you use the A-B-C-D Systems Thinking Approach as a "new orientation to life" and all projects?*

* Essential reading for all the tools in this chapter

The Systems Thinking Approach:
Where's Your Focus? on the crises of today or the opportunities of tomorrow?

Tool #26 "Organization as a System" Model

Application of Systems Dynamics #1: Holism; #4: Input-Output Model; and #10: Subsystems

In this chapter we describe a primary application of the third concept of systems thinking, the **A-B-C-D Systems Framework,** or "The New Orientation to Life." In Chapter I, we discussed at length the A-B-C-D model as an overall systems concept. In this chapter, we demonstrate how it applies to an organization as a system, as a way to *create alignment and attunement and give you a competitive edge.*

The following paragraphs explain this model. Refer to it time and again so that you fully understand it. You must completely understand it in order to use the tools that follow.

A. The Organization as a System

Phase A: Customer Value

Systems thinking *begins with the end in mind* (as Steven Covey says). *Outcomes, purposes, missions, visions, goals, objectives, ends* are all words to describe this phase about the outcomes of the organization as a system (we define it as the *Customer Edge*). Defining who your customer is and what he or she wants and then positioning the organization to have a unique competitive edge with the customer instead of the competition is critical. It is **the first** and foremost strategic and systems thinking task any organization must completely define.

Obviously, any organization trying, as a system, to satisfy the customer must deal with the environment in which the organization exists. Good strategic thinking helps the organization look at future environmental trends to define where the organization wants to be.

Phase B: Success Measures

This phase deals with the **feedback loop**—the Key Success Factors. *These are the quantifiable outcome measures of success* that should be constantly fed back into the organization. (They are sometimes called *goals* and *objectives.*) Feeding back quantifiable measurements of how the organization is functioning is *the key to organization learning* as well as success. You must guide corrections and adjustments throughout the year in order to make sure you are achieving **Customer Value.** Whether you call them *goals*, or *objectives*, or *key success indicators*, or *critical success factors,* it is all about *building a scoreboard of organizational success* measurements and feeding the status of these back into the organization so it can learn and correct its actions.

Phase C: Create the Strategic Edge

This phase is where inputs into *the organization as a system* come in. The $64,000,000-dollar question for organizations is *"What are the core strategies that we need to adopt?"*

These are the primary ways we will be achieving organizational outcomes (especially customer-value). This is strategic thinking at its very best. The tools in Phase C were chosen to show all aspects of strategic planning that lead to developing these core strategies. Strategic planning, however, includes parts of Phase A, parts of Phase B, and parts of Phase C.

In addition, Phase C deals with the conversion of strategic plans into business plans and then into annual department plans for every aspect of the organization. *A strategic plan is a blueprint and a living, breathing document*. **Operational or annual department plans are what you implement.** You do not implement a strategic plan. It is the framework or blueprint for creating the business and operational plans. Phase C inputs into *the organization as a system model* are crucial in defining the core strategies and department annual plans that are necessary to implement change throughout an organization.

Phase D: Strategic Change Management Process

The throughput, or processes, of the *organization as a system* must react to organizational change of all types in today's dynamic world. Thus, this chapter covers four main components. It details the inner workings of a living, breathing organization in systems and horizontal interdependent process terms (much like TQM and reengineering) rather than through separate functional boxes in analytic organizational charts.

The #1 master component of Phase D is to create a Strategic Change Management Process. This is the guiding leadership and management mechanism that ensures integrated and systemic change. Defining and putting in place *change processes and structures* is key to that success.

The second major component of Phase D deals with the operational or technical processes—**Creating the Process Edge.** This is done through *the alignment of the delivery processes* of the organization. In our model of the *organization as a system,* you can see that the alignment of the delivery processes is not a straight line. Instead, it occurs more in keeping with our Rollercoaster of Change (Systems Concept #4). In this model *the alignment of delivery processes* is part of a *web of relationships* that create effective or ineffective delivery processes. The more operational or technical parts of an organization are usually the focus of most change efforts (to their detriment). The five parts *above* this thick wavy black line concern the alignment of delivery processes.

The third major component of Phase D deals with throughputs or processes of *the organization as a system* that create **The People Edge.** *Creating the people edge through the attunement of people's hearts and minds* is crucial to creating customer value. It is also the other half of this *web of relationships* that ultimately creates your organizational culture. When it comes to the alignment of delivery processes we have separated this social side of the attunement of people's hearts and minds from the technical or operational side. Both are inextricably combined into this phase as a web of integrated relationships inside the organization to create customer value. Without it, we don't have synergy and may even have discord. "Fit" becomes a dirty three-letter word in systems thinking, because the components are only supposed to help assist and integrate. *Remember: The whole is primary and the parts should only be optimized as a secondary consideration.*

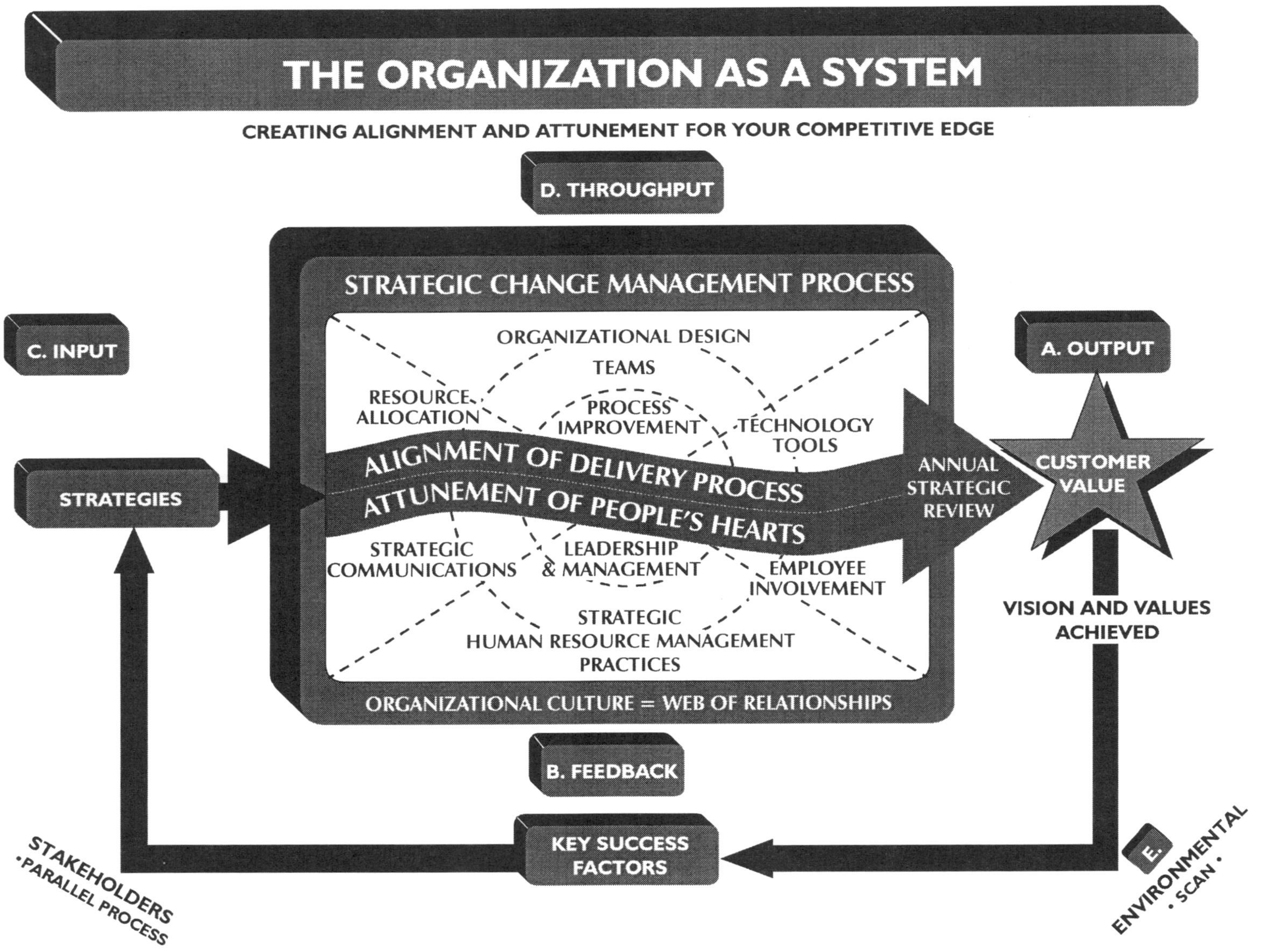

4th Edition • Adapted from General Systems Theory and Haines Associates—
Our experiences, literature searches, and continual client feedback.

1420 Monitor Road, San Diego, CA 92110 • (619) 275-6528 • FAX (619) 275-0324
E-mail csmhaine@sprynet.com

Suggestions for Use:

1. Use "The Organization as a System" model to conduct a high-performance organizational survey and assessment on the status of each component and its relationship to every other component.

2. **Based on extensive best practices research**, we suggest that you try to use the Organizational Systems Model in the following ways:
    1. A template, model, or diagnostic tool.
    2. A framework for thinking and analyzing the organization (or department).
    3. Questions to ask as you make decisions to change items/tasks in the organization (i.e., implement the strategic plan).
    4. A common framework for thinking, communicating, and working together to change parts of the organization and achieve the vision.
    5. An increased awareness, sensitivity, and understanding of how an organization works and how the parts should fit together in support of the vision/customers.
    6. A tool to diagnose the status of your effectiveness in achieving your organization's "fit, alignment, and integrity" to your vision and to your desired culture.
    7. Exquisite simplicity, a macro model; use it to get a handle on organizational changes.
    8. To eliminate biases.
    9. To give you a focus through organizational complexity.
    10. Bird's eye view/framework to look at the overall organization
        - multiple cause and effect
        - a balanced way to cover the waterfront
    11. Help focus in on areas needing work
        - set priorities for work
        - clear linkages/interdependence to other functions, tasks
    12. Road map—how not to get lost in organization complexity
        - know where you are and how to navigate to success
        - 21st century road map vs. 1700s map
    13. Diagnose problems/solutions in organizations and how one thing affects all others in order to increase one's chances of success. This is especially true when attempting a *culture* change.
    14. To explain, teach executives/managers how to manage/lead strategic planning/strategic change.
    15. A way to guide any large-scale change and to improve individual/team performance and links to the vision/values, direction.
    16. To have more confidence in your implementation.
    17. To learn how multicauses have multieffects
        - simple cause/effect is obsolete
    18. Help avoid strategies/actions based on a systems diagnosis, solid solution.

B. A-B-C-D—Change Checklist

The Organization as a System model can be used to develop an integrated set of tasks needed to achieve a desired change. We do it by checking each component for its relationship and impact on the desired change.

- We can also use this method to evaluate the status of the desired change,
- or use it to decide who should be on a task force to guide this change (people support what they help create).

For example: Any change in one strategy of a firm will result in changes to every other part of the organization as a system.

Suggestions for Use:

1. **Fit of Components:**

   Analyze the fit of all parts of the Organization as a System Model.

   - Does it fit with your strategic plan?
   - Does it have internal consistency, i.e., your model should fit the:

     a. Overall level of an integrated system's approach/collaboration within the organization
     b. Operational tasks of quality and service
     c. Leadership and management skills and practices
     d. Technology, communications, and other resource allocation
     e. Structure and organizational design
     f. Human resource management practices, including (1) policies and procedures, and (2) performance and reward systems, including staffing/promotions
     g. Informal organizational culture/teams
     h. Feedback loop and renewal systems, including continuous improvement process
     i. Change management system to ensure change is managed well

(continued)

Suggestions for Use: *(continued)*

A High-Performance Work Organization (The Organization as a System)

Summary of Best Practices Research:

A diagnostic tool for understanding and managing accelerated change.

← *Paradigm Shift* →

	Type Organization / Organization as a System	**A.** Reactive Organization	**B.** ***Industrial Age*** Responsible Organization (Traditional)	**C.** ***Systems Age*** 21st Century High-Performance Organization (Traditional)
A. Output	1. Achievement of Results	Survival Level & Conflict Only	Profitability OK or within Budget	Customer Value (★ Results)
B. Feedback	2. Feedback Loop	Rarely Used (Closed System)	Financial/ Operational Measures Only	KSFs/Annual Strategic Reviews/ Org'n Learning
A–C. Strategic Planning	3. Strategic Planning	Survival/Confusion Day-to-Day	3-Year Forecasts/ Operational Planning	Integrated Strategic Management System
D. Alignment (of delivery processes)	4A. Operational Tasks (Quality/ Service) 4B. Technology 4C. Resources 4D. Organizational Design 4E. Team Development 4F. Business Processes	A. Firefighting/Fix It (Low Quality) B. Out of Date C. Squeaky Wheel D. Fragmented E. Adversarial/ Individual Focus F. Personal Control	A. Maintain Only/ Obsolete Tasks B. Piecemeal Technology C. Incrementalism D. Hierarchy and Bureaucracy E. Functional Teams Only F. Bureaucratic/ Department Controls	A. Reputation for High Quality/ Service B. Technology Fit/ Organization C. Resources Clearly Focused D. Networks/Flat Strategic Alliances E. Cross-Functional Self-Managed F. Customer-Focused (Value Chain)
D. Attunement (of people's hearts and minds)	5A. Leadership & Management 5B. Employee Involvement 5C. Strategic Communications 5D. Human Resources 5E. Culture Change	A. Enforcing Blaming (Incompetence) B. Avoid Blame/ Wait C. Minimal/ Negative D. Poor People-Management E. One Man Rule	A. Directing/ Controlling B. Obedient Doers C. Formal/ Newsletter D. Low Risk E. Command and Control	A. 6 Competencies (All System Levels) B. Empowered C. Strategic/ Positive/Open Book D. Empower Employees to Serve Customer E. Participative Leadership (Facilitate/ Support)
D. Strategic Change Management	6. Strategic Change Management	Avoid Pain Only (No Follow-Through)	Isolated Change Projects	Transformational Change/Proactive
	7. Annual Strategic Review	Not on Radar Screen	Department Goals and Objectives	Strategic Plan—Living and Breathing Updated Document
E. Environment	8. Environmental Scanning	Rarely – Closed System	Today Only	Future/Full SKEPTIC

(continued)

Suggestions for Use: *(continued)*

A High-Performance Organization Survey

Directions: (1) Please circle the number that best describes your organization the way it is today. Then total up the scores at the bottom.

(2) In addition, run a line down the page connecting each circle. The result is probably a zigzag showing where your organization's emphasis has been (high #'s) and not been (low #'s). The extent of your zigzag is the extent of your lack of congruence and fit with your outputs.

		Reactive Organization				Responsible Organization				21st Century High-Performance Organization		Comments
		A				B				C		
A.	**Output**											
	1. Achievement of Results	1	2	3	4	5	6	7	8	9	10	
B.	**Feedback**											
	2. Feedback Loop	1	2	3	4	5	6	7	8	9	10	
A–C.	**Strategic Planning**											
	3. Strategic Planning	1	2	3	4	5	6	7	8	9	10	
D.	**Alignment—Delivery**											
	4A. Operational Tasks (Quality/Service)	1	2	3	4	5	6	7	8	9	10	
	4B. Technology	1	2	3	4	5	6	7	8	9	10	
	4C. Resources	1	2	3	4	5	6	7	8	9	10	
	4D. Organizational Design	1	2	3	4	5	6	7	8	9	10	
	4E. Team Development	1	2	3	4	5	6	7	8	9	10	
	4F. Business Processes	1	2	3	4	5	6	7	8	9	10	
D.	**Attunement—People**											
	5A. Leadership and Management	1	2	3	4	5	6	7	8	9	10	
	5B. Employee Involvement	1	2	3	4	5	6	7	8	9	10	
	5C. Strategic Communications	1	2	3	4	5	6	7	8	9	10	
	5D. Human Resources	1	2	3	4	5	6	7	8	9	10	
	5E. Culture Change	1	2	3	4	5	6	7	8	9	10	
D.	**Strategic Change Mgmt. Process**											
	6. Strategic Change Management	1	2	3	4	5	6	7	8	9	10	
	7. Annual Strategic Review	1	2	3	4	5	6	7	8	9	10	
E.	**Environment**											
	8. Environmental Scanning (SKEPTIC)	1	2	3	4	5	6	7	8	9	10	

TOTAL SCORE = ________ (160 points possible)

A. High-Performing Organization = 110 to 160 points
B. Responsible Organization = 60 to 110 points
C. Reactive Organization = 0 to 60 points

(continued)

Suggestions for Use: *(continued)*

2. **Strategic Change Impact Exercise**

   (Using the A-B-C-D Phases and the Organization as a System Model)

   What components of your organization will/should be impacted by the major change/ strategy you propose? Which change/strategy? ____________________

Which Components Are Impacted?

Phase A

1. ________ Vision
2. ________ Mission
3. ________ Organizational Values
4. ________ Organizational Culture
5. ________ Organizational Identity/Image and Positioning
6. ________ Key Environmental Stakeholders (List):

   ____

   ____

   ____
7. ________ Strategic Plan
8. ________ Quality Services
9. ________ Customer Service
10. ________ Quality Products
11. ________ Customer Choices
12. ________ Lower Cost Products/Services
13. ________ Speed/Responsiveness

Phase B

14. ________ Key Success Factors—Outcome Measures (List):

    ____

    ____

    ____

Phase C

15. ________ Other Core Strategies (List): ____________

    ____
16. ________ Dept. Annual Plans

(continued)

Suggestions for Use: *(concluded)*

Which Components Are Impacted? (concluded)

Phase D

17. ________ Operating Tasks
18. ________ Leadership Development System/Skills
19. ________ Empowerment
20. ________ Key Internal Stakeholders (List): ____

    ____

21. ________ Staffing Levels (Recruitment/Selection)
22. ________ Facilities/Equipment—Physical Resources
23. ________ Strategic-Communication Processes
24. ________ Resources (Financial)
25. ________ Technology
26. ________ Organizational Structure/Design
27. ________ Job Design/Definition
28. ________ Employee Involvement
29. ________ Strategic Business Units (SBU)
30. ________ Succession Planning
31. ________ Reward System (Pay/Non-Pay)
32. ________ Performance Appraisal
33. ________ Training and Development
34. ________ Business Processes
35. ________ Policies and Procedures
36. ________ Team Development
37. ________ Annual Strategic Review (and Update)
38. ________ Change-Management Structures

Phase **E**

What's changing in the environment?

39. ________ To support us:

    ____

    ____

    ____

40. ________ To defeat us:

    ____

    ____

    ____

Note: Use this to build a Comprehensive Change Management Action Plan.

Tool #27 Reinventing Strategic Management (Planning and Change)

Application of the A-B-C-D Systems Framework

"Reinventing Strategic Management" (Planning and Change) is a copyrighted Centre for Strategic Management process and a different way to use systems thinking and the A-B-C-D framework. Use it to tailor and create various strategic planning processes and integrate them into strategic change.

➥ **For example:** There are many uses of the four phases.

Use the Four Phases of Systems Thinking:

A Creating Your Ideal Future (Output)

B Measurements of Success (Feedback Loop)

C Converting Strategies to Operations (The Input to Action)

D Successful Implementation (Throughput/Actions)

E and Environmental Scanning (ongoing)

Potential Uses (Be sure to go beyond planning into strategic change on each use)

1. **Comprehensive Strategic Plan:** A comprehensive strategic planning process for an entire organization will require 10 to 16 days offsite to complete steps 1 through 10, tailored to the organization. (This is beyond our scope here. However, the 10-Step Model is shown on page 185. For more information on this full process and a full 4-page Executive Summary, call the Centre at 619-275-6528.)

2. **Strategic Planning Quick:** A shortened noncomprehensive version of strategic planning for an entire organization will require 5 days offsite (minimum).

3. **Business Planning:** To conduct a shortened 3-year business planning process for a line business unit or major support function/section/program (i.e., element of the larger organization), you will need 5 to 10 days, depending on whether #1 above is first accomplished.

4. **Micro Strategic Planning:** To develop a strategic plan for a small organization or business, you will need 2 days offsite; the rest can be accomplished without meetings.

5. **Strategic Life Plan:** To conduct a personal (person, family, couple) life plan, see Tool #28.

6. **Strategic Human Resource Management:** To create "the ***people edge***" in your organization, see Tool #29.

7. **Leadership Development System:** To enhance your leadership roles and competencies for a competitive business edge, see Tool #34.

8. **Organizational Systems Model:** To systematically diagnose any change effort and dramatically increase your probability of success, see Tool #26.

9. **Team Effectiveness:** To comprehensively focus on all aspects of teams to dramatically enhance their outcomes and effectiveness, see Tools # 31, 32, and 33.

The Different Uses

1. Comprehensive Strategic Plan

Tailored to Your Needs (Reinventing Strategic Management)

Instructions: Based on your current understanding of the Reinventing Strategic Planning and Change Management Models (i.e., Strategic Management), please list the importance (H-M-L) of developing each potential deliverable for your organization.

Strategic Planning—Steps #2–5

1. __________ Environmental Scanning (SKEPTIC)
2. __________ Vision
3. __________ Mission
4. __________ Values
5. __________ Driving Force(s)

5a. __________ Rallying Cry

6. __________ Key Success Factors
7. __________ Current State Assessment

7a. __________ Scenario/Contingency Planning

8. __________ Core Strategies/Actions/Yearly Priorities

Business Units—Step #6

9. __________ SBU/MPAs Defined

9a. __________ Business/Key Support Plans (3-Year Mini Strategic Plans)

Annual Plans—Step #7

10. __________ Annual Plans/Priorities/Department Plans
11. __________ Resource Allocation/Budgeting (including guidelines)

Individuals/Teams

12. __________ Individual Performance Management System—Tied to Strategic Planning

12a. __________ Rewards and Recognition System—Tied to Strategic Planning

Bridge the Gap—Step #8

13. __________ Plan-to-Implement Day

(continued)

1. Comprehensive Strategic Plan *(concluded)*

Focus on the Vital Few ("STAR" Results)—Align Delivery—Step #9

14a. _________ Quality Products and Services

14b. _________ Customer Service

14c. _________ Organization Structure/Redesign

14d. _________ Business Process Reengineering (BPR) to lower costs/improve response to customer *(customer focused)*

14e. _________ Blow Out Bureaucracy (and Waste)

14f. _________ Speed/Responsiveness

Management Development—Attunement of People/Support Systems—Step #9

15a. _________ Professional Management and Leadership Competencies, Skills and Practices Workshop (trainer-coach-facilitator)

15b. _________ Skills created through the Managing Strategic Change Workshop

15c. _________ HR Programs/Processes (E.D.C.)

15d. _________ Values/Cultural Change

15e. _________ Strategic Budgeting

15f. _________ Information Technology (T.S.G.)

Yearly Update—Step #10

16. _________ Annual Strategic Review and Update

17a. _________ Teamwork for Executive Team

17b. _________ Teamwork for Department Teams

17c. _________ Teamwork for Cross-Functional Relationships/Teams

2. Strategic Planning Quick is depicted on the next page.

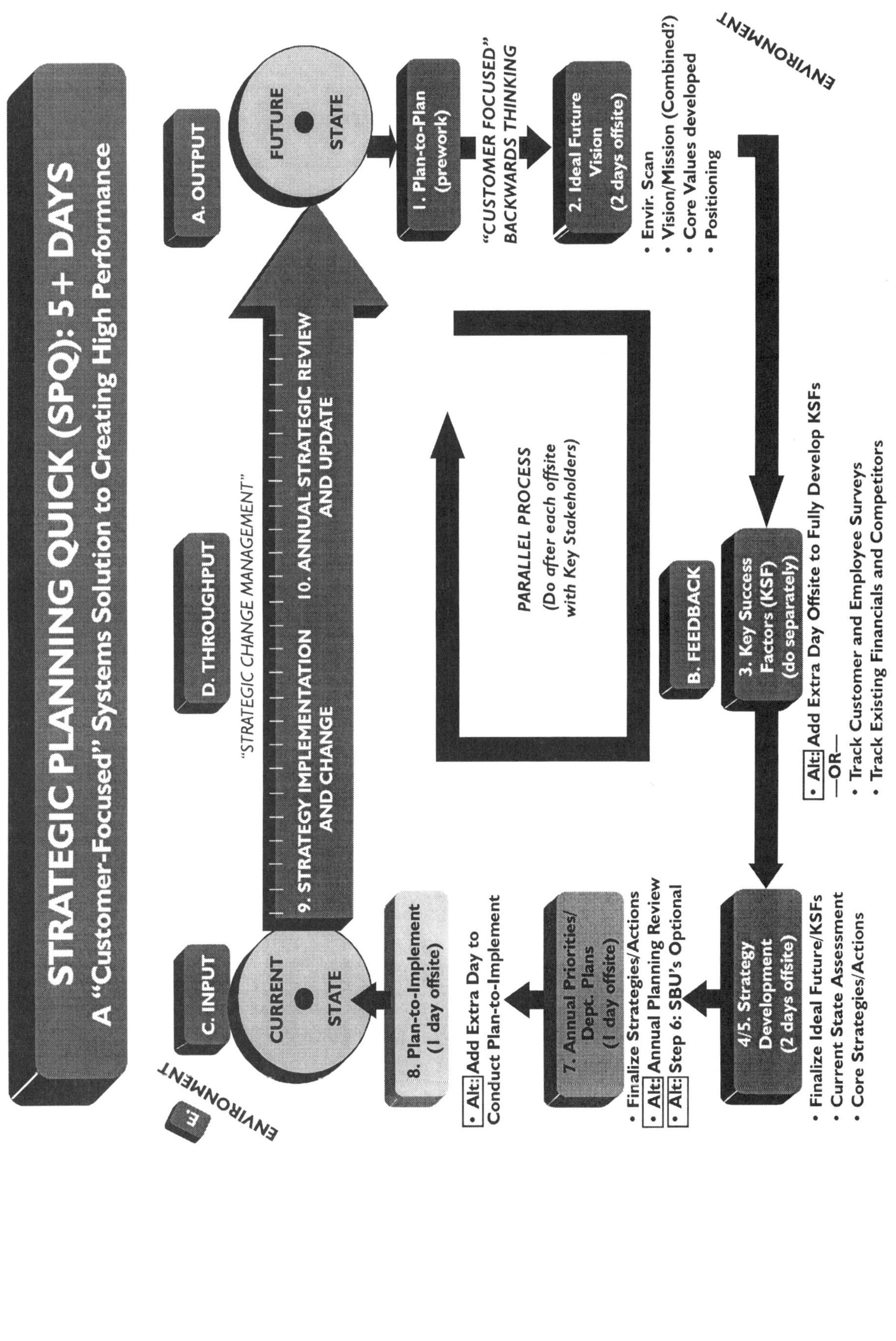

Adapted from Steiner (1979), our experiences, a 1991 "Best Practices" literature search, and client feedback ever since.

3. 3-Year Business Planning

For all Strategic Business Units and Major Organizational Support Units

Step #1: Create Your Own Ideal Future Vision Phase A

- Duration—2 days
- Conduct educational briefing and Plan-to-Plan/Corporate Strategic Plan review.
- Refine or develop your vision, mission, and values in draft form (Step #2), using corporate's as a guide.
- Develop corporate goals with outcome measures of success (alternative).*
- Develop key stakeholder parallel process.
- You may need to skip Phase B success measures at first, due to time constraints.

Step #2: Convert Strategies to Operations Phase C

- Duration—2 days
- Finalize your ideal future vision (Step #2).
- Conduct current state assessment (Step #4).
- Develop your core strategies (Step #5) and top priority action items for the next year—*"the glue".*
- Set up second key stakeholder feedback.

Step #3: Strategy Implementation and Change Phase D

- Duration—1 day every two months, at first
- First set of tasks: finalize core strategies/actions (Step #5 and #7).
- Set up quarterly meeting of the Strategic Change Leadership Steering Committee (Step #9) to maintain plan and success/decide on Step #6.
- Conduct plan-to-implement (Step #8).

***Notes: Feedback Loop Phase B**

- Key Success Factors not recommended due to time limits.
- Instead, monitor core strategies and existing financials, and survey customers and employees.

4. "Micro" Strategic Planning

For Smaller Organizations

Step #1: Create Your Own Ideal Future Vision (1-day offsite) Phase A

- Conduct educational briefing and plan-to-plan before the offsite. (Include key stakeholder parallel process and environmental scanning.) Phase E
- Refine or develop your vision, mission, and values in draft form. (Step #2)
- Develop a key success factor process outside the offsites. Phase B
- Set up current state assessment, to be accomplished between Steps #1 and #2. Phase C

Step #2: Plan-to-Implement Your Own Future Successfully (1-day offsite) Phase D

- Finalize your ideal future vision. (Step #2)
- Present/review current state assessment. (Step #4)
- Develop your core strategies (Step #5) and action items.
- Set up annual planning/budgeting process to follow this micro strategic planning.

Step #3: Strategy Implementation and Change (1 day each quarter) Phase D

- First set of tasks: finalize core strategies and annual plans. (Steps #5 and #7)
- Set up quarterly meeting of the Strategic Change Leadership Steering Committee (Step #9) to maintain plan success; decide on Step #6; conduct plan-to-implement (Step #8).

Note: **Feedback Loop** (accomplish outside the three planning steps above) Phase B

- KSFs not recommended due to "micro" process.
- Instead, monitor core strategies and existing financials; plus survey customers and employees.
- Do this outside the planning steps/offsites above; once completed, present to Board/planning team for final approval.

Tool #28 Strategic Life Planning

Application of Seven Levels of Living Systems and The A-B-C-D Systems Model

Look before, or you'll find yourself behind.

—Benjamin Franklin

The clarity of an individual's search for meaning is important to the organization's success as well as the individual's success. The better the match, the better the results will be, organizationally and professionally. Thus, managers need to help employees develop not only a career path but also *a Strategic Life Plan* to stimulate employee initiative and focus their energy. The A-B-C-D framework within your environment is fully applicable to this goal, as shown in simplified form below and in more detail on the next page.

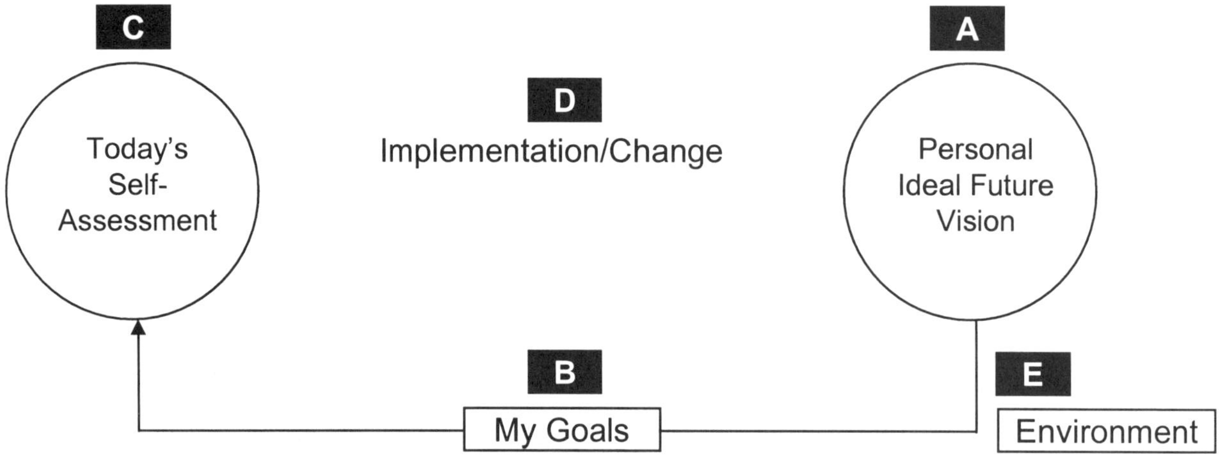

My vision for myself in the Year __________ to __________.

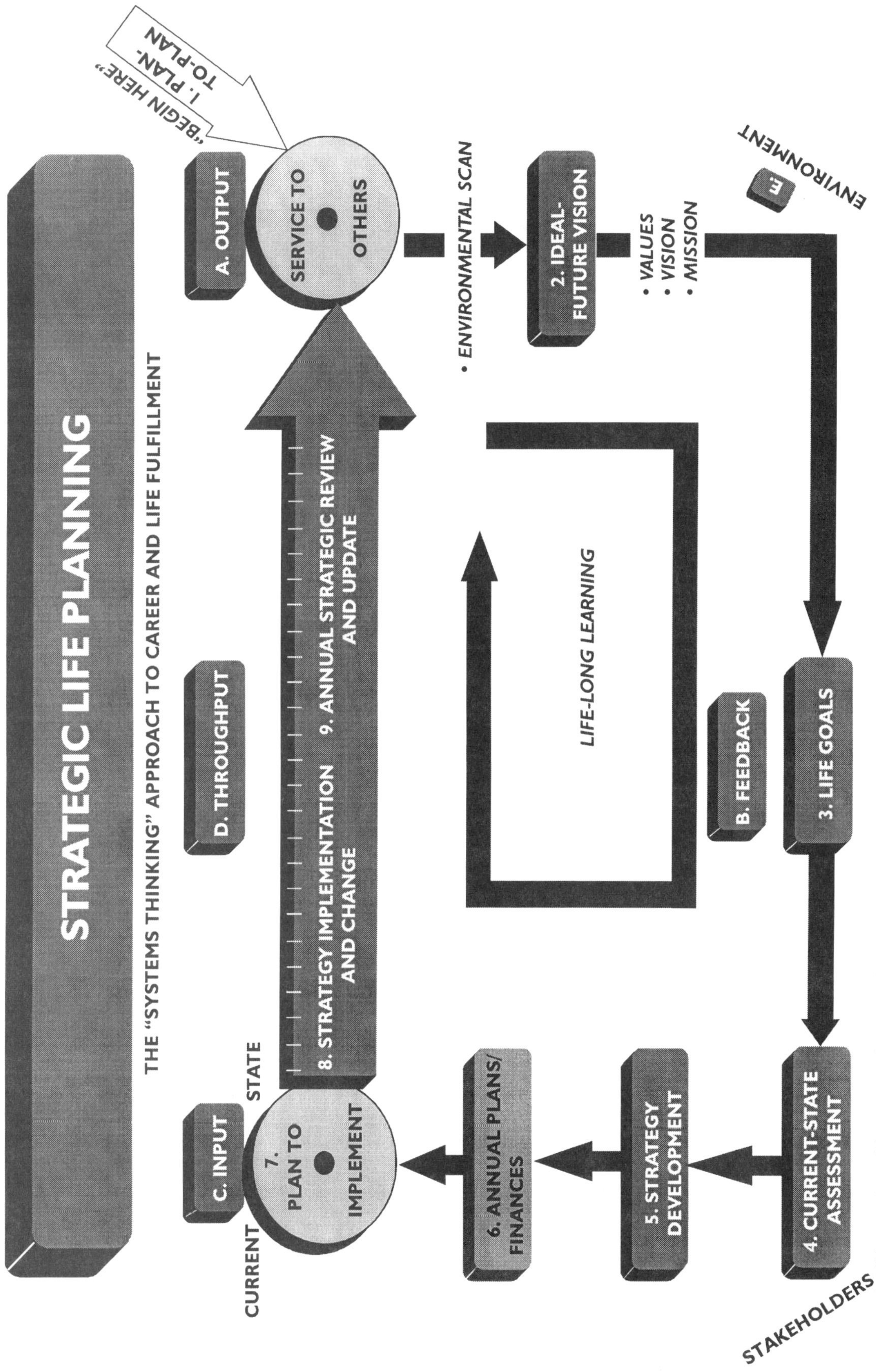

4th Edition • Adapted from General Systems Theory, and Haines Associates, our experiences, a "Best Practices" Literature search, and client feedback ever since.

1420 Monitor Road, San Diego, CA 92110 • (619) 275-6528 • FAX (619) 275-0324
E-mail: csmintl@san.rr.com • www.csmintl@.com

Start with Personal Visioning—"*Backwards Thinking*"

Use the following worksheets to begin putting Strategic Life Planning into practice in *your* life.

Worksheet I: Personal Vision Exercise

1. Brainstorm your personal vision; then consider: "How will I know I have achieved my vision?" Provide answers, using the chart below.

Roles	Vision	Measures of Success at Year ________
Personal		
1. Physical Health		
2. Mental/Learning		
3. Emotional/Spiritual (Ethical)		
Financial		
4. Lifestyle/Wealth		
Professional		
5. Job/Career		
Interpersonal		
6. Social/Friends		
7. Community/Service		
8. Immediate Family (Home, Spouse)		
9. Extended Family (Parents, Siblings)		

2. Now try to get your vision down to a single statement.

3. Think of what your rallying cry should be, and put it into eight words or less.

Worksheet II: Personal Values Exercise

Rank the following values from 1 to 15, with 1 being the most important to you and 15 being the least important to you.

Values	Actual	Desired
1. Having good relationships with colleagues	________	________
2. Professional reputation/respect	________	________
3. Achievement of organization/unit goals	________	________
4. Teamwork and collaboration	________	________
5. Leisure time for enjoyment/fun	________	________
6. Wealth and prosperity	________	________
7. Fitness and health	________	________
8. Contribution, service to society, community	________	________
9. Acknowledging others' achievements	________	________
10. Autonomy/freedom to act	________	________
11. Personal growth	________	________
12. Time with family/close friends	________	________
13. Ethical behavior	________	________
14. Excitement and challenge	________	________
15. Spiritual/religious time	________	________

Note: If a person's vision and values don't match the organization's, you have a *motivation gap*. Identify such gaps and deal with them personally and organizationally.

4. Now continue on and complete the rest of the A-B-C-D Phases of Strategic Life Planning (see model; call the Centre at (619) 275-6528 for a complete book and workbook on *Strategic Career Life and Planning,* if desired).

Tool #29 HR Strategic Planning

Application of Systems Dynamics #4: A-B-C-D Input-Output Model; and Seven Levels of Living Systems

Use a systems thinking approach to creating a HR strategic plan combining both the A-B-C-D model and the HR Systems Content Model.

A. Human Resource Strategic Planning

The People Systems to Create a High-Performance Organization

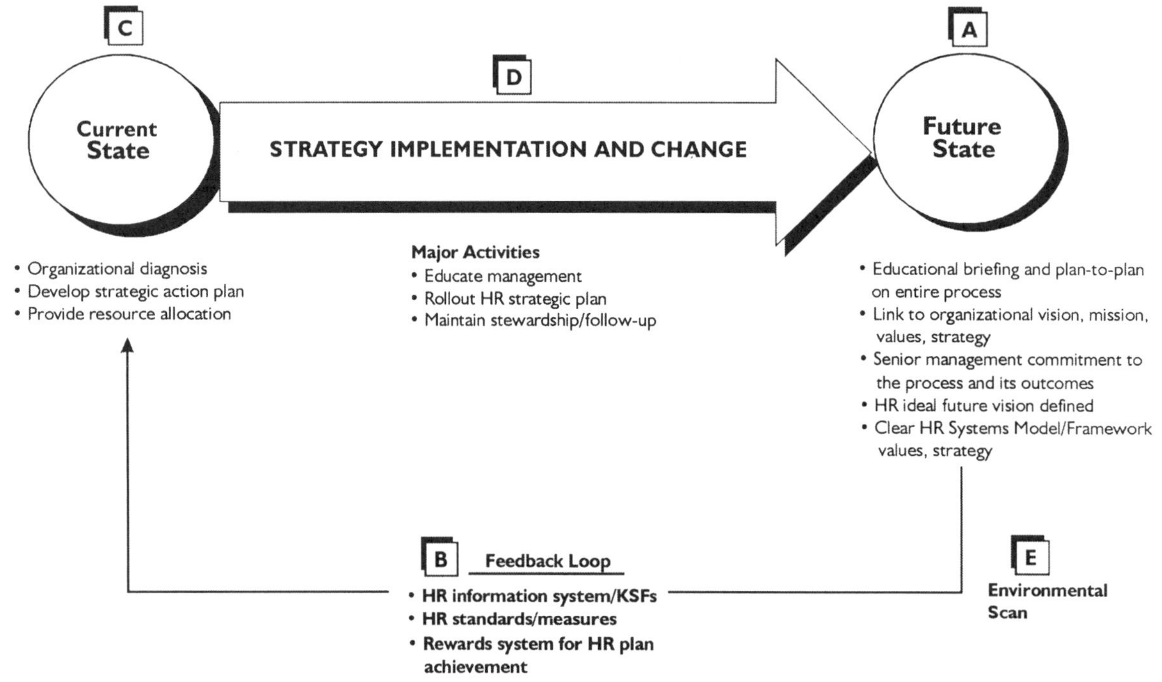

Suggestions for Use: **Human Resource Strategic Planning**

The People Systems to Create a High-Performance Organization

Note: This follows the same steps as strategic planning for an organization. The main difference is that you do strategic planning for the HR function/department, but not the entire organization.

Phase A Future State

- Conduct educational briefing and plan-to-plan on entire process.
- Link to organizational vision, mission, values, and strategy. (Internal environment Phase E)
- Scan the external environment. (Phase E)
- Obtain senior management commitment to the process and its outcomes.
- Define Human Resource ideal future vision.
- Develop clear Human Resource Systems Model/framework. (Use our A-B-C-D framework.)

Phase B Feedback Loop

- Develop HR information systems/Key Success Factors on HR based on the HR Systems Model.
- Set HR standards, measures.
- Use surveys to measure them.
- Institute rewards system for HR plan achievement.
- Get stakeholder involvement and input on this as well.

Phase C Current State

- Conduct organizational diagnosis on HR system effectiveness and its fit with the other tracks.
- Develop strategic action items to support the plan.
- Make sure that the HR strategic plan includes a consideration of all aspects of the HR Systems Model.

  i.e. — succession/manpower planning
  — career development
  — hiring, assimilation, start-up
  — ER/HR policies
  — union–management relations
  — organization and management development
- Provide resource allocation to support the desired changes.

(continued)

Suggestions for Use: **Human Resource Strategic Planning** *(concluded)*

The People Systems to Create a High-Performance Organization (concluded)

Phase D Strategy Implementation and Change—Major Activities

- Educate management on HR systems and organizational behavior.
- Rollout/communicate the HR strategic plan.
- Become/maintain stewardship of the HR strategic plan, organizational cultures, values.
- Ensure fit/integration/coordination with any other major improvement processes (i.e., systems fit, alignment, and integrity).

B. HR as a System

Are all of your HR programs and processes linked to your organization's strategic plan (especially vision, values, and strategies)? The Centre has developed a Strategic HR Management Systems Model. It addresses such issues as people-flow and movement over time.

See the HR Systems Model that follows, as well as a comprehensive list of HR practices/programs to help you assess your best practices in HR.

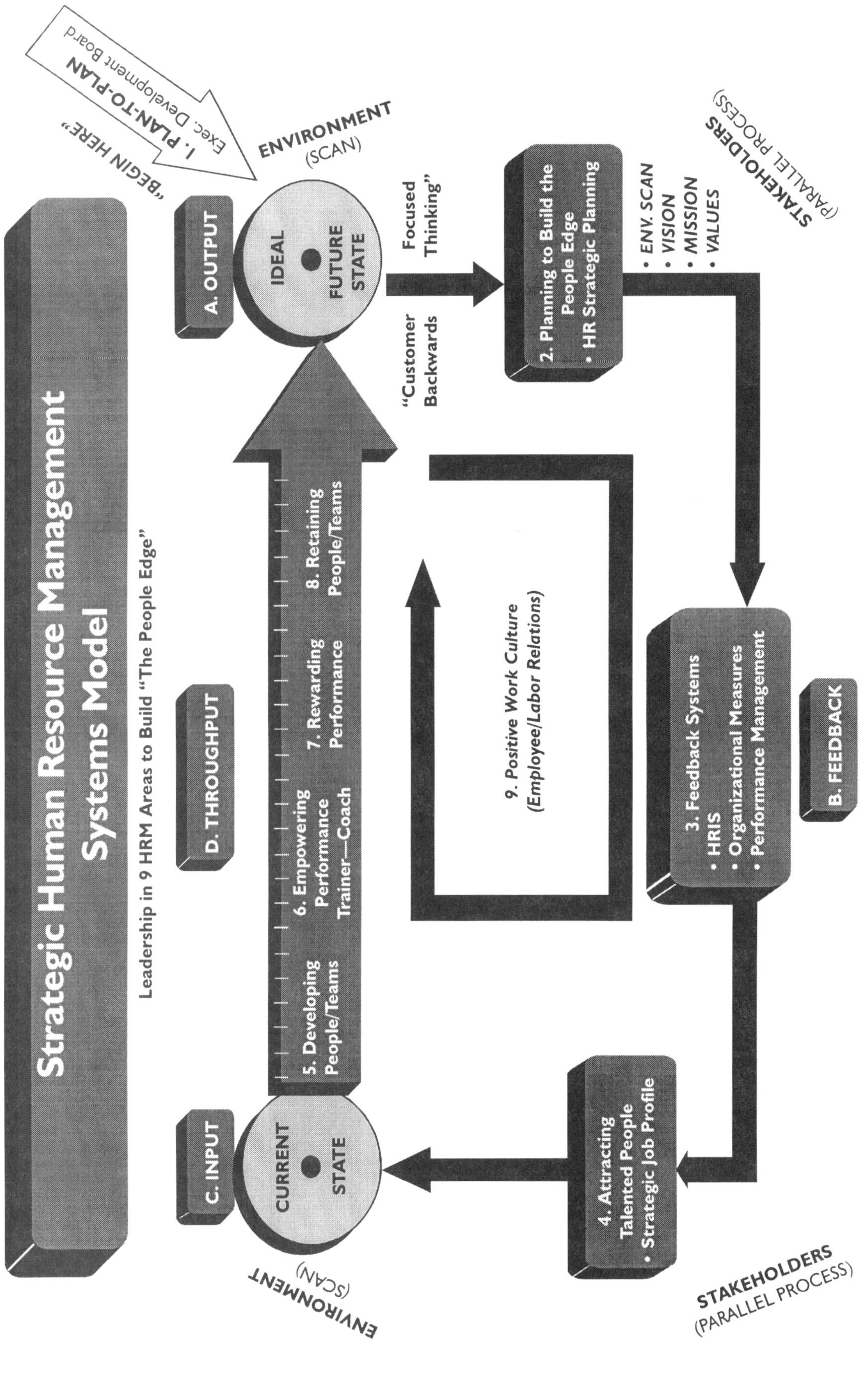

Adapted from General Systems Theory and Haines Associates 1978.
Based on 1984 and 1992 literature searches and client feedback ever since.
CSM has offices in the USA • Canada • Australia • New Zealand

1420 Monitor Road, San Diego, CA 92110
(619) 275-6528 • FAX (619) 275-0324

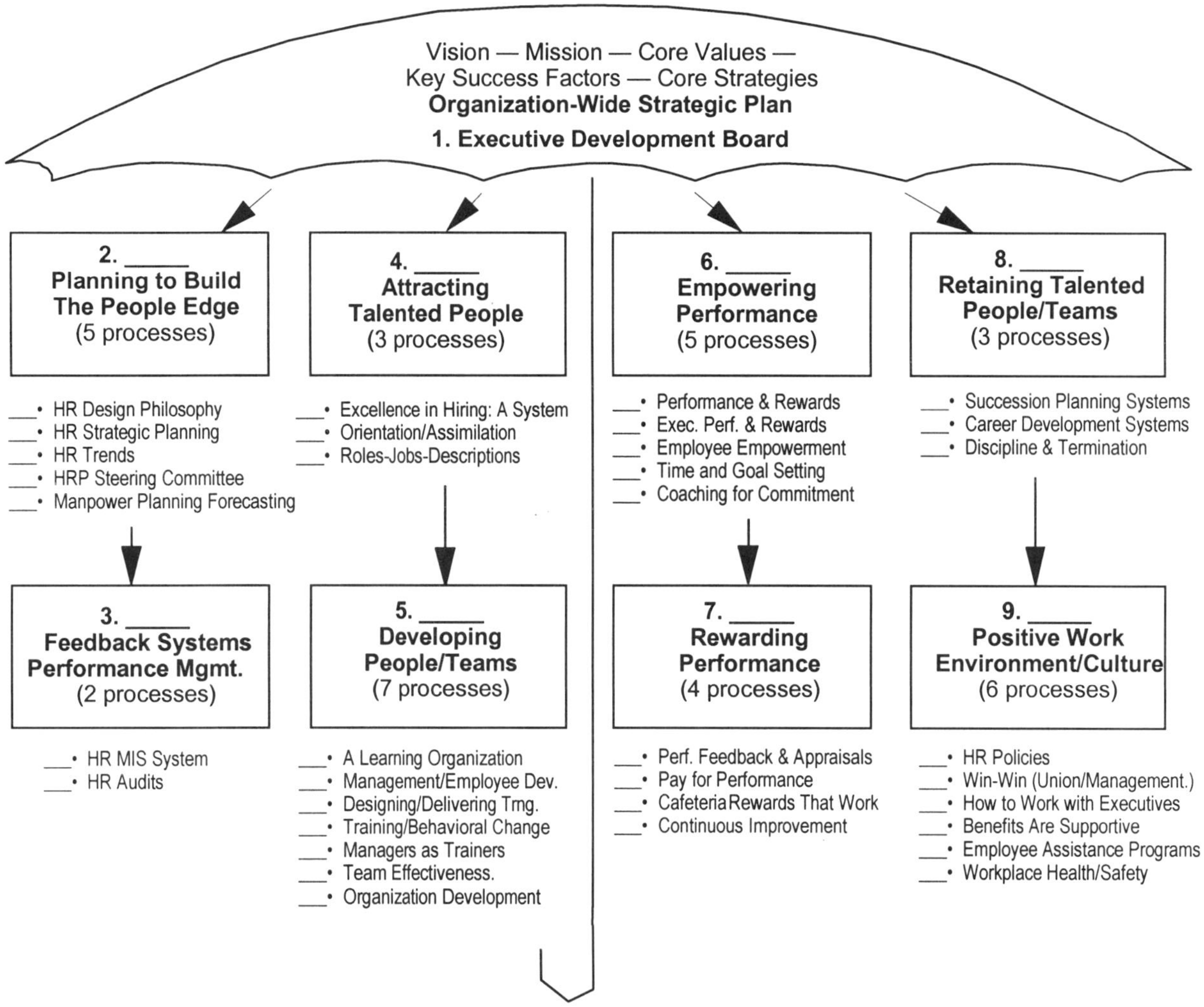

Suggestions for Use:

1. Use the detailed list on the next three pages (based on the above figure) to do a comprehensive assessment of your organization's "people practices."

2. After the comprehensive assessment, what actions do you need to do as a part of your strategies and actions in your HR strategic plan?

8 Areas and 35 Key Human Resource Management Processes

Instructions: Fill out the status of each HRM process today using a scale of 1–10.

Processes	Current State Assessment					Score
	(1) Reactive Organization —Survival Only		(5) Responsible Organization —Traditional Control		(10) 21st Century High-Performing Organization —Proactive Empowerment	
#1 Planning						**#1 Planning**
1. Organization's HR Design Philosophy Clear	(1)	2 3 4	(5)	6 7 8 9	(10)	Total Score: ______ 5 processes = ____ (avg.)
2. HR Strategic Planning	(1)	2 3 4	(5)	6 7 8 9	(10)	
3. HR Trends: Year 2000 Clear	(1)	2 3 4	(5)	6 7 8 9	(10)	
4. HRP Steering Committee Established	(1)	2 3 4	(5)	6 7 8 9	(10)	
5. Manpower Planning and Forecasting Completed	(1)	2 3 4	(5)	6 7 8 9	(10)	
#2 Feeding Back						**#2 Feeding Back**
6. HR MIS System in Place	(1)	2 3 4	(5)	6 7 8 9	(10)	Total Score: ______
7. HR Audits Done Regularly	(1)	2 3 4	(5)	6 7 8 9	(10)	2 processes = ____ (avg.)
#3 Attracting						**#3 Attracting**
8. Excellence in Hiring: A System in Place	(1)	2 3 4	(5)	6 7 8 9	(10)	Total Score: ______ 3 processes = ____ (avg.)
9. Smart Start (Orientation/ Assimilation) Done	(1)	2 3 4	(5)	6 7 8 9	(10)	
10. Roles—Jobs—Descriptions Clear	(1)	2 3 4	(5)	6 7 8 9	(10)	
#4 Empowering						**#4 Empowering**
11. 21st Century Performance and Rewards System in Place	(1)	2 3 4	(5)	6 7 8 9	(10)	Total Score: ______ 5 processes = ____ (avg.)
12. Exec. Performance and Rewards System in Place	(1)	2 3 4	(5)	6 7 8 9	(10)	
13. Employee Empowerment and Performance Allowed	(1)	2 3 4	(5)	6 7 8 9	(10)	
14. Practical Time and Goal-Setting Tools Used	(1)	2 3 4	(5)	6 7 8 9	(10)	
15. Coaching for Commitment and Results Used	(1)	2 3 4	(5)	6 7 8 9	(10)	

(continued)

8 Areas and 35 Key Human Resource Management Processes (continued)

Processes Continued	Current State Assessment					Score
	(1) Reactive Organization —Survival Only		(5) Responsible Organization —Traditional Control		(10) 21st Century High-Performing Organization —Proactive Empowerment	
#5 Rewarding						**#5 Rewarding**
16. Performance Feedback	(1)	2 3 4	(5)	6 7 8 9	(10)	Total Score: ______
17. Pay for Performance: Failures/Solutions Found	(1)	2 3 4	(5)	6 7 8 9	(10)	4 processes = ____ (avg.)
18. "Cafeteria" Rewards That Work	(1)	2 3 4	(5)	6 7 8 9	(10)	
19. Continuous Improvement/ Suggestions Rewarded	(1)	2 3 4	(5)	6 7 8 9	(10)	
#6 Developing						**#6 Developing**
20. A Learning Organization Created	(1)	2 3 4	(5)	6 7 8 9	(10)	Total Score: ______
21. Management/Employee Development System Exist	(1)	2 3 4	(5)	6 7 8 9	(10)	7 processes = ____ (avg.)
22. Designing and Delivering Training (Adult Learning)	(1)	2 3 4	(5)	6 7 8 9	(10)	
23. Training/Behavioral Change Reinforced	(1)	2 3 4	(5)	6 7 8 9	(10)	
24. Managers as Trainers: A How-To Guide Established	(1)	2 3 4	(5)	6 7 8 9	(10)	
25. Team Building and Effectiveness	(1)	2 3 4	(5)	6 7 8 9	(10)	
26. Organization Design and Development	(1)	2 3 4	(5)	6 7 8 9	(10)	
#7 Retraining						**#7 Retaining**
27. Succession-Planning Systems Institutionalized	(1)	2 3 4	(5)	6 7 8 9	(10)	Total Score: ______
28. Career Development Institutionalized	(1)	2 3 4	(5)	6 7 8 9	(10)	3 processes = ____ (avg.)
29. Progressive Discipline and Terminations Effective	(1)	2 3 4	(5)	6 7 8 9	(10)	

(continued)

8 Areas and 35 Key Human Resource Management Processes (concluded)

Processes Concluded	Current State Assessment					Score
	(1) Reactive Organization —Survival Only		(5) Responsible Organization —Traditional Control		(10) 21st Century High-Performing Organization —Proactive Empowerment	
#8 Supporting						**#8 Supporting**
30. HR Policies (Supporting Service vs. Control)	(1)	2 3 4	(5)	6 7 8 9	(10)	Total Score: ______
31. Win-Win (Union/ Management Relationship	(1)	2 3 4	(5)	6 7 8 9	(10)	6 processes = ____ (avg.)
32. How to Work with Senior Executives Clear	(1)	2 3 4	(5)	6 7 8 9	(10)	**Grand Total (350 possible) ______**
33. Benefits as Supportive	(1)	2 3 4	(5)	6 7 8 9	(10)	**35 processes =**
34. Employee Assistance Programs Established	(1)	2 3 4	(5)	6 7 8 9	(10)	**____ (avg.)**
35. Workplace Health/Safety	(1)	2 3 4	(5)	6 7 8 9	(10)	

Tool #30 Hiring and Promotions as a System

Application of Systems Dynamics #9: Hierarchy; and the A-B-C-D Systems Model

Make sure every selection decision you make is successful. Take the guesswork out of selection each time and every time with the A-B-C-D Systems Thinking Approach.

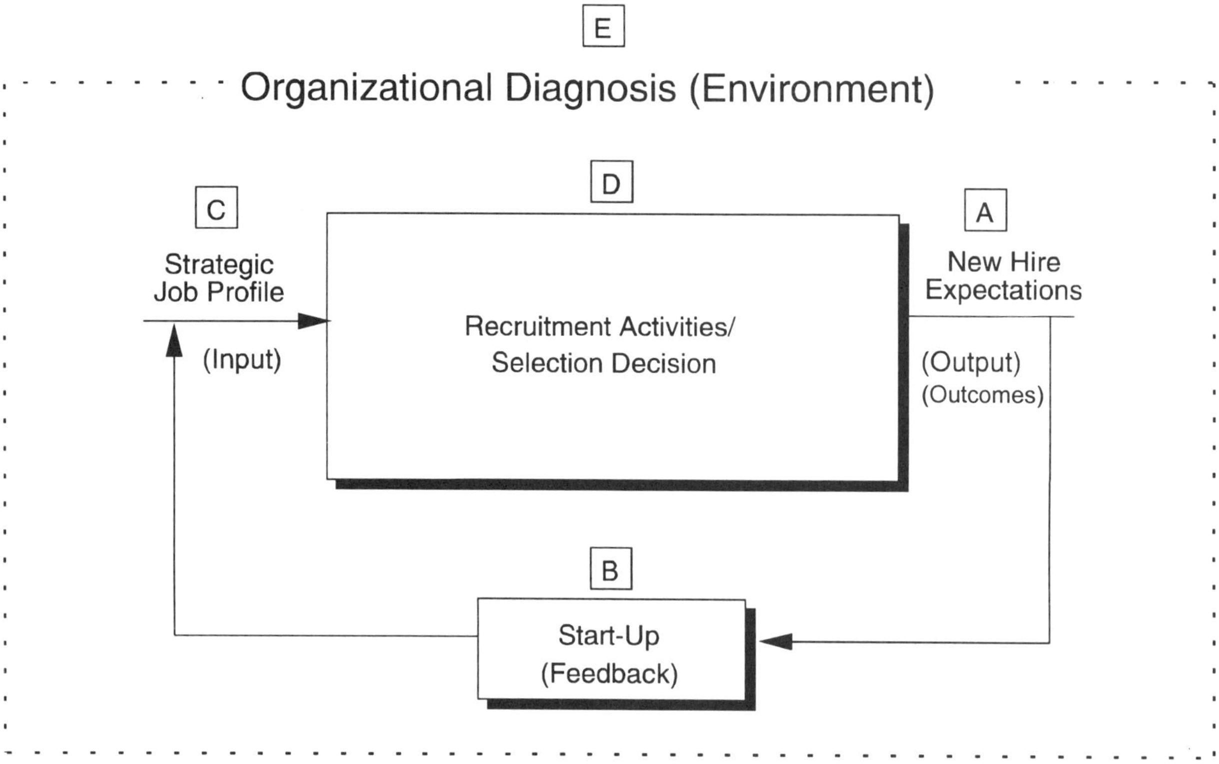

Build a Strategic Job Profile (SJP)

This is the beginning of your search for the right person. Start by defining your outcomes (Phase A) and expectations of the new hire; then convert it to your Strategic Job Profile. Use it as your input to drive decision making (Phase **C**).

1. Title?

   Pay range/expected offer?

   Expected start date?

2. Responsibilities and design of job?
3. Key other jobs and reporting relationships (3-way: up, down, and sideways) and fit with this job?
4. Hiring manager's goals/expectations for this job?
5. What is the supervisor's managerial style/personality?
6. What are the initial priorities/tasks of this job?
7. What challenges/problems exist with this job?
8. What resources are available (people, money, materials) to do the job?
9. Qualifications/knowledge, experience required for this job?

   a. Required? b. Preferred?

10. What personal values are desired of this person for the job?
11. What mix of skills are needed?
    - technical __________
    - interpersonal __________
    - managerial/leadership __________
    - conceptual/strategic __________

    = 100%

12. What type of personality/communication style is desired in this job (i.e., driver, expressive, amiable, analytical)?
13. How does this job fit in the life cycle of this organization?
14. What organizational strategic thrust(s) must this person agree with and help implement?

____ ____________________

Hiring Authority Date

The Selection Decision Process Phase D

1. Decision meetings held? (See below, "Successful Hiring")

2. Fast vs. right?

3. Reference checks/secretaries/back doors—whose responsibility?

4. Resumes verified, especially education?

5. Dinner/informal interview (get to know the person)?

6. Criteria is Strategic Job Profile?

7. Biases of your own—overcome?

8. Reasons why not to hire (when you "like them")?

Successful Hiring (Best Practices) is most effectively done through: Phase D

- multiple interviews
- a group-decision process
- comparing perspectives
- full references
- checking past successes/behaviors as a guide to future success/behavior

➥ **For example:** Selection Decision Matrix

When hiring for a key position in your organization, place 2 to 4 finalists into a "Selection Decision Matrix" and compare each finalist against your decision criteria.

SELECTION DECISION MATRIX				
	FINALISTS SKILLS (H-M-L)			
STRATEGIC JOB PROFILE	**1.**	**2.**	**3.**	**4.**
1. Job Design 2. Roles (3-way) 3. Expectations, Goals				
4. Initial Priorities 5. Challenges, Problems 6. Resources Available				
7. Supervisor Style 8. Qualifications, Knowledge, Experience 9. Personality, Values				
10. Management Style 11. Mix of Skills: 12. Technical 13. Interpersonal 14. Management/Leadership 15. Conceptual/Strategy				
16. Compensation 17. Employment Contracts				

Suggestions for Use:

1. Note: Successful hiring is most effectively done through the following best practices:
   - A clear, strategic job profile
   - Multiple interviews
   - A group-decision process meeting
   - Use of the selection matrix
   - Comparing perspectives
   - Full references
   - Checking past success/behaviors as a guide to future success/behavior
2. This systems approach can also be used for promotion. Add performance reviews and supervisory recommendations to your list of considerations. Also pay attention to the outcomes of the job the person now holds and the outcomes expected in the new position.

Tool #31 The Team as a System

Application of Systems Dynamics #4: Input-Output Model; and Seven Levels of Living Systems

Teams are crucial to success in creating the high-performance organization. Thus, teams of all types need clarity in their outcomes and regular feedback on the status of their progression toward these outcomes.

- ➥ **For example:** Common learning/feedback events for the team as a whole are key to team effectiveness.
- ➥ **For example:** This is just as true for families as it is for organizations. Families need to learn from their intense experiences of living together how they are making life pleasant and successful for one another, as well as what is dysfunctional. They also need to learn how they can change.

How does team effectiveness occur? As always, a regular feedback loop is the key. Teams and families rarely take the time to process a significant event and how people felt about it. Post-mortems, debriefs, checkups, and feedback/reinforcement sessions are rarely held.

Teams and Team Learning

Our A-B-C-D Systems Model is one way to look at teams as a system.

Suggestions for Use:

The team model below can help focus your energies and attention.

Effective Team Learning—Ask yourself and your teammates to answer the following questions. Then, create an action plan for needed improvements.

Phase A: Team Outputs—Our Shared Ideal Future

1. What should we achieve?
   - Shared vision
   - Values
   - Clear mission

   Does the team identify/clarify its vision, values, and mission and is it beginning to see its purpose in light of the larger organization?

Phase B: Feedback—Results/Measures, Content/Process, Team Learning

2. How are we doing? What feedback from the environment do we get?
   - Key Success Factors
   - Environmental scan/SKEPTIC
   - Customer satisfaction

   Is the team aware of its environment and does it take this into consideration all the time? Is feedback constantly sought?

Phase C: Inputs—Assessments and Strategies (Priorities)

3. Where do we stand today vs. our mission? What is the gap?

3a. What key strategies (goals) and short-term priorities do we have to make to progress towards our mission?

- Team SWOT assessment
- Individual performance assessment
- Focused few strategies/goals
- Top 10 action priorities

3b. Are team members clear and do they agree on the short-term collective and individual priorities, time frames, and accountability?

Phase D: Throughput

4. Who does what? Are the structures, roles, and responsibilities clear?

- Team structure
- Individual roles and objectives
- Team support and expectations/time frames

Do team members define the team's interdependencies and determine which tasks require coordination? In addition, are roles and responsibilities reviewed and procedures and expectations/time frames clarified?

4a. How do we make decisions and procedures that optimize quality and acceptance?

Healthy Norms:

- Meeting management
- Planning processes
- Conflict management
- Reward system
- Problem solving
- Decision making/consensus

Has the team developed healthy norms and procedures for solving problems, making decisions, and managing all its processes and procedures?

4b. How effectively do we work together? Are our relationships healthy and honest?

- Work style
- Communications style
- Strengths and limitations
- Process skills
- Interpersonal feedback

Are our working relationships regularly examined and more productive ways of working together established individually and collectively?

Phase E: The Environment

5. This is very important to team effectiveness. Look at two different areas.

- What organizational factors and people impact this team?
- What is changing in the external environment that impacts this team?

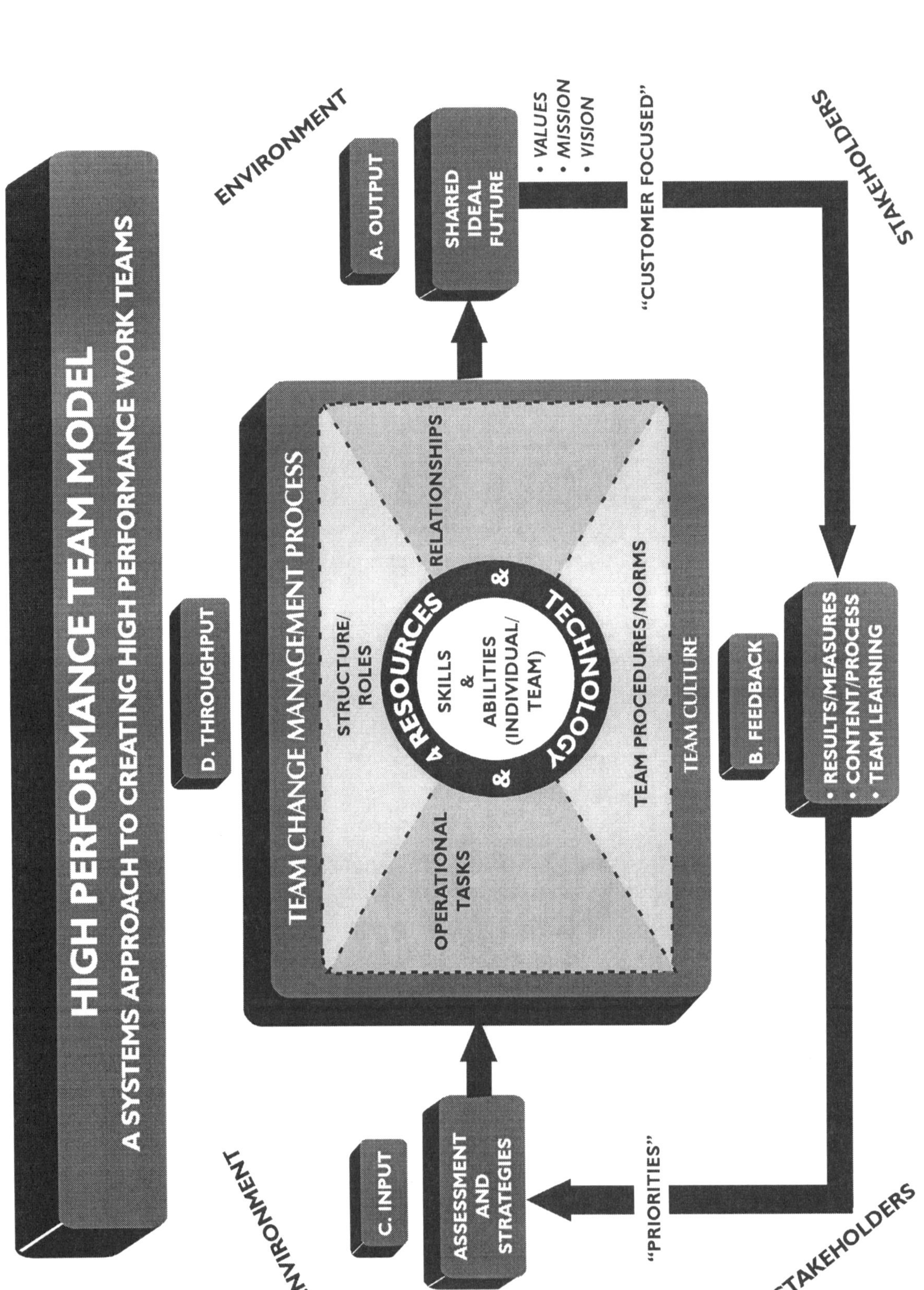

Adapted from General Systems Theory and Haines Associates, 1979; and client feedback ever since.

1420 Monitor Road, San Diego, CA 92110 • (619) 275-6528 • FAX (619) 275-0324

Tool #32 Systemic Team Building

Application of Systems Dynamics #4: A-B-C-D Input-Output Model

Systems thinking is the method for **problem solving and team building.**

Step 1: Define the ideal state in the future. Phase A

Step 2: Develop feedback mechanisms and norms to learn/grow as individuals/as a team. Phase B

Step 3: Diagnose where you are now. Phase C

Step 4: Action plan how to get from Today C to the Future A.

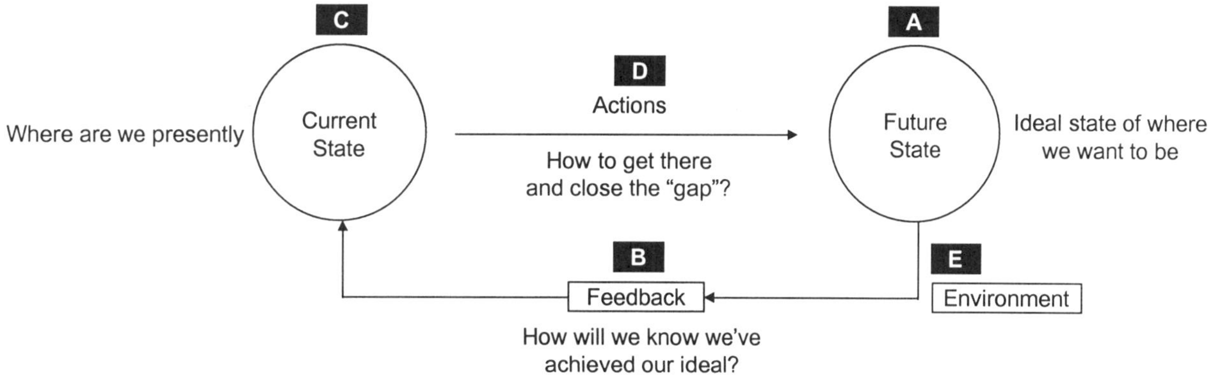

Make your next team building and development more systemic, thorough, and long-lasting with this A-B-C-D Systems Approach.

Suggestions for Use:

High-performance teams are the way to run a business. You need team development of all types and at all levels of the organization, in the following order:

Phase A: Future State

- Conduct education briefing and plan-to-plan on entire process.
- Make sure you have senior management's personal commitment and willingness to undergo personal growth and guided self-change.
- Clarify ideal future vision for teams.
- Develop clarity on levels and types of teams desired, by priority (i.e., project teams, functional teams, cross-functional teams, self-managed teams).
- Link to organizational vision, mission, and values.

Phase B: Feedback Loop

- Team standards/inter/intra-team feedback
- Stakeholder involvement and input
- Follow-up/reinforcement systems in place
- Continual improvement/renewal philosophy in place
- Rewards systems to reinforce desired changes
- Best-practices research

Phase C: Current State

- Conduct a team diagnosis of each team and its fit with the other tracks.
- Develop strategic action items to support the plans for team development.
- Provide resource allocation to support the desired changes.

Phase D: Strategy Implementation and Change—Major Activities

- Make certain everyone learns and understands the team development model.
- Conduct team-building process for teams selected with regular follow-up checkpoints.
- Become skilled in meetings management and role clarification.
- Become skilled in group dynamics, process, and facilitation.
- Become skilled in team leadership and management functions.
- Become skilled in interpersonal and influence management, as well as communications.
- Become skilled in ethical persuasion, decision making, and conflict resolution.
- Develop a proactive management fit and coordination with outside impactors, the other six tracks, and any other major improvement projects (i.e., systems fit, alignment, and integrity).

Phase E: Environmental Scan

- Continually keep watching and gathering feedback on team effectiveness from the two main environments: (1) external to the team but inside the organization, and (2) the external environment.

Team building effectiveness is accomplished by the A-B-C-D phases:

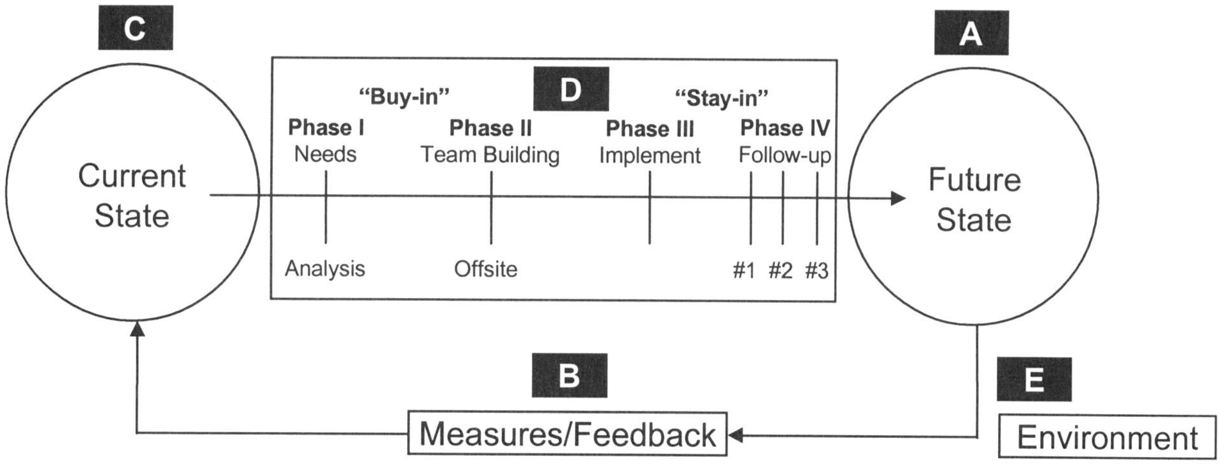

Details of the Team-Building Process

Phase I—Data Gathering and Data Analysis/Synthesis

- Personal interviews/other methods
- Observation on the job and studying records
- Requires time to gather input from other specialists and people with relevant information on team
- Requires time for the consultant to collate data into a summary report
- Preparation of client (team leader) for the offsite meeting

Phase II—Offsite Meeting

- Definition of Phase A clear future vision
- How will we know we are "there"? Phase B
- Presentation of findings in "summary report"
  - — Exactly that—what we looked for, what we found
  - — Assimilation/analysis of data—what it means
  - — Problem identification, action planning
- Decisions/action planning:
  - — Given the implications of being at Phase C and desiring to be a Phase A, what needs to happen to get there? (i.e., Phase D)
  - — Result: Plan of specific actions that need to occur and in what order, involving how many people, by when

Phase III—Implementation of Action Plan Phase D

- Accomplish task (i.e., achieve goals).
- Begin to build independence from consultant; instead, do self-diagnosis of your team effectiveness on an ongoing basis.

Phase IV—Monitoring/Follow-Up (Feedback Loop = Phase B)

- Minimum of two half-day team meetings with consultant within 4–6 weeks and within 3 months following first offsite meeting in order to assess results to date and further actions needed; can be onsite or offsite as needed
- Continually assess environmental changes. Phase E
- Consultant meets periodically with staff as process consultant.
- Consultant works with designated person to monitor progress of action plan developed at first offsite meeting.
- Involvement of consultant in specific action steps as appropriate

Tool #33 Cross-Functional Teams

Application of Systems Dynamics #10: Subsystems

Cross-functional teams are the key to success, productivity, and meeting the customers' needs. Do you use them? How? How are they trained and/or rewarded?

Why are cross-functional teams so key? Because, while we usually organize our organizations vertically by functions, it is through natural horizontal and cross-functional collaboration and teamwork that work actually gets accomplished. (Remember the "throughput" phase of General Systems Theory.)

➥ **For example:** Cross-functional, team-oriented organizations are more cooperative and less hierarchical in nature.

Some characteristics include:

- Self-directed work teams
- Flattened organization
- Low differentiation, hierarchy, and perks between management and workers
- Lateral, cross-functional teamwork promoted
- Empowerment, autonomy, delegation promoted
- Management titles more supportive vs. directive (i.e., advisor, coach, leader, coordinator)
- People rewarded based on what they contribute and achieve vs. what they control
- Pay for position and reward for performance (titles and rewards)

A. New Paradigm of Titles

> *Old titles like foreman, supervisor, manager, and executive are giving way to facilitator, coordinator, coach, and leader. The attitude is shifting from "their job is to make me successful" to "my job is to help them be successful." Words like* direct, control, order *are being replaced by* enable, facilitate, help, share.
>
> —Cliff McIntosh
> *Current*, Quetico Centre, July 23, 1990

Suggestions for Use:

1. Check your job titles. Do they still reflect the old "command and control" paradigm?

B. Overall Cross-Functional Teamwork—The Horizontal Organization

Suggestions for Use:

1. Because of the natural way work gets done, becoming "cross-functionally excellent" is a must.
2. Whenever possible, create cross-functional teams, or at least involvement and input from all other relevant functions.
3. When creating department annual plans, be sure to list and recognize others who will be involved or impacted by your actions.
4. Personally, look for ways to integrate your knowledge and skills with other functions. Join, listen, and learn how an entire organization works. **Narrow specialists are out! "Systems Interpreters" are in!**
5. Assess your organization while you are experimenting with more and more cross-functional teamwork. Check out the chart that follows; circle where you are among the four levels (from #1 individual focus to #4 self-directed work teams) on all ten areas of teamwork emphasis in a systems view of teamwork.
6. Analyze your results by scanning the page. Do the circles fall predominately in one area—or are they a real mixed bag?
7. What changes do you need to make? Create an action plan to address them.

ACTION	WHO	WHEN

Cross-Functional Teamwork—The Horizontal Organization

Phase	Type of Teamwork / Cross-Functional Teamwork Emphasis	#1 Individual Focus	#2 Functional/ Dept. Teamwork	#3 Some Cross-Functional Teamwork	#4 Self-Directed Work Teams
Phase A	1. Shared Vision/ Strategies	Senior Management's Job Only	Dept. Mission & Plans Only	Sharing of Dept. Plans/Regular Follow-up Mtgs.	Every Dept./Level Uses Strategies as Organizing Focus
Phase B	2. Organization-Wide Strategies (or goals)	Specific KRAs for My Job	Dept. Goals Only	Project Teams for Certain Strategies	All Have Strategy Sponsorship Teams
	3. Leadership/ Management Skills	Traditional Boss—Subordinate Skills	Participative Management Skills	Trainer-Coach Facilitation Skills for Managers (T-C-F)	T-C-F Skills at all Levels—"Every Employee a Manager"
Phase C	4. Core Business Processes	Individual Job Focus	Department Processes	Some TQM/BPR	Organize Company Around These
	5. Supplier/Customer Contact	Only If in Your Job Description	Certain Departments Only as Interface	On Special Occasions or Cross-Functional Projects	Normal Part of Everyone's Job in Cross-Functional Teams
	6. Organization Design—Hierarchy	Standard Vertical Bureaucracy/ Job Descriptions	Emphasis on Department Teamwork and Team Building	Cross-Functional Projects/ Tasks Often Set Up	Cross-Functional Teams with Shared Leadership/Mgmt. (Team Advisors)
	7. Physical Set-up Location	Offices/Cubicles for Individuals	Each Department Separate	Project Meetings and War Rooms	Cross-Functional Team Members in Same Location
	8. Resources, Communications, and Technology	Based on Your Job and Need to Know	Openness and Participation in Department Resources	Access to Cross-Functional Project Resources, Communication, and Technology	Open Book Management across Organization—Info Available to All
	9. Rewards System	Adversarial/ Individual Focus	Department Teams Only Rewarded	For Cross-Functional Projects	Standard Cross-Functional Team Rewards
Phase D	10. Percentage of Organization Managed by Cross-Functional Teams	0%	10%	20–40%	50% +

C. Outside-In; Strategy Sponsorship Teams

Organize and manage from the outside-in, from the customer back into the organization (backwards thinking), to be certain that all processes and procedures are designed to meet the customer's needs. Set up Strategy Sponsorship Teams so strategies are directed toward the customer instead of functional turf battles.

Managing from the customer → In through Strategy Sponsorship Teams

From the "Outside → In" Is What Systems Thinking Is All About

Switch the focus from hierarchy and "turf" to the customer.

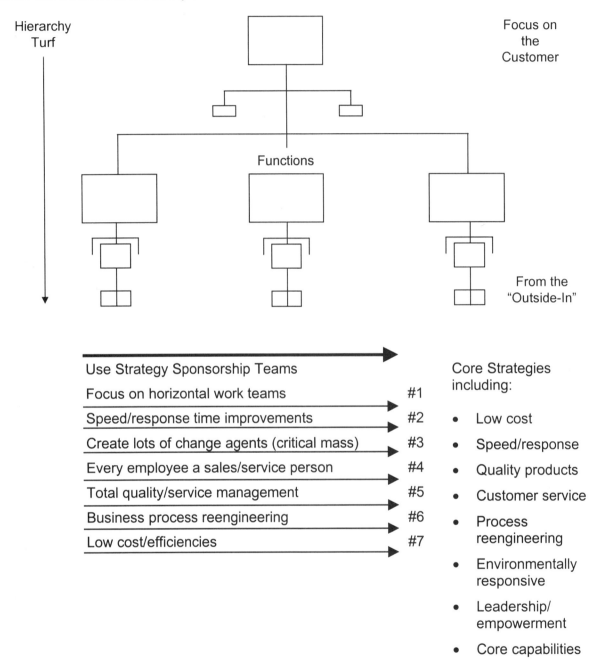

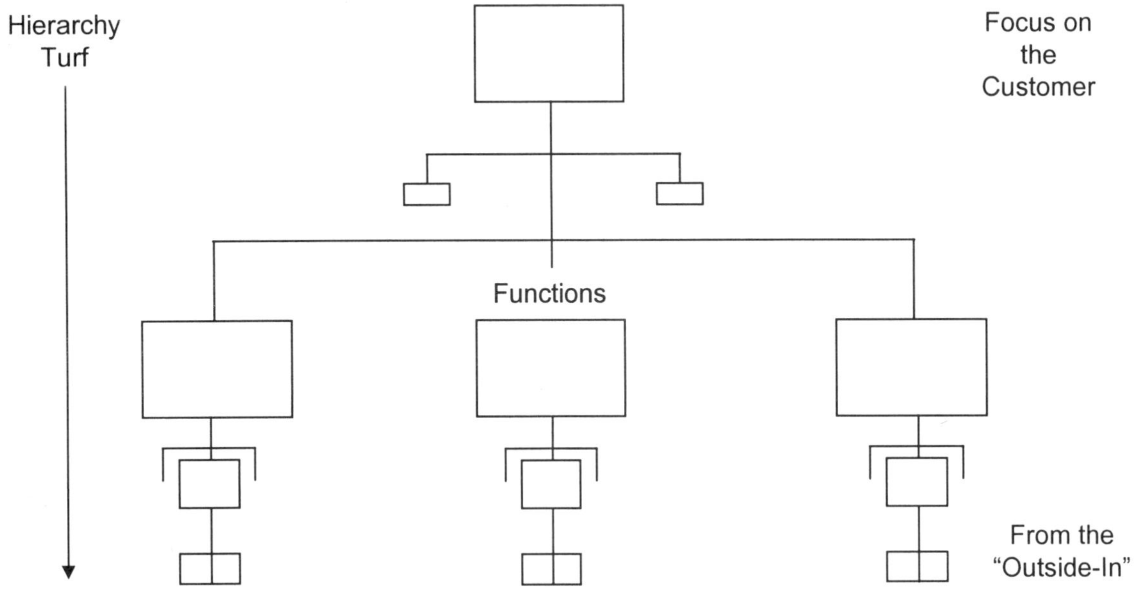

Use Strategy Sponsorship Teams

- Focus on horizontal work teams #1
- Speed/response time improvements #2
- Create lots of change agents (critical mass) #3
- Every employee a sales/service person #4
- Total quality/service management #5
- Business process reengineering #6
- Low cost/efficiencies #7

Core Strategies including:

- Low cost
- Speed/response
- Quality products
- Customer service
- Process reengineering
- Environmentally responsive
- Leadership/ empowerment
- Core capabilities

Suggestions for Use:

To organize from the outside-in, give responsibility and accountability for each core strategy/major change project to both the line organization and Strategy Sponsorship Teams (SSTs).

Strategy/Project	SST Champion	SST Team Member
1.		
2.		
3.		
4.		

Roles of these SST champions—to "keep the strategy/major change alive"

1. To be kept informed of the status of the core strategy's actual implementation.
2. To actively support and perform a leadership role in advocating this core strategy/major change across the organization.
3. To cajole/agitate and otherwise push and influence the people responsible for implementing this core strategy/major change to keep it moving forward (i.e., reverse the entropy that usually occurs with achieving change within a day-to-day context).
4. To advise and recommend actions needed to achieve this core strategy/major change.
5. To actively track and monitor the major change/core strategy's success and report on it at quarterly SCLSC meetings.

SST for Each Core Strategy/Major Change (sponsors, leaders, champions)	**Line Manager** (Still accountable for all core strategies)
1. Accountable to be "devil's advocate"; to cajole, push, lead, agitate for these to change/succeed. 2. Report quarterly to the SCLSC on the status of the core strategy/major change. Use the KISS Method; mostly verbal reports/dialogue are desired. 3. Receive all department plans for this core strategy/major change. Review/ critique them. 4. Support and work with line managers on coordination and achievement of this core strategy/major change. Do it so line manager has no surprises at the quarterly SCLSC meeting. 5. Can increase in size beyond the strategic planning committee membership if needed.	1. Continue to be accountable/responsible for actions/results. 2. Develop annual department plans for your area of responsibility around each core strategy in order to support/ contribute to and help achieve each one. 3. Track, monitor, correct, and reward achievement of the actions. 4. Work with and keep SST informed of actions/priorities of the annual plan company-wide. 5. Can be a member of SST as well. 6. Participates in the quarterly SCLSC meeting discussions/future actions.

Possible Secondary Role for SST

6. Can grow beyond SST concept into proactive coordination or task force (halfway to becoming accountable).

SST Non-Role (Absolutely)

7. *Do not* interfere with the line managers' direct accountability and allow them to assume a passive role. **This is wrong!**

D. Teamwork in Alliances and Partnerships

Alliances and partnerships in systems may be more effective ("stick to your knitting") than vertical hierarchy organizations.

➥ **For example:** *In Post-Capitalist Society*, Peter Drucker writes that "organizations will concentrate on their core tasks. For the rest, they will work with other organizations in a bewildering variety of alliances and partnerships."

Some networking and strategic alliance concepts to include in your core strategies:

1. Achieve vertical "control" through alliances/common visions and values vs. vertical ownership.
2. Only do what you do well (focus—focus—focus).
3. Let others do the rest through strategic alliances based on teamwork and trust
   - — separate organizations
   - — clear guidelines about control
   - — lowered barriers to entry in these other areas
   - — information networks to do the controlling

4. Often it is best to be led by one big fish with his or her own pond and other little fish in the alliance. In partnerships it is more equal—which is best for you?

5. Promote the good of the entire network/alliance.

Some key alliance strategies include: (1) Market Agreements/Dual Marketing; (2) Joint Ventures; (3) Franchising; (4) Private Label; (5) Buyer-Seller; (6) Consortia; (7) Common Standards; (8) Research Alliances; (9) Technology/Market Access.

Which are right for you?

- ➥ **For example:** Is your personal time management out of whack, and are your days too full and stressful? If so, maybe there are things you don't do well/shouldn't do. Can you ask, delegate, hire others to do those things you dislike? Align with someone else who likes to do these things.

- ➥ **For example:** The 28 core members of the Mitsubishi group are bound together by cross-ownership and other financial ties, interlocking directorates, long-term business relationships, and social and historical links. (In Japan they refer to alliances as *keiretsus.*)

Suggestions for Use:

1. Building effective teamwork in alliances and networks is a difficult, time consuming, and dynamic task. However, since they are part of your core strategies, they are often necessary, especially if you wish to expand internationally in today's global world.

2. There are books and books on this issue. Understand these issues before you take such chances.

3. Look long-term at everyone's missions and visions. They must be compatible to yours and mutually beneficial.

4. Most alliances fail because of differences in value systems, causing a failure of **cross-company** teamwork.

Tool #34 Leadership Development as a System

Application of Systems Dynamics #4: Input-Output

If we know one thing today . . . it is most managers are made, not born . . . There has to be systematic work on the supply, the development, and the skills of tomorrow's (top) management . . . It cannot be left to change . . .

—Peter F. Drucker

Thinking of leadership development *as a system* instead of just providing training programs is a whole new way to think. And each leader and each organization needs to think this way, since leaders and managers are the only true sustainable edge over the long term. A system of development is one of the best ways to develop this competitive edge, individually and collectively.

The ultimate competitive advantage (and the foundation for all else) is a company's leadership practices.

➥ **For example: Leadership is needed at all levels of any organization.**

- Executive leadership
- Managerial leadership
- Supervisory leadership
- Professional/technical leadership
- Team leadership
- Operator leadership

➥ **For example: Practice control and discipline—*Start with yourself as a leader.***

He who knows much about others may be learned, but he who understands himself is more intelligent. He who controls others may be powerful, but **he who has mastered himself is mightier still.**

—Lao-Tsu, Tao Teh King

➥ **For example:** Senior management defensiveness is one big barrier to leadership development. This seems to be a very common situation in change programs, where managers reason defensively and "change" becomes just a fad. Change has to start at the top, as defensive senior managers are likely to disown any transformation in behavior or reasoning pattern coming from below.

Source: Adapted from Chris Argyris, *"The ForeSight Intrapreneur"* #3, 1991.

Strategic Leadership Development System Concepts

("The People Edge")

- **Core concepts of leadership**
  - — Leadership is the responsibility of senior management.
  - — It is usually carried out and led through an Executive/Employee Development Board (EDB).
  - — It uses the Individual Development Plan concept.
  - — It is tied to the strategic plan (especially strategies and values).

- **Alignment of people processes**

  The EDB's role is to align the following processes to your strategic plan in order to create "the people edge" at the executive and lower management levels.

  1. selection/hiring
  2. promotion/succession planning
  3. executive development
  4. management development
  5. career development/life planning
  6. rewards; both intrinsic and extrinsic

- **Individual Development Plan (IDP) concept**

  This must cover at least three levels of management:

  1. executives
  2. middle management
  3. first-line supervisors

- **Core skills and values**

  While the continuously changing environment creates the need for a living, breathing, flexible leadership development system, it also requires a set of core skills, such as:

  - — self-mastery
  - — coaching/counseling
  - — learning how to learn/reflection time
  - — training others/mentoring others
  - — facilitating groups/teams
  - — handling disagreements constructively

  It also requires that leaders value

  - — integrity
  - — curiosity
  - — discovery
  - — dialogue

Suggestions for Use:

Building a Strategic Leadership Development System

See the model on page 222.

1. **Plan-to-Plan**
   - Read Centre for Strategic Management summary article on "Leadership" as preparation.
   - Hold executive briefing on leadership.
   - Form Leadership Development Board and support team.
   - Review *best practices research* on leadership.
   - Tailor the Strategic Leadership Development System to your needs.
   - Make commitment to proceed.
2. **Shared Leadership Vision—Phase A**
   - Clarify organizational vision—values—strategic plan.
   - Establish leadership vision, principles, and mind-sets tied to the strategic plan, and the external environment. (Phase E)
   - Tailor the leadership competencies/outcomes.
3. **Reinforcement and feedback systems—Phase B**
   - Leadership progress/success factors
   - Best practices benchmarks
   - Create/refine feedback vs. six competencies of "Centering Your Leadership"
4. **Assessment of collective leadership competencies—Phase C**
   - Self—others (360%)
   - Competency maps
   - Other tailored assessments—leadership styles, etc.
5. **Leadership development strategies (and actions)—Phase D**
   - Master Personal Development Plan (PDP) inventory/format
   - Modular development options
   - Resources, timing, and reinforcement
   - PDP administration and support structures
   - Rewards, recognition, and succession planning tied to development
   - Performance appraisal tied to strategic plan and development

Plan-to-Implement

6. **Plan-to-Implement—Leadership Development Board**
   - Expectations
   - Kickoff planning
   - Buddy system
   - Develop coaching/mentoring skills

6A. **Personal development plans**
   - Established for each executive—with individual priorities
   - Individual skills assessment/leadership styles instruments
   - 1–3 years in length
   - Clear sign-off of authority

7. **Implement leadership development**
   - Implement coaching/mentoring
   - Sharing/spreading our learning
   - Track, report, adjust
     — quarterly reports
     — supervisor reviews
     — performance appraisal ties

8. **Annual leadership review (and Update)**
   - Yearly revisions/updates

Create a Culture for Life-Long Learning	
Positive Culture	**Key Stakeholders/Environmental Scan**
• Stairway of Learning	• Customers
• Supportive, challenging environment	• Suppliers
• Positive reinforcement	• Board of Directors
	• Employees
	• Others

Note: Call the Centre to receive a four-page article describing this process in detail: (619) 275-6528.

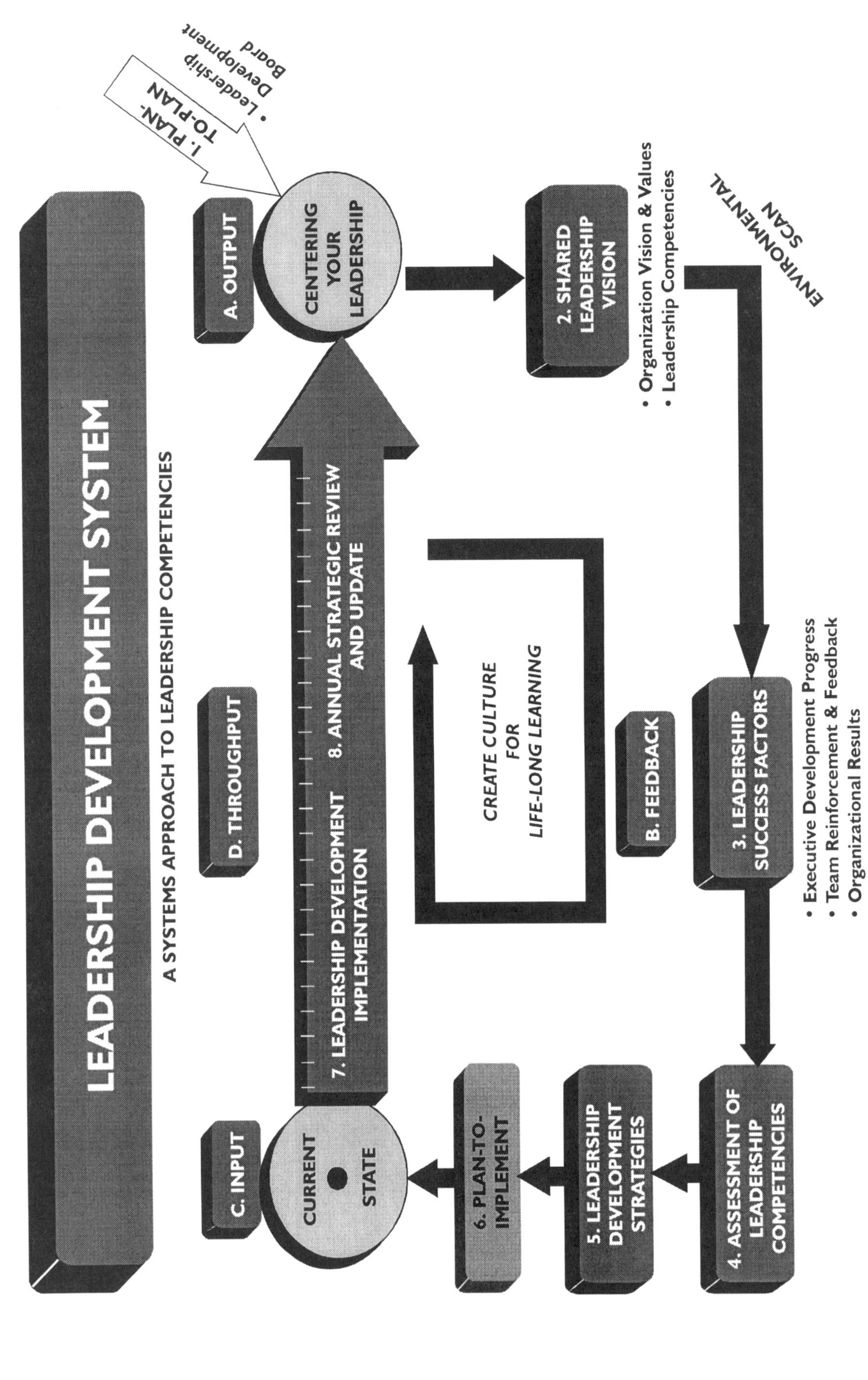

Adapted from General Systems Theory and CSM Working Papers.
Based on 1995 literature search and client feedback ever since.

Tool #35 TQM as a System

Application of Systems Dynamics #1: Holism; and #3: Input-Output Model

Deming conceived TQM as a "Total System." Our systems thinking approach puts the "T" back in TQM.

➥ **For example:** Deming's 14 Steps to Quality are very well known.

1. Drive out fear.
2. Eliminate quotas and numerical goals.
3. Break down all barriers between departments.
4. Eliminate inspection. Learn to build products right the first time.
5. Institute a vigorous program of education and self-improvement.
6. Remove barriers that rob workers of their right to pride of workmanship.
7. Institute leadership: The aim of leadership should be to help people do a better job.
8. Eliminate slogans, exhortations, and production targets.
9. Adopt a new philosophy. This is a new economic age. Western managers must awaken to the challenge, learn their responsibilities, and take on leadership for change.
10. End the practice of awarding business based on the price tag. Move toward a single supplier for any one item. Base this long-term relationship on loyalty and trust.
11. Improve constantly and forever the system of production and service.
12. Put everybody to work to accomplish the transformation.
13. Institute job training.
14. Create constancy of purpose toward improvement of product and service to become competitive and to stay in business and to provide jobs.

Source: *USA Today*, November 15, 1990.

Deming's ideas have been reduced to a checklist, not a system (like our A-B-C-D Systems Model) or the power of the Four Concepts of Profound Knowledge, which Deming also articulated.

THE POWER OF PROFOUND KNOWLEDGE

To provide you with a better understanding of Profound Knowledge as Dr. Deming described it, we include his four elements: (Note Element #1)

1. **Theory of Systems**. Systems and processes are synonymous.
2. **Theory of Variation**. Variation is everywhere.
3. **Theory of Knowledge (Learning)**. "This should have been the most important course that you ever attended."
4. **Theory of Psychology**. Everybody wants to feel important. Actions that you might take on physical, logical, and emotional levels to help individuals and teams feel important are key.

Adapted from Bill Scherkenbach's website www.scherkenbach.com

A. TQM as a System

Suggestions for Use:

1. If you want to put the "T" back in TQM, use our A-B-C-D Systems Model and fill in all 14 points and anything else you need to create a systems approach.

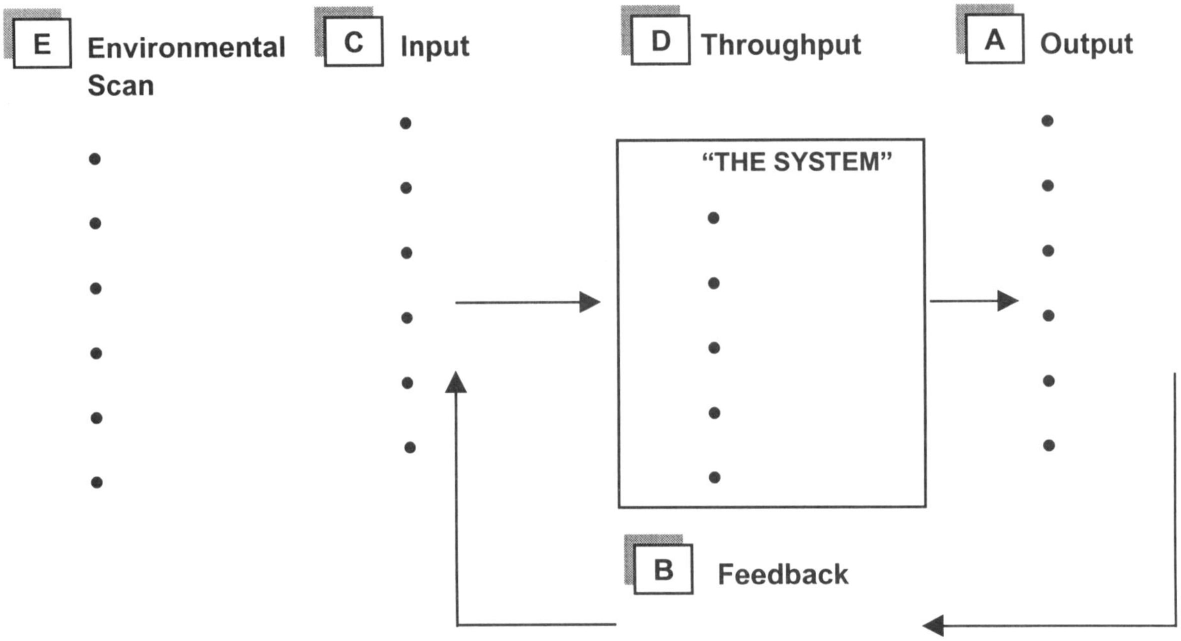

2. To make this true "TQM process" work, look at this list of strategic quality/continuous improvement processes based on our best-practices research.

Instructions: Please answer the following questions (yes or no) regarding your organization's status. Does your organization currently have . . . ?

_______ 1. a formal strategic planning document (beyond vision)? Is it used to run your business?

_______ 2. quantifiable outcome measures of success for the plan (and not just financial ones)?

_______ 3. three-year business plans for your major units or departments (including line units as well as Human Resources)?

_______ 4. a formal annual plan for the organization (not just a budget)?

_______ 5. a formal change management–type steering committee, led by your CEO (or equivalent) to manage your quality improvement effort?

_______ 6. five or more quality/service business process improvement–type teams with membership cross-functionally (i.e., horizontally) across the organization? Are senior and middle managers on the teams, too?

_______ 7. customer-service training? Does top management attend, too?

_______ 8. a formal "customer-recovery strategy" for front-line employees?

_______ 9. leadership training? Does top management attend, too? Quality improvement tools training, too?

_______ 10. formal personal leadership plans (PLPs; not department plans alone) for top management members to lead your effort?

_______ = Total # of yes answers. You need 8–10 yes's to have a high-performance continuous improvement effort: Otherwise you may be in ***Trouble!***

B. Strategic Management (A-B-C-D) Leads the Way for TQM

(Sample TQM = Total Quality Management (System) using Systems Thinking)

Strategic planning is an important organizational intervention. It will help you develop a shared vision of your future and the values, culture, and business strategies you need to get you there.

It is a way to

- accelerate/advance the TQM changes you want to make
- tie in and increase the importance of other major changes that should be (but usually aren't) part of the TQM corporate strategies, with total buy-in/ownership by the organization

Prework:	**Step #1**	**Plan-to-Plan**
		(Educate, organize, and tailor the process)
OUTPUTS: A	**Step #2**	**Vision and Mission**
	1.	Who: customer focus
	2.	What: quality, service, response, environmental, cost, profitability
	3.	Why: stockholders, stakeholders, customers, society

	Step #3	**Core Values**
	4.	Self-directed work teams
	5.	Employee empowerment/creativity
	6.	Continuous improvement
	7.	GE's Workout (blowout bureaucracy); reinvent government
	8.	Communications effectiveness; drive out fear
FEEDBACK: B	**Step #4**	**Key Success Factors**
	9.	Benchmarking/measurement systems (world-class comparisons)
	10.	Employee and customer satisfaction surveys
	11.	Market research
	12.	Executive compensation and other rewards
INPUTS: C	**Step #5**	**Core Strategies**
	13.	TQM/TQL—some of Deming's 14 Points
	14.	Service management/quality service
	15.	Speed and response time
	16.	Business process improvement/reengineering
	17.	Improved sales and market-driven culture
	18.	Cost efficiencies, reductions, and productivity improvements
	19.	De-layering
	20.	People as our competitive business advantage
	21.	Culture change
	22.	Organization structure/design
THROUGHPUTS: D	**Steps #6–10**	**Operational Planning and Implementation**
	23.	Annual/operations/tactical planning
	24.	Annual budgeting
	25.	Performance management/evaluation system
	26.	Strategic Change Steering Committee/transition management/Q.M.B.S.—P.A.T.s
	27.	Annual strategic reviews and updates, management meetings
ENVIRONMENT: E		
	28.	What is changing in the environment (SKEPTIC)?

C. Fishbone Diagrams—A Variation of the A-B-C-D model

TQM devotees use fishbone diagrams as a variation of the A-B-C-D model to see specific cause/effect relationships. Once the relationships are clear, you can allocate the resources (money, people, equipment, etc.) based on your outcomes. In planning, create a set of fiscal year action priorities (15–25 items) to allow you to budget for the *future.*

➡ **For example:** At the Centre for Strategic Management, our business model looks like this:

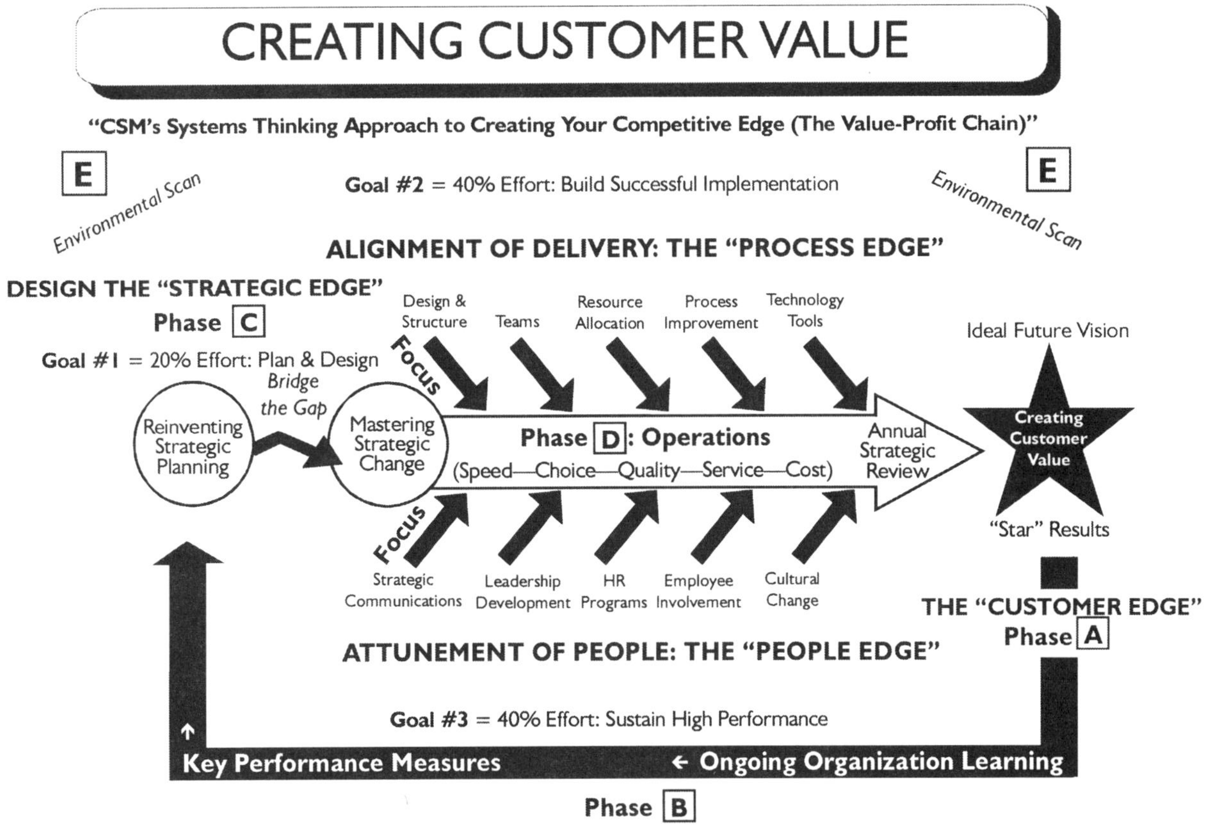

Suggestions for Use:

1. A fishbone design is a similar way to use the A-B-C-D input-output model. It works the same way.
   - [A] Determine your outputs within the environment. [E]
   - [B] Build a feedback loop.
   - [C] Determine your inputs.
   - [D] Determine your priority actions, and then match the alignment of the delivery processes and the attunement of people's hearts and minds to these priorities!
     1. Just connect each organizational component with the main strategies first.
     2. Then build supporting actions and budgets to fund each key action priority.

D. Business Processes—The Key to TQM—Phase D

The core of TQM is Phase D; the organization's business processes. Do you know what your key 7–10 business processes are (underneath your functional departments). They need to link together horizontally and cross functionally to create an integrated organization-system; this will better serve the customer.

Programs vs. Processes

- **Programs** are like campaigns—they have beginnings and ends.
- **Processes** are different. They are ongoing so they naturally conform to the laws of entropy. (They run down and die over time without continual reinforcement, renewal, and improvement.)

Business Process Reengineering Defined

Business processes are a set of activities that cross the boundaries of functional departments.

The organization must be seen as a set of processes that produce outputs of value to a customer, not as a set of functions.

The outcome of a business does not usually rest with an individual or a specified functional area. Employees play a part in one or more business processes.

The problem with most organizations today is that they see themselves as a group of functions, rather than as processes. Ask people on the street what they do in their companies, and they will tell you which department they work in.

Reengineering isn't working

Blowing out bureaucracy through reengineering is principally a cost-reduction project. However, when it is part of a customer-focused systems change process, it is quite effective and successful. We read all the time that reengineering "isn't working."

Common criticisms are:

- Lack of measurable results
- No strategic focus
- Brutal cuts only—"survival syndrome"
- Great-sounding programs that don't connect to the business of serving the customer
- Low cost "appreciation" versus real skill building for future success

➥ **For example:** Typical processes to reengineer (all based on customer needs and wants)

I. **External Customer (Phase A)**

1. **Product development focused on the customer's wants and needs** (includes focus groups, surveys, market research, analysis, segmentation, brainstorming, design purchasing, engineering, prototype manufacturing).
2. **Customer identification to order/sale** (includes marketing, segmentation, research, advertising, promotion, prospecting sales, closing).
3. **Order fulfillment** (includes credit, order entry, assembly, setup, suppliers, procurement, packaging, shipping).
4. **Customer service** (includes receipt of product/service, complaints, repairs, customer treatment, speed, and response time).
5. **Product life-cycle** (includes reduce, reuse, recycle, reclaim, dispose).

II. **Other Customers—stockholders/owners/government/management (still Phase A)**

6. **Financial management** (includes taxes, governments, cash management inventory, investments, profit/loss, balance sheet, and capital requirements).
7. **People management** (includes recruiting, hiring, orienting, developing, rewarding, motivating, promoting, retaining, and terminating).
8. **Public and investor relations** (includes PR, contributions, communications, reports, relationships, stockholders, media, and community).

Suggestions for Use:

Score yourself (H-M-L) on how your efforts to improve processes are succeeding.

_______ 1. Are you clear on what your business processes are?

_______ 2. Are you clear on which business processes are your top priorities?

_______ 3. Are you working to reengineer all these top processes?

_______ 4. Is the reengineering team composed of at least three functional departments (cross-functional teams)?

_______ 5. Is the change based on a clear understanding and explicit list of customer "wants"?

_______ 6. Does each reengineering team have a senior executive as sponsor and champion?

_______ 7. Have the teams been trained on project management, teamwork, and conflict management?

(continued)

_______ 8 Do they have the technical tools to accomplish their tasks?

_______ 9. Is the reengineering linked back to senior management through the Leadership Steering Committee on a regular basis?

_______ 10. Has your organization set targets to reduce waste?

_______ 11. Have you done "Blow Out Bureaucracy" workshops?

_______ 12. Is there a conscious core strategy adapted by the organization?

_______ 13. Is problem-identification rewarded or penalized?

_______ 14. Is automation considered during reengineering?

_______ 15. Are there rewards and recognition for eliminating waste?

_______ 16. Has benchmarking been done on the process being reengineered?

_______ 17. Does each individual have a QIDW plan as part of this, including all executives and the CEO?

Tool #36 — Systems Solution vs. Problem Solving (Through the A-B-C-D Systems Framework)

Application of Systems Dynamics #3: Input-Output Model

Use a more systems-oriented "solution seeking" (vs. problem-solving) model that focuses on objectives or outcomes and on alternative solutions. It should also help in troubleshooting the solutions for system side effects (i.e., all four phases of systems thinking). Analyze and solve problems within the context of your desired outcomes.

A. Solution-Seeking Model

Phases	Sequence
C	1. Problem/issue identification—root causes; not simple cause and effect.
Systems Solutions	**Now use Systems (and Backwards) Thinking:**
E A B	2. Set ideal desired objectives/goals or multiple outcomes that also solve the root causes (usually a weakness in analytic thinking) within your environment • With quantifiable measures of success
C	3. Brainstorm alternative strategies/actions to achieve these ideal outcomes/desired solutions. • There's always a third alternative. Find it. • Be sure to collect data and facts about the issues.
C	4. Develop tentative strategies and integrated action plans. **Double back:**
E B	5. Troubleshoot the integrated action plans (usually a weakness in analytic thinking). • Examine your biases and assumptions. • Check the environment around the decision, both internally and externally. • Include a "parallel process" to increase buy-in ownership and correct systems solutions. • Remember the "relationships" of all parts to each other and the overall objectives.
Recycle ↑ D	6. Implement the action plans with speed and flexibility. • Include rollout and communications.
E B	7. Continually provide feedback on how close you are coming to meeting your goals within a complex and changing environment.

In Short . . .

The world can no longer be comprehended as a simple machine. It is a complex, highly interconnected system.

The Basic Trouble . . .

Is that most people are trying to solve the problems of a complex system with the mentality and tools that were appropriate for the world as a

Simple Machine

—Ian Mitroff

Suggestions for Use:

1. Learn the "solution seeking" model.
2. Use it instead of a traditional problem-solving model.
3. Focus especially on the weak areas in most problem solving—#2, #3, and 5 (Phases A and B)

B. Five Why's to Better Solution Seeking

Ask yourself the 5 Why's every so often so that you are clear on the outcomes/results you want for every part of your life. The "Why" question takes you further along the continuum from *activities* to *outputs* to the ultimate societal *outcomes*.

➥ **For example:** For a salesperson:

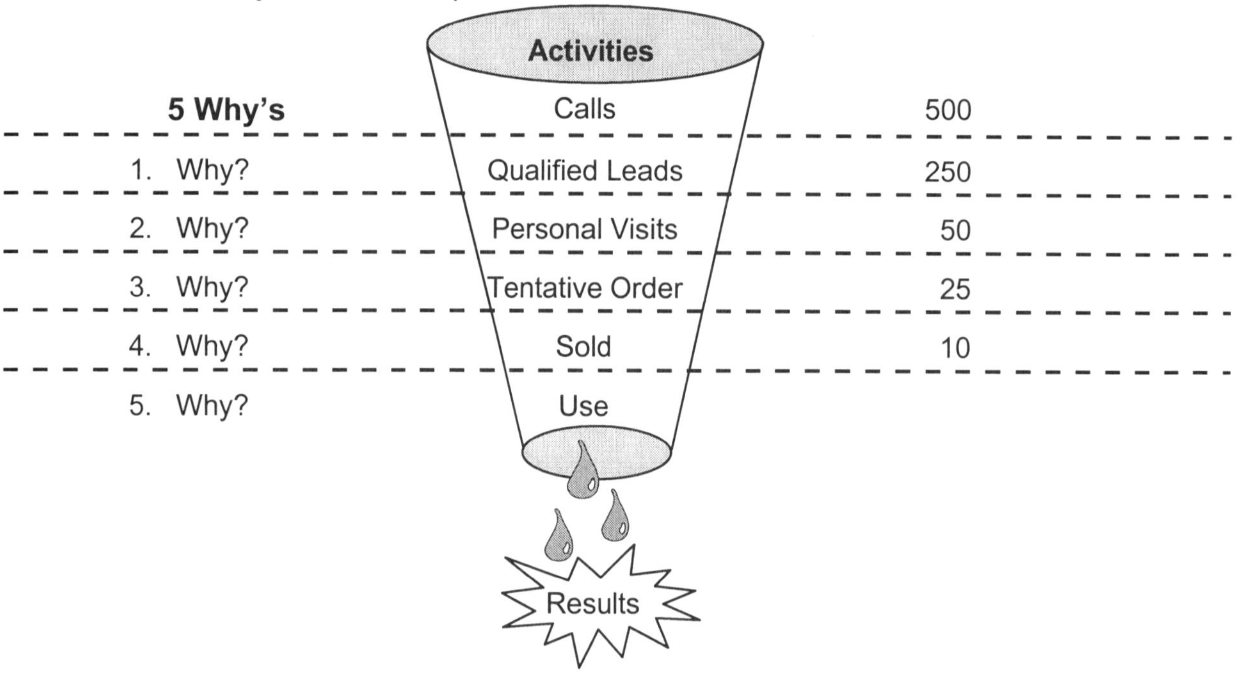

➡ **For example:** Look at the activities you did for yourself (not for your job) today. Now ask the 5 Why's. Are the results you will receive from these activities part of your ideal future vision?

Suggestions for Use:

1. Whenever you aren't sure if an activity or task makes sense, ask "why" for understanding and clarity.
2. If you aren't sure what the purpose, goal, or outcome of a meeting or project is, ask "Why are we discussing this?"
3. The more "why's" you ask, the closer you will get to the outcomes.

Tool #37 Organization Design as a System

Application of Systems Dynamics #9: Hierarchy

Make sure your next reorganization project is thorough, comprehensively thought-out, and well executed. There is no perfect organization structure and design, so there will always be system trade-offs.

➥ **For example:** Organizational design and redesign is an underutilized way to change complex systems and bureaucracies to better fit your goals and vision.

A. The Systems Thinking Approach to Redesign

Suggestions for Use:

Phase A Future State

- Conduct an educational briefing and plan out the entire process.
- Link structure to organizational vision, mission, values, and strategy.
- Ensure senior management commitment to the process and its outcomes.
- Define the organizational design and ideal future vision.
- Develop a clear understanding of the concept.

Phase B **Feedback Loop**

- Set standards, measures, Key Success Factors.
- Use surveys.
- Focus on continuous improvement process, renewal, learnings.
- Get stakeholder involvement and input.
- Build a reward system to reinforce the desired changes.

Phase C **Current State**

- Conduct an organizational diagnosis on the organizational design, as well as its fit with the other tracks/strategic plan.
- Develop an organizational design strategy.
- Develop strategic action items to support the plan, including a consideration of:
  - — work flow/mapping
  - — "workout" of bureaucracy
  - — work simplification
  - — networks/alliances
  - — integration, differentiation issues
  - — centralized/decentralized philosophy (which functions go where?)
  - — job design, enrichment
  - — empowerment, power shifts
  - — organizational levels, spans of control
  - — bureaucracy, policies
  - — organizational life cycle
  - — organizational headquarters role (control vs. service)
- Allocate the resources needed to support the desired changes.

Phase D **Strategy Implementation and Change—major activities**

- Educate management on organization design and its many tools and techniques.
- Rollout/communicate the changes to be made in a sensitive, caring way (but persist in the changes).
- Follow up the organizational design changes with needed role changes/skills in leadership and team development.
- Ensure clarity/completion of activities in the (A) future state; (B) feedback loop; and (C) current state.
- Ensure fit, integration, and coordination with other tracks and any other major improvement projects (i.e., systems fit, alignment, and integrity).
- Set up a steering committee to guide the redesign process.

Phase E **Environmental Scanning**

- What is changing in the environment? Conduct a full environmental scan.

B. Indepth Understanding—Interdependent Subsystems

(Application of Systems Dynamics #10: Subsystems)

"Are we micro smart, yet macro dumb?"

Focus on achieving a balanced fit (or optimum result) of each component of an organization, fitting it together with all others to create a synergistic positive effect on the whole organization's results. Stop turf battles and dominant departments.

- Don't maximize a single component—maximize the whole and desired outcome.
- The corollary to this is the need for each of us as individuals to balance all parts of our lives—our bodies, our minds, and our spirits.

➡ **For example:** If one department in an organization tries to maximize the achievement of its mission at the expense of other departments, the overall organization will achieve suboptimal results. It will not come near achieving its goals as the parts/departments won't fit together properly to maximize its whole.

➡ **For example:** Do you consider your personal or business's total portfolio or business units when you are about to decide on specific issues within the portfolio?

Synergy in Business

The Art of Making 1 + 1 = 3

Synergy has become the not-so-secret weapon of business success. Managers of giant corporations as well as small enterprises have learned to creatively combine the resources at their disposal to dramatically increase productivity, profitability, and market performance.

A New Way of Thinking

1st Thought: At the Macro, Strategic Level (Systems Thinking):

- Look at the total portfolio of business areas, lines, projects, elements

vs.

2nd Thought: Now look at the Micro Level (Incremental, Analytic, Reductionistic Thinking):

- An individual project, product, service, business level

The Fit Issue

1. **Excellence** is doing 10,000 little things right (i.e., fitting them with 10,000 other little things) to achieve the desired result.
2. **The key** is follow-through; is it consistent with your purposes? with your vision, mission, and values? We must be musicians who listen to the music—not just technicians/mechanics.

3. **The key** is to find out how to lock in employees and customers emotionally.
   - 15% of actions are rational/left-brained.
   - 85% of actions are emotional/right-brained.

4. **The biggest problem with "fit"** is the tendency for most things to immediately fly apart again or become technical. Be careful not to put short-term profits before long-term image and values.

5. **A values audit** looks at the image and culture of the organization regarding perceptions vs. reality.

In summary, what's the key issue in our systems framework?

The key is fit and linkage, not the "best answer/technique" per department/box.

"Excellence is a matter of doing 10,000 little things right."

Alignment and Paradigms

A paradigm shift in one aspect of an organization (i.e., mission, strategy, vision, culture) causes the need for paradigm shifts in every aspect of that organization (i.e., staffing, structure, technology, leadership, etc.)

- if -

you believe in a systems view of organizations.

C. Interdependent Subsystems (continued)

Don't deal with any one subsystem separately and alone; subsystems are all interconnected. Interdependency and relationships are the reality of life. Work multiple subsystems at once or in sequence for effective results.

➥ **For example:** In organizations, work is usually done across functional departments. Changing one department (such as the customer services department) alone won't really result in the desired outcome. Avoid this "silo" mentality. You need to understand and coordinate with other departments in order to be effective. In fact, it really helps if you *both* have the same overall corporate goal in mind.

In families, if there is a problem with one member, it is often assumed that this person is the only problem. In reality, the web of family relationships contributes mightily to the problem and must be solved in order to solve the one individual's so-called problem. See the concept of "co-dependency" and books on this subject for even more details.

➥ **For example:** To successfully implement a strategic plan, the following professions and fields must work together:

1. Decision sciences
2. Motivational theory/behavioral science
3. Organization design, structure, job design
4. Project management
5. Transition management, organization development
6. Human resources/development
7. Planning
8. Budgeting/finance
9. Quality control
10. Customer service
11. Communications
12. Marketing

Question: How do you bring it all together?

Suggestions for Use:

1. Get everyone to recognize that interrelationships are a reality of life.
2. Identify the interdependencies between all departments.
3. Focus especially on each department's mission and where its customers are. Often departments have other departments as their customers.
4. Have frequent meetings with interdependent departments to honor and discuss these linkages.

D. Alternate Idea: Design Your Own Systems Model

If all of the systems tools we've detailed in this book are not right for you, design your own input → output model. The key is to *have a systems model as a way to think*.

Suggestions for Use:

1. Build your own systems model, based on the major changes you are making. You can use this Systems Model only if you adapt it to your situation.

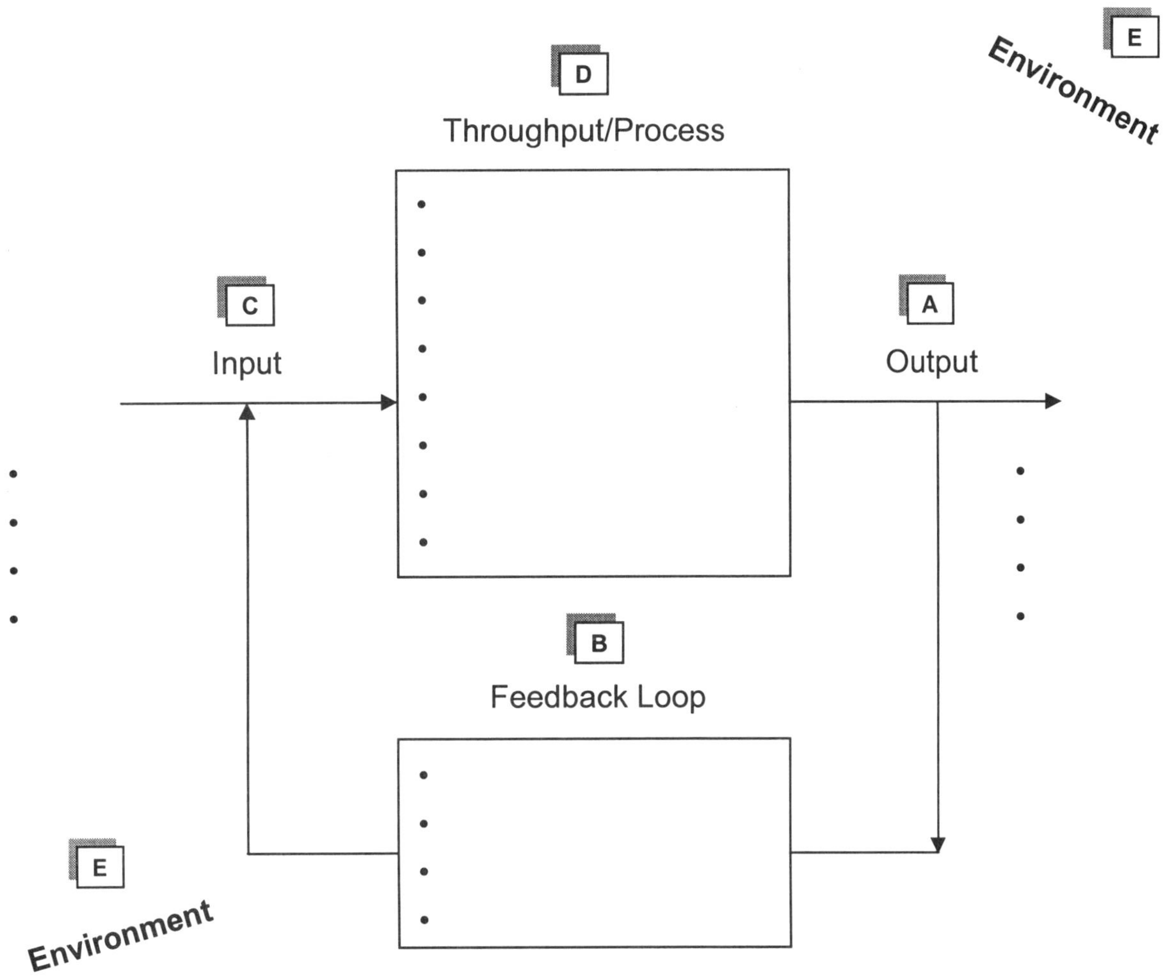
E
Environment
D
Throughput/Process
C
Input
A
Output
B
Feedback Loop
E
Environment

Tool #38 Project Management—Simplicity

Application of Systems Dynamics #3: Input-Output Model

Begin with the end in mind.

—Steven Covey

Problems created at one level of thinking can't be solved at the same level of thinking.

—Albert Einstein

No matter what kind of a project you are managing, keep in mind that our A-B-C-D model is actually a "new orientation to life" and, as such, is applicable to your project.

Suggestions for Use:

1. Set out the A-B-C-D-E framework.
2. Use it as a guide to address all five phases and their associated questions.
3. Share it and gain consensus with
   a. all key project members
   b. all project sponsors and stakeholders

A **Desired outcomes:**

1.

2.

3.

B **Key success measures:**

1.

2.

3.

4.

5.

(continued)

C Project/Charter/Task Force strategies/actions:

Strategies	*Actions*
1. Products and services	
2. Primary customers	
3. Marketplace/revenue impact	
4. Competitor implications	
5. People implications	
6. Return on investment	

D Charter/Task Force timeline for implementation:

Beginning date Milestones Ending date

Details:

E Within what environments:

CHAPTER VI
APPLICATION: SEVEN LEVELS OF LIVING SYSTEMS

Includes tools to guide learning and change at six different levels of organizational functioning.

Tool No.	The Applications
39	"Glue" and the Cascade of Planning — *How do you "cascade" a strategic plan down throughout the organization so that accountability is clear?*
40	Six Leadership Competencies — *What are the six natural leadership competencies (and 30 associated skills) leaders are likely to need?*
41	Total Rewards Systems—All Levels — *What nonfinancial rewards do employees want that are also inexpensive to give?*
42	Methods of Communication — *How would you rate the effectiveness of communication? (from low to high)?*
43	HR and Training Roles—In Strategic Management — *What roles can all staff executives play to help their organizations?*

OPPORTUNITIES VS. PROBLEMS

Stay opportunity-focused.

One opportunity can change the course of a business,

while

solving all the problems

just gets you back to zero.

—Fred Chaney

Tool #39 "Glue" and the Cascade of Planning

Application of Systems Dynamics #10: Subsystems; and Seven Levels of Living Systems

Develop your strategic plan, operations plans, and project plans using the A-B-C-D phases and different levels of living systems, including regular/annual strategic reviews and updates.

- **Link all levels of your organization together through a "cascade" of planning** from corporate to business unit to departments to teams to individuals.
- Use your core strategies (shorter term desired results) and your core values (guides to behavior) as organizing principles—your "glue."

A. The Cascade of Planning

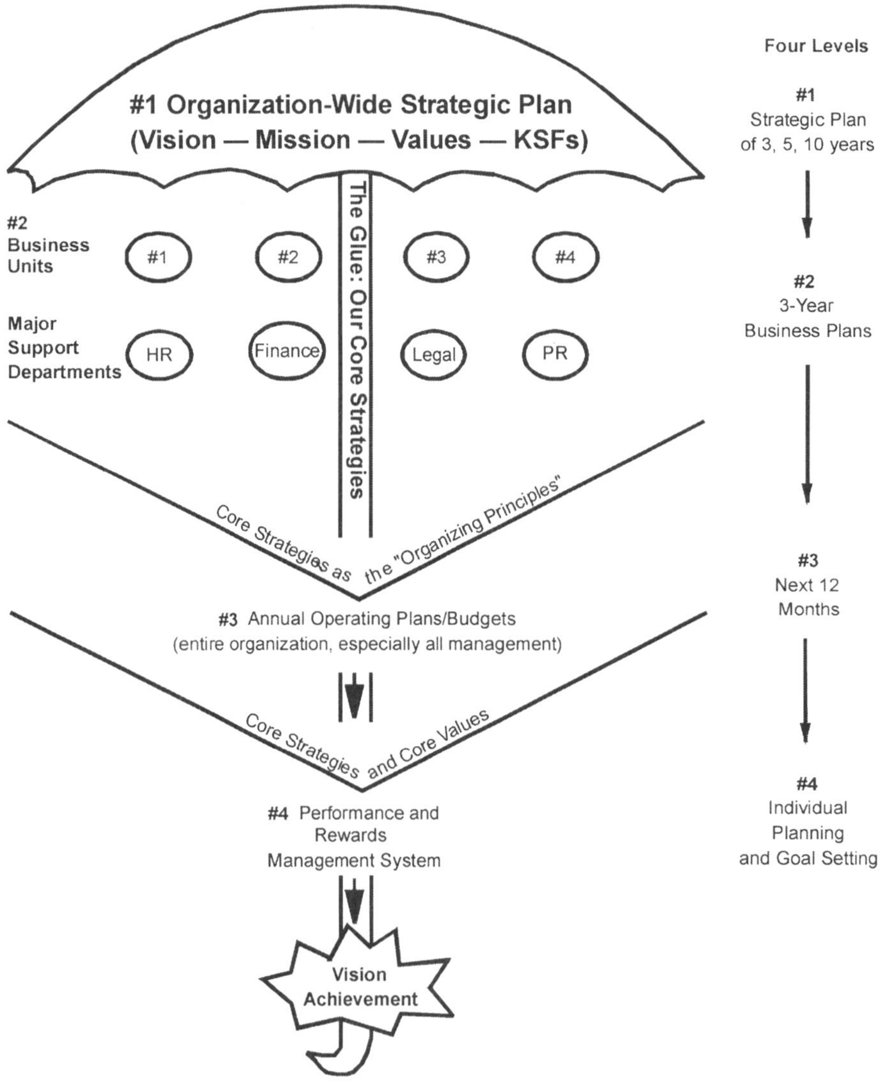

Suggestions for Use:

1. Use your core strategies as the "glue" to connect all departments to the strategic plan.
2. We also recommend that you eliminate the concepts of department annual objectives, and individual key result areas (KRAs). Instead, substitute the organization's overall core strategies for each of them.
3. With so many choices in outcomes and technologies, remember to **focus on the future** as well as the present, and set priorities at all levels.

➥ **For example:** In planning your personal life (as well as for your organization), remember that you absolutely must focus—focus—focus on a smaller number of core strategies that lead to success. That isn't easy today. Less is more!

B. Annual Department Plans

Suggestions for Use:

1. Set priorities and focus on the three most important actions over the next 12 months *under* each *core strategy.* (*Rule of 3* again)
2. Use the format. *Don't try to be all things to all people—it doesn't work.*
3. **Priority of Annual Action Items**—In terms of ensuring overall success this year, what top priority action items need to be accomplished?
4. **Personally:** Know your future vision and core strategies, and how to achieve them. Then list your top three actions to accomplish each strategy.
5. The next year, focus—focus—focus; you plan strategically, but you will implement departmentally.

Core Strategies	Who Is Responsible?	Who Else to Involve?	When Done?	Status
Core Strategy #1				
1.				
2.				
3.				
Core Strategy #2				
1.				
2.				
3.				
etc.				

➥ **For example:** Organizations are generally hierarchical. However, the work gets done horizontally, across functions.

Suggestions for Use:

1. If the same core strategies are used throughout, all department plans will be easier to develop.
2. Each department's annual plan should be developed at the department level, using the same format.
3. These draft plans should be shared and analyzed in a large group meeting with as many members of management participating as is possible and practical. Interestingly enough, the column on the form with the most comments is usually "Who Else to Involve?"
4. After department plans have been shared and there is feedback, have them finalized.

C. Performance Appraisals

Performance appraisals are not done effectively in most organizations. A "performance management system" is what is needed.

Suggestions for Use:

1. If you are serious about your strategic plan, tie it to the performance appraisal.

   Set up the appraisal with three pages:

   Page 1: Your organization's core strategies (i.e., results)

   Page 2: Your organization's core values (i.e., behaviors)

   Page 3: The individual's career development priorities
2. The Key Results Areas (KRAs) of every job description should be linked to the organization's glue—its core strategies and core values.
3. The performance appraisal will be four pages long.

   Simplified:

   Page 1: Cover sheet

   Page 2: Performance vs. applicable core strategies

   Page 3: Performance and adherence to the core values

   Page 4: Career growth and development plans (as well as overall evaluation)

Until you tie the strategic plan to your day-to-day decision making and annual performance appraisal, it will not be fully successful.

D. Business Unit—Level of Operations

Organizations often have smaller independent units called *strategic business units*. In the public sector, they can be called *major program areas*. However, there is no such concept or terminology on this key issue.

SBUs/MPAs Explained

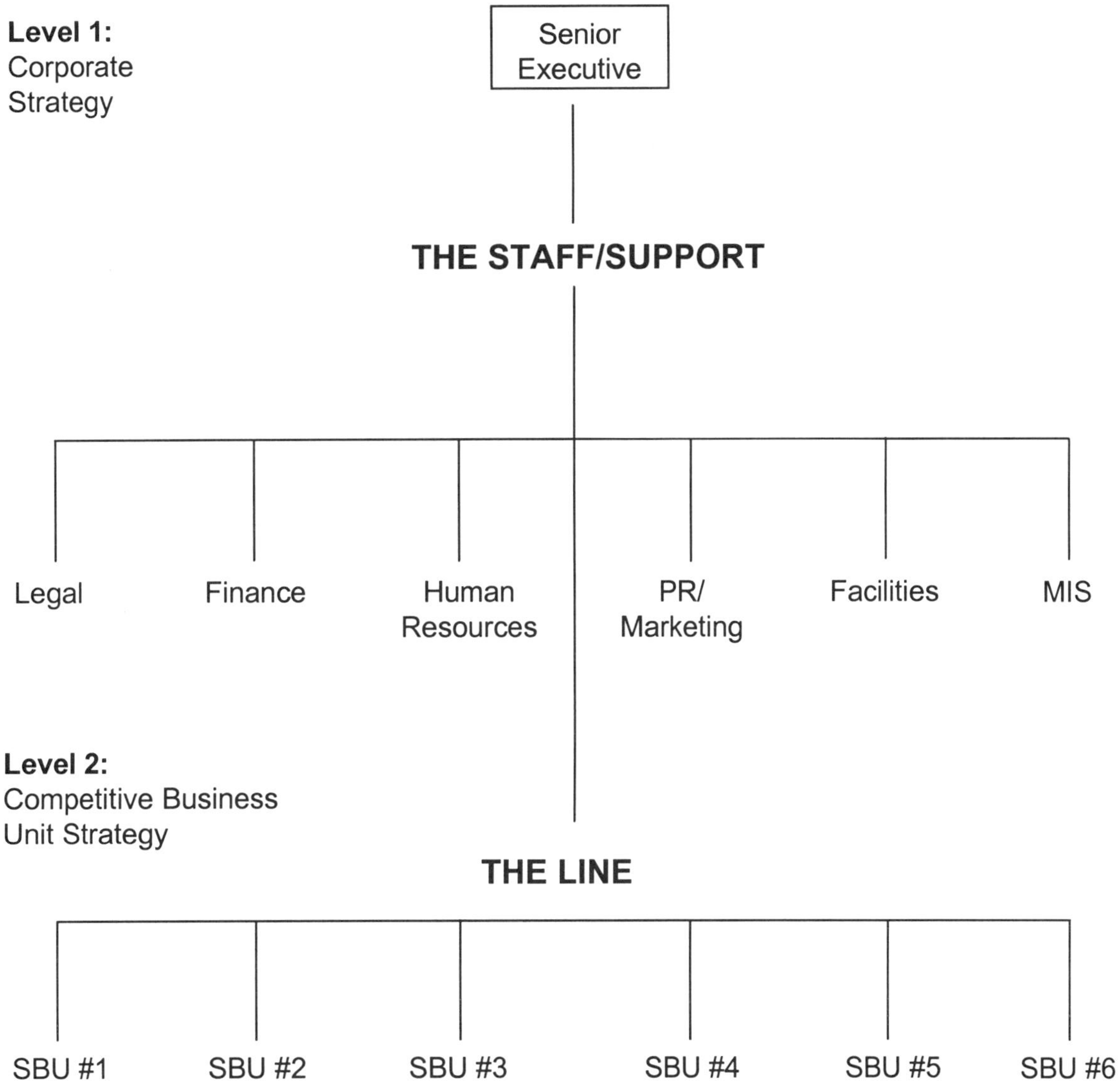

➥ **For example:** Be clear on why all strategic business units and major program areas fit under the one organization.

➥ **For example: Many organizations are "micro smart" and "macro dumb."** Each program or business unit seems a good idea from an individual ("micro") analysis. However, when you look at the entire *portfolio* from a total (macro) perspective, it is often clear where the priority programs/business units exist.

Suggestions for Use:

1. Each business unit/program area also needs its own strategic plan.
2. The main differences between these and the organization's plan are that:
   - These plans have to fit into the total overall strategic plan.
   - They usually cover a period of three years or less.
   - They are much more specific regarding customers, competitors, products, and services.
3. Be clear on why this strategic business unit or major program area is part of the overall organization. Does it still fit and make sense or not? What are the reasons?
   - Are core units or programs based on your driving force(s) and core strategies?
   - Add others for a specific reason—related, profitable, interest, expertise, conglomerate.

E. Negative Sum Game in Business Units

A "zero-sum" game is where neither side gains anything. A "negative sum" game is where both sides/departments lose (i.e., lose-lose). Watch out for the "negative sum game" being created between departments vs. the needed coordination in organizations. It occurs when we force departments to suboptimize the whole by maximizing their own part or turf. The debating of allocation of (1) overhead or (2) setting pricing/cost transfers between units, causes fights and conflicts over what is best; a zero-sum game. It is a waste of time and counterproductive.

It appears to be a "zero-sum" game as there is no added revenue gained as a result of this game. However, it becomes a "negative sum" game due to the time, cost, and conflict wasted internally instead of being focused on the customer.

➥ **For example:** Executives should control overhead costs through other means—such as budget reviews, process improvement, internal customer satisfaction, etc. The basic principle here is accountability = responsibility = areas I control within my system. Don't hold me accountable for something I don't control.

Suggestions for Use:

1. Discuss the Standard Income Statement below with executives and come to a collective agreement regarding accountability and responsibility in your organization.
2. The Gross Profit Margin should be where you hold line management or the business units accountable (#4).
3. If headquarters administrative costs (#5) are not the responsibility of the business unit, decide who/how to get accountability/responsibility there as well.

Standard Income Statement (Profit and Loss):

#1. Sales Revenue		________
#2. C.O.G.S. (Cost of Goods Sold)	–	________
#3. Strategic business unit operating costs (General and Administrative Expenses) (G/A)	–	________
#4. Gross Profit Margin	=	________
#5. Headquarters operating expenses (G/A) (indirect expenses/ overhead not allocated to the strategic business unit)	–	________
#6. Strategic business unit profit before taxes	=	________
#7. Taxes	–	________
#8. NIAT	=	________

Tool #40 Six Leadership Competencies

Application of Seven Levels of Living Systems

What competencies and skills might a leader need to implement a Strategic and Integrated Leadership Development System?

We believe that six areas are needed (three systems levels and three "collisions" of systems levels = 6 areas).

Our research covered the work of 27 popular authors, and included many books on leadership development. None addressed the issue of leadership development competency in terms of an integrated system.

➥ **For example:** Look at this issue in systems terms, and you will understand where leadership skills and competencies are needed.

A. A Systems THINKING Approach to Leadership Competencies:

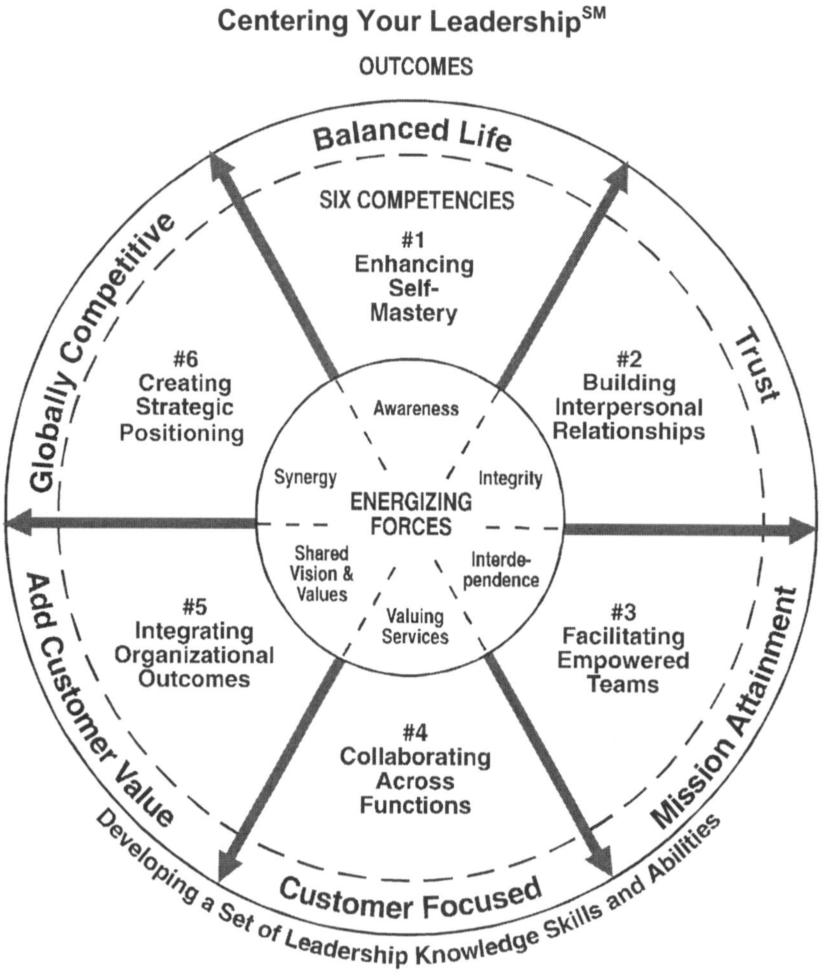

Once these six natural leadership competencies have been acknowledged, look at the skills making up these competencies. The list, as you might imagine, can be quite extensive. However, using a Delphi technique, along with our own research, we reduced our lists to the five main skills most people and organizations need (30 total). See the survey on the next page for details.

Suggestions for Use:

1. Take the survey of 30 skills on the next pages.

2. Use this to create *individual* development options for each manager/supervisor taking this survey. These might include the following:

______	public seminars	______	temporary job assignment
______	executive seminars—universities	______	job placement
______	customized, in-house training	______	task forces
______	mentoring—shadowing—guiding	______	visits to vendors, field, headquarters
______	professional associations	______	reading lists
______	conferences	______	buddy system support
______	committees	______	training others
______	practicums—action learning	______	goal-setting
______	intern programs	______	body-mind-spirit assessments
______	job rotation		

Question: Which of these do we prefer in our organization?

3. Once you've done your needs assessment and listed your development options, each executive/manager (i.e., leader) should complete a "Personal Development Plan."

4. Now you're ready to integrate this into our Strategic Leadership Development System.

Leadership Development Competencies

I. Optional Instructions: #1 ❑ How skilled are you in these corporate leadership skills?

#2 ❑ How well does the person you are rating do now?

______________________________ (name)

#3 ❑ How well does your organization and its management do these now?

II. Instructions Please circle the number or N/A that applies.

Topic	Current State Assessment					N/A	Score and Comments
	(1)		(5)		(10)		
Self or Others:	No Skills		Some Skills		High Skills	Not Applicable	
Management of Organization	—Reactive Organization		—Responsible Organization		—21st Century High-Performing Organization		
	—Survival Only		—Traditional Control		—Proactive Empowerment		
Level #1—Enhancing Self-Mastery (Personal)							**Level #1**
1. Personal and life goal setting	(1)	2 3 4	(5)	6 7 8 9	(10)	N/A	Total Score: ______
2. Balancing life (body-mind-spirit)	(1)	2 3 4	(5)	6 7 8 9	(10)		5 processes = ____ (avg.)
3. Acting with conscious intent	(1)	2 3 4	(5)	6 7 8 9	(10)		
4. Ethics and integrity displayed	(1)	2 3 4	(5)	6 7 8 9	(10)		
5. Accurate self-awareness	(1)	2 3 4	(5)	6 7 8 9	(10)		
Level #2—Building Interpersonal Relationships							**Level #2**
6. Caring about others	(1)	2 3 4	(5)	6 7 8 9	(10)		Total Score: ______
7. Effectively communicating with others	(1)	2 3 4	(5)	6 7 8 9	(10)		5 processes = ____ (avg.)
8. Mentoring, coaching, and improving performance	(1)	2 3 4	(5)	6 7 8 9	(10)		
9. Managing conflict/ negotiations effectively	(1)	2 3 4	(5)	6 7 8 9	(10)		
10. Supporting innovation and creativity	(1)	2 3 4	(5)	6 7 8 9	(10)		

(continued)

Leadership Development Competencies (continued)

Topic	Current State Assessment					N/A	Score and Comments
	(1)		(5)		(10)		
	No Skills		Some Skills		High Skills	Not Applicable	
Self or Others:	—Reactive Organization		—Responsible Organization		—21st Century High-Performing Organization		
Management of Organization	—Survival Only		—Traditional Control		—Proactive Empowerment		
Level #3—Facilitating Empowered Teams							**Level #3**
11. Practicing participative management	(1)	2 3 4	(5)	6 7 8 9	(10)		Total Score: ______
12. Facilitating groups effectively	(1)	2 3 4	(5)	6 7 8 9	(10)		5 processes = ____ (avg.)
13. Delegating and empowering others	(1)	2 3 4	(5)	6 7 8 9	(10)		
14. Training and developing others	(1)	2 3 4	(5)	6 7 8 9	(10)		
15. Building an effective team around them	(1)	2 3 4	(5)	6 7 8 9	(10)		
Level #4—Collaborating across Functions							**Level #4**
16. Installing cross-functional teamwork	(1)	2 3 4	(5)	6 7 8 9	(10)		Total Score: ______
17. Integrating business processes	(1)	2 3 4	(5)	6 7 8 9	(10)		5 processes = ____ (avg.)
18. Institutionalizing systems thinking and learning	(1)	2 3 4	(5)	6 7 8 9	(10)		
19. Valuing/serving others in the organization	(1)	2 3 4	(5)	6 7 8 9	(10)		
20. Managing people/HR management processes	(1)	2 3 4	(5)	6 7 8 9	(10)		
Level #5—Integrating Organizational Outcomes							**Level #5**
21. Organizing effectively	(1)	2 3 4	(5)	6 7 8 9	(10)		Total Score: ______
22. Strategically communicating organization-wide	(1)	2 3 4	(5)	6 7 8 9	(10)		5 processes = ____ (avg.)
23. Cascading planning and accountability	(1)	2 3 4	(5)	6 7 8 9	(10)		
24. Leading cultural change	(1)	2 3 4	(5)	6 7 8 9	(10)		
25. Designing and organizing effective change structures	(1)	2 3 4	(5)	6 7 8 9	(10)		

(continued)

Leadership Development Competencies (concluded)

Topic	Current State Assessment					N/A	Score and Comments
	(1)		(5)		(10)		
Self or Others:	No Skills		Some Skills		High Skills	Not Applicable	
Management of Organization	—Reactive Organization		—Responsible Organization		—21st Century High-Performing Organization		
	—Survival Only		—Traditional Control		—Proactive Empowerment		
Level #6—Creating Strategic Positioning Externally							**Level #6**
26. Scanning global environment	(1)	2 3 4	(5)	6 7 8 9	(10)		Total Score: ______
27. Reinventing strategic planning	(1)	2 3 4	(5)	6 7 8 9	(10)		5 processes = ____ (avg.)
28. Networking and managing external alliances	(1)	2 3 4	(5)	6 7 8 9	(10)		
29. Positioning the organization in the marketplace	(1)	2 3 4	(5)	6 7 8 9	(10)		
30. International sophistication/effectiveness	(1)	2 3 4	(5)	6 7 8 9	(10)		
Level #7—Energizers							**Level #7**
31. Level 1—Perception of self-awareness	(1)	2 3 4	(5)	6 7 8 9	(10)		Total Score: ______
32. Level 2—Reputation for integrity	(1)	2 3 4	(5)	6 7 8 9	(10)		6 processes = ____ (avg.)
33. Level 3—Recognition of interdependence with others	(1)	2 3 4	(5)	6 7 8 9	(10)		
34. Level 4—Values providing service to others	(1)	2 3 4	(5)	6 7 8 9	(10)		
35. Level 5—Understands/agrees with the organization's vision and values	(1)	2 3 4	(5)	6 7 8 9	(10)		
36. Level 6—Believes in mutual influence and synergistic efforts	(1)	2 3 4	(5)	6 7 8 9	(10)		

Grand Total: _______ (360 possible) / 36 = _______ (average)

B. The Special Role of Leadership

"Managerial Malpractice"*—defined as maintaining and using managers who are unqualified, poorly trained, misguided, or inadequately prepared.*

—Source: *Stop Managing, Start Coaching!*
by Jerry W. Gilley and Nathaniel W. Goughton,
Training & Development, August 1996.

Let's put an end to managerial malpractice. Instead, let's take the initiative and be leaders in our personal and organizational lives. Leadership is a contemplative art, requiring lifelong learning, application, feedback, and more learning. Every single organization should have a strategic leadership development system like we describe here. It is the best guarantee of success, according to the literature, and is one of just three factors common to every successful organization analyzed in a massive 1994 Ernst and Young/American Quality Foundation Study involving four countries, four industries, and almost 1,000 organizations.

➥ **For example:** The Foundational Systems Thinking Question is: What is it that I contribute to the problem as a leader? Secondly, can I change and be a positive and proactive leader?

Again, what am I doing *(or not doing)* that is causing the problem?

➥ **For example:**

1. The only thing we can change is our own behavior; we cannot change anyone else's. The word "behavior" in layman's language means simply *what we do.*

2. We must assume responsibility for our own destiny. We cannot blame anyone else for our misfortunes. The key word here is *we.*

Systems Thinking—Our Own Worst Nightmares

An inherent assumption of the systems thinking worldview is that problems are internally generated—that we often create our own worst nightmares.

—Adapted from Innovation Associates, Inc.

Linear Thinking—"Who Is Responsible?"

Linear thinkers are always looking for a thing or person who is responsible. Systems thinkers take on greater responsibility for events because, from their perspective, everyone shares responsibility for problems generated by a system.

—Adapted from Peter M. Senge, "The Fifth Discipline"

C. Interdependence—The Learning Organization

Systems thinking makes understandable the subtlest aspect of the learning organization—the new way individuals perceive themselves and their world. At the heart of a learning organization is a shift of mind-set, from seeing ourselves as separate from the world to *connected* to the world, from seeing problems caused by someone or something "out there" to seeing how *our own actions* create the problems we experience. A learning organization is a place where people are continually discovering how they create their own reality. And how they can change it.

—Adapted from Peter M. Senge, 1990

Suggestions for Use:

1. Look at yourself first for a solution to any problem.
2. We often ask the wrong question. The old question was "What are your problems?" The new question has to be "What are we doing that's causing the problem?"
3. The only thing an organization can change is the behavior of its people. Thus, if we can identify the behavior that is getting in the way of success, then we can either stop doing it or do something else.
4. Remember: We cannot change the external world around us; we can only change how we react to it.

D. Leadership Self-Renewal

Focus on feedback about actual status vs. desired outcomes; process/activity feedback alone won't help. Solicit as much feedback as you can. *"Feedback is the breakfast of champions."*

➥ **For example:** Feedback on process improvement is the goal of much TQM work. This feedback is fine, but outcome feedback is also needed.

Suggestions for Use:

1. There are many, many ways to use the feedback concept successfully. Only your imagination and desire limit it.
2. Successful Life-Long Learning (Feedback and Renewal)

   Use the following list to obtain full and successful life-long learning, feedback, and renewal.

Self: Self-renewal is the process an organization goes through when it continually revamps and adapts itself to constantly changing circumstances *before a crisis occurs*.

- Only an "inadequate" manager accepts things as they are.
- Leaders and managers seek to revise process and structure to reflect changing realities.

Leaders do this through many of the system's model components:

I. **Environment**

1. Think in broader terms as to environmental impact.
2. Monitor the customer's changing needs and wants.
3. Regularly evaluate products, markets, and the competition before changing decisions and direction. Information is a competitive weapon!
4. Set up an environmental scanning system.

II. **Outputs**

5. Institute yearly incremental and evolutionary changes in response to market changes so that there will be no need for revolutionary change.
6. Make the vision, mission, and values crystal-clear and reiterate them frequently (along with the rationale). Create a course employees can identify and commit to.

III. **Strategies**

7. Set goals and strategies and revise them as needed.
8. Ignore "sunk-cost" or cost only mentalities.
9. Promote mobility, flexibility, quickness, and smallness as a strategic weapon.

IV. **Feedback**

10. Have an objective feedback system that continuously provides you with honest, unprocessed, unfiltered information. Listen! Really listen!
11. Use an anonymous feedback process (company-wide and with customers) regularly—perhaps each year—and encourage curiosity.

V. **Managerial Tasks**

12. Think constantly in terms of renewal, change, and continuous improvement; model these things at the very top.
13. Confront uncertainty—don't deny it.
14. Don't shoot the messenger bearing bad news. Reward honesty in reporting failures, mistakes, and screw-ups.
15. Welcome and reward errors, as long as people learn from their mistakes.
16. Honor and reward disagreements and resistance before decision making. Consider facts and opinions to be friendly. Skeptics are our best friends!

17. Persevere and be fanatical and committed. Hold fast to the renewal culture desired, despite the fears of habit-seekers and supporters of the status quo.
18. Have a permanent issue-management or corrective-action team play devil's advocate.
19. Businesses that want to stay ahead will need to learn self-renewal and to manage continuous change.
20. Put in place a Strategic Change Leadership Steering Committee to ensure successful management of change.

VI. **Organization/Staffing**

21. Provide a mix of internal promotions, external hires, and personnel rotation across departments and units to prevent inbreeding.
22. Empower all employees to take initiative. Share some decision making with non-management employees.

VII. **Systems/Infrastructure**

23. Highly value risk-taking and innovation. Push teamwork and trust vs. power and office politics. Explicitly reward and promote these positive values.
24. Reward those who are fully committed to renewal and penalize those who are not, no matter how competent they are at tasks.
25. Consistently and comprehensively base decisions upon the values held throughout the company, its areas, its programs, and its systems. Your values represent stability; do not tolerate disloyalty to those values.

VIII. **Informal Culture**

26. Place a heavy emphasis on intangibles such as vision, values, and motivation. Sound the rallying cry and make sure that the entire organization is involved; it should "own" and integrate these things. Communicate this consistently.
27. Educate the entire company about the renewal effort. Involve active senior management and create training programs.
28. Make sure all parts of the Organization as a Systems Model align with the strategic plan. After all, you **do** want to create a high-performance organization, don't you?

Tool #41 Total Rewards Systems—All Levels

Application of the Seven Levels of Living Systems

Financial and nonfinancial rewards for individuals, teams, and the entire organization must be timely, meaningful, and significant. They are key to your success! Link them to your strategic plan.

➥ **For example:** Early in my career Henry Migliore, Dean of the business school at Oral Roberts University, showed me a nationwide survey (see the Employee Needs Questionnaire on page 261). I have since replicated these results using the Questionnaire over 200 times.

A. Top Three Job "Needs" of Employees (in no particular order)

1. Recognition for doing good work
2. Freedom for independent thought and action
3. Opportunity for personal growth

Other "Needs"

4. Higher salary and/or more benefits (almost always fourth)
5. Promotion to a better job
6. Job security
7. Satisfying the boss's wishes
8. Prestige and status

Survey source: Dr. H. Migliore, Dean, Oral Roberts Business School; the author's own surveys generated the same results in Asia, Europe, and the United States.

B. Effective Rewards (Best Practices) Are:

- Timely
- Significant
- Personally meaningful
- Competing against oneself only
- Multiple winners

Source: Stephen G. Haines, 1984 (as updated).

Note: The practice of "pay for performance" is often contrary to what the five best practices show is needed or effective. In addition, a different type of reward—a "nonfinancial" reward—is what is needed.

C. Nonfinancial Rewards

Some innovative nonfinancial rewards that meet the top three job "needs" of employees include:

I. **Recognition**
- Administrative Recognition Program (ICA)—after the fact
- Thank you cards; letters, letters, letters; pictures; plaques; newsletters
- Team celebrations; dinners
- Inter-team projects, celebrations
- Tokens—on-the-spot
- Academy Awards
- On-the-spot rewards
- Seniority; service awards
- Senior management visits
- Company parties; meetings

II. **Freedom/Independent Thought and Actions**
- IBM Presidents Club; Seoul Olympics (80/20 Rule)
- Production team awards
- ICA sales meetings; awards quarterly
- Self-managed work teams
- Flex-time; part-time
- Task forces; project teams; quality
- Empowerment; delegation

III. **Growth and Development**
- Training attendance
- Career development (IJP)
- Job design (plan—do—control)
- Job rotation; pay for knowledge
- Customer/vendor trips
- Professional development; associations

D. Financial Rewards

- Fixed/variable compensation (no merits)
- Restricted stock; Cliff Vesting
- Benefits—401K, pension, time off
- Corporate/unit profit sharing
- Deferred compensation—CD rates
- ESOP (Employee Stock Ownership Plans)
- Immediate leader awards
- Stock purchase plans

Employee Needs Questionnaire

WHAT DO EMPLOYEES WANT FROM A PERFORMANCE MANAGEMENT SYSTEM?

List in priority rank order (1–10) your needs from your current job.

Priority		Need	Doing it now?
Survey Results	Yours		
		1. Higher salary and/or more benefits	
		2. Recognition for doing good work	
		3. Food, clothing, and shelter	
		4. Satisfying the boss	
		5. Promotion to a better job	
		6. Personal growth and development	
		7. Safety in your work environment	
		8. Prestige and status	
		9. Job security	
		10. Opportunity for independent thought and actions (freedom)	

Tool #42 Methods of Communication

Application of Systems Dynamics #5: Feedback; and Seven Levels of Living Systems

In today's dynamic and fast-paced environment, it is getting more difficult to communicate frequently and effectively. (This is as true at home as it is at work.) High-tech communication methods such as faxes, e-mail, and answering machines are supposed to make communication easier. However, effective communication requires two partners, the sender and the receiver. Too much of our quick communication today is one-way. The sheer volume of e-mail, paper, and other one-way communication drowns out our ability to really hear and understand. And since we often *hear with our eyes*, one-way communication is relatively ineffective by itself alone. We have developed the "Stairway of Communications Effectiveness" to illustrate what we mean.

A. The Effectiveness of Communication

➥ **For example:** The volume of one-way e-mail is sometimes overwhelming. It is truly fast, but there is no feedback, no visual clues, no tone of voice, etc. This lack of feedback makes it an impersonal medium, much more vulnerable to *flaming* e-mail and angry, conflict-generating words than two-way, face-to-face communication. Without feedback, the receiver can easily misconstrue the meaning of what is written, which can escalate conflict. Helpful two-way communications are just plain ignored in today's blizzard of messages and paper.

Suggestions for Use:

1. Analyze your communication methods. Better yet, ask a trusted friend or colleague to help you.
2. Which methods do you usually use?
3. Which two-way communication do you underuse?
4. Which one-way communication do you overuse?
5. What changes do you need to make to be a more effective communicator?

Ladder of Communication Effectiveness

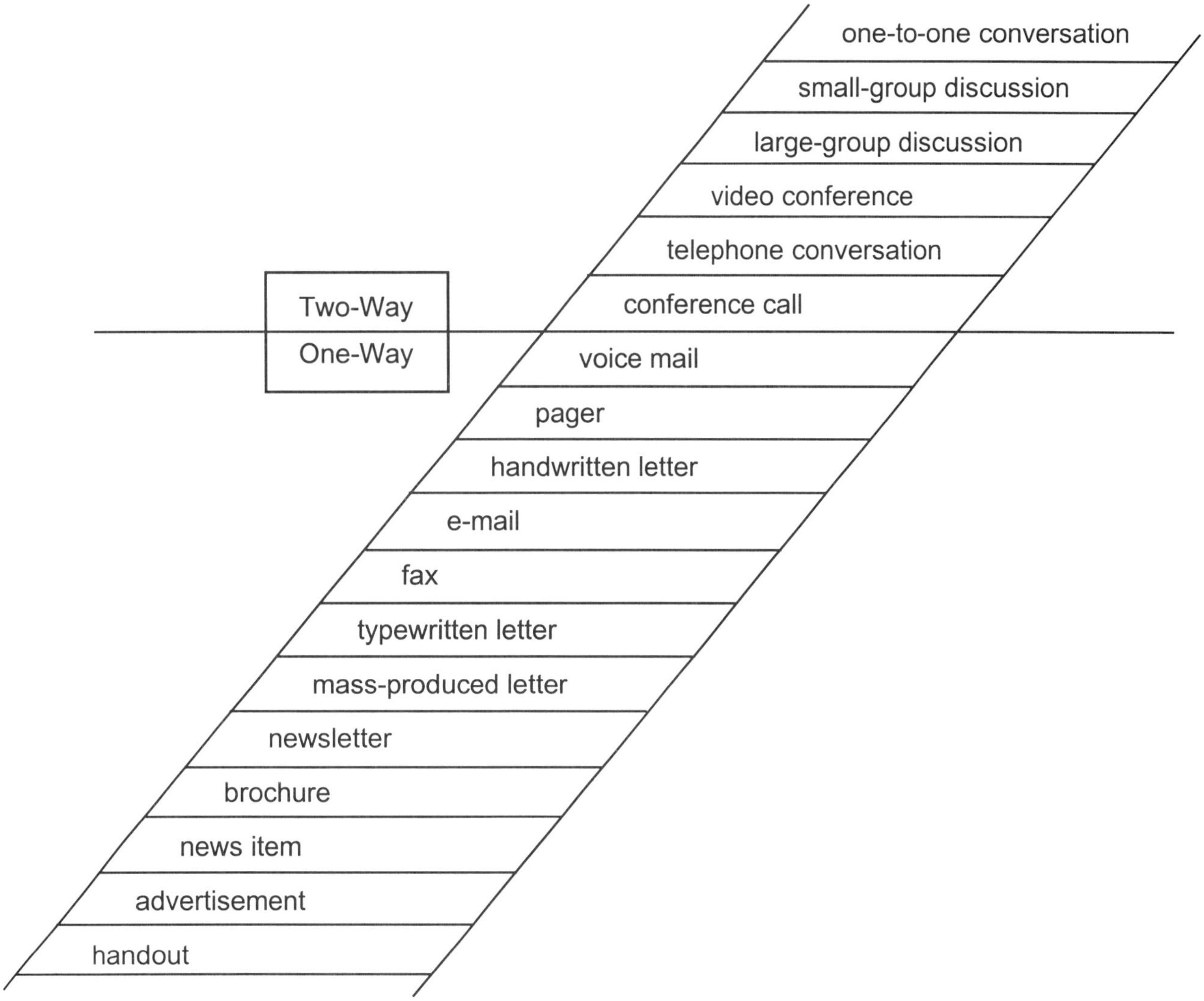

B. Repetition—Repetition—Repetition

People don't hear and certainly don't understand everything you say to them. Or they may not believe it. Make "stump speeches" and repeat things over and over again if you want to help people through a change. This is especially true when emotions are high or the changes are difficult.

Communication Methods

Words =	7%
Tone =	38%
Body Language =	55%
Total =	100%

What you do speaks louder than what you say!

We Remember Approximately

- 10% of what we *read*
- 20% of what we *hear*
- 30% of what we *see*

- 50% of what we *see* and *hear*
- 70% of what we *say* and *do*

- 90% of what we *explain as we do*

Repetition Increases Understanding

- 1st time = 10% retention
- 2nd time = 25% retention
- 3rd time = 40–50% retention
- 4th time = 75% retention

➥ **For example:** This is just as true at home with children and family members as it is at work.

Suggestions for Use:

1. People need to hear things three to four times, especially if there is emotion/change involved.
2. Use more than one of your senses whenever you communicate (as many as possible).
3. Teach what you want to learn yourself.
4. Two-way communication is much better than one-way communication.
5. Remember to communicate with body language/tone of voice as well as words.

C. Strategic Communications Matrix

Set up a Strategic Communications Matrix and/or a "Rollout Plan Matrix" for communicating strategically to all stakeholders about your changes. Remember to communicate at all levels, starting with key stakeholders.

Strategic Communications Matrix

How / **Who**	Face-to-Face (Small group)	Large Group Meeting	Video	Voice Mail	E-Mail	Written Letter	Feedback
Middle Management							
1st Line Supervisor							
All Departments							
All Employees							
Key Stakeholders (list)							

➥ **For example:** Matrices are great to show relationships between systems and /or systems concepts.

Suggestions for Use:

1. Set up a matrix of the components/systems you want to analyze.
2. Compare each component on each side with all others on the other side (i.e., each box of the matrix); draw the needed conclusions.
3. Develop action plans as a result of what you see.

Tool #43 HR and Training Roles—In Strategic Management

Application of the Seven Levels of Living Systems

There are four strategic roles for Human Resource and Training executives. These correspond to four different levels of living systems (corporate, business unit, function, implementation).

A. Human Resource Roles

➥ **For example:** The Human Resources Role in Strategic Management

	Business Strategy Levels		HR Strategic Role
1.	Organization-wide strategy *What business are we in?*	1.	People/organization placement/changes and succession
2.	Business unit strategy (SBU) *How do we create a competitive advantage?*	2a.	Employee-driven strategies *Create a competitive advantage through employees.*
		2b.	HR support/involvement in any other strategies
3.	Functional department strategies *Learning to be efficient.*	3.	Human resource strategic plans
4.	Strategic management *Making strategy work!*	4.	Change/transition management
		4a.	HR practices

Note: This list is also similar to the four strategic roles that support departments play (i.e., Finance, Legal, Marketing, PR, MIS, Facilities, etc.).

B. Training Roles

➥ **For example:** Training Roles in Strategic Management

Four ways to be involved and to influence senior executives:

1. As a coordinator, facilitator, or member of a strategic planning and change management support cadre.

2. By modeling and conducting a strategic planning/change management process for the Training and Human Resource Development function.

3. Through a strategically aligned management development system and programs.

4. By focusing on implementation and change management—support the vision, values, and strategies of the organization-wide strategic plan.

Suggestions for Use: In Analyzing Staff Departments

1. *Question*: What is your role in the organization? Are you happy with it?

2. If not, how can you move up to the next level?

3. Discuss this with appropriate colleagues.

4. Develop the department mission statement and share it with your "customers." You want them to agree with your role.

5. Then develop strategies and action plans, and assign actions with timelines to achieve your goals.

CHAPTER VII
APPLICATION: THE ROLLERCOASTER OF CHANGE^{SM}

The applications in this chapter focus on the concept most essential to guiding organizational change: that systems follow a natural cycle of life and change. As we saw earlier, this concept can be expressed as the *Rollercoaster of Change*^{SM}. We look here at the Rollercoaster's many uses, particularly its application for self, interpersonal, team, and organizational change.

Tool No.	The Applications
44	The Rollercoaster of Change^{SM} — *What is the natural, normal, and legitimate emotional way change occurs?*
45	The Rollercoaster of Self-Change — *How does change occur naturally for me as a person?*
46	The Rollercoaster of Interpersonal Change — *How does change occur between people?*
47	The Rollercoaster of Team Change — *How does a team undergo change?*
48	The Rollercoaster of Organizational Change — *How does an organization undergo change overall?*
49	Cutting and Building Success Strategies — *How does the Rollercoaster apply to organizational business strategies?*
50	Six Natural Phases of Change — *How does large-scale change occur in six predictable phases?*
51	The Natural Life Cycle — *How does the Rollercoaster apply to the life cycle of organizations?*
52	Performance Management System and Cycle — *How does this natural cycle apply to managing performance in an organization?*
53	People-Edge System and Cycle — *How can I use the circular nature and life cycle of change to develop the people in my organization into a competitive business advantage?*
54	Annual Strategic Review Cycle — *How does the yearly cycle of the earth apply to updating plans?*

Simple Answers:

For every complex problem there is a simple answer and . . . it is always wrong!

—H. L. Menkin

Tool #44 The Rollercoaster of Change

Application of Natural Cycles of Change; and the Seven Levels of Living Systems

Systems move in natural cycles and circles, but many people think and try to work in straight lines. Keep in mind that the **Rollercoaster of Change**SM is in many ways a natural and normal part of planning and change.

We see straight lines and structure, but reality is really made up of circles, because of our language, which is left-to-right.

The cycles of change, input, throughput, output, and feedback from the environment repeat endlessly throughout all seven levels of living systems and their interactions with other systems.

A. The Rollercoaster of ChangeSM

- **For example:** When people go through change, it isn't along a straight line from A to B. Their emotions take them on a rollercoaster ride. It's perfectly normal, so acknowledge its existence and allow it to occur. Help others through it, too.

- **For example:** We call this the Rollercoaster of ChangeSM and have been able to see many different uses for it. **In fact, when people are going through change, just the knowledge of its existence is very helpful to people.** This means it is natural and normal to be depressed during change; just don't live there over time.

Persistence . . . Hang In THERE!

Nothing in the world can take the place of persistence. Talent will not; nothing is more common than unsuccessful men with talent. Genius will not; unrewarded genius is almost a proverb. Education will not; the world is full of educated derelicts. Persistence and determination alone are omnipotent.

—Calvin Coolidge

A basic truth of management—if not of life—is that nearly everything looks like a failure in the middle . . . persistent, consistent execution is unglamorous, time-consuming, and sometimes boring.

—Rosabeth Moss Kanter, July 1990

ALL CHANGE IS A LOSS EXPERIENCE

1. **Loss** creates a feeling of depression for most people. One loses preferred modes of attaining and giving affection, handling aggression, dependency needs—all those familiar routines which we have evolved and usually taken for granted.
2. **Loss** is a difficult experience to handle; particularly if what one leaves behind is psychologically important.
3. **All loss** must be mourned and the attendant feelings disgorged if a restitution process is to operate effectively.
4. **Most** organization change flounders because the experience of loss is not taken into account. To undertake successful organizational change, an executive must anticipate and provide the means of working through that loss and all four phases of it.

Adapted from Harry Levinson, *Psychological Man*

Rollercoaster of Change℠ and the Systems Thinking Approach
"Persevere"—The Key to Strategic Change

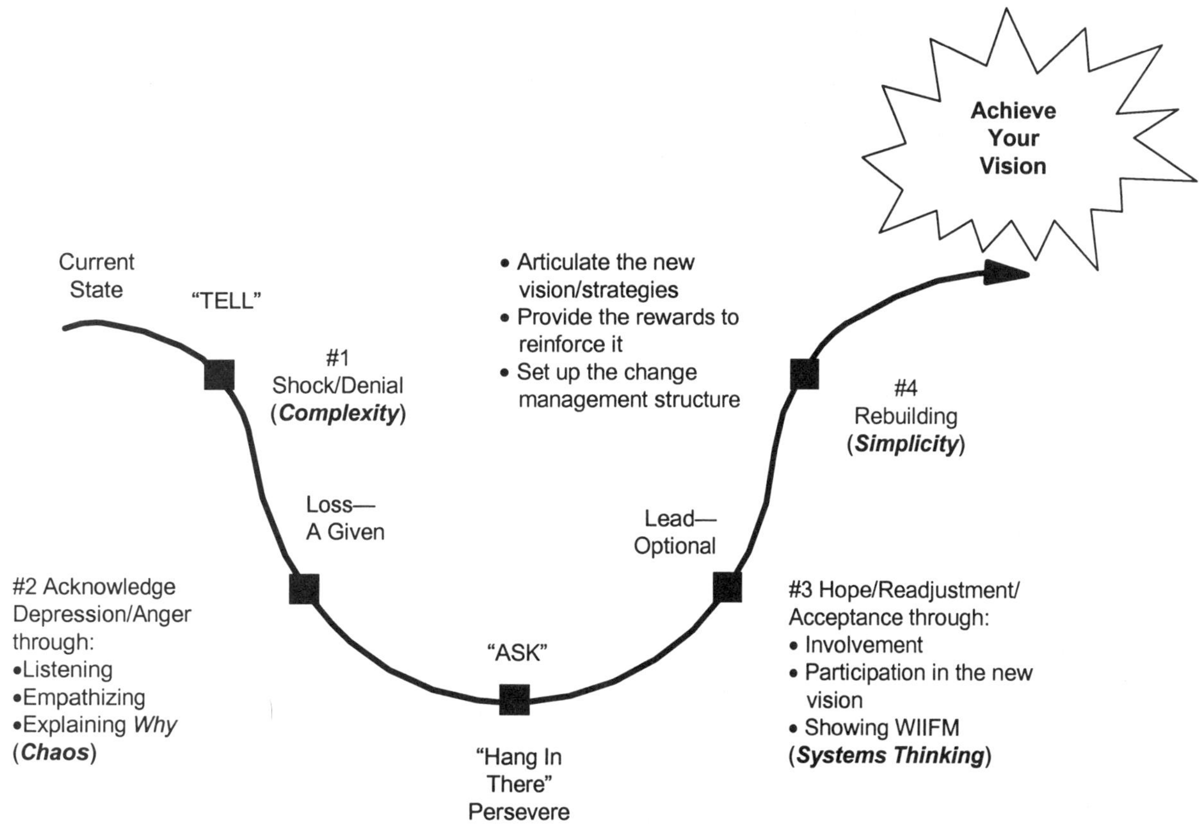

Chaos and Complexity

Chaos and complexity are a normal and natural part of the process of change, of discovering new ways of being and achieving new visions.

Answer these major questions in any change effort:

1. Not "if" but "when" will we start to go through shock/depression?
2. How deep is the trough? Is it different for each person? (Implications?)
3. How long will it take? Are employees and management at the same stage?
4. Will we get up the right side (optional) and rebuild?
5. How do we manage the change proactively?
6. At what level will we rebuild?
7. What new skills do we need to accomplish this?
8. How many different rollercoaster rides will we go on and experience in this change?
9. Are there other changes/rollercoasters occurring?
10. Will we hang in and persevere at the midpoint (bottom)? How?
11. How will we deal with normal resistance? (Push or pull?)
12. How will we create a critical mass to support and achieve the change?

B. Indepth Understanding: Many Uses of the Rollercoaster

All you need to know in predicting, leading, and managing every type of change in our lives is that you will be on a rollercoaster ride.

➥ **For example:** Learning, coaching, training, planning, team building, etc., are all just different types of change; there is a rollercoaster ride for each of them.

➥ **For example:** Personally and professionally, whatever you do in today's world probably involves some form of change. We may not call it that, but that's what it is. So being an expert on the natural, normal, and predictable cycle of change that occurs in this world is essential.

➥ **For example:**

- Planning is really "planning for change."
- Organizations change when people change, so change is really personal and involves change, in our own behavior—not changing others.
- We can't really change others. If we want others to change, we need to change our own behavior and our own relationships with others. Then the relationships can be further changed.

Suggestions for Use:

1. Internalize the idea of the rollercoaster and its sequences. Of course, be sure to remember that any model is only a simplistic representation of a complex reality.

2. Teach and share this model with key people whenever you are involved in any type of change. Make sure people realize that it is natural, normal, and expected that things will get worse and that there will be a loss of energy (Stage 2—Anger/Depression) before things get better (Stages 3 and 4).

3. Once you know the fundamentals, look at the next few tools and apply the curve and the different terminology and actions to your specific situation.

Tool #45 The Rollercoaster of Self-Change

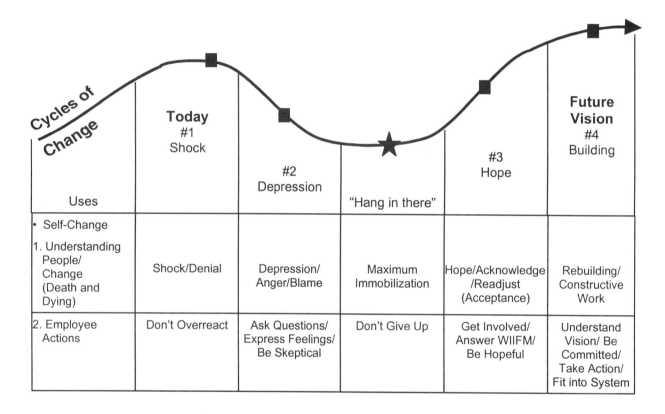

Application of Natural Cycles of Change;
and the Seven Levels of Living Systems

A. Self-Change

"Self-change" is the first key level of living systems we need to focus on, professionally and organizationally. Using the rollercoaster for self-change, our ride looks like this.

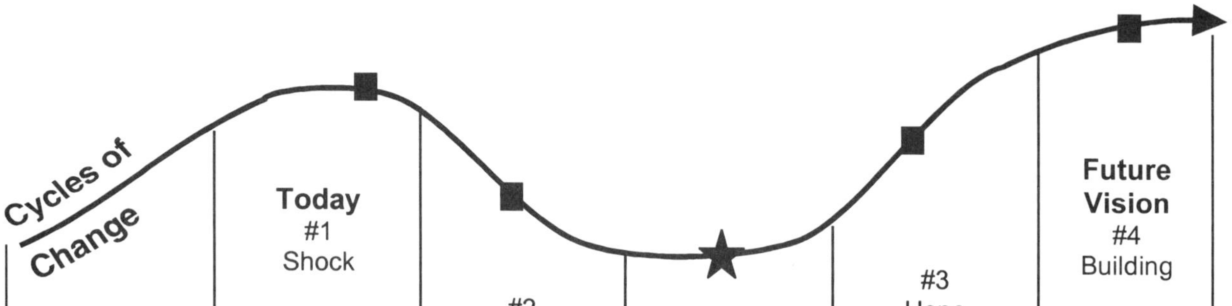

Uses	**Today** #1 Shock	#2 Depression	"Hang in there"	#3 Hope	**Future Vision** #4 Building
• Self-Change 1. Understanding People/ Change (Death and Dying)	Shock/Denial	Depression/ Anger/Blame	Maximum Immobilization	Hope/Acknowledge /Readjust (Acceptance)	Rebuilding/ Constructive Work
2. Employee Actions	Don't Overreact	Ask Questions/ Express Feelings/ Be Skeptical	Don't Give Up	Get Involved/ Answer WIIFM/ Be Hopeful	Understand Vision/ Be Committed/ Take Action/ Fit into System

➥ **For example:** Before I can help someone else in my family, team, department, or organization, I have to first get to Phase #3 (hope) at a minimum.

Suggestions for Use:

1. Know this curve well because it is normal and natural in today's world.
2. Recognize that you are always somewhere on this curve; wherever it is, you are still okay.
3. Don't deny your feelings and emotions when you are in Phase #2. Acknowledge and honor them.
4. Take care of yourself when in Phase #2. Adopt coping behaviors—take time off, eat healthily, get enough sleep, and exercise.
5. As an employee, follow the advice during each cycle; and don't overreact!

B. Executive Misperceptions

Executives plan and lead change, so they usually go through change before their employees. Thus, the change sequence affects executives, then supervisors, then the rest of the employees.

Executives often have feelings about the change that are at the opposite end of the curve from their employees ("If I feel good, they are angry and upset"). **This is one place where executive intuition is usually wrong.**

"If it's right for me, it's wrong for my employees."

The Rollercoaster of Change^SM^

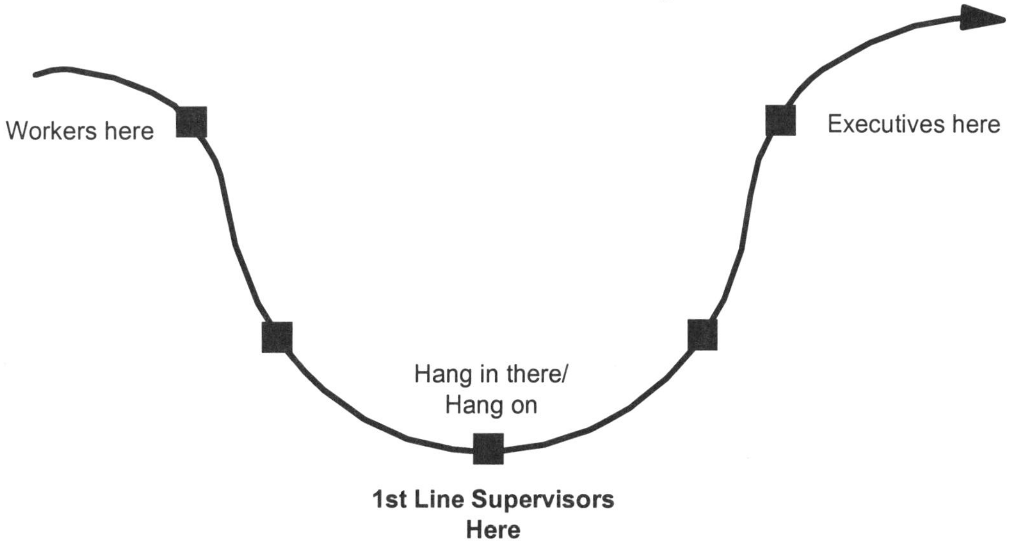

➥ **For example:** No matter what the change is, you must recognize that Stage #2 feelings of anger, depression, emotions, etc., are natural and normal. Just don't live there forever! Often the best thing you can do is learn about this rollercoaster and share where you and others are on it. It's legitimate to be anywhere on it!

However, you should keep moving from #2 → #3 → #4. You will experience temporary setbacks and move backwards at times, but take comfort in the fact that executives generally go through this before supervisors, and supervisors before workers. So you weren't the only one!

➥ **For example:** Parents usually go through the stages before their children.

Suggestions for Use:

1. Recognize the reality. Your intuition may be wrong.
2. Realize that everyone goes through this cycle and stages at different rates and depths.
3. Help yourself through it first.
4. Be ready to assist others at any step at any time.
5. Learn the skills of the helpful coach and involve others through this curve.

Tool #46 The Rollercoaster of Interpersonal Change

Application of Natural Cycles of Change; and the Seven Levels of Living Systems

Interpersonal skills are among your most valuable assets. Since change is constant for you and nearly everyone else you come in contact with, see how these five interpersonal rollercoaster suggestions apply to your life. While the terms are different, it is the same rollercoaster. It is predictable and it is a guide for you to use when going through the rollercoaster interpersonally.

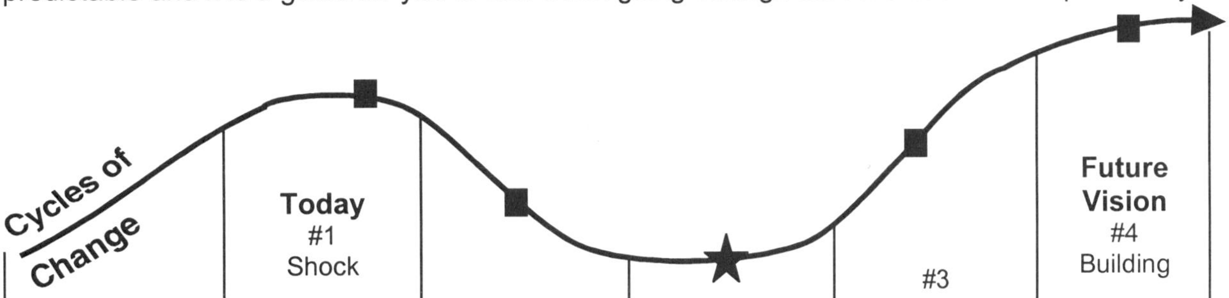

Uses	**Today** #1 Shock	#2 Depression	"Hang in"	#3 Hope	**Future Vision** #4 Building
• Interpersonal Changes 1. Relationships	Inclusion Desire	Control Issues	Growth Desire	Openness	High Performance
2. Proper Structure of Management Interactions with Employees	High Directive/ Low Supportive	High Directive/ High Supportive	Transition/ Persistence	High Supportive/ Low Directive	Low Supportive/ Low Directive
3. Situational Leadership (new leadership skills)	Tell/Direct (train)	Sell/Ask (coach)	Persevere	Participate/ Involvement (facilitate)	Delegate within System (empower)
4. Manage-ment's Specific Tasks	Change Self First/Appreciate/ "Everyone Changes at Different Rates and Depths	"Skeptics Are My Best Friends"/ Empathize/ Listen/Explain Why/Face-to-Face Meetings	Be Consistent/ Model the Way	Seek Involvement/ Show WIIFM/ Challenge the Process/ Celebrate the Heart	Shared Vision/ Articulate Again and Again/ Enable Others/ Systems Fit, Alignment, and Integrity
5. Coaching	Contact/Purpose	Chaos or Compatibility	Continuous Relationship	Contract/Norms	Collaboration/ Work

➥ **For example:** Issues of inclusion, control, growth, openness, and performance are issues for all of us as we interact with others every day. They are natural and normal and go on all the time, minute by minute.

Suggestions for Use: **Personally and Professionally**

1. Study these five situations and decide for yourself, in practical terms, how you can be flexible when dealing with others.
2. Be clear on how to interact with others so that there is more inclusion and less need to control. Control often stifles growth.
3. Examine your level of openness. Do you share with others first, or hold your cards close to your vest?
4. Are you willing to be open to feedback (even if it hurts) so you can continue to learn, grow, and be more effective?
5. As a supervisor or parent, realize that you need both telling/expert skills and style and also asking/active listening skills. Most of us tend to be good at one or the other in our interpersonal relationships.
6. Learn to be flexible. Match up your interpersonal style to the needs of the other person and the situation they are in. The long-term popularity of Hersey/Blanchard's Famous "Situational Leadership" model was no accident.
7. Use the model above as a template and guide to improving your coaching skills. The rollercoaster concept is the only concept you need to know. Use it when coaching others (i.e., learn effective listening skills; maintain the relationship, even when strong corrections/sanctions are necessary; build healthy norms between you, including a clear sense of purpose/outcomes).

Tool #47 The Rollercoaster of Team Change

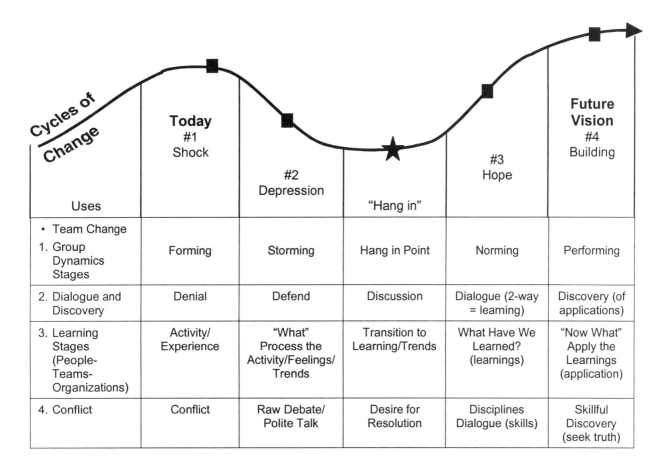

Application of Natural Cycles of Change; and the Seven Levels of Living Systems

In organizations, in families, in communities, and in sports teams, productive work gets done by groups of people who become teams and go on to work together effectively. Whenever you get together in a new group (and often in existing groups), it is natural and normal for you to take the rollercoaster ride to become an effective team.

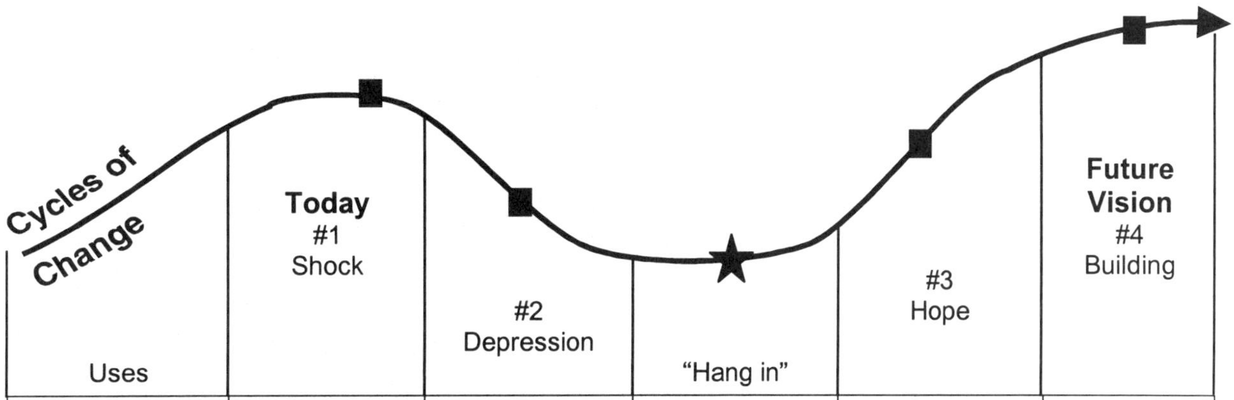

Uses	**Today** #1 Shock	#2 Depression	"Hang in"	#3 Hope	**Future Vision** #4 Building
• Team Change 1. Group Dynamics Stages	Forming	Storming	Hang in Point	Norming	Performing
2. Dialogue and Discovery	Denial	Defend	Discussion	Dialogue (2-way = learning)	Discovery (of applications)
3. Learning Stages (People-Teams-Organizations)	Activity/ Experience	"What" Process the Activity/Feelings/ Trends	Transition to Learning/Trends	What Have We Learned? (learnings)	"Now What" Apply the Learnings (application)
4. Conflict	Conflict	Raw Debate/ Polite Talk	Desire for Resolution	Disciplines Dialogue (skills)	Skillful Discovery (seek truth)

➥ **For example:** Most people assume (wrongly) that if they put groups of people together for a meeting, they will be forming an effective team that can immediately do productive work. Nothing could be further from the truth. Each group goes through the same rollercoaster sequence until they become an effective team at Stage #4. The chart above gives a path to follow to transverse the rollercoaster naturally and successfully.

Suggestions for Use: Personally and Professionally

1. Since most productive work today requires that teams function effectively, internalize the four stages of team/group dynamics: Form, Storm, Norm, and Perform.

2. Learn techniques to speed things up on this rollercoaster/learning curve of effective teamwork. Spend time when forming a team to define:
   - your purpose(s)
   - your norms of acceptable behavior
   - goals and timetables
   - roles and accountabilities and their interdependencies
   - how to get feedback to continually improve the team

3. Work with each of the teams you are part of to learn how to maintain intellectual honesty and the dialogue and discovery of better solutions that come with it. Learn to *"leave your shield at the door"* and stop defending all your ideas and taking issues personally. You can either defend your position/ideas or expand your range of information for better decision making, but not both.

4. "Consensus" means that I can *"actively support"* the decision that is made. Work toward making this an effective tool in your team situation.

5. Effective conflict resolution also involves these phases as well. Stifling anger and emotions in the name of politeness and logic is to suppress conflict and its potential benefits. What are its benefits?

6. "Adults learn best by doing" is a basic truism (so do children, by the way, but that's another book on the problems in education). To learn from anything you are doing (formal training program, meeting, etc.), learn to seek feedback and insights for improvement at the end of each activity by asking three key questions:

   #1 ***What*** just happened?

   #2 ***So What*** can we learn or generalize from all of this?

   #3 ***Now What*** can we do differently or improve by applying these learnings?

What—So What—Now What!

Tool #48 The Rollercoaster of Organizational Change

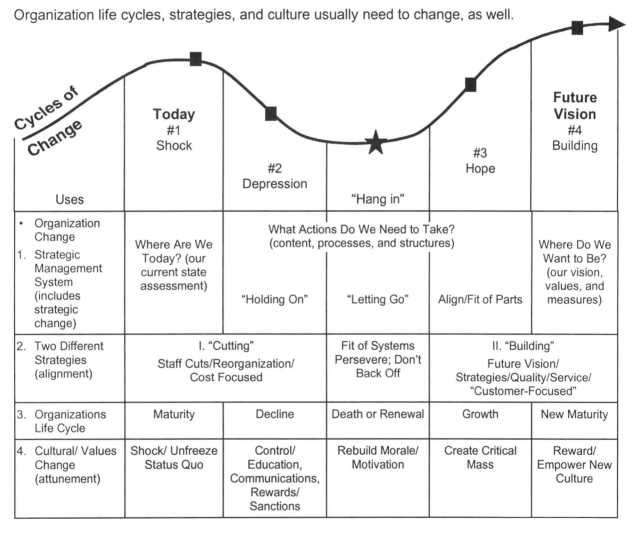

Application of Natural Cycles of Change;
and the Seven Levels of Living Systems

While organizations change when people change, there still is a collective set of behavioral changes that organizations need to undergo organization-wide to deal with constant and dynamic environmental changes. This is the ultimate level of living systems for improved organization effectiveness. And just as within the hierarchy of the Seven Levels of Living Systems, organizational change includes all the rollercoaster dynamics of the previous four rollercoaster tools and levels.

Organization life cycles, strategies, and culture usually need to change, as well.

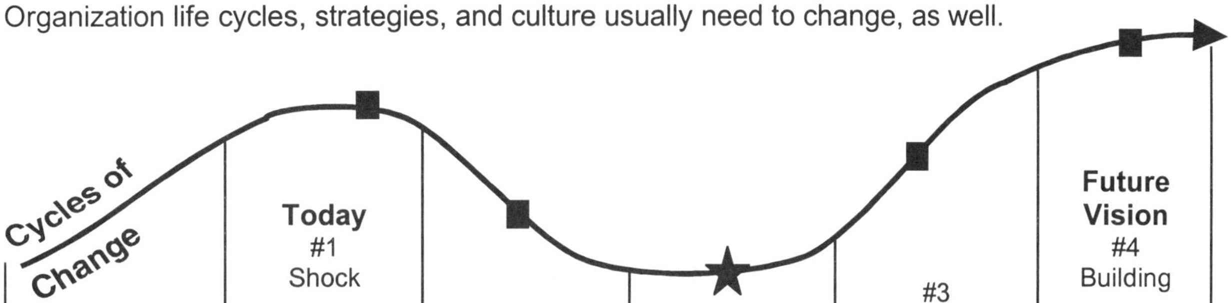

Uses	**Today** #1 Shock	#2 Depression	"Hang in"	#3 Hope	**Future Vision** #4 Building
• Organization Change 1. Strategic Management System (includes strategic change)	Where Are We Today? (our current state assessment)	What Actions Do We Need to Take? (content, processes, and structures) "Holding On"	"Letting Go"	Align/Fit of Parts	Where Do We Want to Be? (our vision, values, and measures)
2. Two Different Strategies (alignment)	I. "Cutting" Staff Cuts/Reorganization/ Cost Focused		Fit of Systems Persevere; Don't Back Off	II. "Building" Future Vision/ Strategies/Quality/Service/ "Customer-Focused"	
3. Organizations Life Cycle	Maturity	Decline	Death or Renewal	Growth	New Maturity
4. Cultural/ Values Change (attunement)	Shock/ Unfreeze Status Quo	Control/ Education, Communications, Rewards/ Sanctions	Rebuild Morale/ Motivation	Create Critical Mass	Reward/ Empower New Culture

➥ **For example:** Most organizations attempt organization-wide change in a piecemeal, haphazard fashion. This is why experts estimate that 70–90% of all major change fails.

Suggestions for Use:

As this book of tools shows, major change requires you to pay close attention to the fit between, and among, all aspects of the web of relationships (i.e., parts/components) in support of the overall objectives of the whole system/organization.

1. This chapter deals with all seven levels of living systems that affect organizations—individual, interpersonal, team/department, cross functions or cross-department, and organization-wide changes. (See other five Rollercoaster Tools.)

2. Chapter 5 deals with the **alignment of your delivery processes,** based on the strategies you need to achieve world-class star results and customer value (Phase A outcomes).

3. Chapter 3 deals with **attunement with people's hearts and minds** in support of the new values and desired culture, as well as customer satisfaction.

4. Chapter 8 deals with the need for a **Strategic Management System** that includes several tools about the Strategic Change Management process.

5. In other words, achieving major, large-scale or transformational change of any magnitude is very, very difficult and has a low probability of success.

6. Your choices include five different rollercoasters that might look like the following page. Which do you want? What price are you willing to pay to achieve change?

TRANSFORMATIONAL CHANGE AND EXCELLENCE

THE FIVE CHOICES OF CHANGE AND LEVELS OF EXCELLENCE

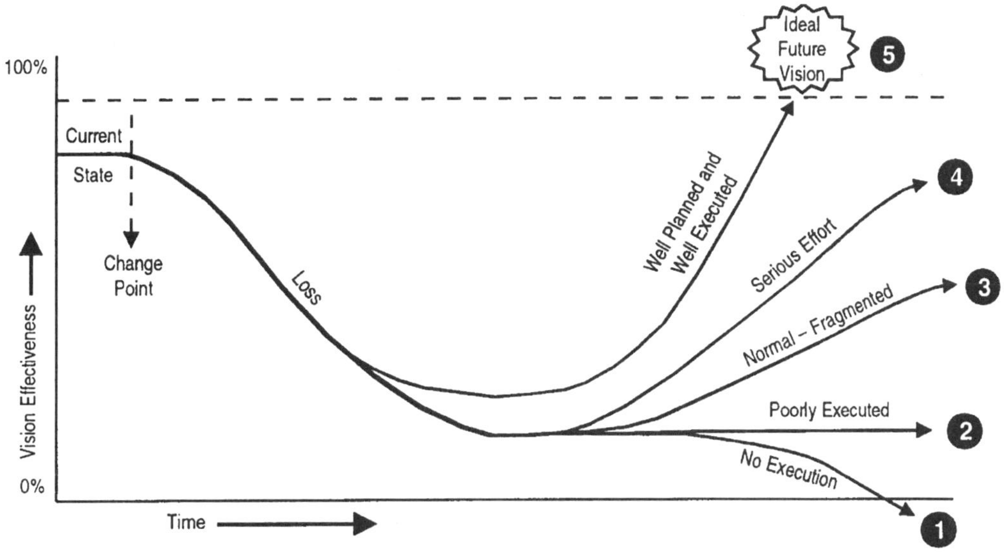

Which will you be?

_____ ❶ **Incompetence**—"Going Out of Business"

_____ ❷ **Technical**—"Dogged Pursuit of Mediocrity"

_____ ❸ **Management**—"Present and Accounted for Only"

_____ ❹ **Leadership**—"Making a Serious Effort"

_____ ❺ **Visionary Leadership**—"Developing an Art Form"

Tool #49 Cutting and Building Success Strategies

Application of Systems Dynamics #11: Dynamic Equilibrium; #12: Internal Elaboration; as well as the Natural Cycle of Change

A. Strategies

A set of strategies for success almost always includes "cutting" and "building" strategies, to both (1) keep expenses under control and (2) to meet customers' needs.

This requires a clear purpose, vision, or mission in which you define your desired outcomes in terms of (1) products/services and (2) customers.

It is crucial that you develop the two different types of strategies shown below:

1. Cost-**cutting**
2. **Building** a future vision

They follow the Rollercoaster of Change[SM] sequence.

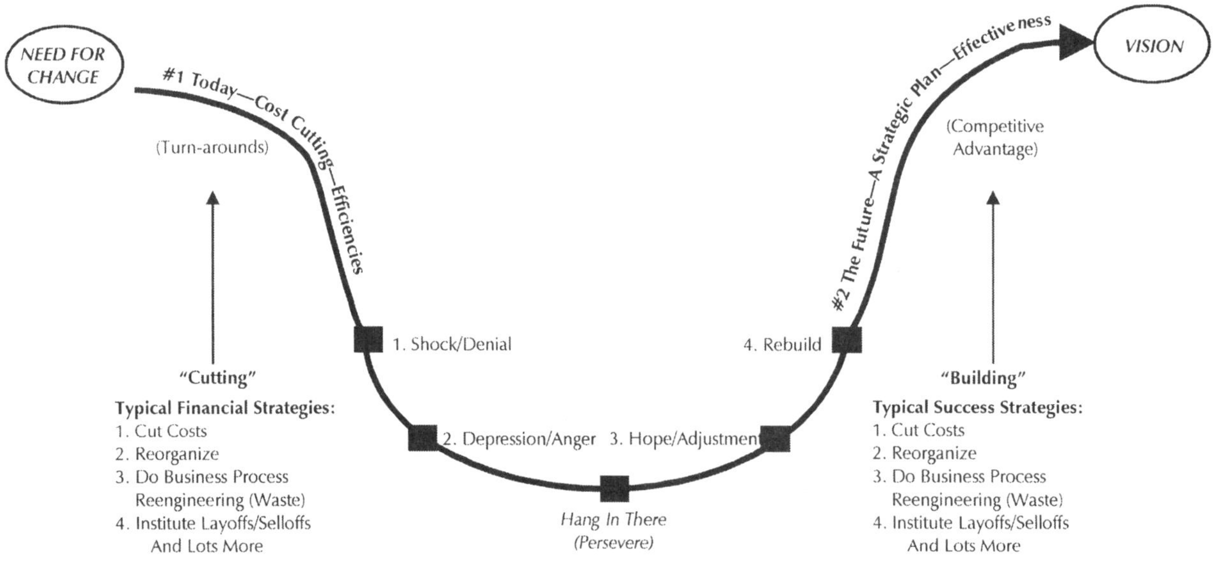

➥ **For example:** What are your strengths in your personal life? What about your organization? Are you willing to spend money to make money, for example, or invest in yourself (education, etc.)?

Suggestions for Use:

1. Develop a clear idea of where you want your organization to be in the future. Be clear about your desired future customers, products, and services.
2. Next, conduct a current state assessment so that you know where you are today.
3. Define the gap between the first two steps.
4. Filling this gap requires a set of strategies. Cutting costs is probably paramount, but where you cut them should depend on what your overall goals are. Make sure you have both:
   - Cost-cutting strategies
   - Building toward the future–type strategies

B. Alternative Application: Preventing Failure

(Application of Systems Dynamics #6: Multiple-Goal Seeking)

Are you clear on the difference between the use of quick-fix and turnaround strategies?

- Long-term success strategies can help you build toward your future; they focus on customers—and their needed products and services—how to win them and keep them.
- Cost reduction is an important, yet analytic, failure-prevention strategy only ("necessary, but not sufficient for success"). Your chief goal should not be to lower costs, but to win and keep customers.

➡ **For example:** Once you cut costs to keep from going bankrupt, what will you do to create success with your customers?

➡ **For example:** To prevent failure with your customers, you need a "Customer Recovery Strategy."

Suggestions for Use:

1. There are times when you must cut costs and patch up customer relations at the same time (i.e., tough economic situation, company turn-around effort).
2. However, you will also need positive, go-forward strategies and actions.
3. Carefully evaluate whether you must do both at once to keep up morale or whether you can do them sequentially.
4. This sequential focusing only on costs/patching up alone is often a big mistake.

Tool #50 Six Natural Phases of Change

Application of Natural Cycles of Change;
and the Seven Levels of Living Systems

Change is natural, and we've seen that its phases are predictable. The phases overlap at times, but are useful in planning and implementing major organizational change because they provide a framework to help guide the organization through stressful times.

Phases	Goals and Major Actions
1. Pre-Change	**Pre-Planning: Goal—Be ready to lead and manage the change effectively.** A. Finalize decisions about the changes. B. Conduct "Plan-to-Implement" (structures, roles, processes, phases). C. Plan out the announcement details of the actual change decision with "military precision."
2. Shock/Denial	**Kick-Off the Change: Goal—To communicate the changes.** A. Communicate the changes openly, along with their rationale, in a "TLC" fashion. Treat people with dignity and respect. B. "Unfreeze" the organization from the old, steady state, using proven techniques to do so. C. Minimize, as much as possible, the inducement and sense of shock, denial, and loss.
3. Anger/ Depression	**Reorganize People: Goal—Deal effectively with the losses, concerns, and emotions that are a natural part of the process.** A. Begin to implement the changes in people, jobs, structures, processes, etc. B. Deal effectively with the anger, depression, and loss, using proven techniques to do so. C. Continually explain the vision, as well as the logic and rationale behind the change.
4. Hang In/ Persevere	**New Team Start-Up: Goal—Clarify new work/team roles and responsibilities.** A. Communicate the expectations and style of the new structures and supervisors. B. Clarify roles and responsibilities of each new team member, and answer "What's in it for me?" questions. C. Decide and agree on new team operational procedures and processes. Begin to build relationships.

(continued)

Phases	Goals and Major Actions
5. Hope/ Adjustment	**Re-Establish the New Direction and Management Systems: Goal—Decide, agree, and communicate plans for the future.** A. Rebuild all management processes and systems to "blow out bureaucracy and waste" and serve the customer better. B. Redo strategic, business, and operational plans and budgets; all need to be based on desired marketplace positioning and changes in strategy/vision. C. Reinforce desired cultural changes through employee involvement and participation in decisions that affect them.
6. Rebuild	**Climb the Learning Curve: Goal—Become a high-performance organization.** A. Conduct follow-up team building and improve cross-functional teamwork to achieve your vision. B. Gather customer feedback and take needed actions to improve customer value. C. Conduct employee surveys and make appropriate changes so you "live" the desired values and culture.

➥ **For example:** Many large-scale change efforts in organizations consist mainly of laying off employees, reorganizing the "org" chart, and then considering the change over with. "Chainsaw" Al Dunlap, former CEO of Sunbeam, was eventually fired, as were many others CEOs who didn't understand the natural realities of change. Their naiveté about the human side of change is almost criminal.

Would you let a surgeon operate on your body if you were aware that he or she knew as little about body processes as some CEOs do about change?

Suggestions for Use:

1. Have all middle and senior management study, discuss, and fully understand the six natural phases of organizational change.
2. If it is a major change, assign a full-time staff assistant/coordinator to support senior management to help them improve skills and credibility.
3. Consider the use of a master-level external consultant to assist with difficult points throughout the change.
4. Combine senior management and support staff into a Change Leadership Team that meets regularly throughout all phases of the change effort.
5. The Leadership Team should use the six natural phases to plan its work, step by step.

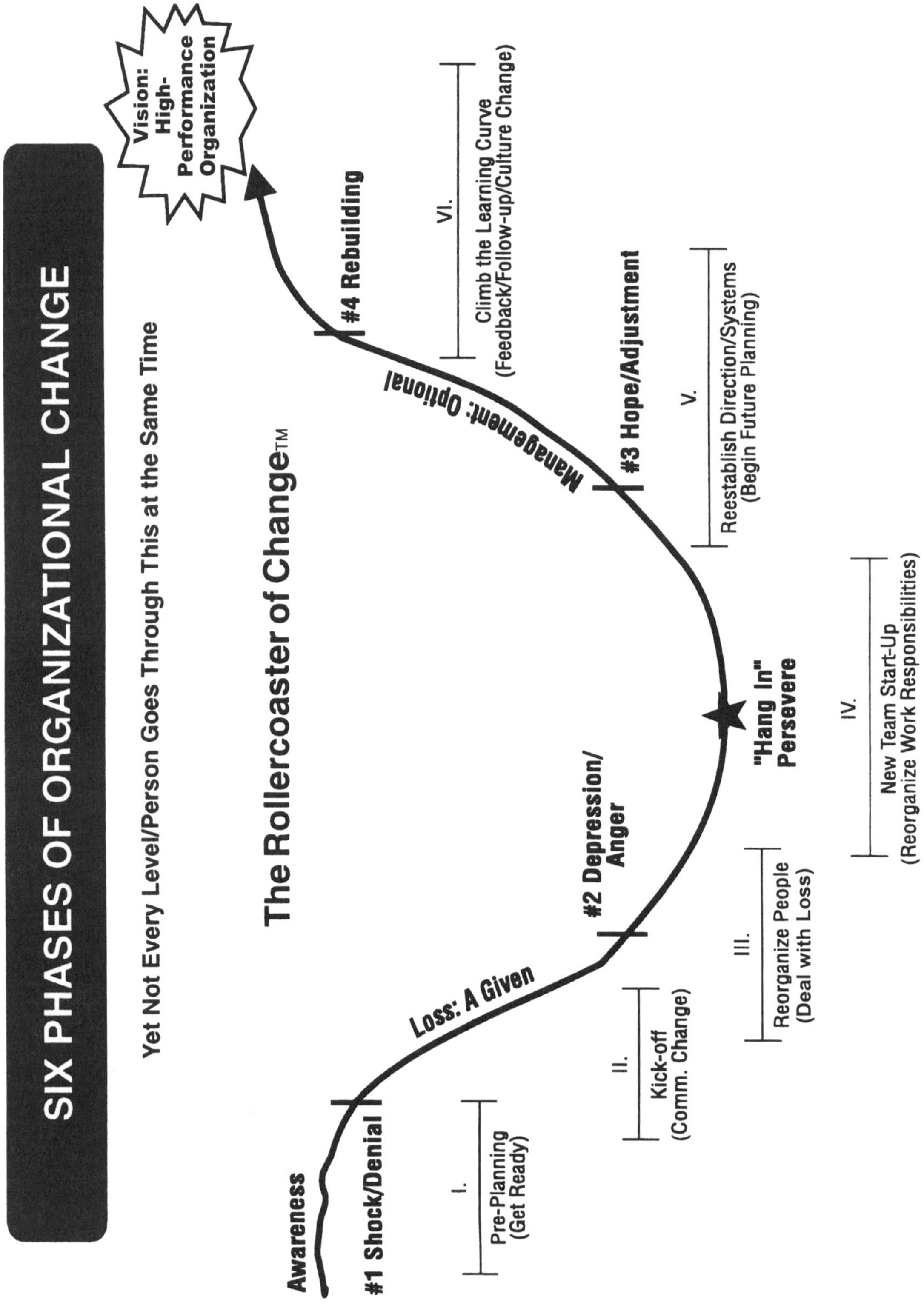
SIX PHASES OF ORGANIZATIONAL CHANGE
Yet Not Every Level/Person Goes Through This at the Same Time
The Rollercoaster of Change™
Awareness
#1 Shock/Denial
Loss: A Given
#2 Depression/ Anger
"Hang In" Persevere
#3 Hope/Adjustment
Management: Optional
#4 Rebuilding
Vision: High-Performance Organization
I. Pre-Planning (Get Ready)
II. Kick-off (Comm. Change)
III. Reorganize People (Deal with Loss)
IV. New Team Start-Up (Reorganize Work Responsibilities)
V. Reestablish Direction/Systems (Begin Future Planning)
VI. Climb the Learning Curve (Feedback/Follow-up/Culture Change)

Tool #51 The Natural Life Cycle

Application of Natural Cycles of Change

As systems, we pass through phases or cycles: birth, growth, maturity, decline, death (or renewal). Nothing lives forever, but you can use strategic planning/thinking to get ahead of the power curve. Just remember that solutions to complex problems take time and need to be appropriate for your place on the life cycle.

Chaos is also part of this decline and, believe it or not, is a natural stage in evolution. Just keep it moving you forward into renewal—not death.

Normal Life Cycle

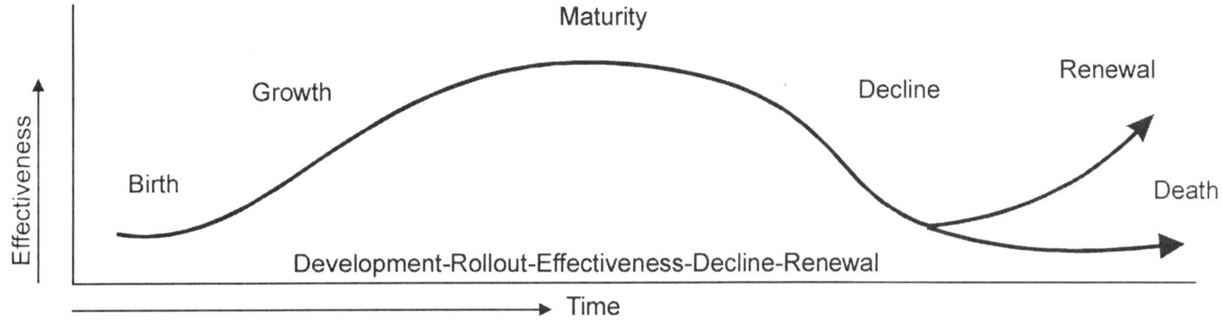

Faster Is Slower

> *All natural systems, whether ecosystems or organizations, have an optimal rate of growth that is far slower than the fast pace most of us think is desirable. The system will compensate for fast growth by slowing down, even if it means death.*
>
> —*The Fifth Discipline,* Peter M. Senge

Natural Systems Are Cycles of Causes and Effects

Farmers know all about natural systems. They can't double-cross nature by planting a crop and harvesting it a week later. Nature requires time and a combination of sunlight, water, temperature, soil, and nutrients in order to do its work. You can't cheat Mother Nature!

- ➥ **For example:** A system is a process . . . with inputs and outputs . . . that tries to move at a certain pace. Organizationally and personally you need to know where you are on your life cycle and build strategies appropriate to it. There is a complete body of strategy literature on this. The only difference is that organizations can renew perpetually if they adapt properly to their environment. People have limits to their renewal; eventually we all die.

Suggestions for Use:

1. This cycle is the way reality is. Just keep in mind the need for constant feedback and environment scanning to fight off decline and enhance renewal opportunities.

2. Use the Organizational Life Cycle Matrix below: Determine where your organization is on both sides of this matrix.

3. ***Question***: Once you've "slotted yourself," determine what it means for your future strategies. Each one of these requires different strategies. See my 1998 book, *Strategy School,* for additional details.

Organizational Life Cycle Matrix

Competitive Position ↓	Company Maturity				
	1. Emerging	2. Growth	3. Mature	4. Declining	5. Renewal
A. Dominant					
B. Leading					
C. Important					
D. Tenable					
E. Weak					

Adapted from Hayden

Tool #52 Performance Management System & Cycle

Application of Systems Dynamics #9: Hierarchy; #10: Subsystems; and Natural Levels of Change

Managing the yearly cycle of performance of individuals and teams is crucial to organizational success. It must be tied to your strategic plan as follows.

➥ **For example:** A Performance Management System is a cycle of change for high performing cultures.

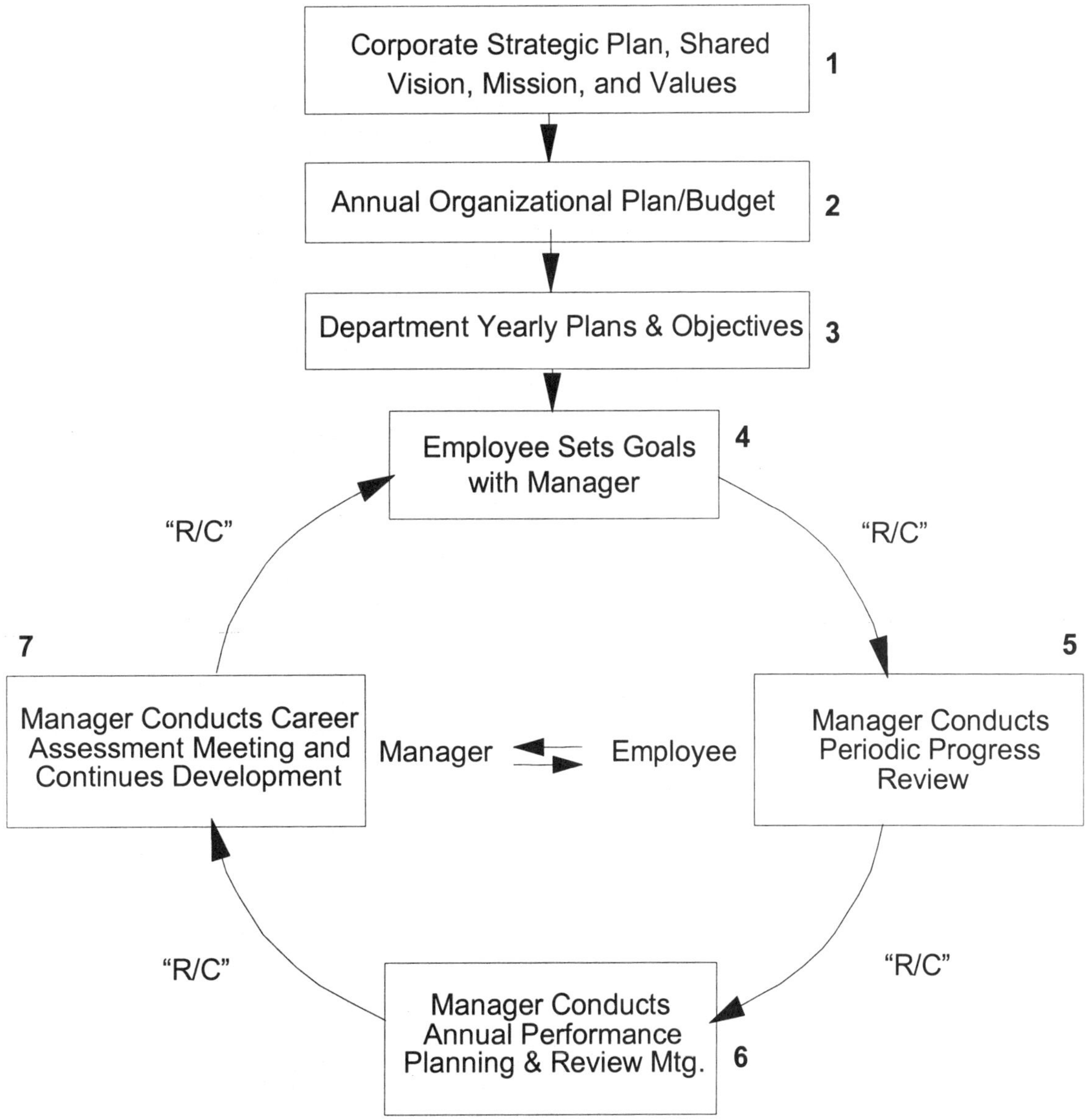

"R/C"—Rewards for Performance and Coaching can and should be given throughout this cycle.

➥ **For example:** Some of the keys to successful performance might include:

1. "No surprises" during the evaluation at the end of the review period.
2. Each person is responsible to manage the performance of only one person—him- or herself. Self-management (or the "every employee a manager" concept) is the key to individual career success and this performance management system.
3. The "every employee a manager" concept means that each person's supervisor merely corrects/critiques the goal-setting and self-evaluation of each individual, until both parties agree on the goals and evaluation. The supervisor will sign it off.
4. A 360° performance appraisal is also an option for full information if it is properly conducted.

Suggestions for Use:

1. Every organization should have this crucial system as it links the strategic plan to each employee and links all levels of the organization together in pursuit of the shared vision.
2. Assess how well you are doing on the "mega-issues" listed on the next page.
3. Assess whether you have all eleven elements of an Empowering Performance Management System.
4. Do you follow all the key steps (C) in your Performance Management System?
5. Integrate the results into an action plan.

What to do	Who	When

A. Mega-Issues of Performance Management in Your Organization

Instructions: On a scale of 1 (low) to 10 (high), rate these issues in your organization.

_______ 1. Are performance goals clear?

_______ 2. How important are these goals to the executives? Does the executive team really model them?

_______ 3. Do we deal positively with the "negative sum" merit increase phenomenon? Especially in a low-inflation economy?

_______ 4. Do we deal with the vulnerability of performance management, which is based on each individual manager's abilities? Can all of our managers do this well?

_______ 5. Reward issues are very susceptible to violations of expectation. Are all our employees educated so they are realistic and motivated about Performance Management?

_______ 6. Do we know what rewards people want? Are we delivering them?

_______ 7. Do we meet the needs of employees for career guidance, assistance, and development?

_______ 8. Is our merit program a true merit plan, or is it just a cost-of-living adjustment?

_______ 9. Do we deal with goal changes in our fast-paced environment?

_______ 10. Do managers confront poor performers at evaluation time?

_______ 11. What terminology do we use? Is it clear and well understood? Is "pay for performance" a helpful term?

_______ TOTAL SCORE (possible 110 points)

B. Elements of an Empowering Performance Management System

Question: Which performance management elements are in place within your organization?

_______ 1. Link to strategic plan/annual organizational goals, strategies, and priorities

_______ 2. Goal-setting process

_______ 3. Coaching process

_______ 4. Annual performance-appraisal process (tied to core strategies/core values)

_______ 5. Career-development process

_______ 6. Link to compensation system

_______ 7. Recognition and nonfinancial rewards system

_______ 8. Training and development support throughout organization

_______ 9. Link to a progressive discipline system (performance consequences)

_______ 10. Executive-level system, management and professional-level system, and non-exempt level system specifics

_______ 11. Tie to organizational learning (succession planning and development system)

C. Key Steps in a Performance Management System

Once your organization has defined its mission and values, written a strategic plan, and set an annual plan/budget, you or other organizational leaders must take the following steps:

Step #3 Establish department plans and objectives for the year tied to the strategic plan, and explicitly explain them to all employees.

Step #4 Make sure each employee sets individual goals with his or her manager and identifies the behaviors expected to achieve these goals, as well as the ways in which goal achievement will be measured. Goals should be checked to see that they are stated in specific terms and that they are obtainable and measurable.

Make sure each manager coaches and counsels his or her employees on a regular basis, as appropriate, to track progress. Incentives and rewards (nonfinancial) can and should be given throughout this cycle.

Step #5 Make sure managers conduct semiformal, periodic, progress reviews with each employee on a monthly or quarterly basis. They should use this time to make any necessary changes in the employee's goal statement and the behaviors or actions necessary to achieve employee goals. Praise and/or encouragement should be freely given and corrections suggested and discussed. Priorities and time schedules should also be reviewed and clarified. Both parties should agree on a summary of expectations for the next period.

Step #6 Make sure each manager conducts a formal employee-performance appraisal meeting on an annual basis with each of his or her employees. Goals and behaviors must be reviewed.

Step #7 Each manager must also meet with each of his or her employees to discuss career goals. Objectives and development needs are discussed in relation to corporate goals and needs.

Return to Step #4. The manager and employee must review the employee's goals at the beginning of each new organizational year.

Tool #53 People-Edge System and Cycle

Application of Systems Dynamics #9: Hierarchy; and #10: Subsystems

Any organization wishing to be successful must obviously pay close attention to people issues. The "Blinding Flash of the Obvious" (BFO) is that without human beings, nothing gets done. The people in an organization frequently end up being the difference between success and failure.

How do you begin creating The People Edge℠?

It is a multiyear and multiphase change process at the least. It is not just having the right culture, although that is key. You must also have the *right people in the right job, with the right skills, at the right time, with the right motivation—within this right culture!*

Whew! How do you do all that?

It isn't easy, and it will take some time. The integrated Systems Thinking Approach is your best chance to do this successfully. When you begin to see that people can give or withhold anywhere from 20–80% of their discretionary effort and still remain employed, it becomes obvious that you will have to institute intensive, large-scale change.

➡ **For example:** Jack Welch, Chairman and CEO of General Electric, did this. Bear in mind that he has led GE for a very long time (17+ years) and started with a sound culture of development to begin with. Welch's successful methods have been the subject of many recent books and business magazine profiles

Start with a strategic plan and our Systems Model of Integrated Change. Use the model on page 298 to follow the many integrated steps, systems, subsystems, and processes (14 overall) that need to be integrated for maximum impact.

Succession Planning and Development

Of course, the core of creating the People Edge℠ is succession planning and management/ leadership development. A checklist on this topic follows the Systems Model of Integrated Change. This checklist helps to make the entire process more specific and practical.

Proactive Succession and Development

Change your organization from:

Openings waiting for qualified people

to

Qualified people waiting for openings.

Suggestions for Use:

1. Review all 14 points of the creating the People Edge[SM] multiyear, multiphase change process. Make sure you understand it before you go on.
2. Then fill out the questionnaire on succession and development.
3. Integrate your results into an action plan.

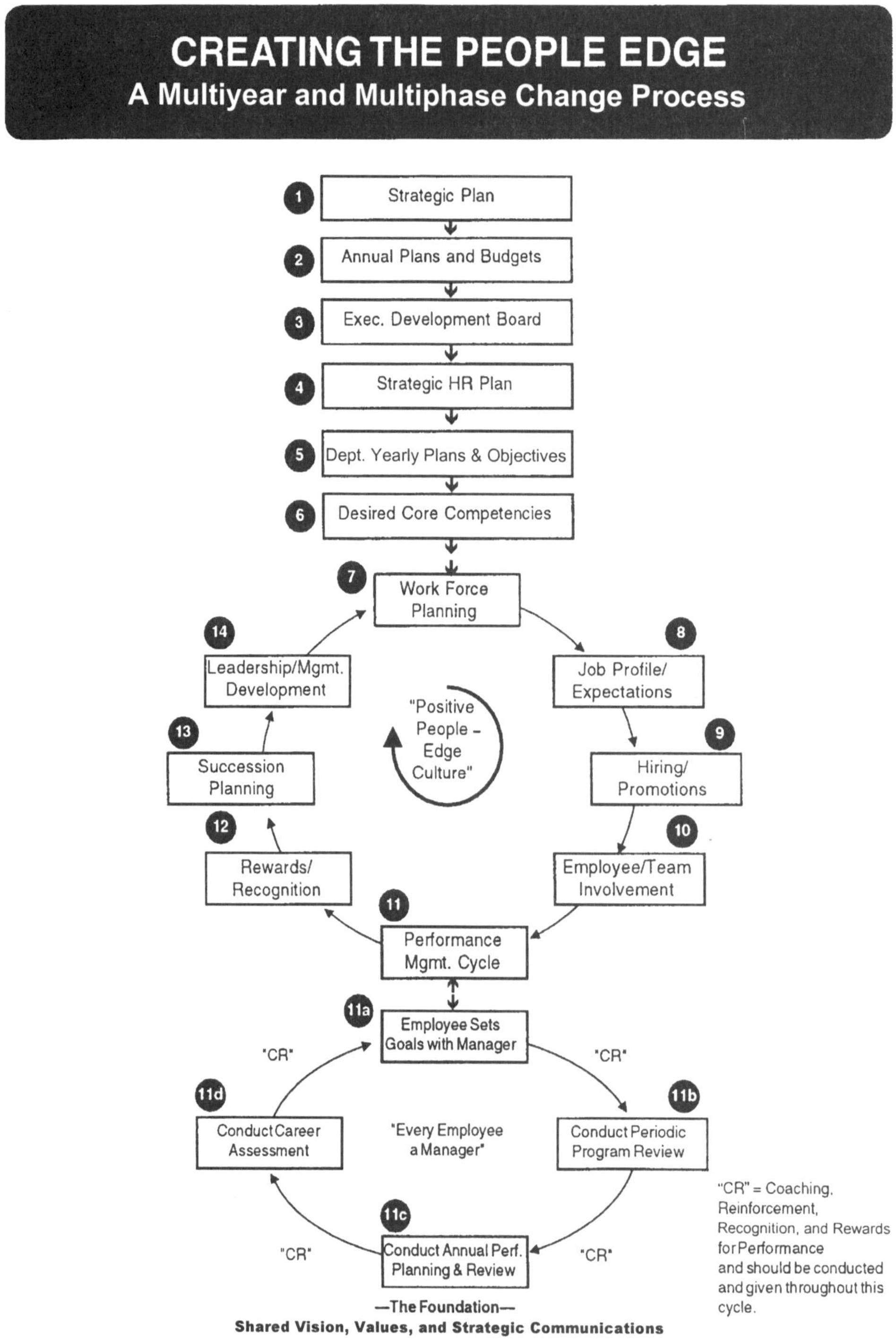
CREATING THE PEOPLE EDGE
A Multiyear and Multiphase Change Process
1 Strategic Plan
2 Annual Plans and Budgets
3 Exec. Development Board
4 Strategic HR Plan
5 Dept. Yearly Plans & Objectives
6 Desired Core Competencies
7 Work Force Planning
8 Job Profile/ Expectations
9 Hiring/ Promotions
10 Employee/Team Involvement
11 Performance Mgmt. Cycle
12 Rewards/ Recognition
13 Succession Planning
14 Leadership/Mgmt. Development
"Positive People - Edge Culture"
11a Employee Sets Goals with Manager
11b Conduct Periodic Program Review
11c Conduct Annual Perf. Planning & Review
11d Conduct Career Assessment
"CR"
"CR"
"CR"
"CR"
"Every Employee a Manager"
"CR" = Coaching, Reinforcement, Recognition, and Rewards for Performance and should be conducted and given throughout this cycle.
—The Foundation—
Shared Vision, Values, and Strategic Communications

People-Edge System

Instructions: In the spaces provided to the left of the items, list your priorities (1 is your highest) to get started building this system. Also list your lowest priorities (18-19-20, with 20 being the lowest). There are twenty items; you do not need to prioritize more than the five highest or three lowest.

_______ 1. Organization-wide strategic plan in place.

_______ 2. Annual plans and budgets in place for all departments, with clear accountability.

_______ 3. Executive/Employee Development Board in place.

_______ 4. Human Resource strategy plan in place.

_______ 5. Human Resource department yearly plans and objectives in place, with clear accountability.

_______ 6. Desired core competencies defined to guide overall hiring.

_______ 7. Workforce planning conducted to identify employee needs over the next one to two years.

_______ 8. Clear and complete job profile and expectations for open jobs.

_______ 9. Process in place for interviews, hiring, selection, and promotion skills; decision-making management involved in change effort.

_______ 10. Management commitment made to solicit, give and receive feedback, and acquire conflict management skills.

_______ 11. Performance Management cycle program and evaluation for each individual.

_______ 11a. Mentoring and coaching skills course for senior management and other managers involved to help them set clear goals and follow up with each employee.

_______ 11b. Performance improvement skills course for senior management and other managers so they can do day-to-day and periodic performance reviews.

_______ 11c. Concurring performance appraisal skills courses for senior management and other managers involved.

_______ 11d. Career development program and form for each individual.

_______ 12. Reward and recognition systems to recognize and reinforce high performance and coaching/development results.

_______ 13. Succession planning/form (for senior management's eyes only).

_______ 14a. Individual Development Plans (IDPs) for each individual.

_______ 14b. Alternate development solutions available for IDPs.

_______ 14c. Needs-analysis conducted and training courses available for common needs.

Tool #54 Annual Strategic Review Cycle

Application of Systems Dynamics #8: Entropy; and Natural Cycles of Change

All organizations and individuals need to take formal time on an annual basis to reassess and readjust their strategic (or life) plans and keep them on track, alive, and up-to-date. Systems run down over time; review is critical to reversing this entropy.

➥ **For example:** Our natural cycles of change are one year (that is how long it takes the earth to circle the sun). Organizations and individuals need to review and update once a year.

Annual Strategic Review (and Update)

A Practical Systems Thinking Approach to Continuous Improvement in Creating Customer-Focused, High-Performing Organizations

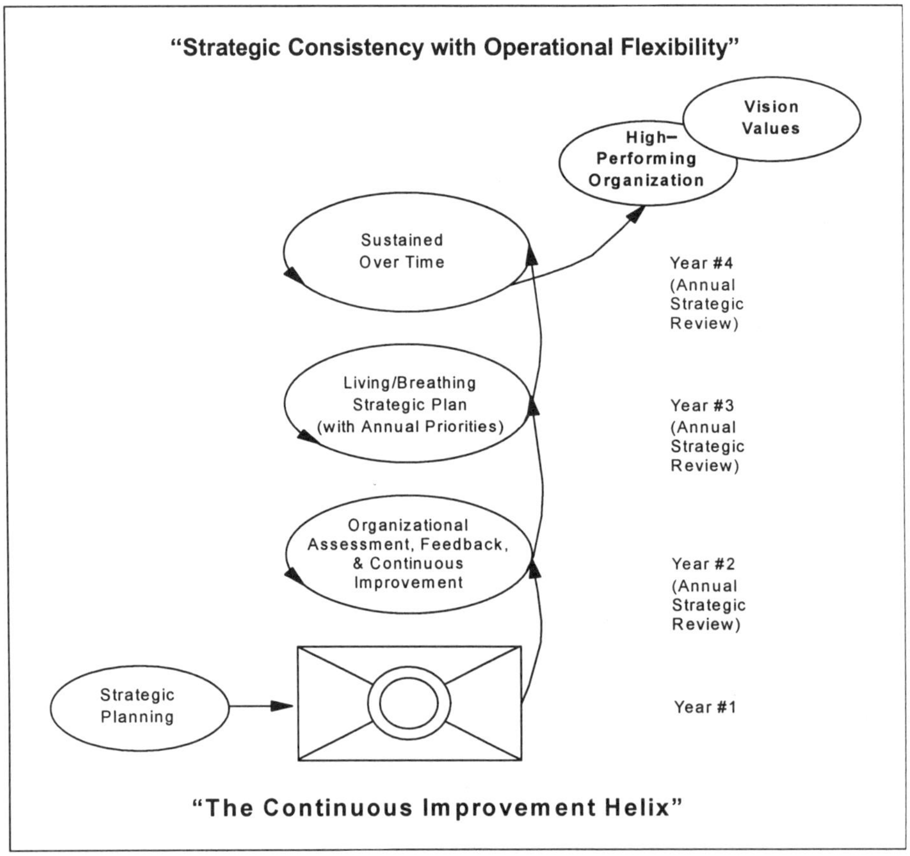

Annual Strategic Review (and Update) Concept

Similar to an annual independent financial audit and update

Goal #1: Assess the Strategic Management process as well as the system itself.

Goal #2: Assess the status and progress of the strategic plan.

This will help you:

1. Update your strategic plan
2. Clarify your annual planning and strategic budgeting priorities for the next year
3. Address any issues raised in either goal
4. Set in place next year's annual plan and Strategic Change Management process

Suggestions for Use:

1. Based on the framework and goals listed above (#1 and #2), each organization (and person/family) needs to conduct an independent yearly follow-up and diagnosis on how they are performing. If you want to learn how to be a customer-focused, high-performance learning organization, you have to do this.
2. *Question*: Where do you see yourself on the matrix below?

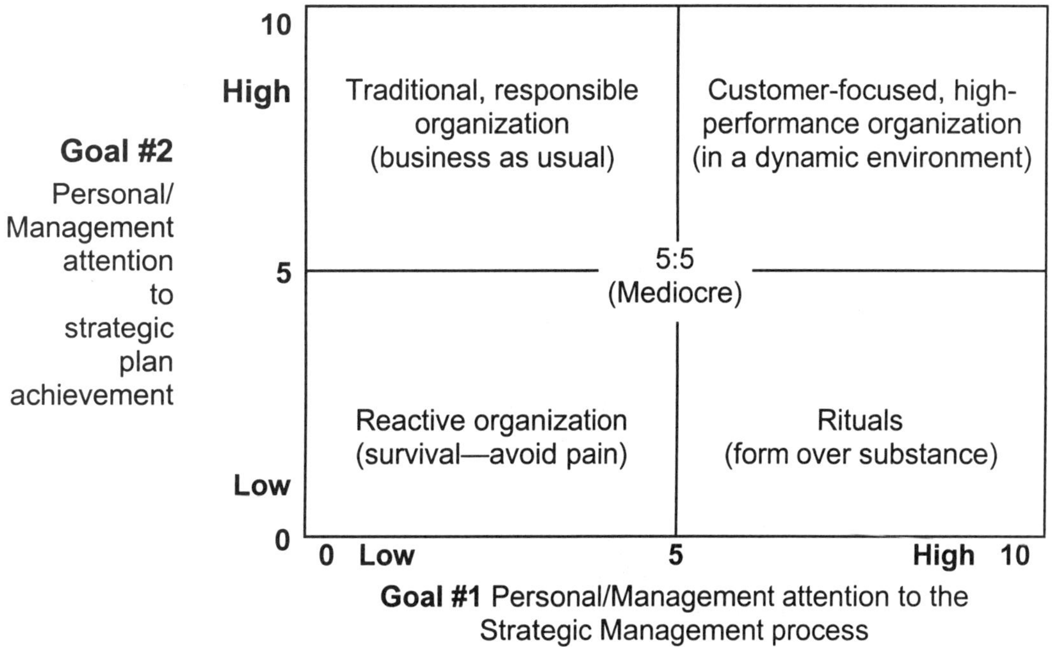

Suggestions for Use:

3. Follow the specific steps and sequence outlined below.

Annual Strategic Update

1st Step: Strategic Update

1. Hold a Strategic Change Leadership Steering Committee two-day session (include senior management and others) to:
   a. Review senior management decisions from plan-to-review session (vision, mission, values, key success factors).
   b. Perform environmental scanning review (opportunities/threats).
   c. Give feedback from annual strategic review (strengths/weaknesses).
   d. Validate and define core strategies.
   e. Develop next year's action priorities (top three) under each core strategy.

2nd Step: Parallel Process

2. Carry out appropriate parallel processes to involve and gain input on the draft plan from as many people/stakeholders as possible.

3rd Step: Strategic Update

3. Conduct a second session (one-day) to:
   a. Finalize the strategic and operations plans. Explore idea of a rolling plan.
   b. Prepare for annual planning and strategic budgeting process.
   c. Reset the Strategic Change Leadership Steering Committee and yearly comprehensive map of implementation.

4th Step: Approval

4. Strategic plan/annual priorities approved, if needed by the Board of Directors.

5th Step: Operations Planning

5. Annual plans developed and shared in a large group annual review meeting (or incorporated into an annual management meeting concept).

6th Step: Strategic Budgets

6. Conduct strategic budgeting using the top three priorities from each core strategy.

7th Step: Strategic Change

7. Restart the Strategic Change Leadership Steering Committee, etc.

> **Change can travel at the speed of thought.**
>
> —Greenpeace

CHAPTER VIII
SUMMARY APPLICATIONS

The applications in this chapter will help you integrate the previous tools in this guidebook into the context of a Strategic Management system. Its guiding systems concept is *holism*, which holds that the whole is more than the sum of its parts; the system itself can only be explained as a totality. Holism requires total, Strategic Management of the organization, and integrating the systems tools is an essential part of that management. It is one of the most fundamental elements of success in today's complex organizations.

Tool No.	The Applications
55	Organizational Culture Change — *What is "culture" and how do you change it?*
56	Strategic Management System — *What would be a good system for managing/leading your organization or business unit in a strategic fashion in a year-year cycle?*
57	Tailor to Your Needs — *How do you fit your unique situation into a systems model for Strategic Management?*
58	Wheel of Detail — *How can you ensure you pay attention to all the details of Strategic Change Management?*
59	Change Management Organizational Structures — *What are the full range of choices available to build the specific change management structures needed for effective change?*
60	Change Management Fail-Safe Mechanisms — *What checks and balances will ensure effective Strategic Management implementation, even with ineffective senior management leadership?*
61	Open Systems Planning — *How do you plan to identify and effectively deal with all the key stakeholders in your internal and external environments?*
62	Socio-Technical Systems — *How do you identify and effectively deal with all organizational issues involved in large-scale change in a simplified way?*
63	Versatile Assessment Tool — *What's a simple way to assess any situation for its systems implications?*
64	Five Key People Management Subsystems — *What are the people processes (or management subsystems) every organization needs to attract and retain the employees necessary to deliver customer value?*

Tool #55 Organizational Culture Change

Application of Systems Dynamics #1: Holism; and #10: Subsystems

A. Organizational Culture

(The way we do business around here)

An organization's culture is a set of interrelated beliefs or norms shared by most of the employees about how one should behave at work and what activities are more important than others. It is a holistic concept that permeates the entire organization; subcultures may also exist.

Assumptions/Philosophy =
our World View
("Weltanschauung")

↓

personal values

↓

organizational values

↓

norms of behavior
(i.e., the standards for action)

↓

individual behavior

↓

Collectively leads to our culture

There are many different subcultures within an organization, as well.

➥ **For example: Typical Organizational Culture Levels**

#1 Top Executive
beliefs/values/philosophies

↓

#2 upper management practices

↓

#3 middle management practices

↓

#4 workers
behaviors/performance/norms

Beliefs/values expressed through action create a culture. *True organizational culture is as it is perceived by the workers.* The key task is to create one desired culture throughout the total organization.

➥ **For example: Adversarial Cultures within an Organization**

It now appears that many communication, productivity, and union problems occur because of significantly different value systems among employee populations.

#1 Managers versus those being managed

or

#2 Line departments versus staff departments

or

#3 Manufacturing versus marketing

or

#4 Headquarters versus field

or

#5 Division versus division

The importance of organizational culture is greater than ever. As companies move away from hierarchical, top-down organizations, a greater number of the decisions individuals make are going to be shaped by the firm's culture. An organization's culture can determine the environment, which helps, hinders, or confuses the achievement of organizational goals. Without careful attention to the impact change has on all aspects of an organization, the drive for competitive advantage can be thwarted by a nonsupportive cultural environment.

In fact,

> When strategy and culture
>
> *or*
>
> vision and culture
>
> **collide**
>
> which wins out?
>
> ***Culture, of course!***

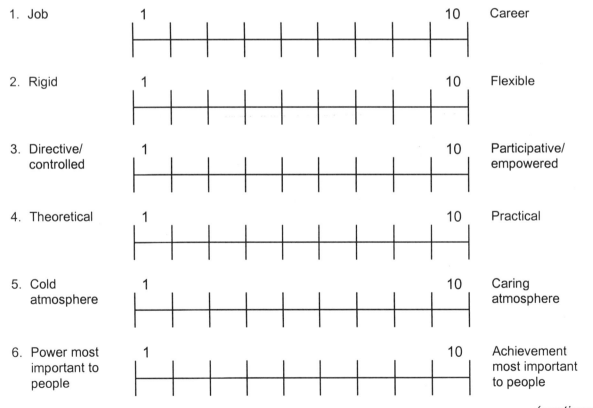

Suggestions for Use: Organizational Culture Questionnaire

Instructions: Answer the following questions.

1. How do you want it to *feel* to work here in the future? Put a "Y" for your answer.
2. How does it *feel* to work here today? Put an "X" for your answer.

1. Job	1	10	Career
2. Rigid	1	10	Flexible
3. Directive/ controlled	1	10	Participative/ empowered
4. Theoretical	1	10	Practical
5. Cold atmosphere	1	10	Caring atmosphere
6. Power most important to people	1	10	Achievement most important to people

(continued)

Suggestions for Use: **Organizational Culture Questionnaire** (continued)

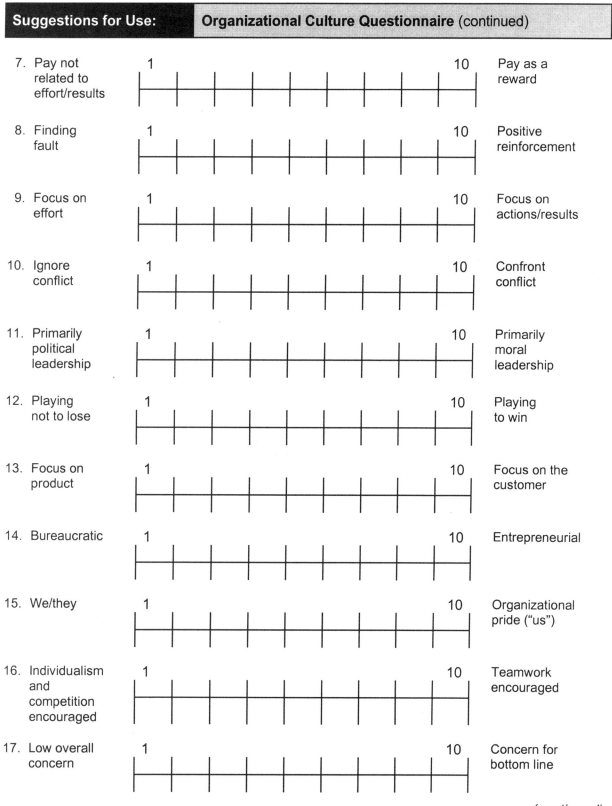

	1									10	
7. Pay not related to effort/results											Pay as a reward
8. Finding fault											Positive reinforcement
9. Focus on effort											Focus on actions/results
10. Ignore conflict											Confront conflict
11. Primarily political leadership											Primarily moral leadership
12. Playing not to lose											Playing to win
13. Focus on product											Focus on the customer
14. Bureaucratic											Entrepreneurial
15. We/they											Organizational pride ("us")
16. Individualism and competition encouraged											Teamwork encouraged
17. Low overall concern											Concern for bottom line

(continued)

Suggestions for Use: Organizational Culture Questionnaire (concluded)

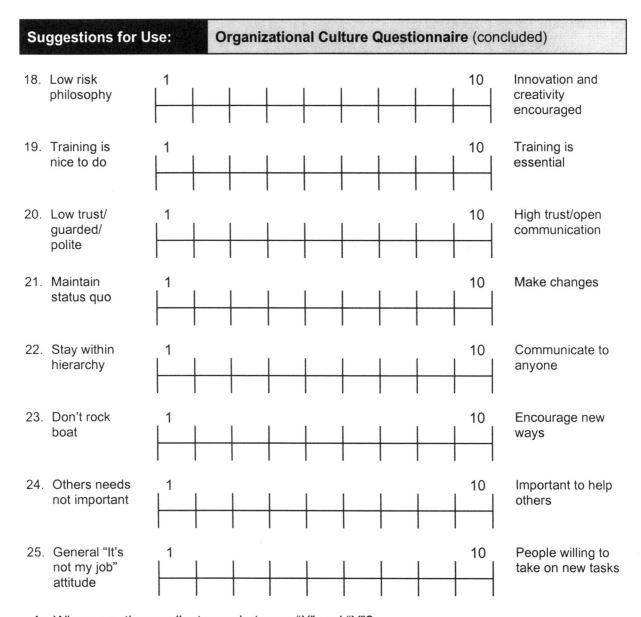

18.	Low risk philosophy	1	10	Innovation and creativity encouraged
19.	Training is nice to do	1	10	Training is essential
20.	Low trust/ guarded/ polite	1	10	High trust/open communication
21.	Maintain status quo	1	10	Make changes
22.	Stay within hierarchy	1	10	Communicate to anyone
23.	Don't rock boat	1	10	Encourage new ways
24.	Others needs not important	1	10	Important to help others
25.	General "It's not my job" attitude	1	10	People willing to take on new tasks

A. Where are the smallest gaps between "X" and "Y"?

B. Which three cultural norms are most in need of improvement? This is where there are the largest gaps.

C. Create an action plan for this list.

D. Look at the surveys across and up/down the organization to see if different cultures exist within the organization. Do *they* need to be changed?

B. Cultural Change—Indepth

Effective cultural change takes two to five years, even with concentrated and continual actions.

We hear this term all the time. However, two key issues are frequently misunderstood:

Misunderstood Issue #1:

- Changing the culture means changing the behavior of an entire organization, so methods must include all aspects of the Organization as a Systems Model. The organization will come apart, change, and come together again to fit into the new desired behaviors.
- In even the best of cases where change is desired, understood, and prepared for, it still takes a minimum of 12 to 18 months for an individual to make the change of habits. How long will it take others who may not have as good an attitude, understanding, or set of skills?

Suggestions for Use:

1. **Criteria for Cultural/Systemic Change Efforts**

   Does the effort meet these tests of systemic change?

   1. Does it include removing political barriers (or is it a quick fix, exhibiting short-term mentality)?
   2. Does it really deal with systemic change (i.e., changing the rules)?

(continued)

Suggestions for Use: *(continued)*

3. Is there ongoing community/key stakeholder involvement?
4. Does it involve shifting money, roles and responsibilities, and staff?
5. Does it involve proactive prevention, as well?
6. Does it involve shared leadership and a collective vision?
7. Does it involve horizontal involvement and leadership?
8. Does it work with a whole system (individual, family, team, community, and organization)?
9. Does it involve systems learning including ongoing feedback, progress reviews, and outcome measures on an ongoing basis?
10. Does it involve a change in what drives the organization?
11. Does it involve a fundamental change in the relationships between or among organizational parts (i.e., a major change in the ways of doing work)?
12. Does it involve a basic cultural change in norms, values, or reward systems?
13. Does it have a contagious, passionate, motivating, catalytic effect on others, spreading the results?

2. **Organizational Checklist for Cultural Systemic Change**

Question: Which of these are present now, and at what level of effectiveness?

(L = low, M = medium, H = high)

1. ______ Committed top leaders; support; modeling; use of power
2. ______ Written description of the changed organization or vision
3. ______ Conditions that preclude maintenance of the status quo or opportunistic timing and "pain"
4. ______ Likelihood of a critical mass of support
5. ______ A medium- to long-term perspective (multiyear)
6. ______ Awareness of resistance and the need to honor it and work with it
7. ______ Awareness of the need for education (top down)

(continued)

Suggestions for Use: *(concluded)*

8. ______ The conviction that the change must be tried; change structures are in place to make it happen

9. ______ Willingness to use resources

10. ______ Commitment to maintaining the flow of information and reinforcement through communications, especially cross-functional

11. ______ Related to the business strategy

12. ______ Organization-wide and all levels

13. ______ No prescribed technologies or solutions

14. ______ Persistence in rollouts, follow-ups, modifications

15. ______ Symbols and language consistent and clear; development of exemplars, pilots, success stories

16. ______ Pay attention to system congruencies; fit issues (7 Track systems framework)

17. ______ Adaptable and developmental learning organization

18. ______ Reward systems changed to reinforce this change (feedback loop)

19. ______ People held accountable for the change or results (rewards, punishment, consequences)

20. ______ Rollercoaster of Change known and used to anticipate problems

21. ______ Executives have skills to use it successfully

Misunderstood Issue #2

- We have underlined the importance of the entire organization changing its behavior, as a consequence of Misunderstood Issue #1. Never underestimate how difficult culture change is. You must attack it hard, fast, and directly, so that people know you are serious. And you must persist and repeat the desired change again and again. The only alternative to perseverance is failure in culture change.

- In order to be clear, articulate the desired organizational values or guiding principles you desire, along with what the supporting new behaviors should be. Then do a 1-2 punch; conduct a values assessment, install the values throughout the organization, and then revamp the rewards/appraisal system to reward and severely penalize everyone, especially senior management, if they do not adopt these new desired behaviors.

C. Why Cultural Change Efforts Usually Fail

Suggestions for Use:

Which of these mistakes are you making? Score this H-M-L (H = yes, all/most of the time; M = yes, at times we do; L = no, we don't usually make this mistake).

________ 1. Underestimate the complexity of our systems

________ 2. Details are lacking

________ 3. Knowledge of change is missing

________ 4. Reinforcers lacking

________ 5. There is little or no accountability

________ 6. Time pressure

________ 7. Resistance to management

________ 8. Battles over turf

________ 9. Change structures are missing

________ 10. Reactive posture

________ 11. Maintain the status quo

________ 12. Stubbornness

________ 13. Control issues

________ 14. Few participative management skills

________ 15. Fatal assumption made that change will occur naturally

________ 16. Failure to redistribute resources

________ 17. Desire to be "politically correct"

________ 18. Initial bias is wrong—training alone won't do it

________ 19. Lack of senior management modeling

________ 20. Too many consultants and philosophies

________ 21. Lack of customer focus

(continued)

Suggestions for Use:	*(concluded)*

________ 22. Skeptics are not involved

________ 23. Poor cross-functional teamwork

________ 24. Unsupportive business and organizational design (Strategic Business Design)

________ 25. Lack of follow-through

________ 26. Middle managers do not have adequate skills

________ 27. Communication is poor and direction is unclear

________ 28. Cherished values violated

________ 29. Lack of debriefing and learning

________ 30. Culturally diverse organization not integrated

________ 31. No game plan

Totals: # of Highs __________; Mediums __________; Lows __________

Note: Use this to build a Change Management Game Plan that will guarantee you will succeed.

Tool #56 Strategic Management System

Application of Systems Dynamics #1: Holism

This is a systems approach to managing all parts of your organization in a more strategic fashion. It uses many of the tools in this book in an integrated fashion.

A. Organizations as Systems

➥ **For example:**

Every organization is perfectly designed to get the results it is getting. Thus, if results are less than desired, the design should be changed. That includes adjusting structure, work processes, linkages, information flows and functions to meet new needs.

—*Keeping Current*, Quetico Centre, 1994

A basic reorientation of our thinking is needed.

In one way or another, we are forced to deal with complexities, with "wholes" or "systems" in all fields of knowledge. This implies a basic reorientation in scientific thinking.

—Ludwig Van Bertalanffy

We now need a strategic management system.

I need to stress at this point that an effective management system is more than just the sum of the parts . . . it is a set of integrated policies, practices and behaviors.

Sometimes having a good management system is confused with having high-quality employees. This is a mistake—the two are quite different in some important ways.

Having high-quality employees does not assure an organization of having a sustainable competitive advantage or even a short-term advantage.

—Edward J. Lawler III
The Ultimate Advantage: Creating the High-Involvement Organization

The winning formula:

Preparation, discipline and talent, ***working within the system,*** *is the winning playoff formula.*

—Michael D. Mitchell
St. Louis *Sporting News,* May 16, 1994

B. Strategic Management System: The Imperative for Survival!

Definition

- A comprehensive system to lead, manage, and change one's total organization in a conscious, well-planned, and integrated fashion, based on our core strategies and *proven research that works* to develop and successfully achieve an ideal future vision.
- *The new way to run the business*—systematic and strategic (based on our strategies).
- The method: interactive and participative.

  (People support what they help create)—a basic truism.
- Is managed as a complete systems change

  (with strategic/annual/individual plans, budgets, and measurements)
- Is successful if it is:
  1. Vision-inspired and shared
  2. Mission/customer-focused
  3. Values/culturally based
  4. Strategically driven
  5. Outcome or results-oriented
- Its hallmark is: *Strategic Consistency yet Operational Flexibility*

  (Focus—Focus—Focus)

C. 15 Key Benefits of a Strategic Management System

Which of these benefits are still missing in your organization?

_______ 1. Taking an organization-wide, proactive approach to a changing global world.

_______ 2. Building an executive team that serves as a model of cross-functional or horizontal teamwork.

_______ 3. Having an intense executive development and strategic orientation process.

_______ 4. Defining focused, quantifiable-outcome measures of success.

_______ 5. Making intelligent budgeting decisions.

_______ 6. Clarifying your competitive advantage.

_______ 7. Reducing conflict; empowering the organization.

_______ 8. Providing clear guidelines for day-to-day decision making.

________ 9. Creating a critical mass for change.

________ 10. "Singing from the same hymnal" throughout the organization.

________ 11. Clarifying and simplifying the barrage of management techniques.

________ 12. Empowering middle managers.

________ 13. Focusing everyone in the organization on the same overall framework.

________ 14. Speeding up implementation of the core strategies.

________ 15. Providing tangible tools for dealing with the stress of change.

________ 16. What else?

D. Strategic Management System Diagnosis

Suggestions for Use:

Question: Which dysfunctional organizational problem do you still face?

Output (Problem List)	What's Probably Missing?	Actions Needed?
(H-M-L) _____ 1. Conflict and survival	Ideal Future Vision (Not shared—plus others below)	
_____ 2. Success unknown (except financial)	Measurement System (Not in place/accountability)	
_____ 3. Confusion and all things to all people	Core Strategies (Not agreed to nor list of Top Priority Actions)	
_____ 4. Low implementation of quality/service	Operational Tasks (No dept. annual plans or accountability/follow-up)	
_____ 5. Incompetence and blaming	Leadership & Management Skills (Nor values on appraisal)	
_____ 6. Low commitment and incrementalism	Resources (Not focused/priorities)	
_____ 7. Bureaucracy and fragmentation	Organizational Design (Unknown or traditional)	
_____ 8. Low risk taking, poor people management	HR & Rewards System (Missing—not tied to values/strategies)	
_____ 9. Adversarial	Interdepartment Teamwork (Not focused upon/rewarded)	
_____ 10. No follow-through	Strategic Change Management System (Missing system and accountability)	

Note: *"Sustaining High Performance,"* by Stephen Haines is devoted to this subject (St. Lucie Press, 1994). The next page provides an overview.

E. Yearly Strategic Management Cycle
(Using the Systems Thinking Approach)

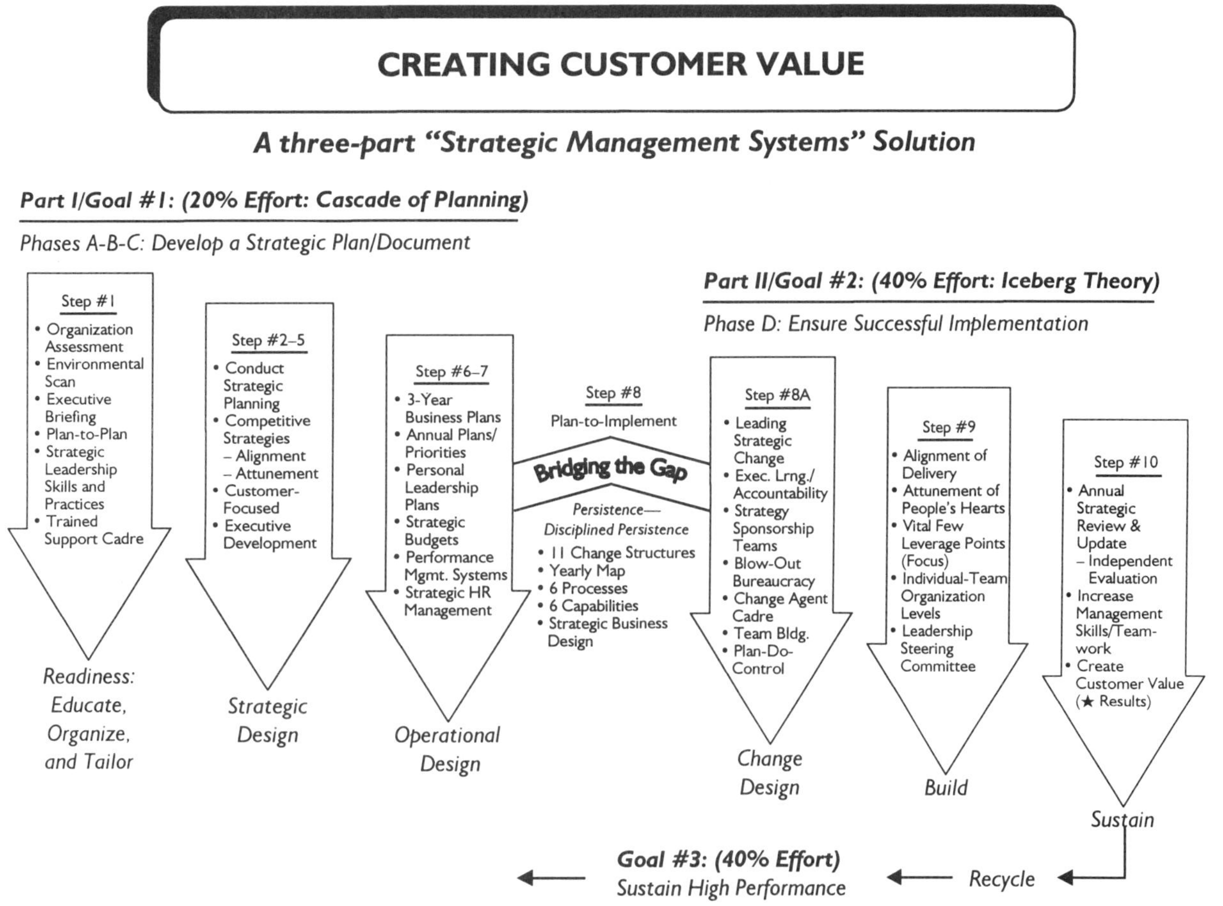

It should be obvious by now that each tool in this book is only part of an overall system of *how to lead and manage an organization in a systematic and strategic fashion.* Good organizations have this system and they review it formally every year as part of an **Annual Strategic Review (and Update)** of their overall direction. This review focuses equally on Phase A: The Customer; Phase B: Feedback and Learning; Phase C: the entire Strategic Plan, as well as the complex and confusing Phase D. It includes the need for a **Strategic Change Management Process** governing and guiding the *alignment of delivery processes* and the *attunement with people's hearts and minds.*

The *Annual Strategic Review* is the way to continually refresh, update, and renew your vision and direction each year along with creating detailed implementation plans. Only by doing this once a year in a formal fashion, along with weekly, monthly, and quarterly follow-up processes, will you have designed, built, and sustained a long-term positive direction. This is what helps you year after year in achieving your ideal future vision. (Phase A all over again!)

And what's your Ideal Future Vision? It should be tied to keeping your customer in mind as **THE** most important outcome of any organization as a system, or any person who wants to live a fulfilling life. In other words, **all these Tools are aimed at helping you Create Customer Value** in your personal and professional endeavors.

Note: The graphic on the next page may help illustrate this circular yearly cycle.

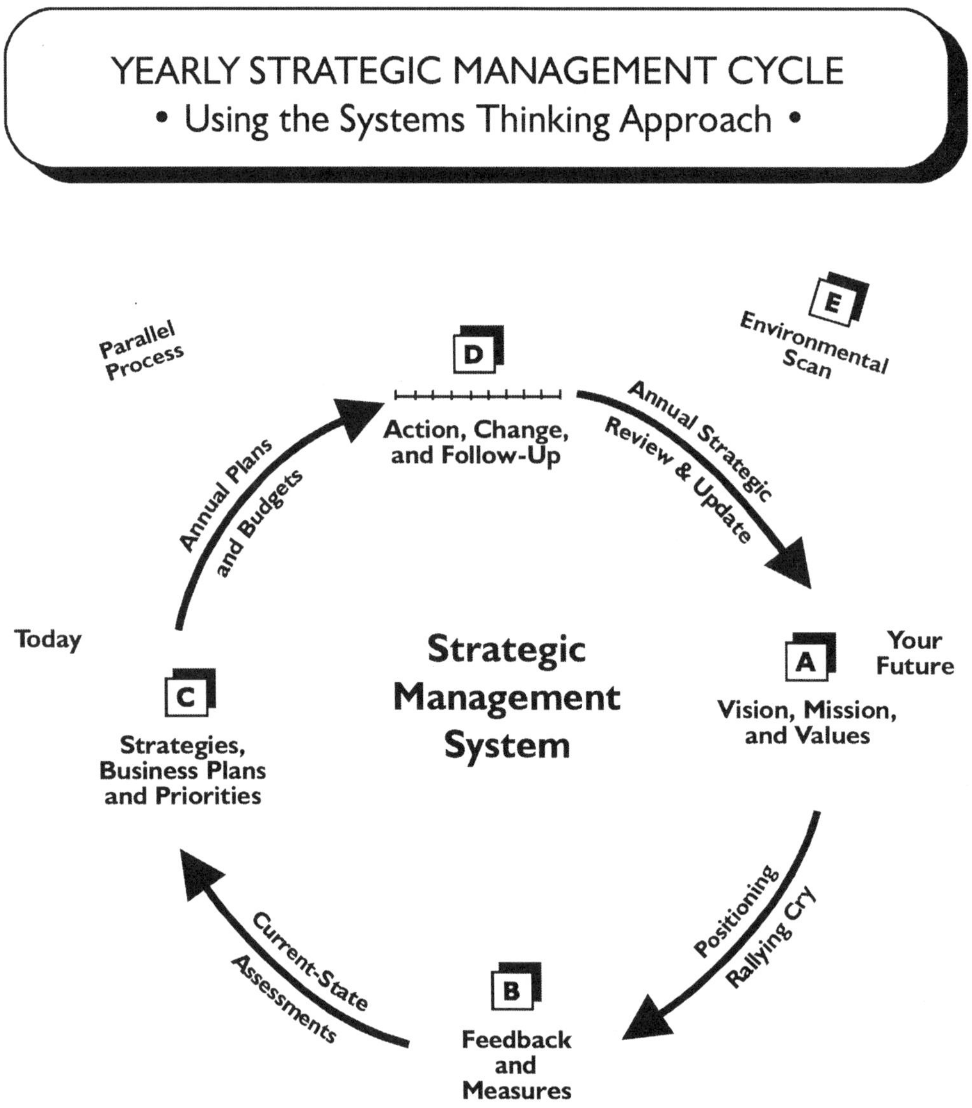

Thinking Backwards to the Future

Tool #57 Tailor to Your Needs

Application of Systems Dynamics #7: Equifinality

Most planning processes reach plateaus. Anyone promoting a systems approach must help you figure how to fit the approach into what already exists in your organization. Otherwise, people are apt to reject this approach as theoretically correct but practically useless. Tailoring it to your needs is essential.

➥ **For example:**

What should you do this year if you already have a supportive mission developed by the previous CEO?

Answer: Tailor the Annual Strategic Review (Step #10) to the new CEO's desires to spend time working on your plan.

Suggestions for Use:

Please list the importance (H-M-L) of adding and installing the following **Strategic Change Management Process** concepts in your organization over the life of your strategic plan in order to achieve your vision and values. (i.e., What do you still need to do?)

Scoring Code: **H** = major need; **M** = smaller need or just refine existing skills processes or program; **L** = not applicable or already in place.

Steps #1–5—Strategic Planning

_______ 1. Environmental scanning system in place?

_______ 2. Key Success Factors with targets set and all tracking systems in place?

_______ 3. Do you have clear data (i.e., employee survey) on your values' strengths and weaknesses and a specific action plan to eliminate these weaknesses within the next one to two years?

_______ 4. Do you have a clear and ongoing system for customer feedback on your strengths and weaknesses vs. customer expectations?

_______ 5. Are realistic yearly organization-wide "must do" action priorities in place with lead accountability, time frames, and resources allocated to them?

(continued)

Suggestions for Use:	*(continued)*

Step #6—Business Planning

________ 6. Do all business units have three-year business plans in place?

________ 7. Do all major support departments have three-year business plans in place?

Step #7—Annual Plans/Budgets

________ 8. Does each major department have annual department work plans in place, using the organization's core strategies and annual action priorities?

________ 9. Have all major department plans been shared and critiqued with the collective management team?

________ 10. Are all "must do" annual priorities funded?

Step #8A—Plan-to-Implement Day

________ 11. Are all your needed Strategic Change Management structures in place, based on all 11 menu options?

________ 12. Do you specifically have in place a Strategic Change Leadership Steering Committee that meets at least every two months?

________ 13. Do you have a yearly comprehensive map of implementation in place, including when you will conduct your annual strategic review (and strategic plan update)?

________ 14. Is your formal organization structure still properly supporting the new direction?

________ 15. Have you reviewed and developed a game plan to tailor the six core change processes to your needs?

________ 16. Have you reviewed and developed a game plan to tailor and install the six basic organizational capabilities/foundations for change?

________ 17. Are your design principles clear and articulated to guide the entire change effort?

________ 18. Do you have a complete rollout plan to get a simplified version (trifold, etc.) of your strategic plan to all employees and to have them understand it?

________ 19. Do you have a game plan to build a critical mass for change, including individual transition support, whole system participation, etc.?

(continued)

Suggestions for Use: *(continued)*

Step #8B—Mastering Strategic Change

________ 20. Do you have the skills throughout your Collective Management Team to successfully lead and manage this transformational change effort?

Step #8C—Executive Development/Accountability

________ 21. Do you have personal leadership plans for all senior executives to show ongoing support for your vision, values, and strategies?

________ 22. Do you have a strategic communications plan to continually reinforce the desired changes again and again (repetition—4 times)?

________ 23. Do you have a leadership development system in place to develop your collective leadership/management as a key to success?

________ 24. Do you have a one-on-one coaching/mentoring process in place for your CEO and senior executives to continually support their growth and management of this change?

________ 25. Does the senior management team need to be a more effective team?

________ 26. Do members of the Collective Management Team need to improve their skills in conflict management?

Step #8D—Strategy Sponsorship Teams

27. List your "alignment of delivery" strategies. Have you conducted a strategic impact exercise for each and do you need Strategic Sponsorship Teams (SSTs) for them in order to coordinate your organization's efforts?

Strategies		Impact Exercise	SST
______	1.		
______	2.		
______	3.		
______	4.		
______	5.		

(continued)

Suggestions for Use: *(continued)*

28. List your "attunement of people's hearts" strategies. Have you conducted a strategic impact exercise for each and do you need Strategic Sponsorship Teams (SSTs) in order to coordinate your organization's efforts?

Strategies		Impact Exercise	SST
______	1.		
______	2.		
______	3.		
______	4.		
______	5.		

Step #8E—Bureaucracy and Funding

________ 29. Do you need to get a fast start and grab people's attention to the change process (cut through old bureaucracy)?

________ 30. Do you have the money to fully fund this strategic change management process?

Step #8F—Internal Change Agent

________ 31. Do you need internal change agent (line and staff) skill development to support this change effort?

Step #8G—Some HR Best Practices (Among Others)

________ 32. Has your performance review/appraisal been redone and has it been well communicated/understood to evaluate everyone on (1) adherence to values, (2) strategic contribution, and (3) learning/growth?

________ 33. Do you have an organization-wide recognition of results system in place to support your core strategies and values?

________ 34. Have you revamped your financial incentive programs to support your strategic plan and Key Success Factors; including organization-wide and team rewards, as well as individual and department incentives?

Step #8H—Teams

35. Does the organization have effective team and teamwork skills:

______ a. within and/departments?

______ b. across departments?

(continued)

Suggestions for Use: *(continued)*

_______ 36. Do the Strategy Sponsorship Teams need more skills to become effective teams?

37. Are there other new teams that need effective team skills? List them:

_______ a.

_______ b.

_______ c.

38. Have the skills for systems thinking and learning (i.e., The Learning Organization) been acquired by:

_______ a. the new teams?

_______ b. the Collective Management Team?

_______ 39. Has the "Plan-Do-Control" task cycle been disseminated to the new teams and the Collective Management Team to help in their work?

40. Have the many uses of the Rollercoaster of Change been taught to:

_______ a. the new teams?

_______ b. the Collective Management Team?

Step #9A—Change Management Process

41. Have the following different employee transition needs been taken into consideration?

_______ a. Individual employee mastery of change/interpersonal skills?

_______ b. Employee involvement, empowerment, and accountability enhanced?

_______ c. Small unit leadership and participative management skills?

_______ d. Whole-system participation to accelerate the cultural change process?

42. Do you have adequate ongoing feedback/debriefing mechanisms in place to assess, continuously improve, learn, and sustain momentum?

_______ a. For executives?

_______ b. For teams?

_______ c. For projects?

_______ d. For meetings?

(continued)

Suggestions for Use:	*(concluded)*

Step #9B—Alignment of Delivery

_______ 43. a. Do the organization's computer and telecommunications technology have a specific change game plan in place to support the Strategic Direction?

_______ b. Has a business process reengineering program been set up to lower costs, improve efficiencies, and better support the customer (better-faster-cheaper)?

Step #9C—Attunement of People's Hearts and Minds

_______ 44. a. Have all your people management/HR processes been assessed/audited and modified to support your strategic direction?

_______ b. Do you have a specific, identified list of each dysfunctional value and barrier to cultural change, along with a game plan to attack each one?

Step #10—Annual Strategic Review

_______ 45. Is the month/dates/sequence of the next annual strategic review (and update) set?

Tool #58 Wheel of Detail

Application of Systems Dynamics #12: Internal Elaboration

"The devil is in the details" is a pretty good way to describe design choices for an integrated Strategic Management strategy. When you select the most appropriate Strategic Change Management strategies, you need to consider several things. How do you know the many options available to you? The "Wheel of Detail" provides the answers.

➥ **For example:**

How do you improve quality and customer service?

Answer: If you don't know what you don't know, the Wheel is a great checklist for what changes are needed first.

Suggestions for Use:

1. What are our needs (H-M-L)? This "wheel" provides many choices of how to meet these needs. Check the current status of the ones you have—and ones you still need.

A. Strategic Change Management "Wheel of Detail"

Explicit Tasks of Steps #8, #9, and #10
(Using the Organization as a Systems Model as a Template)

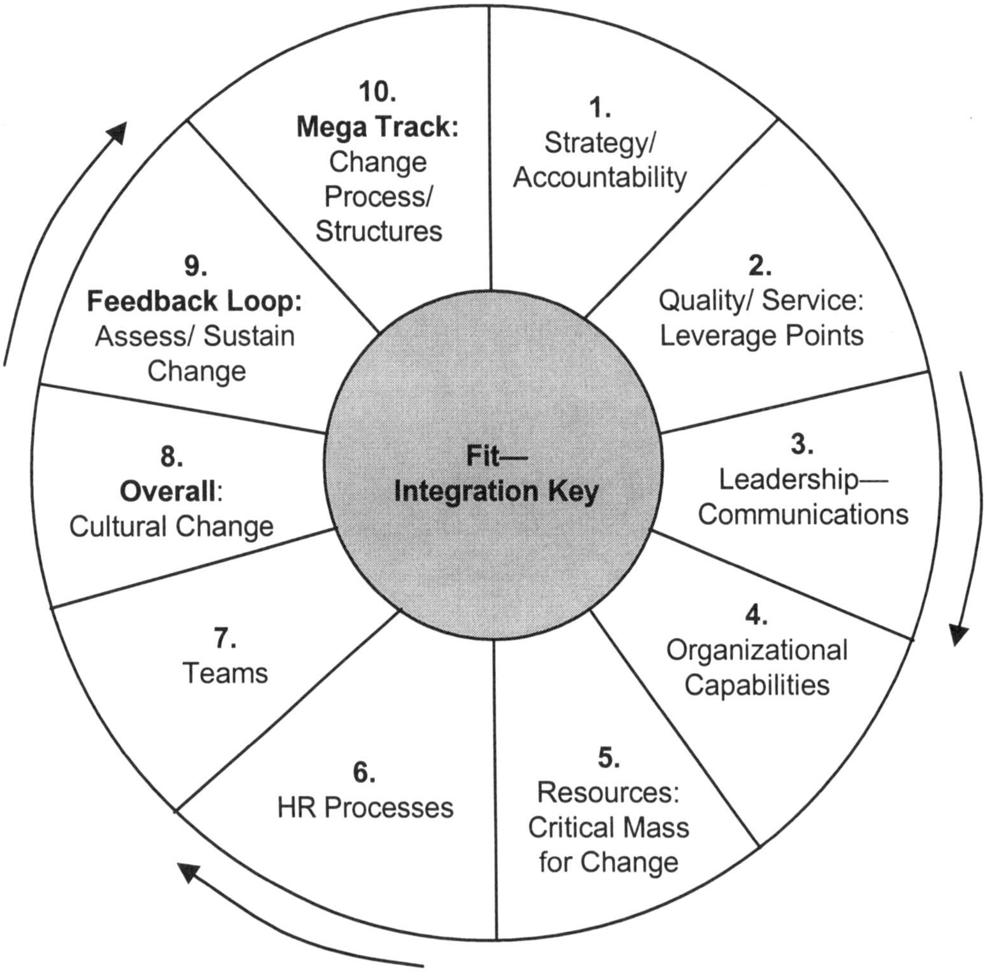

"The devil is in the details"

Designing an Integrated Management Strategy

A change of this magnitude cannot be described as a single change; in reality it is a constellation of changes that are both discrete and interdependent, and that must be managed simultaneously.

Success in managing fundamental change includes moving the organization to a mode in which both (1) learning and (2) improving the quality of performance are equally valued.

B. Mastering Strategic Change Explicit Tasks

(Not left to chance—or good intentions—use multiple leverage points to change behaviors)

Question: What are our needs? Prioritize them using a 1-2-3 scale with the top priority receiving a 1.

1. **Strategy/Accountability**

1. ______ **Finalize the strategic plan;** develop an initial rollout and communications plan and include quick actions so people know you are serious.

2. ______ **Establish an organization-wide annual plan** that reflects the strategic planning action priorities for the first year of each core strategy. Hold senior management accountable for this list.

3. ______ Require **three-year business plans** for all major functions; this will help create a critical mass for change, involvement, and ownership.

4. ______ Build all **department/division/unit annual plans** around the organization-wide annual priorities/goals.

    ______ • Schedule a peer review of these plans at an annual review meeting.

5. ______ **Maintain consistency and accountability** toward the new vision; provide sanctions to those who don't follow it, especially middle/senior management, and replace anyone if not openly committed to change.

2. **Quality/Service (Leverage Points)**

6. ______ **Conduct a strategic business organizational design assessment** and restructuring project (checklist for reorganizing tasks).

7. ______ Create a **customer-focus on service/quality** effort throughout the entire organization; address issues of standards, training, rewards, etc.

8. ______ Blow out bureaucracy through **employee empowerment,** waste, obsolete tasks, cost-cutting, changes to controls, policies, and/or business process reengineering.

    ______ • Then re-design your information systems.

9. ______ Use the budget as a leverage point for change; **use strategic budgeting** to fund the top yearly priorities; set up RFPs, etc.

10. ______ **Begin thinking about your "organizational processes and systems"** as potential transition tasks.

3. **Leadership/Strategic Communications**

11. ______ **Senior management's personal commitment** to a set of tasks with a mission to implement this strategic plan and lead the Strategic Change Leadership Steering Committee (i.e., personal leadership plan, stump speech, etc.).

12. ______ Continually communicate and build **organization-wide commitment** to the vision, values, and core strategies (over and over again), along with the rationale; reduce rumors—hold stakeholder meetings/updates, etc.

13. ______ Continually **increase the range and depth of leadership and management practices** on an ongoing basis as the only true competitive advantage over the long-term. Use best management practices and focus especially on the skills of trainer—coach—facilitator.

14. ______ **Realign financial management** and controls to support the new direction (delegation/empowerment).

15. ______ Have the **CEO or senior management lead** the Steering Committee and Strategy Sponsorship teams.

4. **Organizational Capabilities**

16. ______ **Conduct "top-down" training and development** (as a minimum) in:

    _______ • Mastering strategic change/transition management skills

    _______ • Visionary leadership practices and skill building (trainer—coach—facilitator)

    _______ • Skills in conflict management and communications

    _______ • Skills in problem solving, decision making, and participative management

17. ______ Focus on **skill development of middle management and first-line supervisors.**

18. ______ Provide your Strategy Sponsorship Teams with **formal and ongoing training** about their core strategy and best practices/benchmarks.

19. ______ **Set up internal staff development** so that you build your own internal cadre of expertise and skills (not just knowledge) to carry out your vision and core values.

20. ______ **Realign the information systems** and controls to support the new direction (strategic use).

5. **Resources: Critical Mass for Change**

21. ______ Focus on changing all three levels of the organization (headquarters and field; waves of change):

    _______ • Organization-wide

    _______ • Team, departments, cross-functional

    _______ • Individuals (including WIIFM)

22. ______ **Develop participative management techniques** for involvement of all organizational members/key stakeholders to build ownership and commitment.

    _______ • Include **time/opportunities to disengage** from the old.

    _______ • **Include forces/projects** and other team collaborations, led by various executives to ensure their leadership/commitment, especially cross-functional teams.

23. ______ **Create a strategy to win wide support and commitment.**

    _______ • Attend to political and cultural dynamics and informal leaders.

24 ______ Continue to use the **parallel process** on decisions that affect key stakeholders.

25. ______ **Fund the strategic change process** itself.

6. **HR Processes**

26. ______ Set up an **Executive/Employee Development Board** to guide all development, careers, succession.

27. ______ **Reexamine all your HR systems,** processes, and procedures, and diagnose their fit vs. the desired culture. Refine as necessary. (Use our HRM Systems Model.)

28. ______ Provide for a **rewards for total performance** diagnosis and revisions project.

29. ______ Revise your performance management system (and specifically your performance appraisal) to **directly evaluate everyone vs. your core strategies and values.**

30. ______ **Review all the potential transition issues.**

7. **Teams**

31. ______ Help your executive team become more effective.

    _______ • Senior management level

    _______ • Middle management—horizontal task forces

    _______ • Others as needed—see major tasks facing any new team

32. ______ Develop effective new teams including **Strategy Sponsorship Teams** as "change agents" for each core strategy.

33. ______ Find ways to help **everyone get involved in team efforts** to make the change happen—including finding out WIIFM (What's in it for me?).

34. ______ Consider **empowering** partial or full self-directed work teams to solve problems and make decisions closer to where the customer is.

35. ______ **Focus on team learning and team rewards** as the key units of success.

8. **Overall: Culture Change**

36. ______ Immediately conduct **cultural/values assessment,** feedback and problem solving, including eliminating fear and other demotivating factors.

37. ______ **Identify and reduce the key barriers to change.** Legitimize skeptics and reduce/eliminate resistance/dysfunctionality.

38. ______ Build a **continuous improvement/problem identification and perseverance mentality** among top/middle management. Build in patience and humility.

39. ______ Hold **senior and middle management strictly accountable** to lead, initiate, and fully/actively support this process and the desired changes. Provide private forums to criticize and be skeptical.

40. ______ Use your legitimate power to directly, specifically, and forcibly **"attack" each value change desired.** Persist and persevere on each over the next 3–5 years (watertight integrity to the new culture).

9. **Feedback Loop: Assess/Sustain Change**

41. ______ Conduct yearly strategic organizational assessment and feedback and problem solving to ensure fit/integration of all components of the organization to the desired vision. (Systems Fit, Alignment, and Integrity)

42. ______ Sustain and institutionalize the desired changes through ongoing surveys, feedback, rewards, follow-up, and reinforcement (including **annual strategic reviews [and updates]** to the vision and plans).

43. ______ Build in **regular evaluation/feedback processes,** including Key Success Factors with coordinator/system, such as (1) employee; (2) customer satisfaction; (3) competitor analysis.

- _______ To identify and surface dissatisfaction with the current state;
- _______ To provide sound data vs. perceptions for problem solving.

44. ______ Develop an **environmental scanning system** and use it on a regular basis.

45. ______ Develop an ongoing best practices research system, including **benchmarks set by your competition** and excellent companies in all industries who have the best practices.

10. **Mega Track: Change Process/Structures**

46. ______ **Develop and institutionalize the primary change management structures/roles** including:

- _______ Personal leadership plans
- _______ Weekly executive committees
- _______ Daily/weekly/monthly "kitchen cabinet" core leadership/support team
- _______ Monthly/quarterly Strategic Change Leadership Steering Committee
- _______ Strategy sponsorship teams for each core strategy

47. ______ **Provide sources of confidence, trust, and stability** for employees throughout the rollercoaster ride of change.

48. ______ **Conduct contingency planning** on troublesome scenarios.

49. ______ **Develop a game plan** on the process of change, including a yearly comprehensive map.

50. ______ Be aware and **responsive to the role of emotions** in the change effort. Listen and explain the why with empathy.

- _______ **Manage all steps in the Rollercoaster of Change** simultaneously to meet differing individual needs.

C. "Wheel of Detail"

EXPLICIT TASKS OF STEPS #8, #9, AND #10

Directions: Fill out columns two and three using High, Medium, and Low for your answers. Note any ideas or comments in the last column.

Explicit Tasks	Emphasis in last 2 Years (H-M-L)	Need for Improvement (H-M-L)	Comments
1. Strategy/Accountability			
2. Quality/Service: leverage points			
3. Leadership and Strategic Communications			
4. Organizational Capabilities			
5. Resources: critical mass for change			
6. HR processes			
7. Teams			
8. Overall: Culture Change			
9. Feedback Loop: assess/sustain change			
10. Mega Track: change process/structures			

Tool #59 Change Management Organizational Structures

Application of Systems Dynamics #9: Hierarchy

Successful change begins with the selection of the correct structures to guide the change. Organizing yourself into the correct structures is a key systems thinking concept around which all desired changes should coordinate and integrate.

➥ **For example:**

The day-to-day organizational chart is set to maintain the status quo. What different structures or infrastructures are needed to make the desired changes? Organizational charts are an impediment to change as they foster the status quo.

Suggestions for Use:

1. What set of choices do you as a leader of change think are needed in this case?
2. Normal structures are usually not set for change. Select the specific structures you feel are crucial to change.

A. Specific Change Management Organizational Structures

Instructions: Circle those structures you feel you need to implement to be successful in your change. Then implement them.

Complex Systems are changed by small interventions

1. Set up a Core Planning Team and a parallel process to involve other key stakeholders with development of your organization's strategic plan.
2. Set up divisional/department planning teams to develop three-year business plans for each SBU/major support department to ensure that the organization's strategic plan filters down and across the organization.
3. Set up an annual management meeting, with social time. It should have three key business components:
   - A look backward at last year's results (KSFs)
   - A look forward (via a large group meeting) to review and critique the annual plans of all SBUs/major support departments
   - Training, speeches, etc., to reinforce your organization's vision, strategies, and core values

4. Gather cross-functional leaders into a quarterly Strategic Change Leadership Steering Committee. Create a parallel process (with key stakeholders) to guide the overall change process and ensure tracking and follow-up on your strategic plan, and to ensure that there is fit, alignment, and integrity of all other major change projects to your vision. Include quarterly business review/KSF and core-strategy discussions.

5. Form the leadership into an Executive Development/Employee Development (EDC) Committee that meets quarterly to plan the succession and development of your top performers and key managers as well as create all HR strategies and rewards systems.

6. Set up a Business Process Reengineering Task Force and Steering Committee to coordinate and streamline business processes for the customer (i.e., speed up processes, reduce costs, improve quality).

7. Set up cross-functional Quality Management Boards (QMBs) to lead the reengineering of strategically important business processes.

8. Set up strategic change project teams of a cross-departmental nature on an ad hoc basis as needed to make sure large, strategic organization-wide projects get a proper focus and priority.

9. Set up strategy sponsorship teams of cross-functional leaders for each core strategy of the organization to build in leadership and support for desired changes.

10. Set up revised weekly staff meetings for top management with a different emphasis:
    - Week 1—Operational issues
    - Week 2—Customer issues
    - Week 3—Strategic plan implementation priorities
    - Week 4—Strategic change process issues
    - Week 5—(1/quarter) EDC meetings (See #5)

11. Set up partnership meetings on a regular basis between different departments/units or warring factions (i.e., union/management NAPs meetings—nonadversarial problem solving; physician/hospital partnership meetings, etc.).

12. Set up quarterly departmental/unit/all-staff meetings in order to:
    - focus on key business issues
    - provide recognition and rewards for those who do what you want (i.e., customer services, cost reductions, etc.)

13. Set up a Peer Rewards Committee to compensate anyone meeting your rewards criteria on a quarterly basis. This would be done at the above all-staff meetings.

14. Set up focus group meetings of both customers and employees (separately) to find out their wants and needs.

15. Design and deliver GE Workout-type bureaucracy busting training/problem solving cross-functional meetings.

16. Create a Key Success Factor Cadre—a cross-functional team of specified KSF coordinators for each KSF measurement led by the overall KSF coordinator. Key responsibility is to develop the KSF matrix and measurement system and report status of it to each SCLSC. Track and report quarterly on vision success in a measurable fashion (year by year).
17. Conduct training and simulations on mastering strategic change to personally experience and to ensure full understanding/appreciation of the complexities of change.
18. Conduct priority-setting meetings to focus budget setting on an annual basis.
19. Set up a complete three-part/three-goal Strategic Management system as a new way to manage the business and organization as a system. Base it on your strategic plan and support this with professional management practices.
20. Set up an independent annual strategic review (and update) of your Strategic Management system and plan.
21. Set up a war room and meet in it to focus on the changes, projects, status, and timelines.
22. Create an Internal Change Management Coordination Cadre—this is the support team to the CEO/Executive Director and the SCLSC to make certain that change management logistics are achieved. They are key to reverse the dreaded "SPOTS" syndrome ("Strategic Plan on Top Shelf . . . gathering dust").
23. Set up self-directed workteams (i.e., horizontal cross-functional) to empower change (once they have the vision and skills). Then delegate signature authority and decision making to staff, who deal directly with the customer. (Train them first.) "Moments of Truth" require the ability to design and implement recovery strategies on the spot.
24. Put in place (1) training and (2) follow-up reinforcement programs (taken first by senior management) on any topic for which change is needed.
25. Appoint account representatives for each customer (if not already organized as such).
26. Create an Automation Steering Group to coordinate all MIS and requests/projects.
27. Hold regular meetings—all functions; all units; all cultures; all levels; all management; all employees.
28. Conduct future searches or search conferences to deal with big issues to create ideal futures, strategies, action plans, and commitments of diverse, yet key stakeholders.
29. Note: Use many of these structures to build effective cross-functional teams as a explicit byproduct of their work.
30. Also set up cross-functional team-building events and/or task forces at every opportunity.
    a. all management meetings
    b. annual senior management retreats
    c. middle management meetings
    d. large-group problem-solving meetings

e. interdepartment team-building events
f. issues meetings
g. social events
h. study sessions
i. all employee meetings
j. close-to-the-customer meetings
k. senior management visitations; job switching for a day or week
l. pirates team (to "steal ideas")
m. in search of excellence; benchmarking teams

B. Possible External Change Structures

1. Advisory Board of Directors
2. Strategic alliances/partnerships
3. Customer/Vendor focus groups
4. Union-Management Committee
5. Community Special Interest Group (SIG) sessions
6. Community forums
7. User groups
8. Industry/Member conferences

Tool #60 Change Management Fail-Safe Mechanisms

Application of Systems Dynamics #11: Dynamic Equilibrium; and #7 Equifinality

The CEO and senior management are often looked to as the only leaders of change. If they are not the strength, does change have a chance to succeed, or will it fail?

These 44 checks and balances are the ways to compensate for what is missing among the executive talent.

Suggestions for Use:

Review this list and make sure you've implemented all those that you need to. Note: * denotes the "must do's" that are most essential to success. Actually, the more of these you set up, the higher your probability of successful implementation.

A. Change Management Fail-Safe Mechanisms (44 Checks and Balances)

Do we have these?

Yes, No, or NI (needs improvement)

_______ *1. Plan-to-plan/executive briefing (first) and "engineer success"—three goals of a Strategic Management system

_______ *2. Parallel process throughout the planning and implementation process (key stakeholder involvement)

— buy-in; stay-in

— build critical mass for change, especially middle management

_______ *3. Three-part Strategic Management system and systems thinking—*a new way to run your business*; the basics; an ongoing process

_______ *4. Vision—mission—core values statements in usable formats; customer-focused

_______ 5. Cultural/values audit and the creation of a culture change action plan—strategic change project

_______ *6. Core values placed on your performance appraisal form

_______ *7. Board of Directors involvement/ownership of the strategic plan; desire to use KSFs for accountability; executive cooperation and regular status/ communications to the Board

_______ 8. A crisp and clear single driving force and associated *rallying cry* that is the essence of your vision; it is the CEO's personal task to institutionalize this

_______ *9. Key Success Factor (KSF) coordinator/cadre and reporting system

_______ *10 Key Success Factor (KSF) Continuous Improvement Matrix fully filled out with targets and measurements

_______ 11. Benchmarking vs. highly successful organizations (*best practices* research)

_______ 12. Establishment of an environmental scanning system (ESS) with specific accountability and feedback mechanisms

_______ 13. SWOT—staff involvement; reality check

_______ *14. Paradigm changes to strategies (from ➔ to) and a focused number of strategies

_______ *15. Strategic Sponsorship Teams (SSTs) set up for each core strategy

_______ *16. Core strategies also used as the Key Result Areas (KRAs) on performance appraisals.

_______ *17. Annual planning format using strategies as *organizing framework* (the "glue")

—links to strategies

—links to values, MBO, and individual goal setting/performance appraisals

_______ 18. Use of SBU *Proforma Matrix* to develop clear financial accountability

_______ *19. Three-year business planning for all SBUs/MPAs to ensure clear competitive strategies; three-year business planning for major support units also (by strategies)—WIIFM (especially a strategic HRM plan for people management)

_______ 20. SBU definition to lead organization design philosophy and efforts, focused on the businesses we are in . . . the customers we serve . . . and the employees we empower to do their best

_______ 21. Development of a priority maintenance system to handle interruptions/new ideas and lack of focus on strategies, business, and product development

_______ *22. Large group annual planning review meeting (critique/sharing)

_______ 23. Strategic change project teams on big, cross-functional ideas

_______ *24. Personal leadership plans (PLP)/commitments developed by the CEO and top three executives of the organization; monomaniacs with a mission

_______ 25. *War Room* with all the changes and timetables on the wall

_______ 26. Contingency planning; *what if* scenarios on key probable events

_______ *27. Annual planning and priority setting first to drive the budgeting process (top three actions per each core strategy); looking at alternative ways to gain funds

_______ *28. One day offsite: Plan-to-implement/executive briefing on *change process*

_______ *29. *Mastering Strategic Change* workshop; simulation taught to all management personnel; indepth understanding of change management

_______ *30. Install different structures for change management, including Strategic Change Leadership Steering Committee (SCLSC) to guide:

—strategic planning implementation

—all change of any nature—the goal is *System Alignment, Attunement, and Integrity*

_______ *31. Yearly comprehensive map on the next 12 months' processes and structures required for change management

_______ *32. Internal coordinator/facilitator and cadre for the change process—to support senior management

_______ 33. Create a critical mass action plan to support the vision, with ongoing communications planned throughout—use the concept of the Rollercoaster of Change[SM]

_______ *34. A rollout/communications strategy plan and reinforcement materials (PR/HR led)

_______ 35. *Organization as a System* framework (Organizational Systems Model); diagnosis and a way to ensure *system's alignment and integrity* to the strategic plan—use the Wheel of Detail

_______ *36. Individual goal setting by all exempt employees tied to the strategic plan . . . then a true performance management system used and modeled by top management as a way to manage individual performance—part of HR strategic planning (the *people edge*) you need

_______ *37. A rewards diagnosis and improvement plan to make sure your rewards support the strategic direction (both financial and nonfinancial)

_______ *38. Set up an executive development committee (EDC) or board (EDB) to manage promotions, executive hiring, and succession plans, as well as development and training . . . all to support the vision, strategic plan, and core values/culture

_______ *39. Creating customer value through Business Process Reengineering (BPR) action plan—strategic change project

_______ *40. Professional management and leadership practices (strategic leadership development system) action plan—strategic change project

_______ 41. Quarterly follow-up meetings to the SCLSC by all departments for all employees; focus on vision, key strategies, and rewards/celebrations

_______ *42. Organization and job redesign and restructuring action plan to be more customer-focused—strategic change project

_______ *43. Creating customer value through total quality/service action plan—strategic change project

_______ *44. Annual strategic review and update (like an independent financial audit and update) of the strategic plan/next year's annual plan and priorities

*Note: Many, many **crucial** *fail-safe mechanisms*!

Tool #61 Open Systems Planning

Application of Systems Dynamics #1: Holism

Teams and organizations today live in a very complex environment, both internally and externally. In order to make sense of it all, it helps to look at each of these specific stakeholders on an individual and then collective basis **once you know your ideal**.

Desired Future Vision (or Destination). This is a classic use of systems thinking: thinking outside first (vision) then inside (internal stakeholder) and outside again. Knowing who your key external and internal stakeholders are and the demands they make on your system (team or organization) is key to good planning and failure prevention.

➥ **For example:**

For a team to be effective, it is not enough to know your goals. Knowing who the key stakeholders are inside the organization (but outside the team) is key to team success. Very often one department (such as Finance) can destroy a process improvement cross-functional team's efforts if it is unwilling to cooperate in funding the effort and in participating in simplifying controls.

Secondly, within a cross-functional team, each internal team member has his or her own goals as the process improvement team relates to department objectives. Knowing and taking into account member demands is key to the success of the team's vision.

Suggestions for Use: **Open System Planning**

Instructions:

1. Identify the level of system you are focusing on. List it in the center of Diagram B below and here as well: ______________________________
2. Have a clear ideal future vision first and list it here: ______________________________

   ____
3. Identify all the key internal parts/living systems within your case studies system (hint—see Seven Levels.) List them below on Diagram A below:
4. Also on Diagram B, identify and list on the "spokes" all the key external stakeholders (other living systems) around your case. Be sure to use all levels of living systems above you in the hierarchy.

Diagram A:

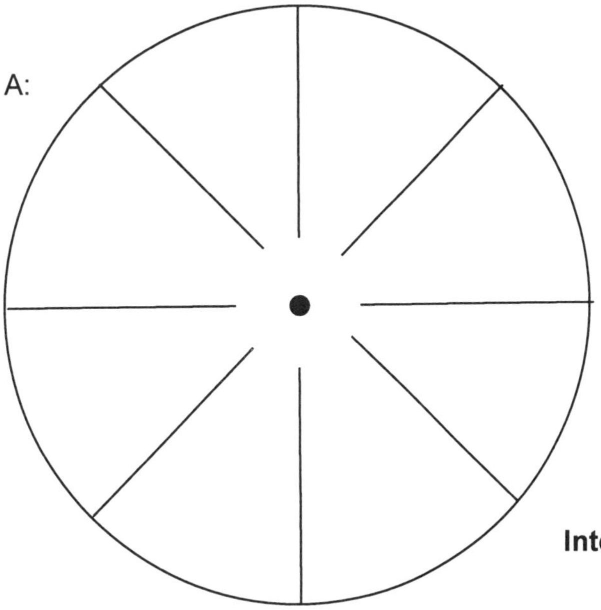

Internal Living Systems

Diagram B:

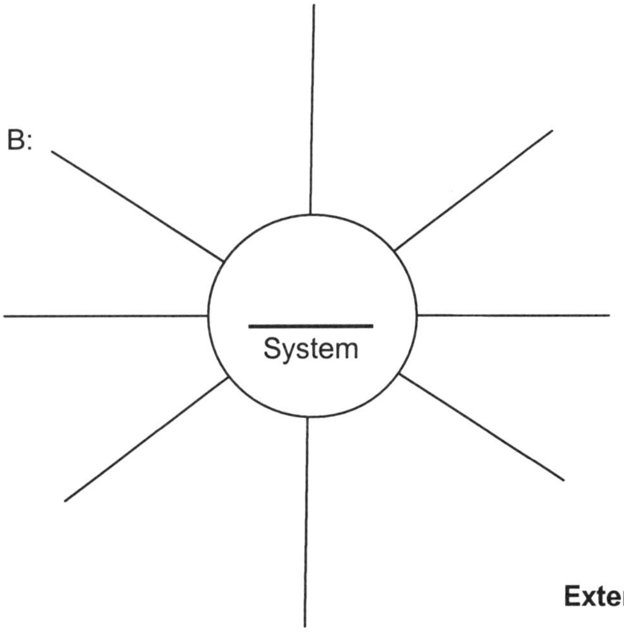

External Living Systems

5. Now fill out the detailed analysis on the next two pages for both of these diagrams (Internal and External Living Systems).

Internal—Open Systems Planning

I. INTERNAL STAKEHOLDERS	Their wants/demands (on you)?	Your responses (today)?	Changes you need to make (for the future)?

External—Open Systems Planning

II. EXTERNAL STAKEHOLDERS	Their wants/demands (on you)?	Your responses (today)?	Changes you need to make (for the future)?

Tool #62 Socio-Technical Systems

Application of Systems Dynamics #6: Multiple Outcomes; and #10: Subsystems/Interrelated Parts

In the earlier days of systems thinking, there emerged from England (Emory Trist and others), the view that all living systems (especially teams and organizations) had both a "technical" (or mechanical) side and a "social" (or human) side. Thus, when looking at change, you needed to focus on both areas. It is a view that is analogous to content vs. process: content is made up of the technical tasks (the "what") to be accomplished; social is the "how to" in getting the job done.

However, updating this concept to current day systems thinking requires considering the system's multiple outcomes or goals as well. Socio-technical without a destination is incomplete. Thus, the "structure" of desired outcomes is key to true systems thinking.

➥ **For example:**

Many process improvement and reengineering efforts have failed (over 70% by some experts' views), many because of a failure to consider people and the commitment of the social or human systems (called employees). However, when looking further at many of these processes, it is their failure to specify their relationship to the desired customer outcomes (not just cutting costs) that is key. In fact, the definition and difficult identification of business processes should all begin or end with the customer as well as cross two or more functions. However, most process improvement efforts fail because they don't even know what the process is.

See the ***Strategic Management*** model our Centre uses as a way to ensure all three factors are included in any process improvement or major change efforts:

1. Strategic Edge where the desired "customer value" is defined

2. People Edge (the social side)

3. Customer Edge (the technical side)

STRATEGIC MANAGEMENT

"Our Only Business"

"Positioning Organizations to Create Customer Value"

❶ Strategic Edge

Creation of a
Strategic Management System:

- Strategic Planning
- Business Planning
- Change Management

"STRATEGIC BUSINESS DESIGN"

❷ People Edge

Attunement with People:

- Leadership Management Development System
- Strategic HR Management
- Executive Coaching and Team Building

❸ Customer Edge

Alignment of Delivery:

- Value-Chain Management and Distribution
- Process Improvement
- Strategic Marketing, Sales, and Service

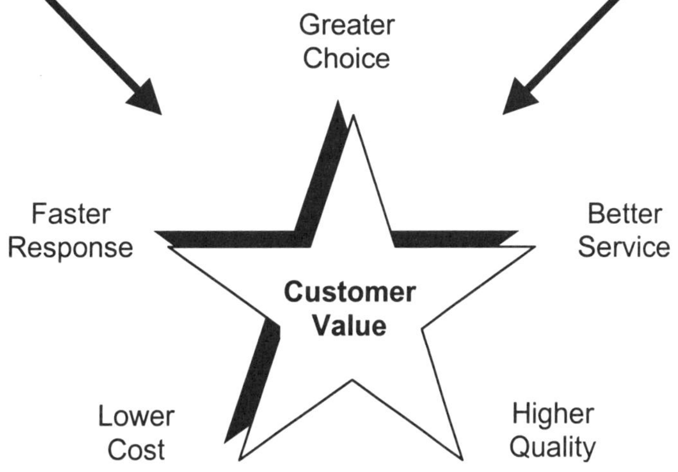

—Our Foundation—

❹ The Systems Thinking Approach

Systems Thinking • Adult Learning • Group Facilitation

Suggestions for Use:	In any change effort, Be sure all three socio-technical factors are clear.
1. *Strategic Edge* What are the desired outcomes? (especially with the customer) 1. 2. 3. 4. 5.	*Technical System* 2. What are the key technical (or change) tasks? *Social System* 3. What are the key social (or human dynamics) that need attention paid to them?

Strategic Change Management: It's Simple

Once You Use the Systems Thinking Approach

The Three Keys:

1. **Have a Shared Direction**
   A. Develop a Strategic Plan
   - have a vision, values and core strategies, and a clear future positioning goal
   - develop clear and focused organization-wide action priorities for the next year

   B. Develop Buy-in and Stay-in to the Plan
   - communicate—communicate—communicate (stump speeches)
   - involvement—participative management—and WIFFM

2. **Develop a Consistent Overall Strategic Business Design**
   A. Conduct a Strategic Business Assessment and Redesign
   - to ensure fit of all the parts, people, and processes of the organization
   - using the overall direction, strategic plan, and positioning as the criteria

   B. Cascade Down Department Work Plans, Budgets, and Accountability
   - use the core strategies, action priorities, and redesign as the glue
   - down and throughout the organization

3. **Successfully Rollout and Implement the Shared Direction and Strategic Business Design**
   A. Know and Adhere to Your Roles
   - **leaders**: to focus on content and consequences
   - **support cadre**: for processes and infrastructure coordination

B. Build Follow-Up Structures and Processes
- to track, control, adjust, and achieve the plan and Key Success Factor results
- to reward, recognize, and celebrate progress and results

Strategic Business Design

"Systematic problems

require

system-wide solutions"

Tool #63 Versatile Assessment Tool

Application of Systems Dynamics #4: Inputs/Outputs

Whenever you are involved in assessing an issue, a problem, or even a new opportunity, how do you learn to identify the systems implications on relationships of all the parts and factors of the organization to each other **in a simple way** . . . and their relationships to the individual, team, or organization's goals, objectives, outcomes, or vision? Tool #63 is a very simple and versatile tool on how to structure your own thinking, that of others, or a team/group problem-solving effort. It will keep you away from the "quick-fix," an analytically direct "one best way" cause and effect.

Starting from where you are (the issue, problem, or opportunities), ask two sets of questions:

I. Beginning Questions

1. What are your goals? mission? purpose? A
2. What helps you achieve these goals? D
3. What hinders you from accomplishing more? D
   (i.e., helps/hinders)

II. Follow-up Root Causes / Cause →Effect "Chain" Questions

1. Why? (does it happen/(inputs)) ← C
2. So what? (is the result/outcome if it continues) → A

Your mental model and theory is your roadblock without our key questions.

"What you look at, is what you see."
(Weisbord's "First law of snapshooting")

What you look for, is what you find.

What theory you use determines what you look for.

➥ **For example:**

When looking at a problem performer, don't assume it is all his or her fault, although the individual must be somewhat at fault and does need to be held accountable.

Instead work with him or her and ask these questions, i.e.,

— Do you know the result **A** of your nonperformance?

— What are its implications?

— What is helping or hindering that achievement?

This includes looking at your own behavior as a supervisor and how it contributes (both good and bad) to this performance.

Secondly, ask the "why" question: Why is this happening? What are some other factors?

Lastly, specifically, look at what you are providing as consequences for his or her performance or nonperformance. Is it any different either way?

Suggestions for Use:

Assessment Form

Instructions: Ask three questions in this order—1st—2nd—3rd

3rd Why? **C**	1st Issue? **B**	2nd So What? **A**

Tool #64 Five Key People Management Subsystems

Application of Systems Dynamics #10: Subsystems/Interrelated Parts

We have all heard the term "MIS" which used to mean a Management Information System, or narrowly, a set of reports generated by computers for senior management on the business operations.

Tool #64 is a newer and broader concept than MIS; that of an overall Strategic Management System (SMS) as detailed here from previous tools. Within this SMS there are **Five Key People Management Subsystems** that are rarely identified, much less properly developed and institutionalized, in order to help senior management lead the organization. Not surprisingly, these management subsystems start with the organization's vision and mission, and are its business management subsystem. For a visual description of this and the other four subsystems, see the drawing on the next page. However, their detailed components or parts are listed below.

Five Key People Management Subsystems

I. Business Management Subsystem

1. Future Vision
2. Mission
3. Strategies
4. Philosophy/Values
5. Social Responsibility Program
6. Organization Culture*

II. Organization Management Subsystem

1. Organization Culture*
2. Organization Structure
3. Organization Rewards
4. Communications, Survey, Involvement Program
5. Integration, Teamwork (inter/intra)
6. Succession Planning*

III. Career Management Subsystem

1. Succession Planning*
2. Professional Management Ladder

III. Career Management Subsystem (continued)

3. Management Health
4. Management Development
5. Career Development*

IV. Performance Management Subsystem

1. Career Development*
2. Day-to-Day Coaching, Counseling, Teaching
3. Performance Appraisals
4. Goal Setting*

V. New Employee Management Subsystem

1. Job Mission, Responsibilities*
2. Job Description, Evaluation
3. Hiring Profile
4. Recruiting, Hiring
5. Orientation, Assimilation
6. Goal Setting

* *Linkages*

Five Key People Management Subsystems

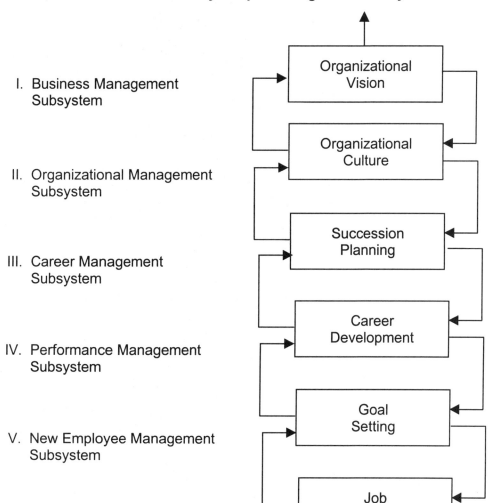

I. Business Management Subsystem

II. Organizational Management Subsystem

III. Career Management Subsystem

IV. Performance Management Subsystem

V. New Employee Management Subsystem

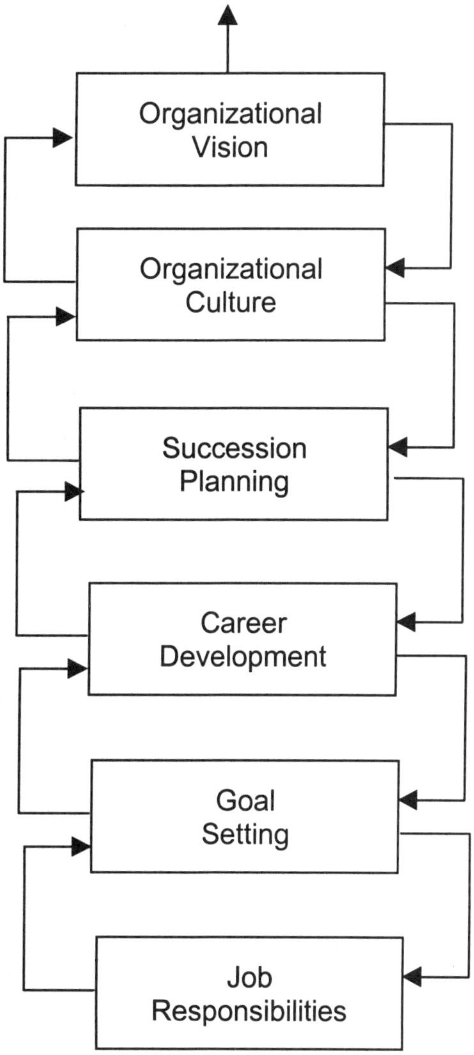

➥ **For example:**

Most organizations structure themselves vertically by functions such as operations, engineering, manufacturing, etc. However, work in all organizations gets done cross-functionally in support of delivering quality products and services to the customer. This is the whole thesis of TQM, Deming, reengineering, and the like as they all focus on the business processes (systems or subsystems) that deliver value to these customers.

In addition to that, however, there is always a people management system that ensures "**the right people are in the right places with the right skills at *the right time.***" That is what these five key people management subsystems accomplish.

Suggestions for Use:

1. Conduct an assessment regarding the current effectiveness of your five key people management subsystems (processes) using the ***Checklist of Key People Management Subsystems Status***.
2. Are you following the best practices in improving these subsystems or processes? Use the following ***Process Improvement Assessment*** as a checklist to action plan improvements.
3. If you already have these subsystems, use the following ***Questions to Ask about Processes*** to ensure your subsystems are as effective as they can be.

Checklist of Key People Management Subsystems Status

Instructions: Fill in your current evaluation (H = high, M = medium, L = low) of your effectiveness regarding these five subsystems. Then list your **Comments/Needed Actions** for each one.

Evaluation		***Comments/Needed Actions***
	I. Business Management Subsystem	
______	1. Future Vision	______
______	2. Mission	______
______	3. Strategies	______
______	4. Philosophy/Values	______
______	5. Social Responsibility Program	______
______	6. Organization Culture	______
	II. Organization Management Subsystem	
Dup.	1. Organization Culture	______
______	2. Organization Structure	______
______	3. Organization Rewards	______
______	4. Communications, Survey, Involvement Program	______
______	5. Integration, Teamwork (inter/intra)	______
______	6. Succession Planning	______
	III. Career Management Subsystem	
Dup.	1. Succession Planning	______
______	2. Professional Management Ladder	______
______	3. Management Health	______
______	4. Management Development	______
______	5. Career Development*	______

(continued)

Checklist of Key People Management Subsystems Status (concluded)

Evaluation		*Comments/Needed Actions*
	IV. Performance Management Subsystem	
Dup.	1. Career Development	________
______	2. Day-to-Day Coaching, Counseling, Teaching	________
______	3. Performance Appraisals	________
______	4. Goal Setting	________
	V. New Employee Management Subsystem	
______	1. Job Mission, Responsibilities	________
______	2. Job Description, Evaluation	________
______	3. Hiring Profile	________
______	4. Recruiting, Hiring	________
______	5. Orientation, Assimilation	________
Dup.	6. Goal Setting	________

Process Improvement Assessment

Proven Best Practices

Instructions: Score yourself (H = high, M = medium, L = low) on your current state of process improvement across the organization.

_______ 1. Are you clear on what your five key people management processes (subsystems) are?

_______ 2. Are you clear on which people processes (subsystems) are your top priorities?

_______ 3. Are you working to reengineer all these top processes?

_______ 4. Is the Process Improvement Team composed of at least three functional departments (cross-functional teams)?

_______ 5. Is the driving force behind each process being reengineered a clear understanding and explicit list of senior management wants?

_______ 6. Does each Process Improvement Team have a senior executive as sponsor and champion?

_______ 7. Have the teams been trained on project management, teamwork, conflict management, and the technical tools they need to accomplish their tasks?

_______ 8. Is the process improvement linked back to senior management through an Employee Development Board on a regular basis?

_______ 9. Does your organization have targets set to reduce "waste"?

_______ 10. Have you done G.E.–type "workout" or "Blow Out Bureaucracy" workshops to "pick" the low hanging waste/fruit?

(continued)

Process Improvement Assessment (concluded)

________ 11. Is there a conscious "core strategy" adapted by the organization to focus in this area?

________ 12. Is problem identification rewarded or penalized?

________ 13. Is automation considered during process improvement?

________ 14. Are there rewards and recognition for eliminating waste?

________ 15. Has benchmarking been done on the process being improved?

________ 16. Does each individual have a QIDW (Quality Improvement in Daily Work) plan as part of this, including all executives and the CEO?

Questions to Ask about Processes

Eliminate

- Does each step add value?
- Can you eliminate the delays? the inspection steps? the filing steps?
- Are some operations rework?

Change

- How can the operation be changed? different methods? technology? equipment?
- Less costly material or service?
- Reduce the frequency of the service? the number of people receiving the service?
- Reduce the time it takes?

Rearrange

- Is the layout the most efficient?
- Can you eliminate transport steps?
- Is the sequence the most efficient?

Combine

- Can any operations be combined? with a supplier's operation? with a customer's?

Simplify

- What is the simplest way to achieve the objective(s) of the process?
- Are instructions easy to understand?

Imagine

- What would be the perfect process?
- How much time would it take?
- Can you flowchart the perfect process?
- Should some parts of the process be examined with a Pareto chart? a run chart? a subprocesses flowchart?

CHAPTER IX
SUMMARY OF SYSTEMS THINKING AND LEARNING

Why Use a Systems Thinking Approach Model?

It provides:

1. A common, better, and more competitive framework for thinking, decision making, communicating, and working together to manage organizational change more successfully.

2. An increased understanding of how the parts of an organization should fit together to support its desired outcomes.

3. A diagnostic tool to assess the degree to which an organization is achieving its desired outcomes.

4. A new **orientation to life** that distills life's complexities into four singular concepts that allow you to successfully cope with all life's details and complexities without losing sight of your goals and destinations.

Language, Communications, and Key Questions

Systems thinking represents a better language and way of being than our old analytic thinking. Systems thinking is like a wide-angle lens on a camera. It gives a better view on your "radar scope" and thus **a more effective way of thinking, communicating, problem solving, and responding!** Otherwise current thinking (and problem solving) can be the source of tomorrow's problems.

Along with the tools, people and organizations need to adopt this systems terminology and key systems questions into their everyday vocabulary. It helps to clarify and simplify your "solutions seeking" and make it more effective and holistic. Some of the key words and phrases in this book include:

The New Language of Systems

1. The Systems Thinking Approach™

2. Input—Throughput—Output—Feedback in the Environment (Four Phases of Systems Thinking)

3. A-B-C-D (The Four Phases in proper order: A = Output; B = Feedback; C = Input; D = Throughput)—It simplifies the mazes, chaos, and messes we see; it helps to see the forest and the trees.

4. And don't forget "E": the Environment. Living systems are open systems, always interacting with their environment.

5. Precondition #1: What entity are we dealing with?
6. The #1 Systems Question: What is our destination or desired outcomes?
7. The #2 Systems Question: What is the feedback to know our status vs. this destination?
8. The #3 Systems Question: What is our ESS (environmental scanning system)?
9. Means vs. ends
10. Multiple-goal seeking
11. Strategic consistency *and* operational flexibility
12. Backward thinking
13. The whole is primary, the parts are secondary.
14. Synthesis vs. analysis is a new relational way of thinking.
15. In the environment, living systems interact in a hierarchy or nest of systems.
16. The reality is that we have messes of problems, instead of separate problems.
17. "Feedback is the breakfast of champions."
18. Negative entropy or positive energy is continuously needed in a system—feedback is key.
19. "Begin with the end in mind" (Stephen Covey).
20. Get outside the nine dots.
21. Relationships and fit are key—processes are important; not separate events.
22. Causes—effects are circular—not one way . . . are not often closely related in time and space.
23. Simplistic, quick fixes do not work for long!
24. Focus on the Seven Levels of Living Systems (especially, #3-individual; #4-team; #5-organization; #6-society; #7-earth) . . . and their collisions and interactions (1:1, team-team, organization-organization).
25. KISS Method—reduces complexity, rigidity, bureaucracy and death.
26. 5 "Whys"—to reach the true/final outcomes/benefits.
27. General Systems Theory—Ludwig Von Bertelenffy

A primer in Systems Thinking Key Questions

Precondition #1:	What entity, system, or "collision of systems" are we dealing with?
Precondition #2:	Within our identified system, what level(s) of the system are we trying to change and what is our purpose or desired outcome?
Systems Question #1:	What are the desired outcomes or destination?
Systems Question #2:	And how will we know we've achieved it? (i.e.: feedback loop of outcome measures)
Systems Question #3:	What will be changing in the environment in the future that will impact us?
Systems Question #4:	What is the relationship of X to Y?
Systems Question #5:	Are we dealing with means or ends? Corollary: Ask the "5 Why's."
Systems Question #6:	What are the new structures and processes we are using to ensure successful changes?
Systems Question #7:	What do we need to do to ensure by-in and stay-in; and to ensure perseverance over time (to reverse entropy)?
Systems Question #8:	What do we centralize (mostly "what's") and what (mostly "how's") should we decentralize?
Systems Question #9:	What are the root causes? (not the symptoms)
Systems Question #10:	How can we go from complexity to simplicity, and from consistency to flexibility, in the solutions we devise?

And: The Foundation Tool and Question:

What is it that I contribute to the problem and can change to be a positive and proactive leader on this?

And: The Ultimate Tool and Question:

What is our common superordinate goal here?

And: Paradigm Shift Tool and Question:

What today is impossible to do, but if it could be done, would fundamentally change what we do?

Without this common language and key systems questions, you can run into problems, as the following fable will attest.

On Joint Military Communications

—Author unknown

One reason the military services have problems with joint operations is that they don't speak the same language.

For example, if you told Navy personnel to "secure a building," they would turn off the lights and lock the doors.

The Army would occupy the building so that no one could enter.

The Marines would assault the building, capture it, and defend it with suppressive fire and close combat maneuvers.

The Air Force, on the other hand, would take out a three-year lease with an option to buy.

In spite of the fact that there is an abundance of partial thinking concepts and seemingly no conscious full systems applications at work, there *are* some places, such as our Centre for Strategic Management, Russ Ackoff's Philadelphia-based association, and Senge's M.I.T.-related Innovation Associates, that are working hard to pioneer the conscientious and consistent use of full systems thinking today.

Research: Places Where Real Systems Thinking Is Happening Today

With the plethora of partial systems thinking concepts emerging, our society is recognizing more and more that the Systems Age, with its systems thinking, is a truism for today's success and growth into the 21st century. For just one example, *good project managers have shifted from linear thinking and begun with the desired destination.*

Other good examples of this are Peter Drucker's recent mission-focused emphasis and Steven Covey's systems thinking point, "Begin with the end in mind," in his book, *Seven Habits of Highly Successful People.*[1]

Royal Dutch/Shell Oil, among others, has discovered that just as mental models can impede learning and business growth, so too can they accelerate them. Shell understands that by helping managers identify their assumptions, it can maintain a real competitive edge (source: *The Fifth Discipline*, Peter Senge).

Scans Report

Working backwards from the end point is one of the problem-solving strategies that students should learn in school. In 1994, the Department of Labor applied this strategy to the problem of redesigning our schools. They turned to industry and businesses and asked them, "What does work require of schools?" Lynne Martin, former Secretary of Labor, formed the Secretary's Commission on Achieving Necessary Skills (SCANS) to find the answer to this question.

[1] Covey, Steven, *Seven Habits of Highly Successful People*. New York; Simon & Schuster, 1989.

- Three foundational skills and five competencies were identified by the SCANS commission, including the foundation skill of *Thinking*: "Thinking creatively, making decisions, solving problems, visualizing, learning how to learn and reason." They also listed *Systems*: "Understanding social, organizational and technological systems, monitoring performance and designing and improving systems." [2]

The Secret of NUMMI

The Japanese company Toyota has taken an interesting, systemic approach to project management through planning and implementation. In the United States, when a project is expected to be operational in twelve months, an average of three months goes into planning, followed by implementation.

On the same project, however, Toyota will typically use about nine months in planning, and then implement a small trial production. By the end of the 12 months, the project will be fully implemented, with almost no hidden snags or slowdowns.

Why does Japan seem to frequently outdistance other industrialized countries, particularly in their business and commercial achievements? Much of it has to do with a willingness to release old, tired paradigms and welcome new ones quickly and efficiently.

A 1986 General Motors top management confidential study of GM and Toyota's NUMMI joint plant in Fremont, California, said, *"It wasn't any one element that made Toyota better, it was* ***their entire system!"***

- The "secret" is not in the individual pieces, although NUMMI employs many management techniques that differ from GM.
- The success of NUMMI's version of the Toyota system lies in the careful integration of practices to manage people, processes, and suppliers into a management system.
- This implies that we can't implement the individual pieces and expect the same result as if we had implemented the entire system. Implementing pieces can result in improvements, and should not be discouraged. However, the "quantum leap" improvement seen at NUMMI only comes after the entire system is in place, ***and in place for some time***.

Performance Survey

Further, if you want to have a high performing organization or unit, just link the hierarchical levels of the organization together to get synergy. Unfortunately as the research below shows, only 20% of all employees see the linkages; **80% don't**.

"Talk is cheap." That's apparent from the results of a survey of more than 500 small and midsize companies conducted by the Oechsli Institute. Many of their employees said management's actions don't support the mission statement and that their company's workers don't understand what's expected of them. Worse, 8 out of 10 managers, salespeople, and operations employees said they were not held accountable for their own daily performance.[3]

---

[2] *T.I.E. News*, Volume 5, Number 1.

[3] Performance survey, January 1992 to September 1992, the Oechsli Institute, Greensboro, NC; Reprinted to *INC.*, March 1993.

Best Practices Report

International Quality Study

The American Quality Foundation and Ernst & Young conducted a massive study in 1994. It was an extensive statistical study of 945 management practices in over 580 organizations (84% response rate) in the United States, Japan, Canada, and Germany. It included four major industries: automotive, banking, computer, and health care industries.

In this study, they defined the best practices that lead to high performance as:

1. Market performance (perceived quality index)

2. Operations (productivity) performance (value-added per employee)

3. Financial performance (ROA)

The survey found only three universally beneficial practices with a significant impact on performance regardless of the starting position of the organization. All the other practices were situational and depended on the “fit” question of organizational life stages, environment, and levels of actual performance (the systems view again).

The three universally beneficial practices were:

1. Strategic planning and deployment/implementation

2. Business process improvement methods

3. Continuous broadening of the range and depth of management (and leadership) practices to make additional gains in performance

Systems Thinking Strikes Again!

Whole Systems Planning

The area of Organization Development has also picked up on the systems view. Procter & Gamble saw it as their competitive edge for over 20 years. David Hanna of Procter & Gamble wrote a volume that detailed much of their techniques entitled *The Dynamics of Organizational Levels: A Change Framework for Managers and Consultants.*

The 1990s saw entire organizations assembling in one room to generate the direction and buy-in to large-scale change. Dannemiller Tyson Associates of Ann Arbor, Michigan, are the leaders in the development and application of their “whole-scale” approach to change. Their book, *Real Time Strategic Change,* is well worth reading as one more excellent systems thinking technique.

Dr. Peter Senge

No book on the techniques of systems thinking would be useful without a discussion of Peter Senge and his best-selling book, *The 5th Discipline.* His “5th Discipline” is systems thinking and he deserves a great deal of credit for repopularizing the concept. However, in discussions with many clients over the past five years, it is the rare person who has actually read the book ("too academic/arcane" are typical comments). While the follow-up book, *The Fifth Discipline Field Book—Strategies and Tools for Building a Learning Organization* has proven more useful, most change practitioners are still confused as to (1) what are the systems thinking concepts, and (2) what are practical tools to implement it? That's precisely why we wrote this book. As a result of this confusion, however, Linkage, Inc., the prominent conference company, will hold its first annual systems thinking conference in April, 2000 to address these issues.

Without trying to fully dissect Senge's system thinking heritage, it is clear he has been heavily influenced by Professor Jay Forrester, his mentor at MIT. Forrester split years ago from The Society of General Systems Researchers to focus on the mathematical side of systems thinking. However, systems thinking is about the synergy, relatedness, integration, and "Unity of Science" for living systems, not a separate scientific discipline.

As a result, Senge's preoccupation with "causal loops" as a technique is part of advancing the field. However, when he focuses on "closed loops" and fails to discuss the environment, he is clearly not looking at open/living systems, but mechanical, industrial mechanisms.

Thus, in summary,

The Centre's Approach *The Complete Guide to Systems Thinking and Learning* *vs.*	**MIT/Senge's Approach** *The Fifth Discipline/ The Fieldbook*
1. Comprehensive systems thinking approach	1. Five excellent separate concepts (yet still piecemeal)
2. Seven Levels of Living Systems	2. Only deals with first and third levels of Living Systems
3. Twelve Characteristics of Systems Theory (Standard Laws of Systems Dynamics)	3. Primarily deals with only a few systems dynamics (causal loops)
4. A-B-C-D-E systems framework	4. No overall systems framework
5. Based on extensive research in General Systems Theory (biology, etc.)	5. Based on Jay Forrester's "Principles of Systems" • Mathematical/sequential • Closed feedback loop • No environmental scan
6. Natural laws and cycles of change (Changing systems—Rollercoaster)	6. Learning focus only

Dr. Margaret Wheatly

Wheatly is the author of two best-sellers in the fields of chaos and complexity entitled *A Simpler Way* and *Leadership and the New Science*. Her contributions to understanding systems thinking are extremely important as she focuses on how self-organizing systems emerge out of chaos and complexity in nature (and should be allowed in organizations as well). However, at the extreme, this is sometimes seen as a belief in anarchy. Organizing living systems toward "what end?" (beyond survival) is a key question here.

Chaos theory is just part of the cycles of change. Chaos theory details how things work in natural systems; not analytically as we order them. The key is: Order can emerge out of chaos.

Order develops naturally from within our universe. And chaos is a natural step in achieving a higher order of things, a more natural order of things. So, accept chaos—it's natural! It's part of the cycles of change (i.e., The Rollercoaster of Change).

Out of the complexity and interdependence of today's technology and society and the chaos of fundamental and turbulent change will ultimately come discoveries of the natural and spontaneous new orders, structure, and visions. But, discover what new orders, structure, and visions?

This "order" is that of the "natural systems" all around us (whether it is our bodies, our team and families, our organizations, society, and many aspects of our natural world and environment).

Thus, chaos and complexity are a natural and normal part of the process of discovering new orders from the natural systems of life. However, only true systems thinking can provide this overall framework and its elegant simplicity (not the new, partial, and "separate" scientific disciplines of chaos and complexity).

Finally, systems thinking is growing everywhere!

Most scientific disciplines are converging on systems thinking. We have identified over 25 (and the list is growing). This includes:

- Cybernetics
- General Systems Theory
- Organization Development
- Physics
- Neuroscience
- Futurists
- Architecture
- Geometry
- Religion
- Ranching and Farming
- Chaos Theory
- Complexity Theory
- Human Resource Management
- Mathematics
- Philosophers
- Education
- Mythology
- Atmospheric and Oceanographic Sciences
- Agriculture
- Gestalt Therapy
- Socio-Technical Systems Theory (Eric Trist)
- Biology
- Astronomy
- Economics
- Art
- Strategic Planning
- Occupational Health
- And many others

Call the Centre for more information, or refer to the bibliography in this book for details.

Obstacles to Systems Thinking and Learning

"Why don't organizations use what we know works?"[4]

(Systems Thinking and Learning)

The author's hypotheses on reasons for the nonuse of proven research on what constitutes best management practices through systems thinking and learning.

If systems thinking is a hard switch to a new thinking concept and a new orientation to life, why is that so? Some obstacles to overcome might include many of the following:

I. Academic Obstacles

1. Ease and desirability of micro/reductionist research projects that are often arcane, irrelevant, or obsolete.
2. Jealousy and/or honest criticism of new and different researchers by other researchers, lowering credibility of research in general.
3. Face validity of action research that follows the natural flow of the universe used in organizations is often criticized in favor of more rigorous academic research criteria using reductionist "scientific" criteria.
4. New reductionistic research is prized versus the collection and weight of previous convergent research to show the systems connections.
5. Research data analysis techniques (i.e., correlation, etc.) are often irrelevant to executives who deal in complex systems.
6. Executives speak finance, academics speak "academise." Neither speak in *systems* terms.
7. Research ignores the business, economic, and human behavior realities and their integration/relationships.

II. Line Management Obstacles

8. Poor role models for managers early in their careers.
9. Executives' ignorance of systems research.
10. Rewards for using proven research and systems thinking are not that significant, or are missing.
11. Delayed cause and effect in management practices often leads to the wrong conclusions and "learnings" by executives.
12. Each organizational situation is so dependent on the context that it obscures the underlying generic systems principles.
13. Executives ignore facts due to perceived irrelevance of academics and research, especially systems theory.
14. Executives ignore facts because their orientation is not necessarily a results-focus for the system they are in, but rather being popular or acquiring power.

---

[4] Who is speaking?

15. Some executives' egos say they alone know best. Taking advice on systems thinking injures their egos. It doesn't fit the macho image.
16. The effect of managerial practices on all employees in an organization is also dependent on the individual practices of each and every supervisor, requiring a culture change to systems thinking.
17. Management's willingness to and ease of accepting average performance and mediocrity vs. demanding integration and adherence or integrity to the overall system—i.e., lack of ***"watertight integrity."***
18. Short-term survival orientation and peer pressure precludes using longer-term systems impacts and effects to aid in achieving excellence.

III. Staff Obstacles

19. The *fit* of all "10,000" actions in an organization working together to make up good management practices is fragmented among numerous staff specialists. They, in turn, try to maximize their job versus the joint optimization in systems thinking—i.e., of all parts fitting together for the overall good of both the company and the employees.
20. Staff specialists are rewarded in many ways for individual job maximization versus this need for fit and joint optimization, which is often unrewarded and/or perceived as a win-lose game by different staff specialists.
21. Lack of results / outcome orientation by staff.
22. Staff specialists are often ignorant of the research regarding best management practices from systems thinking.
23. Staff specialists often have conflicting personal objectives vs. organizational outcomes.
24. The most knowledgeable staff specialists may not be able to translate their knowledge to line executives or may lack the interpersonal skills necessary to influence senior management on good policy/practices from systems thinking.

IV. Organizational and Profit Obstacles

25. Executives focus on and are reinforced in regard to short-term quarterly profit at the expense of long-term, subtler systems implications and employee motivation.
26. Executives are often promoted or change jobs in two to four years prior to seeing the real, longer term delayed cause and effects of poor management practices.
27. Executives face many decisions in a high-pressure environment, making it difficult to maintain good management practices and the overall long-term systems' best interests.
28. Organizational values often are not explicit, agreed upon, or well communicated. Thus, everyone does not have the potential to follow the desired organization values of good management practices to create the desired culture.
29. Some executives' personal values do not fit with the underlying values of overall good management practices.
30. The misguided perception of Frederick Taylor's "scientific management" in western society has, unfortunately, been based on two false assumptions. They are: (a) employees are like machines and are interchangeable parts—not a significant factor in a competitive business advantage; and (b) the breakdown of organizational

units into the smallest units (with specialists) is the way to get synergy in an organization (i.e., 1 + 1 + 1 + 1 = 5 when it usually equals 3 due to the higher "transaction" costs).

31. Boards of Directors often fail to focus on this issue of overall systems integration and best management practices. Unfortunately, these best management practices in organizations are too complex to fully understand.

V. Other Common Strategic Obstacles and Mistakes

32. Failing to integrate planning and change at all levels.
33. Keeping planning separate from day-to-day management.
34. Developing vision, mission, and value statements as fluff, and stopping there.
35. Having yearly weekend retreats and calling them strategic planning.
36. Failing to identify and complete an effective implementation/strategic change process and follow through on any major change effort.
37. Violating the "people support what they help create" premise and seeing change as mechanical.
38. Failing to make the "tough choices" to keep integration and integrity to the overall system.
39. Lacking a scoreboard of outcomes; measuring what's easy, not what's important and a key result.
40. Failing to define and strategize regarding the fit and integration of strategic business units or major program areas to the entire organization.
41. Neglecting to benchmark yourself against the competition and your customers (other systems).
42. Dealing with each change as an isolated event.
43. Having confusing terminology and language between different functions.

Benefits of Systems Thinking and Learning

Systems thinking has some primary, far-reaching benefits that give us:

1. An overall framework and way to make sense out of life's complexities, and any system. Remember, all living things *are* systems. It helps us see patterns and relationships.

2. A way to learn new things more easily—its basic rules are simple and consistent—they stay the same from system to system.

3. A better way to integrate new ideas together within the systems context.

4. A clearer way to see and understand what is going on in any organization or any system, and its environment. Complex problems become easier to understand, as do the interrelationships of parts and multiple cause-and-effect cycles.

5. A new and better way to create strategies, problem-solve, and find leverage points—keeping the outcome/vision/goal in mind at all times.

6. The key systems thinking questions and A-B-C-D template with which to correctly begin any diagnostic or discovery work—problem solving; solution seeking.

7. It engages teams and people in a deeper thought process, analysis, and definition of more root causes that provide longer lasting results. It enables groups to generate multiple choices and different solutions rather than just quick-fix answers when working with difficult problems.

8. It helps get at the deeper structure and relationship or process issues that aren't obvious with the "quick-fix" mentality.

9. It enables us to challenge our inaccurate assumptions and mental models residing deep within ourselves that guide our thinking, acting, and problem solving. When they hold us back, it usually means that new, creative, and broader, more long-lasting solutions don't get identified and implemented.

10. It enables us to see the dynamic interactions and relationships of both:
    - the elements of a system, and
    - systems colliding with other systems at the same time; thus making better decisions with a clearer understanding of the consequences.

11. A better framework for diagramming, mapping, diagnosing, analyzing, problem solving, and decision making of any system—department, unit, organization, or otherwise.

12. A way to manage the complex "systems age," i.e., focusing on the whole, its components, and the interrelationships of the components rather than supposedly isolated and independent problems and parts.

13. A common framework and model for thinking and communicating with the same language to work better together to make positive change in any system to achieve your desired outcomes.

14. In short, a new orientation to life!

Systems-Oriented Organizational Benefits

Some of the attributes you can expect to find in a systems-oriented organization that might not exist in a more mechanistic one include:

- A shared vision and values of the overall organization's future and culture.
- Better cross-functional communication and cooperation to serve the customer.
- Teamwork within and across functions.
- Cross-functional task forces and project teams/empowerment and self-initiative towards the overall organizational mission.

- Integrity of the various parts and departments of the organization fitting and working together for the good of the whole.
- An alignment of business/work processes horizontally across the organization that meet the needs of the external customers (and ties in suppliers).
- Focus on system-wide core strategies rather than functional or department goals or individual key results areas.
- Fewer levels of hierarchy and management; greater operational flexibility and empowerment.
- Lower territorial orientation and more job movement across functions.
- Development of management and leadership skills and practices to collaborate with, influence, coach, and facilitate others rather than control/power orientation.
- Core values explicitly managed to achieve the desired culture.

Lastly, systems thinking gives us a better language, a better way of thinking and being. Its principles are much like a wide-angle lens on a camera; they give us a better view on our radar scope—thus, a more effective way of thinking, communicating, problem solving, and acting. Without systems thinking, we face a situation in which:

Today's thinking (and problem solving) is the source of tomorrow's problems.

If we truly want to move forward toward a better, stronger future, we must begin to make substantial changes in terms of how we look at our world. As astute Canadian futurist Cliff McIntosh said, "The central 21st century issue is [the] invention and mastery of systems that provide the good life and ensure the survival of life on Earth." (Unfortunately, Cliff died before helping with this issue in the 21st century.)

As Edward Cornish said, "We ourselves create our future . . . the future is not something imposed upon us by fate or other forces beyond our control. We ourselves build the future both through what we do and what we do not do. Once we recognize our power over the future, we inevitably begin to anticipate the consequences of what we do and to do those things that will improve our future; in short, we begin to act wisely." [5]

Summary and Bottom Line—Four Concepts Revisited

"Systems thinking is a discipline for seeing wholes, a framework for seeing patterns and interrelationships. It's especially important to see the world as a whole as it grows more and more complex.

"Complexity can overwhelm and undermine: 'It's the system. I have no control.' Systems thinking makes these realities more manageable; it's the antidote for feelings of helplessness.

"By seeing the patterns that lie behind events and details, we can actually simplify life." [6]

---

[5] Cornish, Edward, *"Responsibility for the Future," The Futurist,* May/June, 1994.

[6] Senge, Peter M., *The Fifth Discipline*. New York: Doubleday, 1990.

Thus, we need to shift from analytic thinking to the systems thinking approach advocated by the author, by Ludwig Von Bertelenffy, and many leading scientists everywhere.

What are the keys needed to be successful in letting go of old ways and grabbing hold of this newer, more effective way? Joel Barker's says we must become "paradigm pioneers." To fully embrace the Systems Age, and to fully integrate our new common sense systems tools for systems thinking and learning, each of us must be willing to:

- Get outside our own borders and rules . . . in other words, *get outside the nine dots!*
- Break our own rules of past success . . . *don't wait until it's broken!*
- Develop new reading habits . . . *suspend your judgment.*
- Be ready for failure; don't avoid it . . . *from it springs the seeds of future success.*
- Actively listen . . . don't prepare your response . . . listen . . . listen . . . *listen!*

When all is said and done, we will only successfully integrate systems solutions to our systems problems when we make the transition from unconscious to conscious systems applications, terminology, and language.

The Systems Thinking Approach is now being applied to organizations. *How you think . . . is how you act . . . is how you are!*

Thinking across boundaries, or integrative system thinking, is the ultimate entrepreneurial act. Call it business creativity. Call it holistic thinking. To see problems and opportunities integratively is to see them as wholes related to larger wholes, rather than dividing information and experience into discrete bits assigned to distinct, separate categories that never touch one another.

Research has associated integrative thinking with higher levels of organizational innovation, personal creativity, and even longer life.

The ability to rethink categories and transcend boundaries is essential for every aspect of business practice today. **To start with, many firms desperately need a new concept of the term "business."**[7]

When we look at resolving today's problems in order to grow and thrive in a brand-new century, we must always remind ourselves that: *how* we approach issues and how we think about them are just as crucial as *what* actions we take. One thing is certain—if we continue to engage an analytic, linear, reductionistic approach, the resulting entropy and degradation will eventually grind our systems to a halt—just look at society's intractable problems today.

There are many, many systems tools and aids presented in this book. However, they are all based on our four basic systems concepts:

- Concept #1: Seven Levels of Living (Open) Systems
- Concept #2: Laws of Natural Systems (Standard Systems Dynamics)
- Concept #3: A-B-C-D Systems Model
- Concept #4: Changing Systems (The Natural Cycles of Life and Change)

---

7 "From the Editor," *Harvard Business Review*, November-December 1990.

We can use these four concepts to make certain we're staying on a systems thinking track and moving *from chaos and complexity to elegant simplicity.*

The beauty of the systems approach is these four simple systems concepts (and the 10 key systems questions) that we can use both as a quick start and reality check and as a focus for our synergistic solution-seeking/visioning.

If we remember to consistently pose these systems questions first—and if we remember every system is an indivisible whole—***we will be well on our way to discovering simplicity through the lost art of systems thinking and learning. We will no longer apply analytic/linear approaches to systems problems***.

Now, see the "cheat sheets" below and on the next few pages to ensure you've got all the basic points, characteristics, etc., of systems thinking.

The Natural Laws of All Living Systems (The Unity of Science)

—A Summary—

I. The Whole System (Six Natural Laws)

Twelve Natural Systems Laws vs.	Typical Analytical Dynamics	Systems Principles	Systems Questions	Example
1. **Holism**—Overall Purpose-Focused Synergy	1. **Parts Focused**—Suboptimal Results	Problems cannot be solved at the level they were created.	• What is our common higher-level (super-ordinate) goal?	Union-management fights and strikes over pay tend to amount to a win-lose game. By moving to the higher-level goal of competing and producing more profitably, both sides can make more money (increase the size of the pie). In your day-to-day life, do you think about your future vision and your higher-level goals?
2. **Open Systems**—Open to the Environment	2. **Closed Systems**—Low Environmental Scan	Systems first require work and alignment from the outside in, not the inside out.	• What is changing in the environment that we need to consider? • Is it relatively open or closed in its environmental interactions?	In organizational terms, this means we must keep scanning the environment for changes in anything from our competition to the political scene. At minimum there are 8 areas we need to keep an eye on. They can be remembered by the acronym SKEPTIC. **S**ocio-demographics "**K**"ompetition **E**conomics/**E**nvironment **P**olitics **T**echnology **I**ndustry **C**ustomers

(continued)

The Natural Laws of All Living Systems (continued)

I. The Whole System (continued)

Twelve Natural Systems Laws	vs. Typical Analytical Dynamics	Systems Principles	Systems Questions	Example
3. **Boundaries**—Open—Integrated/Collaborative	4. **Fragmented**—Closed—Turf Battles	The entity to be changed must be clear.	• What entity (system or "collision of systems") are we dealing with, and • What are its boundaries? • What levels of the overall entity do we want to change?	Are you trying to change yourself, your department, a business process, a partnership, or the entire organization?
4. **Input/Output**—How Natural Systems Operate	4. **Sequential**—Piecemeal/Analytic	Focus on the multiple future outcomes first, then *"work backwards"* to today in order to move forward to this future.	• Are we dealing with the ends (the *what*) or with the means (the *how*)?	What is the difference between teaching and learning? Teaching is one key way to accomplish learning; it is a set of means. Learning is the outcome; it is the end-goal of teaching. Schools often focus too much on teachers and teaching; they need to keep in mind the desired outcome—the student's actual learning. Teachers and trainers of all types should ask themselves how do students best learn, not just how to teach.
5. **Feedback**—on Effectiveness/Root Causes from the Environment	5. **Low Feedback**—Financial Only, Direct Cause/Effect Feedback only	As an input, feedback requires receptivity; it calls for us to be flexible and adaptable.	• How will we know we have achieved the desired outcomes? • What are our outcome performance measures?	Look at feedback as a gift—be open and receptive to it; even encourage it. Ask for feedback from all your customers, your employees, your direct reports and peers, and anyone who can help you learn and grow as a person, as a professional, as a leader of your organization.

(continued)

The Natural Laws of All Living Systems (continued)

I. The Whole System (concluded)

6. **Multiple Outcomes**— Goals	6. **Conflict**— Artificial Either/Or Thinking	Systems are naturally goal-seeking and will self-organize to do so.	• What are the desired outcomes? (That is, *Where do we want to be in the future?*)	Organizational outcomes often include the needs of customers, employees, and stockholders, as well as the community, suppliers, etc. Asking this question sends us into "*backwards thinking*," which keeps us from focusing on only isolated events. The question *"Is it x or y?"* is usually based on an incorrect assumption: that there is only one answer in every case. This mistaken assumption occurs in organizations, teams, families, and interpersonal relationships. This often results in needless conflict, differences of opinions, and hard feelings.

II. The Inner Workings (Six More Natural Laws)

7. **Equifinality**— Flexibility and Agility	7. **Direct Cause-Effect**— One Best Way	There are many different ways to achieve the same desired outcomes. Principle: People support what they help create.	• What should we centralize, and • What should we decentralize?	Today's leadership paradigm calls for a new way of looking at organizations. It requires a much higher level of maturity and wisdom—a middle ground between abdicating responsibility and being *"all controlling"*—with a focus on **inter**dependence.
8. **Entropy**— Follow-up/ Inputs of Energy/Renewal	8. **Decline**— Rigidity and Death	If entropy is not reversed (by follow-up/input of more energy) the system will die. (So will the change project.)	• What must we do to ensure buy-in and stay-in over time (perseverance), and thus avoid entropy?	While human beings obviously have a finite life cycle, it doesn't have to be this way for neighborhoods, communities, and organizations. For them, the renewal process that reverses the entropy is key to long-term success.

(continued)

The Natural Laws of All Living Systems (continued)

II. The Inner Workings (continued)

9. **Hierarchy—** Flatter Organization/ Self Organizing	9. **Bureau-cracy—** Command and Control	All systems are linked to other systems (some larger, some smaller) in the hierarchy. Multilevel systems are too complex to fully understand and manage centrally.	• How can we move from complexity to simplicity, and from rigidity to flexibility, in the solutions we devise? • What levels of the overall entity do we want to change?	Large-company divisions often do not know the multiple outcomes of the overall system. This is why such divisions tend to be perplexed by "higher-up" decisions and vice-versa. Simplicity is needed: the application of the Rule of Three, i.e., — Individual: Body, mind, spirit — Learning: Skills, knowledge, feeling/attitude — Human Realities of Interactions: Structure, content, process
10. **Interrelated or Sub-Component Parts—** Relationships/ Involvement and Participation	10. **Separate Parts—** Components/ Entities/Silos	The whole is more important than the parts; relationships and processes are key.	• What is the relationship of x to y and z?	In organizations, the question is not, *How can I maximize my job or department's impact?*; it is, *How can we all work and fit together in support of the overall objectives of the organization?* To that end, each year all major departments need to share their annual plans with senior executives and middle managers and other professionals to ensure everyone knows what everyone else is doing, and to give others a chance to critique those plans. This is actually a large group team-building process.

(continued)

The Natural Laws of All Living Systems (concluded)

II. The Inner Workings (concluded)

11. **Dynamic Equilibrium**—Stability and Balance/Culture —or— disequilibrium at the edge of the polarities/ extremes	11. **Resistance to Change**—Myopic View/ Ruts	The steady-state equilibrium, however much we want it, can be dangerous in a changing world. If you are doing things the same way you did five years ago, it's probably wrong.	• What new processes and structures are we using to ensure successful change?	Designing, building, and sustaining a customer-focused high-performance learning organization for the 21st century requires a balance in how organizations spend their time and energy among content, processes, and structure. Above all, what we need to avoid is *content myopia.* Content Myopia—The Failure to Focus on Processes and Structures Remember: Change is dependent on process and structures!
12. **Internal Elaboration**—Details and Sophistication	12. **Complexity**—and Confusion	Root causes and their effects are usually not linked closely in time and space.	• What multiple causes lie at the root of our problem or concern? (That is, *What are the root causes*?)	On the organizational problem-solving front, such thinking leads to the search for fast, convenient solutions—quick fixes—as if we were dealing with simple mechanical objects, not unwanted outcomes in a system within systems.

The Natural Laws of All Living Systems

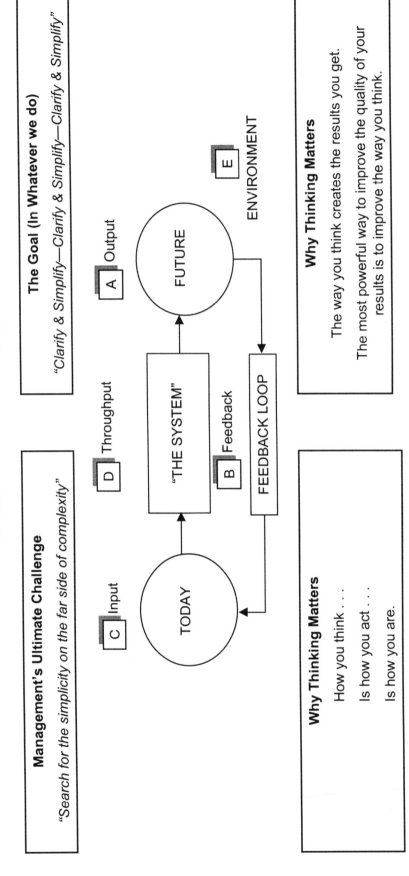

Management's Ultimate Challenge

"Search for the simplicity on the far side of complexity"

The Goal (In Whatever we do)

"Clarify & Simplify—Clarify & Simplify—Clarify & Simplify"

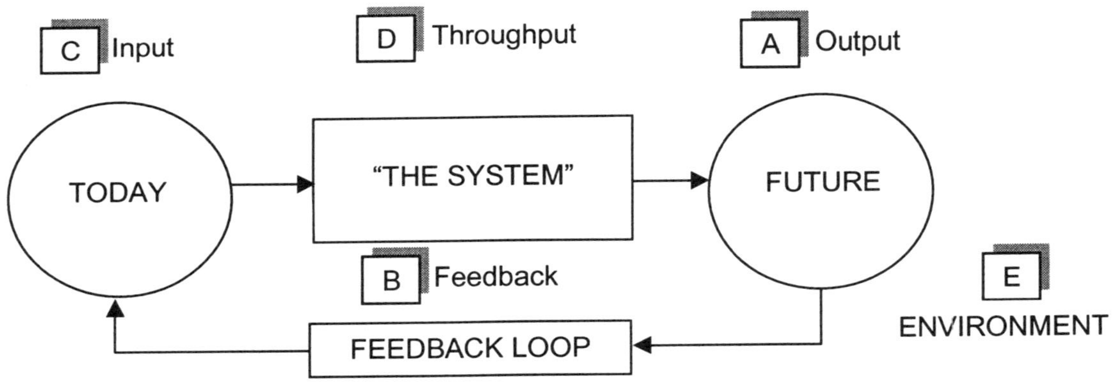

Why Thinking Matters

How you think . . .

Is how you act . . .

Is how you are.

Why Thinking Matters

The way you think creates the results you get.

The most powerful way to improve the quality of your results is to improve the way you think.

Analytic vs. Systems Thinking

(Strategic Consistency yet Operational Flexibility)

(Outside—Inside—Outside Again: Both Are Then Useful)

Success Key: *Organizational Systems Fit, Alignment, and Integrity*

Analytic Thinking *(Analysis of Today)*	vs.	**Systems Thinking** *(Synthesis for the Future*
1. We/they	vs.	1. Customers/stakeholders
2. Independent	vs.	2. Interdependent
3. Activities/tasks	and	3. Outcomes/ends
4. Problem solving	and	4. Solution seeking
5. Today is fine	vs.	5. Shared vision of future
6. Units/departments	and	6. Total organization
7. Silo mentality	vs.	7. Cross-functional teamwork
8. Closed environment	vs.	8. Openness and feedback
9. Department goals	and	9. Shared core strategies
10. Strategic planning project	vs.	10. Strategic Management system
11. Hierarchy and controls	and	11. Serve the customer
12. Not my job	vs.	12. Communications and collaboration
13. Isolated change	vs.	13. Systemic change
14. Linear/begin-end	vs.	14. Circular/repeat cycles
15. Little picture/view	vs.	15. Big picture/holistic perspective
16. Short-term	and	16. Long-term
17. Separate issues	vs.	17. Related issues
18. Symptoms	and	18. Root causes
19. Isolated events	and	19. Patterns/trends
20. Activities/actions	and	20. Clear outcome expectations (goals/values)
In Sum: Parts are Primary	**vs.**	**The Whole is Primary**

STOP **Using Analytic Approaches to Systems Problems!**

In Systems Thinking—the whole is primary and the parts are secondary

vs.

In Analytic Thinking—the parts are primary and the whole is secondary

The bottom line is:

What we think, or what we know, or what we believe

is, in the end, of little consequence.

The only consequence . . . is what we do!

Take the lost art—*these four basically simple concepts*—

and go forward to your destinations

. . . make a difference in today's world!

Bibliography

Aburdene, P. & Naisbitt, J. (1992). *Megatrends for Women*. NY: Villard Books.

Ackoff, R. (1974). *Redesigning the Future: A Systems Approach to Societal Problems*. NY: John Wiley & Sons, Inc.

Ackoff, R. (1991). *Ackoff's Fables: Irreverent Reflections on Business and Bureaucracy*. NY: John Wiley & Sons, Inc.

Argyris, C. & Schon, D. (1978). *Organizational Learning: A Theory of Action Perspective*. Reading, MA: Addison-Wesley.

Augros, R. M. & Stanciu, G. N. (1984). *The New Story of Science*. NY: Bantam Books.

Baker-Miller, J. (1976). *Toward a New Psychology of Women*. Boston, MA: Beacon Press.

Band, W. A. (1994). *Touchstones: Ten New Ideas Revolutionizing Business*. NY: John Wiley & Sons, Inc.

Barker, J. A. (1992). *The Future Edge: Discovering the New Paradigms of Success*. NY: William Morrow and Company, Inc.

Barlett, D. L. & Steele, J. B. (1992). *America: What Went Wrong*? Kansas City: MO: Andrews and McMeel.

Barry, R. (1993). *A Theory of Almost Everything*. Chatham, NY: Oneworld.

Bateson, G. (1980). *Mind and Nature*. NY: Bantam Books.

Beatty, Jack. (1998). *The World According to Peter Drucker*. NY: The Free Press.

Bennis, W., Benne, R., Corey, C. & K. [Eds.]. (1976). *The Planning of Change*. NY: Holt, Rinehart and Winston.

Blank, W. (1995). *The 9 Natural Laws of Leadership*. NY: AMACOM Books.

Bohm, D. (1980). *Wholeness and the Implicate Order*. London: Ark Paperbacks.

Boulding, K. E. (1964). *The Meaning of the 20th Century*. NY: Prentice-Hall.

Briggs, J. & Peat, F. D. (1989). *Turbulent Mirror: An Illustrated Guide to Chaos Theory and the Science of Wholeness*. NY: Harper and Row.

Brinkerhoff, R. O. & Gill, S. J. (1994). *The Learning Alliance: Systems Thinking in Human Resource Development*. San Francisco: Jossey-Bass Publishers.

Bucholz, R. A. (1993). *Principles of Environmental Management: The Greening of Business*. NY: Prentice Hall.

Buckley, W. (1967). *Sociology and Modern Systems Theory*. NY: Prentice-Hall.

Capra, F. (1976). *The Tao of Physics*. NY: Bantam Books.

Capra, F. (1983). *The Turning Point: Science, Society and the Rising Culture*. NY: Bantam Books.

Carnevale, A. (1991). *America and the New Economy*. San Francisco: Jossey Bass Publishers.

Casti, J. L. (1994). *Complexification: Explaining a Paradoxical World Through the Science of Surprise*. NY: Harper Collins.

Chandler, A., Jr. (1962). *Strategy and Structure: Chapters in the History of the American Industrial Enterprise*. Cambridge, MA: The MIT Press.

Chopra, D. (1989). *Quantum Healing: Exploring the Frontiers of Mind and Body Science*. NY: Bantam Books.

Churchman, C. W. (1968). *The Systems Approach*. NY: Dell Publishing.

Coates, J. F. & Jarratt, J. (2nd printing 1990). *What Futurists Believe*. Bethesda, MD: The World Future Society.

Cohen, J. & Stewart I. (1994). *The Collapse of Chaos.* NY: The Penguin Group.

Colburn, T., Dumanoski, D. & Meyers, J. P. (1996). *Our Stolen Future*. NY: Dutton Signet.

Cornwell, J. [Ed.]. (1995). *Nature's Imagination.* Oxford University Press.

Covey, S. (1989). *The 7 Habits of Highly Effective People*. NY: Simon & Schuster.

Csanyi, V. (1989). *Evolutionary Systems and Society*. Durham, NC: Duke University Press.

Cummings, T. G. (1980). *Systems Theory for Organization Development*. NY: John Wiley & Sons.

Cummings, T. G. & Srivastva, S. (1977). *Management of Work: A Sociotechnical Systems Approach*. San Diego, CA: University Associates.

Cziko, G. (1995). *Without Miracles: Universal Selection Theory and the Second Darwinian Revolution*. Cambridge, MA: The MIT Press.

Davenport, T. H. & Prusak, L. (1998). *Information Ecology*. NY: Oxford University Press.

Davidson, M. (1983). *Uncommon Sense*. Los Angeles: J. P. Tarcher, Inc.

Davies, P. C. W. & Brown, J. (1988). *Superstrings: A Theory of Everything*? Cambridge, U.K.: Cambridge University Press.

DeGeus, Arie. (1997). *The Living Company*. Cambridge, MA: Harvard Business School Press.

Denton, D. K. (1991). *Horizontal Management: Beyond Total Customer Satisfaction*. NY: Lexington Books.

Dettmer, H. W. (1996). *Goldratt's Theory of Constraints.* Milwaukee, WI: ASQC Quality Press.

Diamond, I. & Orenstein, G. F. [Eds.]. (1990). *Reweaving the World: The Emergence of Ecofeminism.* San Francisco: Sierra Club Books.

Dibella, A. J. (1998). *How Organizations Learn.* San Francisco: Jossey-Bass Publishers.

Drucker, P. (1993). *Post-Capitalist Society.* NY: Harper Business.

Drucker, P. (1995). *Managing in a Time of Great Change.* NY: Dutton.

Duncan, W. L. (1994). *Manufacturing 2000.* NY: AMACOM Books.

Earley. J. (1997). *Transforming Human Culture—Social Evolution and the Planetary Crises.* Albany, NY: State University of New York Press.

Eberly, D. (1994). *Building a Community of Citizens.* Lanham, MD: University Press of America.

Eberly, D. (1994). *Restoring the Good Society: A New Vision for Politics and Culture.* Grand Rapids, MI: Baker Book House.

Eisler, R. (1987). *The Chalice and the Blade: Our History, Our Future.* San Francisco: Harper and Row.

Eisler, R. & Loye, D. (1990). *The Partnership Way: New Tools for Living and Learning.* San Francisco: Harper Collins.

Feininger, A. (1986). *In a Grain of Sand: Exploring Design by Nature.* San Francisco: Sierra Club Books.

Ferber, M. A. & Nelson, J. A. (1993). *Beyond Economic Man: Feminist Theory and Economics.* Chicago, IL: The University of Chicago Press.

Ferguson, K. (1994). *The Fire in the Equations: Science, Religion & the Search for God.* Grand Rapids, MI: Eerdmans.

Fombrun, C. J. (1992). *Turning Points: Creating Strategic Change in Corporations.* Los Angeles: R. R. Donnelly & Sons Company.

Forrester, J. W. (1969). *Urban Dynamics.* Norwalk, CT: Productivity Press.

Forrester, J. W. (1971) *World Dynamics (2nd ed.).* Norwalk, CT: Productivity Press.

Forrester, J. W. (1971). *Principles of Systems.* Norwalk, CT: Productivity Press.

Forrester, J. W. (1971). *World Dynamics.* Cambridge, MA: Wright-Allen Press.

Forrester, J. W. (1975). *Collected Papers of Jay W. Forrester.* Norwalk, CT: Productivity Press.

Fox, M. & Shelldrake, R. (1996). *The Physics of Angels.* San Francisco: Harpers.

Frankel, V. (1959). *Man's Search for Meaning.* Boston, MA: Beacon Press.

Galbraith, J. R. (1993). *Organizing for the Future: The New Logic for Managing Complex Organizations*. San Francisco: Jossey-Bass Publishers.

Gell-Mann, M. (1995). *The Quark and the Jaguar.* NY: W. H. Freeman.

George, C. (1968). *The History of Management Thought*. Englewood Cliffs, NJ: Prentice Hall.

Glass, L. & Mackey, M. C. (1988). *From Clocks to Chaos*. Princeton, NJ: Princeton University Press.

Gleick, J. (1987). *Chaos: Making a New Science*. NY: Viking.

Goodman, M. R. (1974). *Study Notes in System Dynamics*. Norwalk, CT: Productivity Press.

Gore, A. (1993). *Earth in the Balance: Ecology and the Human Spirit*. NY: Penguin Books.

Griffin, S. (1982). *Made from This Earth*. NY: Harper and Row.

Hainer, S. (1984). "Unpublished Doctoral Dissertation." Philadelphia, PA: Temple University.

Haines, S. G. (1995). *Successful Strategic Planning*. Menlo Park, CA: Crisp Publications.

Haines, S. G. (1995). *Sustaining High Performance*. Delray Beach, FL: St. Lucie Press.

Haines, S. G. (1999). *The Manager's Pocket Guide to Systems Thinking and Learning.* Amherst, MA: HRD Press, Inc.

Haines, S. G. (2000). *The Complete Guide to Systems Thing and Learning*. Amherst, MA: HRD Press, Inc.

Hall, N. [Ed.]. (1994). *Exploring Chaos*. NY: W.W. Norton & Co.

Hamel, G. & Prahalad, C. K, (1994). *Competing for the Future*. Boston, MA: Harvard Business School Press.

Handy, C. (1989). *The Age of Unreason*. Cambridge, MA: Harvard Business School Press.

Handy, C. (1994). *The Age of Paradox*. Cambridge, MA: Harvard Business School Press.

Handy, C. (1998). *The Hungry Spirit: Beyond Capitalism: A Quest for Purpose in the Modern World*. NY: Broadway Books.

Hanson, B. G. (1995). *General Systems Theory Beginning with Wholes: An Introduction to General Systems Theory*. Washington, DC: Taylor and Francis.

Harman, W. & Hormann, J. (1990). *Creative Work: The Constructive Role of Business in a Transforming Society*. Indianapolis, IN: Knowledge Systems.

Hart, R. D. & Cooley, S. L. (1997). *A Nation Reconstructed.* Milwaukee, WI: ASQC Quality Press.

Hawken, P. (1993). *The Ecology of Commerce: A Declaration of Sustainability.* NY: Harper Business.

Heisenberg, W. (1958). *Physics and Philosophy.* NY: Harper Torchbooks.

Helgesen. S. (1990). *The Female Advantage: Women's Ways of Leadership.* NY: Doubleday.

Henderson, H. (1992). *Paradigms in Progress.* Indianapolis, IN: Knowledge Systems.

Henton, D., Melville, J. & Walesh, K. (1997). *Grassroots Leaders for a New Economy: How Civic Entrepreneurs Are Building Prosperous Communities.* San Francisco: Jossey-Bass Publishers.

Herbert, N. (1985). *Quantum Reality: Beyond the New Physics.* NY: Anchor Doubleday.

Herrnstein, R. J. & Murray, C. (1994). *The Bell Curve.* NY: Free Press.

Hersey, Paul (1984). *The Situational Leader.* NY: Warner Books.

Huntington, S. P. (1996). *The Clash of Civilizations and the Remaking of World Order.* NY: Simon and Schuster.

Itzkoff, S. W. (1994). *The Decline of Intelligence in America: A Strategy for National Renewal.* NY: Praeger.

Jantsch, E. (1975). *Design for Evolution: Self-Organization and Planning in the Life Human Systems.* NY: George Braziller, Inc.

Jantsch, E. (1980). *The Self-Organizing Universe.* Oxford: Pergamon Press.

Jaques, E. (1989). *Requisite Organization: The CEO's Guide to Creative Structure and Leadership.* Alexandria, VA: Cason Hall & Co. Publishers.

Johnson, R. A., Kast, F. E. & Rosenzweig, J. E. (1963). *The Theory and Management of Systems.* NY: McGraw-Hill.

Kaku, M. & Thompson, J. T. (1995). *Beyond Einstein (Revised).* NY: Anchor Books.

Kanter, R. M. (1977). *Men and Women in the Corporation.* NY: Basic Books.

Kauffman, S. (1995). *At Home in the Universe.* NY: Oxford University Press.

Keil, L. D. (1994). *Managing Chaos and Complexity in Government: A New Paradigm for Managing Change, Innovation, Organizational Renewal.* San Francisco: Jossey-Bass Publishers.

Klir, G. (1969). *An Approach to General Systems Theory.* NY: Van Nostrand.

Klir, G. [Ed.]. (1972). *Trends in General Systems Theory.* NY: Wiley-Interscience.

Knowles, M. S. (1984). *Andragogy in Action.* San Francisco: Jossey-Bass Publishers.

Kolb, D. A. (1983). *Experiential Learning: Experience as the Source of Learning and Development*. NY: Prentice Hall.

Kuhn, T. (1970). *The Structure of Scientific Revolutions (2nd ed.)*. Chicago: University of Chicago Press.

Langdon, D. G. (1995). *The New Language of Work*. Amherst, MA: HRD Press.

Lanza, R. [Ed.] et al. (1996). *One World: The Health and Survival of the Human Species in the 21st Century*. Santa Fe, NM: Health Press.

Laszlo, E. (1972). *Introduction to Systems Philosophy*. NY: Gordon & Breach.

Laszlo, E. (1972). *The Advance of General Systems Theory*. NY: George Braziller

Laszlo, E. (1972). *The Systems View of the World*. NY: George Braziller.

Laszlo, E. (1994). *Vision 20/20*. Langhorne, PA: Gordon & Breach.

Laszlo, E. [Ed.]. (1991). *The New Evolutionary Paradigm*. NY: Gordon & Breach.

Lawler, E. E., III. (1992). *The Ultimate Advantage: Creating the High-Involvement Organization*. San Francisco: Jossey-Bass Publishers.

Lawler, E. E., III (1996). *From the Ground Up: Six Principles for Building New Logic Corporation*. San Francisco, CA: Jossey-Bass Publishers.

Leopold, A. (1980). *A Sand County Almanac: With Other Essays on Conservation from Round River*. NY: Oxford University Press.

Levinson, H. (1976). *Psychological Man*. Cambridge, MA: The Levinson Institute

Lincoln, Y. S. [Ed.]. (1985). *Organizational Theory and Inquiry: The Paradigm Revolution*. Beverly Hills, CA: Sage.

Linstone, H. A. with Mitroff, I. I. (1994). *The Challenge of the 21st Century: Managing Technology and Ourselves in a Shrinking World*. NY: State University of New York Press.

Lovelock, J. E. (1987). *Gaia*. NY: Oxford University Press.

Lyman, F. (1990). *The Greenhouse Trap*. Boston, MA: Beacon Press.

Margenau, H. & Barghese, R. A. [Eds.]. (1992). *Cosmos, Bios, Theos*. La Salle, IL: Open Court.

Markley, O. W. & McCuan W. R. (1996). *America Beyond 2001: Opposing Viewpoints*. San Diego, CA: Greenhaven Press.

Martin, J. (1995). *The Great Transition*. NY: AMACOM

McNeill, D. & Freiberger, P. (1994). *Fuzzy Logic*. NY: Touchstone, Simon & Schuster.

Meadows, D., et al. (1979). *The Limits to Growth*. The Club at Rome.

Merchant, C. (1981). *The Death of Nature: Women, Ecology, and the Scientific Revolution*. San Francisco: Harper & Row.

Mesarovic, M. [Ed.]. (1967). *Views on General Systems Theory*. NY: John Wiley & Sons, Inc.

Miller, E. J. & Rice, A. K. (1967). *Systems of Organization*. London: Tavistock Publications.

Mische, M. A. [Ed.]. (1996). *Reengineering: Systems Integration Success*. Boston, MA: Auerbach.

Montuori, A. & Conti. (1993). *From Power to Partnership*. San Francisco: Harper Collins.

Morrison, I. & Schmid, G. (1994). *Future Tense: The Business Realities of the Next Ten Years*. NY: William Morrow.

Nadler, G. & Hibino, S. (1994). *Breakthrough Thinking (Rev. 2nd ed.)*. Rocklin, CA: Prima Publishing.

Naisbitt, J. (1982). *Megatrends: Ten New Directions Transforming Our Lives*. NY: Warner.

Naisbitt, J. (1994). *Global Paradox: The Bigger the World Economy, the More Powerful Its Smallest Players*. NY: William Morrow.

Naisbitt, J. & Aburdene, P. (1986). *Reinventing the Corporation*. NY: Warner Books.

Naisbitt, J. & Aburdene, P. (1990). *Megatrends 2000: Ten New Directions for the 1990's*. NY: William Morrow and Company, Inc.

Nirenberg, J. (1993). *The Living Organization: Transforming Teams into Workplace Communities*. Homewood, IL: Business One Irwin.

Oshry, B. (1995). *Seeing Systems: Unlocking the Mysteries of Organizational Life*. San Francisco: Berrett-Koehler Publishers.

Pegels, C. C. (1998). *Handbook of Strategies and Tools for the Learning Company*. Portland, OR: Productivity Press.

Peters, T. (1987). *Thriving on Chaos*. NY: Knopf.

Petersen, J. L. (1994). *The Road to 2015*. Corte Madera, CA: Waite Group Press.

Pfeiffer, J. W., Goodstein, L. D. & Nolan, T. M. (1989). *Shaping Strategic Planning: Frogs, Dragons, Bees and Turkey Tails*. San Diego, CA: Pfeiffer & Company.

Prigogine, I. & Stengers, I. (1984). *Order Out of Chaos*. NY: Bantam Books.

Quinn, D. (1992). *Ishmael*. NY: A Bantan/Turner Book.

Quinn, J. B. (1992). *Intelligent Enterprise: A Knowledge and Service Based Paradigm for Industry*. NY: The Free Press.

Rashford, N. S. & Coghlan, D. (1994). *The Dynamics of Organizational Levels : A Change Framework for Managers and Consultants*. Menlo Park, CA: Addison-Wesley Publishing Company.

Ray, M. & Rinzler, A. [Eds.]. (1993). *The New Paradigm in Business: Emerging Strategies for Leadership and Organizational Change*. NY: Jeremy P. Tarcher/Perigee Books.

Richardson, G. P. (1991). *Feedback Thought in Social Science and Systems Theory*. Philadelphia, PA: University of Pennsylvania Press.

Roberts, E. B. [Ed.]. (1981). *Managerial Applications of System Dynamics*. Norwalk, CT: Productivity Press.

Ross, H. (1996). *Beyond the Cosmos*. Colorado Springs, CO: NAVPRESS.

Rothschild, M. (1990). *Bionomics: Economy as Ecosystem*. NY: Henry Holt & Co., Inc.

Rubinyl, P. (1997). *Unchaining the Chain of Command.* Menlo Park, CA: Crisp Publications.

Rummler, G. & Brache, A. P. (1990). *Improving Performance*. San Francisco: Jossey-Bass Publishers.

Scarre, C. (1995). *Beyond Einstein: The Cosmic Quest for the Theory of Everything.* NY: Anchor.

Schneider, S. H. (1997). *Laboratory Earth: The Planetary Gamble We Can't Afford to Lose*. NY: Basic Books.

Senge, P. M. (1990). *The Fifth Discipline: The Art and Practice of the Learning Organization*. NY: Doubleday/Currency.

Senge, P. M., Roberts, C., Ross, R. B., Smith, B. J. & Kleiner, A. (1994). *The Fifth Discipline Field Book—Strategies and Tools for Building a Learning Organization*. NY: Doubleday/Currency.

Shrode, W. A. & Voich, D., Jr. (1974). *Organization and Management: Basic Systems Concepts*. Homewood, IL: Irwin, Inc.

Simon, H. A. (1957). *Models of Man*. NY: Wiley.

Sims, H. P. & Gioia, D. [Eds.]. (1986). *The Thinking Organization*. San Francisco: Jossey-Bass Publishers.

Spitzer, Q. & Evans, R. (1997). *Heads You Win!: How the Best Companies Think*. NY: Simon & Schuster.

Stacey, R. D. (1992). *Managing the Unknowable: Strategic Boundaries between Order and Chaos*. San Francisco: Jossey-Bass Publishers.

Stead, E. & Stead, J. (1992). *Management for a Small Planet*. Newbury, CA: Sage.

Steiner, G. (1979). *Strategic Planning*. NY: The Free Press.

Talbot, M. (1986). *Beyond the Quantum.* NY: Bantam Books.

Tarrant, J. (1976). *Drucker, the Man.* Boston: Cahners Books.

Terry, R. (1995). *Economic Insanity.* San Francisco: Berrett-Koehler.

Theobald, R. (1992). *Turning the Century: Personal and Organizational Strategies for Your Changed World.* Indianapolis, IN: Knowledge Systems, Inc.

Toffler, A. (1970). *Future Shock.* NY: Random House.

Toffler, A. & Toffler, H. (1980). *The Third Wave.* NY: Bantam Books.

Toffler, A. & Toffler, H. (1995). *Creating a New Civilization: The Politics of The Third Wave.* Atlanta, GA: Turner Publishing, Inc.

Trist, E. & Emery, F. (1973). *Toward a Social Ecology.* London and NY: Plenum.

Vaill, P. B. (1996). *Learning as a Way of Being.* San Francisco: Jossey-Bass Publishers.

Vickers, G. [Ed.]. (1972). *A Classification of Systems.* Washington, DC: Yearbook of the Society for General Systems Research/Academy of Management Research.

Volk, T. (1995). *Metapatterns.* NY: Columbia University Press.

Von Bertalanffy, L. (1968). *General Systems Theory.* NY: Braziller.

Waldrop, M. M. (1992). *Complexity: The Emerging Science at the Edge of Order and Chaos.* NY: Touchstone.

Weinberg, S. (1992). *Dreams of a Final Theory.* NY: Pantheon Books.

Weisbord, M. (1992). *Discovering Common Ground.* San Francisco: Jossey-Bass Publishers.

Wheatley, M. J. (1992). *Leadership and the New Science.* San Francisco: Berrett-Koehler Publishers.

Wheatley, M. J. & Kellner-Rogers, M. (1996). *A Simpler Way.* San Francisco: Berrett-Koehler Publishers.

Wick, C. & Leon, L. S. (1993). *The Learning Edge: How Smart Managers and Smart Companies Stay Ahead.* NY: McGraw-Hill.

Wiener, N. (1961). *Cybernetics: Or Control and Communication in the Animal Machine (2nd ed.).* Cambridge, MA: The MIT Press.

Wilbur, K. [Ed.]. (1985). *The Holographic Paradigm and Other Paradoxes.* Boulder, CO: Shambala Press.

Wilczek, F. & Devine, B. (1988). *Longing for the Harmonies.* NY: W. W. Norton and Co.

Wilson, E. O. & Kellert, S. R. [Eds.]. (1993). *The Biophilia Hypothesis*. Washington, DC: Island Press.

Wolf, F. A. (1988). *Parallel Universes*. NY: Touchstone Books.

Wolf, F. A. (1989). *Taking the Quantum Leap*. NY: Harper and Row.

Yankelovich, D. (1981). *New Rules*. NY: Random House.

Yankelovich, D. (1991). *Coming to Public Judgment: Making Democracy Work in a Complex World*. Syracuse, NY: Syracuse University Press.

Zohar, D. (1990). *The Quantum Self: Human Nature and Consciousness Defined by the New Physics*. NY: William Morrow and Co.

Zuboff, S. (1988). *In the Age of the Smart Machine*. NY: Basic Books.

Zukav, G. (1979). *The Dancing Wu Li Masters*. NY: Bantam Books.

About the Author

Stephen G. Haines
CEO, Entrepreneur, and Strategist, Facilitator, Systems Thinker, and Author

Stephen G. Haines is the founder and president of the Centre for Strategic Management® in San Diego, California. He is internationally recognized as a leader in the field of strategic management and change. Steve has over 26 consecutive years of CEO-level experience with over 200 CEOs in complex and diverse international situations, and been a member of eight top management teams. He has had corporate responsibilities for all aspects of organizational functions, including planning, operations, marketing, PR, communications, finance, HR, training, and facilities. He has held executive positions at MCI, Exxon, Sunoco, Marriott Corporation, and ICA—a $14 billion diversified financial services firm. Preceding that, he served as senior vice president at Freddie Mac, a $32 billion financial institution.

Steve personally serves senior management and boards in a wide variety of private and public sectors. His career focus is using his extensive "best practices" research to lead dozens of major consulting projects. These have included mergers and acquisitions, high growth, turnarounds, restructurings, and strategic transformations. Steve specializes in strategic planning and transformational change. These changes always include a strong emphasis on enhancing leadership competencies through executive coaching, leadership development, HR management, and executive team building. These organization-wide changes also include the realignment of delivery processes and the attunement with people's hearts and minds needed to create customer value.

Prior to founding the Centre for Strategic Management in 1990, Steve was president and co-owner of University Associates Consulting and Training Services (a pioneer in the development of human resource practitioners and their organizations). He was the architect of its renewal before devoting full-time work to strategic management and change through the Centre.

Steve Haines holds an Ed.D. (ABD) in management from Temple University and an M.S.A. in organization development (minor in financial management) from George Washington University. He holds an undergraduate degree in engineering from the U.S. Naval Academy at Annapolis, MD (minor in foreign affairs) and is a graduate of the U.S. Department of Defense Human Goals Institute. As a former Naval Officer, he has flown Navy jets, piloted ships, and served in Vietnam.

Steve is today's new breed of "world class executive consultant" providing value-added advice as a master strategist and business expert, a systems thinker, and a leader with enormous skills in facilitation of difficult executive groups. He is an accomplished keynoter, as well as a prolific author.

As an international consultant to top executives, Steve is able to share extensive corporate research and experience in best practices with clients and attendees of seminars and international conferences where he is a popular keynote speaker on CEO and Board issues. He has taught over 70 kinds of seminars and authored six books and 50 articles, and served on nine boards of directors. He is the co-leader of the Banff Centre for Management's two-week leadership course for top executives and develops strategic management and transformational change frameworks and processes for the Centre. His interests include family and community service, sports, sailing, travel, photography, art, and design.